CRIMINAL PROCEDURE

CRIMINAL PROCEDURE

165701

STEPHEN COUGHLAN

Professor of Law
Dalhousie University

Published in 2008 by

Irwin Law Inc.
14 Duncan Street
Suite 206
Toronto, ON
M5H 3G8

www.irwinlaw.com

ISBN: 978-1-55221-014-7

Library and Archives Canada Cataloguing in Publication

Coughlan, Stephen Gerard, 1957–
    Criminal procedure / Stephen Coughlan.

(Essentials of Canadian law)
Includes bibliographical references and index.
ISBN 978-1-55221-014-7

1. Criminal procedure—Canada—Textbooks. I. Title. II. Series.

KE9260.C69 2008   345.71'05   C2008-904720-6
KF9620.ZA2C69 2008

The publisher acknowledges the financial support of the Government of Canada through the Book Publishing Industry Development Program (BPIDP) for its publishing activities.

We acknowledge the assistance of the OMDC Book Fund, an initiative of Ontario Media Development Corporation.

Printed and bound in Canada.

1 2 3 4 5   12 11 10 09 08

SUMMARY
TABLE OF CONTENTS

DETAILED
TABLE OF CONTENTS

CHAPTER 12:
APPEALS   351

FOREWORD

Professor Coughlan set out to provide in this book a survey of the structure, architecture, and competing values of criminal procedure. He has succeeded marvelously.

The structure of Canadian criminal procedure consists of a complex set of statutory rules. But its architecture is shaped by ancient common law principles and deep societal values, many of which have been both preserved and given new life by the *Canadian Charter of Rights and Freedoms*. The subject is, as Professor Coughlan astutely observes, one in which important questions of legal principle and societal values underlie almost every question. The complex technicality of the subject must be mastered, but not to the neglect of the underlying fundamental principles and deeply held values that are in play. The book succeeds in striking this difficult balance, never neglecting the rules but never failing to place them in the broader context of the underlying principles and values.

This compact volume will not appeal to those seeking a digest of all the reported decisions, although it neglects none of the leading authorities. But it will be a most welcome resource for both those new to the subject and for those with more experience who are facing a novel problem. For the student or the junior practitioner, this book provides a concise and admirably clear account of the subject. The structure of each topic is succinctly set out, the complex bodies of caselaw are summarized with clarity and precision, and there is careful attention to cross-referencing related areas. In short, this book offers a quickly accessible and sure-footed guide over tricky terrain. But that is not all. For those with more experience, it provides a concise yet sophisticated review of the underlying principles of the law—quick access to the "big picture"—which can be so helpful in coming to terms with new problems and formulating or responding to new arguments. While this is a short book, it is not one just for beginners.

One of life's most satisfying experiences is to watch a gifted student, through sustained hard work, fulfill his potential. Steve Coughlan has provided all of his former teachers at the Dalhousie Law School, including this one, with that experience. This book is further evidence of his talent and his industry.

Justice Thomas A. Cromwell
Nova Scotia Court of Appeal
April 2008

ACKNOWLEDGEMENTS

No book is ever exclusively the product of the author, and that mould has not been broken with this one, so many "thank yous" are in order, though it is a delicate task not to ignore important people while at the same time not thanking the entire academy. Many people have contributed to whatever merits this book has, though its demerits remain my own.

A central pleasure of returning to teach where one has been a student is the opportunity to work, as a colleague, with those who have formerly been one's instructors — though that implies a more stark division between the roles than actually exists in practice. In particular it was a pleasure to work in a variety of capacities with Tom Cromwell, now the Honourable Justice Cromwell of the Nova Scotia Court of Appeal, whose ongoing patience with me has extended to reading this manuscript and kindly agreeing to write the foreword. In addition, my law school professors in Criminal Procedure and Criminal Law — Bruce Archibald and Dick Evans, respectively — have been valued colleagues for many years, from whom I have continued to learn. I should also single out former Dean Dawn Russell, without whose many years of I would never have been in a position to pursue an academic career.

My understanding of the subject matter of this book is enhanced greatly by Don Stuart and Tim Quigley — not only because of their own authoritative texts in these areas, but also through my work with the two of them on other projects. Both are unselfish scholars whose advice and assistance has helped not only me but many others interested in criminal law across the country.

This particular book owes its genesis to Patrick Healy, now the Honourable Judge Patrick Healy of the Cour du Québec, who was its original architect, and much of its current structure and content is still owed to his initial idea or to discussions with him about it. I am also grateful to Jeff Miller at Irwin Law for his commitment to this project, and to Dan Wiley for his invaluable technical assistance.

Finally, let me thank my partner in so many things, my wife, Dale Darling, for her ongoing encouragement and support.

*To Denise and Gerry Coughlan,
my mother and late father, for all their inspiration.*

CHAPTER 1

INTRODUCTION

In this book, criminal procedure will be taken to mean the body of rules and principles that govern the investigation, prosecution, and adjudication of any offence enacted by Parliament for which an accused person would have a criminal record if found guilty by a court exercising jurisdiction under the *Criminal Code*.[1] That is, it governs the procedural aspects relating to indictable and summary conviction offences enacted by Parliament pursuant to its legislative authority in matters of criminal law.

This definition of the subject excludes many procedural aspects of penal law. For example, criminal procedure does not include law that

---

1   Unless otherwise indicated, all statutory references in this book are to the *Criminal Code* of Canada, R.S.C. 1985, c. C-46 [*Code*]. All references to sections of the *Canadian Charter of Rights and Freedoms*, Part I of the *Constitution Act, 1982*, being Schedule B to the *Canada Act 1982* (U.K.), 1982, c. 11 [*Charter*] will be preceded by "*Charter.*" See *Criminal Records Act*, R.S.C. 1985, c. C-47, s. 3, which refers to a conviction of an offence under an Act of Parliament or a regulation made under an Act of Parliament. The procedure prescribed in the *Code* applies to all indictable offences and all offences punishable on summary conviction that have been enacted by Parliament. Notwithstanding the broad definition of this book's scope, the criminal jurisdiction of the Canadian military is excluded from consideration here, but it should be noted that this includes a distinctive body of procedural and evidentiary law. Also excluded from consideration is criminal procedure as it applies to young persons under the *Youth Criminal Justice Act*, S.C. 2002, c. 1. For discussion of the latter issue, see Nicholas Bala, *Youth Criminal Justice Law* (Toronto: Irwin Law, 2002).

is enacted for the enforcement of offences that are created by provincial or territorial legislatures and within their constitutional competence.[2] Nor does criminal procedure govern all offences enacted by Parliament. The *Contraventions Act*[3] was created to provide a non-criminal mechanism for the enforcement of some regulatory offences. Further, there are many penal matters that are largely administrative in nature, such as disciplinary offences within the Armed Forces or the Royal Canadian Mounted Police, and procedural law for the enforcement of those offences is properly considered part of administrative law.[4] Similarly, although correctional law is related to the administration of criminal justice, its substantive content has more to do with administrative law than with criminal procedure.[5]

This is a formal and conventional statement of the subject of this book. But something more is desirable to introduce the themes that animate this area of the law. Criminal procedure comprises an enormous array of rules and principles in the administration of criminal justice. Many are highly technical and have narrow application. Others, such as "due process," raise fundamental issues of principle and influence virtually all aspects of procedural law. It would be foolhardy to suggest that all of these rules and principles have resulted in a clear and rational system that expresses agreed values.[6] But it would be foolish not to recognize that both the most picayune rules and the grandest principles are important. For instance, what do we mean by "justice"? Hundreds of years of history attempt to offer an answer of one sort, but section 2 of the *Criminal Code* offers an answer of an entirely different kind. Taken together, these fiddly details and these fundamental values express the standard of justice in Canadian criminal procedure.

What, then, is criminal procedure about? Martin Friedland opened his study of double jeopardy with this claim: "The history of the rule

---

2   See for example, *Provincial Offences Act*, R.S.O. 1990, c. P.33; *Code de procédure pénale* du Québec, R.S.Q. c. C-25.1. In every province or territory there is analogous legislation.

3   S.C. 1992, c. 47. Among other features, liability for a contravention does not entail a criminal record: s. 63.

4   *National Defence Act*, R.S.C. 1985, c. N-5, Part III; *Royal Canadian Mounted Police Act*, R.S.C. 1985, c. R-10, Part IV.

5   *Corrections and Conditional Release Act*, S.C. 1992, c. 20.

6   For a sustained critique of the lack of clarity and the complexity in the law, see Tim Quigley, *Procedure in Canadian Criminal Law*, 2d ed. (Toronto: Thomson Carswell, 2005). This point was often made in working papers and reports of the Law Reform Commission of Canada. See, for example, *Our Criminal Procedure* (Ottawa: Law Reform Commission of Canada, 1988) and *Recodifying Criminal Procedure* (Ottawa: Law Reform Commission of Canada, 1991).

against double jeopardy is the history of criminal procedure. No other doctrine is more fundamental or all-pervasive."[7] The same claim could likely be made, in the same terms, for many other principles of the criminal law, such as *habeas corpus*, the presumption of innocence, or protection against self-incrimination. It matters little whether such a claim could be made for any one principle because what connects them all, as well as all of the technical rules, is another idea. The history of criminal procedure is the history of rules and principles that constrain or affirm the state's power to place a person in jeopardy of investigation, prosecution, and punishment for the commission of a criminal offence. No concept is more fundamental or pervasive in criminal procedure than jeopardy in this broad sense.

The interests of individuals can come into conflict with those of the state in many ways. Restricting discussion solely to the criminal realm, there are issues around the circumstances of a person who is suspected, accused, or found guilty of criminal wrong-doing. A person is in jeopardy of prosecution if an investigation produces reasonable grounds to believe that an offence has been committed and the evidence is sufficient to proceed. A person on trial is in jeopardy of conviction and a criminal record if found guilty. A person found guilty is in jeopardy of a sentence, and that sentence might involve not only a criminal record, but also a loss of liberty. In this sense jeopardy exists whenever the state invokes the power of the criminal law against a person suspected or accused of wrong-doing, and it describes the risk of lawful intrusion or deprivation that such a person faces.

It is not possible to think about jeopardy in the manner just described without also thinking of broader principles of legality, legitimacy, and fairness. If the state is entitled to use its power to enforce the criminal law, and if an individual person might be subject to the intrusion implied by investigation, prosecution, and conviction, a fuller notion of jeopardy requires attention to rules and principles that define the legitimate use of the state's power and, at the same time, the value of individual liberty and security of the person. These concerns are not exclusive to the criminal law, obviously, but they are the central concerns of criminal procedure. Indeed, the negotiation and re-negotiation of due process are constant themes of criminal procedure. There is a constant tension between the interest of the state to ensure the collective security of its subjects and the interest of those subjects in liberty and privacy.

---

7   Martin Friedland, *Double Jeopardy* (Oxford: Clarendon Press, 1969) at 3.

Jeopardy and due process are not subjects of general agreement. The law governing criminal procedure, to borrow a phrase from the late Justice Brian Dickson, as he then was, not only lies in "a field of conflicting values;"[8] it *is* a field of conflicting values. In the years preceding the *Charter*[9] it was argued by many that the law did not accord sufficient protection to persons in jeopardy.[10] Certainly the *Charter* has forced everyone involved in the administration of criminal justice to reconsider the relation between the power of the state to enforce the law and the protection of persons who might be put in jeopardy.[11] Since 1982 there has been no more powerful engine of law reform than the *Charter* and, as a result, there have been profound changes in the law relating to criminal procedure. This has occurred as the courts have given meaning to specific provisions of the *Charter*. The guarantee against unreasonable search and seizure in section 8, the right to counsel in section 10(b), and the right to trial within a reasonable time in section 11(b) have significantly altered the manner in which the police conduct their work and the manner in which prosecutors present their case in court. The right of the accused to make full answer and defence to the prosecution case has also led to important changes in the handling of criminal cases, not least of which is the right of the accused generally to have disclosure of the prosecution case before trial.

Interpretation of the *Charter* is not the sole or direct cause of all recent developments in criminal procedure. Important developments have been influenced by the *Charter* in a somewhat more indirect manner. For some time before 1982, and for some time thereafter, notions of jeopardy and due process were typically thought to concern a conflict between the interests of the state and the interests of the accused. Comparatively little attention was given to the notion that third parties, who might not share the interests of the state or those of the accused, deserved recognition and enforcement of their interests within the law on criminal procedure. Most notable among these are the victims and

---

8   *R. v. Sault Ste. Marie*, [1978] 2 S.C.R. 1299 at 1310.

9   Above note 1.

10 See, for example, Stanley A. Cohen, *Due Process of Law* (Toronto: Carswell, 1977); Ed Ratushny, *Self-Incrimination in the Canadian Criminal Process* (Toronto: Carswell, 1979); Walter Tarnopolsky, *The Canadian Bill of Rights*, 2d ed. (Toronto: McClelland & Stewart, 1975). Since its creation in 1964, the Canadian Civil Liberties Association has been a vigilant advocate of such protection.

11 The literature is vast, but see, for example: David Paciocco, *Getting Away with Murder* (Toronto: Irwin Law, 1999); Kent Roach, *Due Process and Victims' Rights* (Toronto: University of Toronto Press, 1999); Kent Roach, *The Supreme Court on Trial* (Toronto: Irwin Law, 2001); and Don Stuart, *Charter Justice in Canadian Criminal Law*, 4th ed. (Scarborough, ON: Thomson Carswell, 2005).

alleged victims of crime.[12] Their interests in privacy and equality have been specifically invoked as the courts and Parliament have redefined important areas of procedure, such as disclosure by the prosecution or the production of evidence. Other parties, including the public, have also intervened to ensure that the administration of criminal justice is conducted in a manner that respects interests such as the freedom of expression.[13]

If it is accurate to state that the rules and principles of criminal procedure is a field of conflicting values, then it is also accurate that there is no dominant set of values within it. Kent Roach has argued that, in addition to concerns for effective crime control and for due process, there may be seen in recent Canadian law a more pronounced concern for the alleged victims of crime and for other third parties than was previously the case.[14] He has argued that this increased concern for victims is sometimes expressed in a manner that favours the values of efficient crime control and, on some occasions, in a manner that favours other values.

In the field of conflicting values that is criminal procedure there are broad areas for both consensus and conflict. In the development of constitutional principles, the adjudication of cases, and the formulation of measures for law reform, there is also frequent reference to the metaphorical idea that the resolution of conflict may be found in "balance." Balance, in the sense of a mathematical equipoise of weights resting upon a fulcrum, rarely exists in a state of nature. In the law, and most conspicuously the criminal law, if there is balance it is always artificial and always delicate. The state of the law at any given point should reflect deliberate and authoritative choices by people about the appropriate distribution of weight to be made among recognized values. A claim to balance is only a claim that a given distribution is acceptable for the moment: there is no claim to balance that can eliminate the conflict of values and the eventual need for redistribution among them.

The purpose of this book is to provide an introduction to the principal features of Canadian criminal procedure. Some topics are treated in elaborate detail and some, such as the amendments dealing with terrorism, are not addressed in any detail. This book should provide a survey of the structure and the architecture of criminal procedure. Within these formal categories, and indeed in almost every aspect of

---

12   See, for example, *R. v. Seaboyer*, [1991] 2 S.C.R. 577; *R. v. O'Connor*, [1995] 4 S.C.R. 411; and *R. v. Darrach*, [2000] 2 S.C.R. 443.

13   See, for example, *Dagenais v. Canadian Broadcasting Corporation*, [1994] 3 S.C.R. 835; and *R. v. Mentuck*, [2001] 3 S.C.R. 442.

14   See Roach, *Due Process and Victims' Rights*, above note 11.

the subject, the reader will be reminded that there are important questions of principle and value that suffuse the law. These questions invite debate, even though debate and argument are not the main themes of the text.

Nevertheless, reconsider the quotation from Professor Friedland above. Double jeopardy refers generally to the idea that a person may not be prosecuted or convicted *twice* for the same offence. Jeopardy on its own, then, refers to the proposition that no person should be investigated, prosecuted, convicted, or sentenced even *once* by the state, except in accordance with rules and principles that express values of legality, legitimacy, and fairness. Those values have changed profoundly between the time when modern criminal procedure began to take shape and today. And, of course, those values continue to evolve today with changes both small and great. This book attempts, in a modest way, to show the past, the present, and the possible future.

FURTHER READINGS

BALA, NICHOLAS, *Youth Criminal Justice Law* (Toronto: Irwin Law, 2003)

COHEN, STANLEY A., *Due Process of Law* (Toronto: Carswell, 1977)

FRIEDLAND, MARTIN, *Double Jeopardy* (Oxford: Clarendon Press, 1969)

LAW REFORM COMMISSION OF CANADA, *Our Criminal Procedure* (Ottawa: Law Reform Commission of Canada, 1988)

LAW REFORM COMMISSION OF CANADA, *Recodifying Criminal Procedure*, Report 33 (Ottawa: Law Reform Commission of Canada 1991)

PACIOCCO, DAVID, *Getting Away with Murder* (Toronto: Irwin Law, 1999)

QUIGLEY, TIM, *Procedure in Canadian Criminal Law*, 2d ed. (Toronto: Thomson Carswell, 2005)

RATUSHNY, ED, *Self-Incrimination in the Canadian Criminal Process* (Toronto: Carswell, 1979)

ROACH, KENT, *Due Process and Victims' Rights* (Toronto: University of Toronto Press, 1999)

ROACH, KENT, *The Supreme Court on Trial* (Toronto: Irwin Law, 2001)

STUART, DON, *Charter Justice in Canadian Criminal Law*, 4th ed. (Toronto: Thomson Carswell, 2005)

TARNOPOLSKY, WALTER, *The Canadian Bill of Rights*, 2d ed. (Toronto: McClelland & Stewart, 1978)

CHAPTER 2

SOURCES OF CRIMINAL PROCEDURE

Broadly speaking, the sources for criminal procedure, as for criminal law more generally, are derived from the constitution, statutes, and common law. However, it is useful to discuss each of those areas in more depth, and to do so it is convenient to distinguish between the sources of police investigative powers on the one hand and the sources of the rules of pre-trial and trial procedure on the other.

A. SOURCES OF POLICE POWER

Deciding the amount of power to be granted to police in a society is a difficult challenge. Police power is one of the most obvious and potentially most intrusive means by which government interferes with the lives of individuals. A society in which police have excessive power risks suppression. However, a society in which police have insufficient ability to investigate and prevent crime risks lawlessness. Both extremes are to be avoided, but there is a broad range between them, with scope for reasonable disagreement over exactly where the right balance lies.

Police powers derive from two main sources: statute and common law. In addition, it is necessary to discuss the extent to which police effectively have powers based on the consent of a person being investigated.

1) Constitution

Any discussion of constitutional law in Canada must consider the question of division of powers under the *Constitution Act, 1867*[1] as well as the impact of the *Canadian Charter of Rights and Freedoms*, introduced as part of the *Constitution Act 1982*.[2] The former issue has relatively little direct impact on the question of police powers. Both Parliament and the provincial legislatures have the jurisdiction to create police forces, and both levels of government have done so. In addition, though, many provinces have contracted with the Royal Canadian Mounted Police (RCMP), the federal police force, to provide policing services within the province. Even in such cases, however, the RCMP remains under federal legislative jurisdiction, so that, for example, a complaint would have to be brought to the appropriate federal body rather than a provincial police complaints board.[3]

Whatever the constitutional basis for their existence, however, the police will rely primarily on rules of criminal procedure set out in the *Criminal Code* in enforcing the criminal law. That matter lies squarely within Parliament's jurisdiction, thanks to section 91(27) of the *Constitution Act, 1867*, which assigns authority over "the Procedure in Criminal Matters," to the federal government. Police in various provinces can have additional powers conferred by provincial statutes. Further, the duties assigned to police by their governing legislation, whether federal or provincial, can sometimes be relevant.[4] Nonetheless, in the vast majority of occasions, section 91(27) means that it is federal legislation that will determine the extent of police investigative powers.

A much more relevant constitutional law question in this context is the role of the *Charter*. Its importance is twofold. First, any law concerning criminal procedure that is inconsistent with the *Charter* may be struck down unless it can be justified as a reasonable limitation upon guaranteed rights by reference to section 1.[5] Second, the inves-

---

1   (U.K.), 30 & 31 Vict., c. 3, reprinted in R.S.C. 1985, App. II, No. 5. [*Constitution Act, 1867*].

2   Being Schedule B to the *Canada Act 1982* (U.K.), 1982, c. 11 [*Constitution Act, 1982*]. Sections 1–44 of the *Constitution Act, 1982* are referred to as the *Canadian Charter of Rights and Freedoms* or, more commonly, as the *Charter*.

3   See, for example, *Alberta (Attorney General) v. Putnam*, [1981] 2 S.C.R. 267.

4   See, for example, *R. v. Godoy*, [1999] 1 S.C.R. 311 [*Godoy*], where the Court looked to the duties of police as set out in s. 42 of the *Police Services Act*, R.S.O. 1990, c. P.15, in order to help determine whether the *Waterfield* test was met. The *Waterfield* test is discussed in greater detail at Section A(3)(b), below in this chapter.

5   *Constitution Act, 1982*, above note 2, s. 52.

tigation and prosecution of crime in each case must be conducted in a manner that is consistent with rights guaranteed by the *Charter*, and failure to do so may give rise to a remedy under section 24.

The *Charter*, especially the rights in sections 7–14 under the heading "Legal Rights," affects all aspects of criminal procedure from police conduct through to bail, trial procedure, and sentencing. Sections 8 to 10, dealing with search, detention, and arrest, are all directly concerned with investigative powers, and they will be discussed at much greater length below. Further, in the absence of more precise guarantees, section 7 may be invoked as a source of "principles of fundamental justice." Although this section has had a greater impact on issues of substantive criminal law than on investigative powers, it has been held to guarantee the right to remain silent, and is a source of constitutional protection against abuse of process.[6]

The *Charter* has certainly enhanced the protection of civil liberties in Canada and the extent of these effects will be reviewed in subsequent chapters. Paradoxically, the *Charter* has also been a direct and indirect cause of the expansion of police powers. It has been a direct cause of this expansion when judicial interpretation of a right in the *Charter* has created a power that did not previously exist in law. This has occurred in the interpretation of section 8, which protects against unreasonable search and seizure, and in the interpretation of section 9, which protects against arbitrary detention.[7] In essence what has happened is that *Charter* analysis has dictated that a lawful search will not be an unreasonable one, and a lawful detention will not be an arbitrary one. In some situations in which an accused has been searched or detained in the absence of any statutory authority, courts have been faced with a choice between finding a *Charter* violation or finding a new common law power authorizing the police action. As will be discussed below, courts have increasingly been inclined toward the latter course of action.[8]

The *Charter* has also been an indirect cause of the expansion of police powers when courts have found particular police action objectionable, but have suggested powers that would still be consistent with guaranteed rights. This type of judicial interpretation has sometimes given Parliament guidance for legislative expansion of police powers. This would appear to be most evident in relation to matters of search and seizure.[9]

---

6   See, for example, *R. v. O'Connor*, [1995] 4 S.C.R. 411 [*O'Connor*].
7   See the discussion in Chapters 4 and 5.
8   See Section A(3)(b), below in this chapter.
9   See, for example, *R. v. Wong*, [1990] 3 S.C.R. 36; *R. v. Wise*, [1992] 1 S.C.R. 527.

2) Statute

The primary source of police powers is the *Criminal Code*. It creates powers for police to directly enforce the law, as well as a great number of powers aimed at investigating crime, such as search warrants and wiretap provisions.

Sections 494–528 of the *Code*, for example, create a statutory scheme allowing police officers (and others) to arrest an accused or compel an accused's appearance in court via a summons or appearance notice.[10] Police arrest powers are quite broad, creating a power of arrest in almost every situation a peace officer might encounter; virtually the only circumstance in which there is no arrest power is where the police officer does not find the accused committing the offence and the offence is only a summary conviction one. Sections 25–33 create related powers, allowing the use of force to execute powers authorized by law, to prevent the commission of some offences, or to prevent a breach of the peace. In some circumstances even the use of deadly force is authorized.

Other provisions in the *Code* create extensive powers for police to search.[11] Section 487 creates the general search warrant provision in the *Code*, allowing a justice to issue a warrant authorizing the search of a "building, receptacle or place" and the seizure of evidence found there. Warrants under section 487 are typically issued when a justice is satisfied that the search will produce evidence with respect to the commission of an offence. However, the provision also allows a warrant to be issued where there are reasonable grounds to believe that the search will find i) something in respect of which an offence has been committed; ii) the whereabouts of a person believed to have committed an offence; iii) property intended to be used to commit an offence; or iv) property relating to a criminal organization. *Code* provisions also authorize the seizure of the material searched for, as well as material in addition to that specified in the warrant.[12] Further, the *Code* contains a general power to seize without a warrant any thing that an officer reasonably believes was obtained by the commission of an offence, has been used in the commission of an offence, or will afford evidence in respect of an offence, provided the officer was lawfully present.[13]

---

10   See the discussion in Chapters 6 and 7.
11   See the discussion in Chapter 4.
12   Section 489(1).
13   The *Code* also creates a few isolated powers to search and seize without warrant; among them are s. 199(2) dealing with common gaming houses (which also creates what amounts to a power of arrest of those found in the common gaming house) and s. 462(2) dealing with counterfeit money.

In addition to the general search warrant provision, a great number of individual police investigative powers have also been incorporated into the *Code*. These include authorizations to

i)   use a tracking device to monitor the location of a person or object;[14]
ii)   install number recorders on a telephone;[15]
iii) perform video surveillance on a location;[16]
iv)   install a wiretap device to monitor telecommunications or private communications;[17]
v)   obtain blood samples;[18]
vi)   obtain handprints, fingerprints, footprints, or impressions of teeth or other parts of the body;[19] and
vii) obtain DNA samples.[20]

Some of these provisions, such as the wiretap and DNA sample items, are part of comprehensive schemes set out within the *Code*, while other powers are defined in a single section.

Beyond these specific warrant provisions, the *Code* also includes section 487.01, which allows a peace officer to apply for a warrant to "use any device or investigative technique or procedure or do anything" that would be an unreasonable search and seizure if it were not done under a warrant.[21] Further, section 487.11 of the *Code* provides that a peace officer may "exercise any of the powers described in subsection 487(1) [search warrants] or 492.1(1) [tracking devices] without a warrant if the conditions for obtaining a warrant exist but by reason of exigent circumstances it would be impracticable to obtain a warrant."

Supporting these various warrant provisions is section 487.1, which allows officers to apply for a warrant to obtain a blood sample or a search warrant by telephone. That provision has also been made applicable in other circumstances; to obtain a search warrant under the *Controlled Drugs and Substances Act*,[22] for instance. Other investigative techniques are also authorized by statute, such as breathalyzer demands and approved screening device tests to investigate impaired drivers.[23]

---

14   Section 492.1.
15   Section 492.2(2).
16   Section 487.01(4).
17   See Part IV of the *Code*.
18   Section 256.
19   Section 487.091. See also the *Identification of Criminals Act*, R.S.C. 1985, c. I-1.
20   Section 487.05.
21   See the discussion in Chapter 5, Section B.
22   S.C. 1996, c. 19, s. 11(2).
23   Section 254.

Sometimes, statutes other than the *Code* also create investigative techniques. Provincial legislation has authorized random stops of vehicles, which are used to check for both mechanical fitness and impaired drivers.[24] Other legislation, both federal and provincial, creates other investigative techniques. Legislation in British Columbia, for example, creates an obligation for a motorist involved in an accident to report the accident to the police.[25] The Ontario *Coroners Act*[26] authorizes taking samples of bodily fluids in the investigation of deaths.[27] The *Customs Act*[28] authorizes searches of people crossing the border to enter Canada.[29] The *Firearms Act*[30] authorizes inspectors without a warrant to enter premises, including dwelling houses, to search for prohibited firearms on reasonable grounds. Although not strictly a police power, various administrative schemes create a power to compel a person to testify, potentially giving self-incriminatory evidence.[31] There are limits placed on the extent to which evidence gained in these administrative manners can be later obtained by the police via a search warrant.[32]

A very broad police power is contained in section 25.1 of the *Criminal Code*. It permits police officers, under various circumstances, to perform acts that would, for any other person, constitute a crime; in other words, it permits the police to sometimes break the law in the course of their investigations.

Given the broad nature of powers given to police statutorily, it is not surprising that, on more than one occasion, the Supreme Court has sounded a note of caution about allowing police to have non-statutory powers too readily. In *R. v. Kokesch*, for example, it was stated that "this Court consistently has held that the common law rights of the property holder to be free of police intrusion can be restricted only by powers

---

24 See *R. v. Ladouceur*, [1990] 1 S.C.R. 1257, considering the application of the *Highway Traffic Act*, R.S.O. 1980, c. 198, s. 189(a)(1).

25 See *R. v. White*, [1999] 2 S.C.R. 417, considering the application of the *Motor Vehicle Act*, R.S.B.C. 1979, c. 288, s. 61.

26 R.S.O. 1990, c. C.37.

27 *R. v. Colarusso*, [1994] 1 S.C.R. 20.

28 R.S.C. 1985 (2d Supp.), c. 1, s. 1.

29 *R. v. Simmons*, [1988] 2 S.C.R. 495; *R. v. Monney*, [1999] 1 S.C.R. 652.

30 S.C. 1995, c. 39 at ss. 102 and 104. There is an obligation to give reasonable notice in the case of a dwelling house.

31 See, for example, *Thomson Newspapers Ltd.* v. *Canada (Director of Investigation)*, [1990] 1 S.C.R. 425, dealing with s. 17 of the former *Combines Investigation Act*, R.S.C. 1970, c. C-23.

32 See the discussion in *R. v. Jarvis*, 2002 SCC 73; *R. v. Ling*, 2002 SCC 74; and *Application under s. 83.28 of the Criminal Code (Re)*, 2004 SCC.42.

granted in clear statutory language."[33] Choosing the balance between protection of individual liberty and the need for public security, and the appropriate power to be given to the police in order to satisfy the latter concern without unduly sacrificing the former, is a process best undertaken in the legislative realm, where there is at least the potential for public debate. Despite expressing this concern on a number of occasions, however, the Court has not in fact consistently shown restraint in extending common law police powers. It is to that topic we now turn.

3) Common Law

There are three senses in which police may be said to have common law powers. First, there are some powers that were historically given to police, and which have continued to exist despite the codification of most police powers. Second, the ancillary powers doctrine allows courts to create and authorize new common law police powers. Finally, there is a sense in which the police have the common law power to do anything that has no negative consequences for the officer concerned and which results in evidence being admitted at a trial. Although this latter "default" sense is not usually spoken of as a common law power, it is a phenomenon that needs to be acknowledged.

a) Historical Common Law Powers
Historical common law powers include the power of the police to search incident to an arrest or to enter a private dwelling in "hot pursuit" of a person fleeing arrest. Both powers are interesting illustrations of common law powers, in particular because of the flexibility of such powers. This feature can be both an advantage and a disadvantage in a system where predictability is a virtue.

The power to search incident to arrest was confirmed in Canadian law by the Supreme Court in *Cloutier v. Langlois*.[34] Relying on British cases dating to 1829, American cases back to 1848, and Canadian cases from as early as 1895, the Court decided that there already existed in Canada, through the common law, a power for police officers to search a person who had been arrested. This power, the Court said,

> holds that the police have a power to search a lawfully arrested person and to seize anything in his or her possession or immediate

---

33   [1990] 3 S.C.R. 3 at 17. See also *R. v. Colet*, [1981] 1 S.C.R. 2.
34   *Cloutier v. Langlois*, [1990] 1 S.C.R. 158 [*Cloutier*].

surroundings to guarantee the safety of the police and the accused, prevent the prisoner's escape or provide evidence against him.[35]

Therefore, even though the *Criminal Code* did not specify such a search power, the police nonetheless had the power to search an arrested person for one of these three purposes.

A feature of the common law, however, is its ability to evolve — sometimes in desirable directions, sometimes not. In the case of search incident to arrest, the scope of the power has gradually shifted without the kind of public debate that would characterize an equivalent change to a statutory power. The original rationale for allowing the police to search for evidence incident to arrest was to prevent the destruction of any evidence that might be in the immediate control of the accused. However, the actual wording of *Cloutier* does not preclude wider searches for evidence, and within a very short time other courts were interpreting the search power to allow recovery, without a warrant, of any evidence relevant to the guilt or innocence of the accused, whether at risk of destruction or not. In *R. v. Speid*, for example, the Ontario Court of Appeal held that a search of a vehicle that was still in the vicinity of the arrest was validly incidental to the arrest, even though it did not take place at the time of the arrest, and despite the fact that a warrant had been refused.[36]

The Supreme Court noted in *R. v. Stillman* that two lines of authority had developed, suggesting that a broader search incident to arrest applied in the case of searching a vehicle.[37] In the context of searches of the person, the Court said that search incident to arrest did not extend beyond discovering evidence which might go out of existence.[38] However, by the time they decided *R. v. Caslake,* the Court had rewritten the allowed purposes for search incident to arrest to

> ensuring the safety of the police and public, the protection of evidence from destruction at the hands of the arrestee or others, and the discovery of evidence which can be used at the arrestee's trial.[39]

In *Caslake,* the Court did not acknowledge that this greater emphasis on gathering evidence was a change to the underlying purposes that were said to authorize the power in *Cloutier.*[40]

---

35   *Ibid.* at para. 49.
36   [1991] O.J. No. 1558.
37   [1997] 1 S.C.R. 607 [*Stillman*].
38   *Ibid.* at para. 41.
39   [1998] 1 S.C.R. 51 at para. 19 [*Caslake*].
40   *Ibid.*

Most recently, the Court has returned to the power to search incident to arrest to determine whether the power includes the authority to conduct strip searches. In *R. v. Golden*,[41] the Court acknowledged that the scope of search incident to arrest had not been fully delineated and, in particular, that whether it contained the power to conduct strip searches had never been settled. In that context, the Court decided further restrictions needed to be imposed. Reasonable and probable grounds are not generally a requirement of search incident to arrest; that is precisely why the separate "incidental" power has arisen, to allow a search flowing from nothing more than the fact of an arrest. However, to do more than conduct a "frisk" search, the Court has now held, police must have reasonable and probable grounds to believe that a strip search is necessary in the particular circumstances of the arrest.[42] Further, the Court held, such searches must be conducted at a police station unless the police have reasonable and probable grounds to believe that the search cannot be postponed. These additional requirements are imposed by the Court to reflect the greater intrusiveness of strip searches and to attempt to maintain the appropriate balance between individual privacy rights and the needs of law enforcement. They are an explicit effort to have the common law develop in accordance with *Charter* principles.[43]

Performing an arrest within a private dwelling house provides another illustration of the common law's ability to evolve, but it also illuminates the difficulty of determining exactly what common law powers the police have. In *Eccles v. Bourque*,[44] for example, the Court confirmed that the police have the power at common law to arrest within a private dwelling and laid down rules for entering the dwelling without the permission of the owner. As noted in *R. v. Landry* "the Court was simply reaffirming common law principles of some considerable antiquity."[45] That case actually dealt with a situation in which a warrant did exist but was technically invalid and so it was felt for a time that the rules created might cover only that situation. In *Landry*, however, the Court held that the rules applied to any warrantless arrest and outside the civil context of *Eccles v. Bourque*.[46] Subsequently in *R. v. Macooh*[47] the Court also held that, at least in cases of hot pursuit, this right extended beyond indictable offences to cover provincial offences as well.

---

41   [2001] 3 S.C.R. 679 [*Golden*].
42   *Ibid.* at para. 98.
43   *Ibid.* at para. 86.
44   [1975] 2 S.C.R. 739.
45   [1986] 1 S.C.R. 145 at para. 19 [*Landry*].
46   *Ibid.*
47   [1993] 2 S.C.R. 802.

In *R. v. Feeney*,[48] however, the Court further decided that the common law rules that had developed in a pre-*Charter* context[49] needed to be re-examined. Although the common law had held that a dwelling house was entitled to particular protection since *Semayne's Case*,[50] those privacy interests had become even more important with the passage of the *Charter*. Warrantless entry into a dwelling, the Court held, should, like a warrantless search, be *prima facie* unreasonable. An exception was allowed for hot pursuit and the issue of whether an exception should be allowed for exigent circumstances was discussed but not settled. Otherwise, warrantless entries to arrest would *prima facie* violate the *Charter*. To deal with the situation, the Court read a warrant provision into the *Code*, a step that has since been undertaken more formally by Parliament.[51]

b) New Common Law Powers — the "Ancillary Powers" Doctrine

A further feature of common law powers is that the boundaries are never closed: it is always possible for new common law police powers to be created. Frequently, this issue arises in the context of a charge against an accused for assaulting or obstructing an officer in the execution of duty when that officer has not been acting under statutory authority. The question therefore becomes whether the officer had any power at common law. The question can also arise when an accused claims a violation of a *Charter*-right, such as that in section 9: the right not to be arbitrarily detained. An accused who has been legally detained has not been arbitrarily detained, caselaw has held, and so, in the absence of any statutory authority, the question becomes whether the detention was lawful due to a common law power.

Canadian caselaw has adopted a test from the British decision in *R. v. Waterfield* to determine this question. The *Waterfield* test asks two questions:

> first, does the conduct fall within the general scope of any duty imposed by statute or recognized at common law; and second, does the conduct, albeit within the general scope of such a duty, involve an unjustifiable use of powers associated with the duty.[52]

---

48 [1997] 2 S.C.R. 13.
49 Although *Landry*, above note 45, was decided in 1986, the facts pre-date the *Charter*.
50 (1604), 5 Co. Rep. 91 a, 77 E.R. 194 (K.B.).
51 Sections 529.1–529.5.
52 *R. v. Waterfield*, [1963] 3 All E.R. 659 (C.A.) [*Waterfield*].

The Supreme Court has relied on this test to support police powers to protect foreign dignitaries,[53] to enter premises without a warrant or reasonable grounds to investigate a shooting,[54] to stop cars randomly to check for impaired drivers,[55] to set up roadblocks,[56] to forcibly enter an apartment to investigate a disconnected 911 call,[57] to detain individuals for investigative purposes, and, in some circumstances, to conduct searches of those individuals.[58]

Many authors have argued that great caution ought to be shown before relying on the common law in this way.[59] First, *Waterfield* itself was not intended by the court to allow the creation of new common law powers, rather it was intended as a way of understanding the limits on existing police powers. In *Waterfield*, the police had attempted to prevent the accused from driving away in a car they wished to examine. The accused drove the car at a constable who was physically blocking his path and was therefore charged with assaulting an officer in the execution of duty. He was found not guilty as the court reasoned that, although an officer's duty might include preserving evidence, the constable was not *authorized* to prevent removal of the car. After setting out what has become known as the "*Waterfield* test," Justice Ashworth immediately distinguishes between police duties and police powers, pointing to the limits on the latter. He refers approvingly to *Davis v. Lisle*, noting that:

> even if a police officer had a right to enter a garage to make inquiries, he became a trespasser after the appellant had told him to leave the premises, and that he was not, therefore, acting thenceforward in the execution of his duty, with the result that the appellant could not be convicted of assaulting or obstructing him in the execution of his duty.[60]

That Canadian law has not been consistent with the original intent of *Waterfield* is most clear from *Stenning*.[61] The facts of *Stenning* are very

53   *R. v. Knowlton*, [1974] S.C.R. 443.
54   *R. v. Stenning*, [1970] S.C.R. 631 [*Stenning*].
55   *R. v. Dedman*, [1985] 2 S.C.R. 2 [*Dedman*].
56   *R. v. Clayton*, 2007 SCC 32 [*Clayton*].
57   *Godoy*, above note 4.
58   *R. v. Mann*, [2004] 3 S.C.R. 59.
59   See, for example, Steve Coughlan, "Police Detention for Questioning: A Proposal—Part I" (1985) 28 Crim. L.Q. 64; Patrick Healy, "Investigative Detention in Canada" [2005] Crim. L. Rev. 98; James Stribopoulos, "In Search of Dialogue: The Supreme Court, Police Powers and the *Charter*" (2005) 31 Queen's L.J. 1; Steve Coughlan, "Common Law Police Powers and the Rule of Law" (2007) 47 C.R. (6th) 266.
60   *Waterfield*, above note 52 at 662.
61   *Stenning*, above note 54.

similar to *Davis v. Lisle*: an officer entered premises without any statutory authority to do so and was assaulted by a person inside. The *Waterfield* test was applied in *Stenning*, finding that, although the officer might have been a trespasser, he nonetheless was in the execution of duty because he was investigating, and therefore the accused *was* guilty of assaulting an officer in the execution of duty.

Further, the actual terms of the *Waterfield* test are broad enough to potentially justify, *post facto*, a very broad range of police behaviour, therefore injecting undesirable uncertainty into the law. The Court noted in *Dedman* that the common law duties of the police include the "preservation of the peace, the prevention of crime, and the protection of life and property."[62] In other words, the police have very broad duties, so it is unlikely that the first branch of the *Waterfield* test will fail to be met in any given case. The second branch of the test, the Court observed in *Godoy*, "depends on a number of factors including the duty being performed, the extent to which some interference with individual liberty is necessitated in order to perform that duty, the importance of the performance of that duty to the public good, the liberty interfered with, and the nature and extent of the interference."[63] While these factors could, in some cases, fail to be satisfied, as interpreted *Waterfield* nonetheless creates a test with the ability to authorize at common law an extremely wide range of police behaviour that has not been statutorily authorized. This is particularly troublesome when one considers the "after-the-fact" nature of such common law powers. When arising in the context of a charge of resisting an officer in the execution of duty, the recognition of a new common law power has the effect of making the accused criminally liable for behaviour that he could not have known in advance to be illegal.[64]

Given the wide range of powers pre-authorized by statute or available to police by warrant provisions in the *Code*, the ability to apply for a telewarrant, and the proliferation of communications technology in society, the need for broad common law powers is quite small. Al-

---

62   *Dedman*, above note 55 at para. 14.

63   *Godoy*, above note 4 at para. 18, quoting from *R. v. Simpson* (1993), 79 C.C.C. (3d) 482 (Ont. C.A.).

64   Further on this issue, see the range of opinions on the Court's approach in *Godoy, ibid.*, in Graeme G. Mitchell, "*R. v. Godoy*: Constitutional Accommodation of Public Service Programs" (1999) 21 C.R. (5th) 217; Don Stuart, "*Godoy*: The Supreme Court Reverts to the Ancillary Powers Doctrine to Fill a Gap in Police Power" (1999) 21 C.R. (5th) 225; and Heather Pringle, "The Smoke and Mirrors of *Godoy*: Creating Common Law Authority While Making *Feeney* Disappear" (1999) 21 C.R. (5th) 227.

though the Court seems to feel some conflict over these powers, *Waterfield* has been used frequently in recent years. Indeed, members of the Supreme Court have acknowledged that "*Waterfield* is an odd godfather for common law police powers" but nonetheless have concluded that "[b]uilding a composite picture of police common law powers by way of narrow precedents is not a quick fix but in the absence of Parliamentary action it is the least worst solution."[65] Further, the view has recently been expressed that this developing practice of relying on *Waterfield* does not mean that "the Court should always expand common law rules, in order to address perceived gaps in police powers or apprehended inaction by Parliament."[66]

c) "Default" Common Law Powers

Courts do not talk about police officers having the power to do anything that will not result in some remedy being granted to an accused, but, nonetheless, a proper understanding of the ability of the police to interfere with the liberty of individuals requires recognition of this phenomenon. It results from a combination of *Charter* and pre-*Charter* law.

Prior to the *Charter*, there was effectively no basis to exclude relevant evidence in Canada. As long as evidence was reliable, the means by which it had been obtained virtually did not matter.[67] Since the *Charter*, section 24(2) allows, in some cases, for the exclusion of evidence. However, section 24(2) depends upon the accused establishing the breach of a *Charter* right: where no *Charter* violation is found, the pre-*Charter* position on evidence still applies. In such circumstances, the evidence will be admitted.

This means that, as it delimits various *Charter* rights and establishes that certain activities by the police will not constitute a *Charter* breach, the Court is effectively authorizing the police to engage in particular activities despite the absence of any statutory power. The clearest example concerns the section 8 right to be secure against unreasonable search and seizure. The Court has held that an accused only has a section 8

---

65 *Clayton*, above note 56 at paras. 75 & 76, Binnie J. concurring in the result.

66 *R. v. Kang-Brown*, 2008 SCC 18 at para. 6. This statement was made by Justice LeBel on behalf of four judges. Justice Binnie, in response, held that it was too late to hold back from expanding common law powers, saying "[w]e have crossed the Rubicon," at para. 22.

67 *R. v. Wray*, [1971] S.C.R. 272. A small residual power to exclude extremely prejudicial evidence of little probative value was articulated in that case. More recently, the Court has begun to speak about this non-*Charter* exclusionary power in a way that suggests it might have greater vigour than it had seemed at the time: see, for example, *R. v. Buhay*, 2003 SCC 30 at para. 40.

right if she has a reasonable expectation of privacy. The Court has also defined various circumstances in which an accused does *not* have such an expectation. There is no reasonable expectation of privacy in electricity consumption records, for example.[68] In most cases, a warrantless search is *prima facie* illegal and will violate section 8 of the *Charter* if not justified in some way. But obtaining an accused's electricity consumption records does not bring into play any reasonable expectation of privacy, and so section 8 is not invoked. Therefore, there are no consequences for police acting without statutory or common law authority: no stay will be issued and no evidence will be excluded, since no *Charter* breach occurred. Although the Court does not describe this as "giving the police the power to obtain electricity consumption records without a warrant," this is a distinction without a difference.

Other cases have found that a guest in an apartment generally has no reasonable expectation of privacy engaged by a search of that apartment,[69] and passengers do not normally have an expectation of privacy in a motor vehicle.[70] These decisions effectively reflect that the police have the power to search apartments and vehicles as long as they are seeking evidence to incriminate a guest or passenger, rather than the tenant or driver. Though no explicit statutory power exists, and no preexisting or ancillary common law power will be invoked, the evidence will be admitted just as though the police were acting with authority.

4) Consent

Cooperation by a suspect is effectively another source of police powers. As Justice Martin noted:

> Although a police officer is entitled to question any person in order to obtain information with respect to a suspected offence, he, as a general rule, has no power to compel the person questioned to answer .... If, however, the suspect chooses to answer questions put to him by the police, his answers are admissible if the prosecution establishes that his statements were voluntary.[71]

This principle, that police need no statutory or common law authority to obtain evidence by making a request of a suspect, can arise in many contexts. It arises, for example, in considering whether an accused has

---

68   *R. v. Plant*, [1993] 3 S.C.R. 281.
69   *R. v. Edwards*, [1996] 1 S.C.R. 128.
70   *R. v. Belnavis*, [1997] 3 S.C.R. 341.
71   *R. v. Esposito* (1985), 49 C.R. (3d) 193 (Ont. C.A.), quoted in *R. v. Hicks* (1988), 64 C.R. (3d) 68 (Ont. C.A.), aff'd [1990] 1 S.C.R. 120.

voluntarily chosen to speak to police, to appear in a lineup, to provide DNA samples, to stop a vehicle, and other situations.

Police conduct lineups quite frequently, for example, but there is no statutory or common law authority allowing them to require an accused to participate.[72] Equally, however, the Court has never decided whether an accused has a positive right to refuse to participate in a lineup.[73] As a result, although a suspect need not agree, evidence that the accused refused to appear in a lineup can be introduced at trial. Further, if the suspect does not participate in a lineup the police are permitted to obtain identification evidence in other ways—by simply showing only the accused to a witness, for example.[74] Since this procedure is typically even less attractive than a lineup for a suspect, most of those asked to appear in a lineup agree to do so. Thus, although there is no power to compel lineups, consent of a suspect is a perfectly adequate source of authority from the police perspective.

There are a number of situations in which there is ambiguity about whether a suspect should really be said to have consented. Police question many people in the course of any investigation, and most of those people are potential witnesses, not suspects. It is perfectly reasonable to assume that such interviews take place by the consent of the person interviewed. In some cases, however, in the midst of an interview, a witness becomes a suspect. Sometimes police decide during an interview that they now have reasonable and probable grounds, where before they had only suspicions. It is clear that at a certain point an interview, that had initially been by consent, crosses over to one where the person being interviewed should be considered detained and therefore entitled to rights under section 10(b) of the *Charter*, for example. It is not entirely clear, however, how to tell when that point has been reached.[75]

Issues also arise around the limits of an accused's consent. For example, the Supreme Court has held that to take a DNA sample provided for the investigation of one offence, and use it for purposes other than those consented to, violates the guarantee against unreasonable search

---

72   *R. v. Ross*, [1989] 1 S.C.R. 3,

73   *R. v. Marcoux (No. 2)*, [1973] 3 O.R. 861 (C.A.) [*Marcoux*].

74   *Ibid.*

75   Note, for example, the Supreme Court's very brief decision in *R. v. Hawkins*, [1993] 2 S.C.R. 157. Although the Newfoundland Court of Appeal had laid out quite considered reasons for its conclusion that the accused was detained, the Supreme Court simply stated that the accused was not detained, without offering any helpful guidance as to how they had reached that conclusion or how other courts might decide such issues in future.

and seizure, specifically in the investigation of another offence.[76] On the other hand, they have also held that if an accused does consensually provide DNA samples without attaching limits to their potential use, then the accused no longer has a reasonable expectation of privacy in the sample and the police are free to use it in any way they wish.[77]

Apart from any issue of limits on consent, it is also important to be certain that the accused's consent is real from the start. The Court has noted that mere compliance is not sufficient to show that the accused is actually consenting. Most people are not aware of the limits of police power, the Court has noted, and are frequently unaware that they could refuse to comply with a request. Therefore, in those circumstances, it cannot really be said that the accused has consented. Thus, pulling a car over to the side of the road when directed to,[78] emptying the contents of a sports bag,[79] complying with a breathalyzer demand without first calling counsel,[80] and so on, cannot automatically be considered consensual actions.

Finally, it is also worth noting that consent, even if given initially, can be revoked. In *R. v. Thomas*, for example, police entered a house where a noisy party was taking place, eventually leading to a confrontation in which they arrested the owner of the house for assaulting a peace officer in the execution of duty. The Court held that the only basis on which the police were in the house was by the consent of the owner, and that consent had been withdrawn before the confrontation arose. Accordingly the police were not acting in the execution of duty and the accused was acquitted.[81]

B. SOURCES OF PRE-TRIAL AND TRIAL PROCEDURE

1) Constitution

a) Division of Powers

As noted above, section 91(27) of the *Constitution Act, 1867* reserves the power to make laws in relation to "the Criminal Law, except the Constitution of Courts of Criminal Jurisdiction, but including the Procedure

---

76   *R. v. Borden*, [1994] 3 S.C.R. 145.
77   *R. v. Arp*, [1998] 3 S.C.R. 339. See the discussion below in Chapter 4.
78   *Dedman*, above note 55.
79   *R. v. Mellenthin*, [1992] 3 S.C.R. 615.
80   *R. v. Therens*, [1985] 1 S.C.R. 613.
81   *R. v. Thomas*, [1993] 1 S.C.R. 835.

in Criminal Matters," to the exclusive legislative jurisdiction of Parliament. Although the effect of this division of power is to make decisions
of Parliament by far the most important to criminal procedure, provincial jurisdiction also has a significant impact. For example, the provinces
are competent to create superior and provincial courts with jurisdiction
within their territorial limits.[82] Judges of the former are appointed by
the Governor General, pursuant to section 96 of the *Constitution Act,
1867,* while judges of the latter are appointed by the appropriate Lieutenant Governor. Both of these federally or provincially appointed judges
can hear criminal matters, even though the subject matter of criminal
law is in federal jurisdiction. Further, while Parliament has exclusive
authority to establish penitentiaries,[83] in which sentences of two years
or more are served, the provinces may maintain jails for shorter terms of
imprisonment.[84] And while Parliament has the authority to make laws
that define police powers in criminal matters, including powers of arrest and search, the provision of police services is a matter that forms
part of the administration of justice within a province or territory.[85]

The allocation of jurisdiction over criminal procedure to Parliament reflects a deliberate policy at Confederation that the criminal law
should be national in scope.[86] This objective is more easily achieved
in statutory law than in judicial decisions, which leave open the possibility of inconsistency among provinces and even within provinces.
It might be noted, however, that statutory law relating to criminal procedure is not uniform in all parts of Canada. For example, the structure
of the courts is not the same in all jurisdictions, nor is the allocation
of jurisdiction to those courts.[87] The courts have also held that some
aspects of criminal procedure may be applied differentially across Can-

---

82 *Constitution Act, 1867,* above note 1, s. 92(14). See also *R. v. Ritcey,* [1980] 1
    S.C.R. 1077.

83 *Constitution Act, 1867, ibid.,* s. 91(28).

84 *Ibid.,* s. 92(6). On the division of penal institutions between federal and provin-
    cial authority, and in particular the division at sentences of two years, see Mary
    Campbell, *"A Most Vexatious Burden": Jurisdiction in Canadian Correctional Law*
    (LL.M. thesis, McGill University, 1997) [unpublished]. See also Martin Fried-
    land, *A Century of Criminal Justice* (Toronto: Carswell, 1984) at 61–62 [Fried-
    land]; and H.G. Needham, "Historical Perspectives on the Federal-Provincial
    Split in Jurisdiction in Corrections" (1980) 22 Can. J. Crim. 298.

85 Section 92(14). See Peter Hogg, *Constitutional Law of Canada,* 5th ed., looseleaf
    (Toronto: Carswell, 2007) c. 19.

86 See Friedland, above note 84 at 47–49. See also the opening words of s. 8 of the
    Criminal Code.

87 Quebec and Nunavut in particular have different structures from most prov-
    inces and territories.

adian jurisdictions. That is, the constitution of Canada does not require uniform application of the law in all parts of the country.[88]

There have been challenges to the validity of provincial legislation on the grounds that it trespasses upon Parliament's exclusive jurisdiction over matters of criminal law.[89] There have also been challenges to federal legislation that created criminal offences on the basis that the particular law reached into the provincial sphere, rather than being a proper exercise of power under section 91(27) of the *Constitution Act, 1867*.[90] In addition, there have been challenges suggesting that some aspects of criminal procedure were not within Parliament's legislative competence according to the division of powers.[91]

One particular division-of-powers-issue that, in the words of the Court, "seems to have 'boiled up' rather late in our constitutional jurisprudence" was the question of whether the constitutional authority to prosecute criminal offences rests with the federal or the provincial government.[92] As a matter of fact, prosecutions were, at the time of Confederation and for a considerable period thereafter, conducted exclusively by the provinces (other than private prosecutions, discussed below). Roughly 100 years after Confederation, Parliament created federal legislation, some of it constitutionally justified as criminal law under section 91(27), which was to be prosecuted by federally appointed prosecutors. For the most part, these consisted then, as they do today, of narcotic offences, now found in the *Controlled Drugs and Substances Act*.[93] This led to a series of constitutional challenges to determine whether appointing prosecutors was constitutionally a matter of criminal procedure under section 91(27) (and therefore federal) or a matter of administration of justice in the province under section 92(14) (and therefore provincial).

---

88 See, for example, *R. v. Turpin*, [1989] 1 S.C.R. 1296; *R. v. S.(S.)*, [1990] 2 S.C.R. 254; and *R. v. Furtney*, [1991] 3 S.C.R. 89.

89 See, for example, *Johnson v. Alberta (Attorney General)*, [1954] S.C.R. 127; *R. v. Westendorp*, [1983] 1 S.C.R. 43; and *R. v. Morgentaler*, [1993] 3 S.C.R. 463.

90 See, for example, *Reference re Firearms Act (Canada)*, [2000] 1 S.C.R. 783; *Reference re Validity of Section 5(a) of the* Dairy Industry Act, [1949] S.C.R. 1; and *Proprietary Articles Trade Association v. Attorney-General for Canada*, [1931] A.C. 310 (J.C.P.C.).

91 See *MacMillan Bloedel Ltd. v. Simpson Inc.*, [1995] 4 S.C.R. 725; *R. v. Romanowicz* (1999), 138 C.C.C. (3d) 225 (Ont. C.A.).

92 *Canada (Attorney General) v. Canadian National Transportation Ltd.; Canada (Attorney General) v. Canadian Pacific Transport Co.*, [1983] 2 S.C.R. 206 at 235 [*A.G. (Canada)*].

93 Above note 22.

Incrementally, the cases worked their way to a conclusion and eventually reached the final decision that the authority to decide who will prosecute criminal offences has always rested with the federal government, and that the fact that provinces had conducted virtually all prosecutions was simply a practical accommodation resting on the abstention of the federal government from appointing prosecutors.[94] As a result, federal legislation that appointed federal prosecutors in the case of some offences did not violate the division of powers.

It is important to recognize, though, that these decisions did not purport to remove any ability for the provinces to appoint prosecutors. Parliament had created a few exceptions to the practice of provincially-appointed prosecutors, and those exceptions were constitutional. Parliament had not opted to take over the task of criminal prosecutions generally (though seemingly the decisions mean that it could), with the result that, as a matter of practice, the great bulk of criminal law offences are prosecuted by provincial authorities. This is reflected in the definition of "Attorney General" in section 2 of the *Code*, which generally defines the term to mean the attorney general of the province where the proceedings are taken. This approach is subject to a few exceptions, such as terrorism offences, where the federal attorney general is also included. Similarly, there are a few provisions such as section 579.1, which give the federal attorney general a power to intervene in some prosecutions, which is roughly parallel to the power to intervene given to provincial attorneys general in section 579.

b)   The *Canadian Charter of Rights and Freedoms*

The impact of the *Charter* on investigative powers was noted above. In fact, it has also had considerable significance on rules of pre-trial and trial procedure. Some of the *Charter*'s "Legal Rights" provisions are aimed directly at such issues, such as section 14, which guarantees the right to an interpreter, or section 13, which protects against having self-incriminating testimony used. Other rights, though somewhat less specific, also have a direct bearing on these type of procedural issues: the section 11(b) right to a trial within a reasonable time, or the section 11(e) right not to be denied reasonable bail without just cause, for example. Further, the guarantee in section 7 of procedures that are in accordance with the principles of fundamental justice has been held to guarantee the right to make full answer and defence,[95] the right to

---

94   See *A.G. (Canada)*, above note 92. See also *R. v. Hauser*, [1979] 1 S.C.R. 984 and *R. v. Wetmore (County Court Judge)*, [1983] 2 S.C.R. 284.

95   See, for example, *R. v. Chambers*, [1990] 2 S.C.R. 1293; *R. v. Rose*, [1998] 3 S.C.R. 262; *R. v. Mills*, [1999] 3 S.C.R. 668 [*Mills*]; and *R. v. McClure*, 2001 SCC 14.

silence,[96] and it is the basis upon which the Supreme Court developed principles relating to pre-trial disclosure by the prosecution.[97]

Another effect of the *Charter* has been a reconsideration of the personal and public interests involved in criminal procedure. Until comparatively recently, criminal procedure was typically conceived as a matter involving the interests of the state and the accused. Civil liberties were understood to refer to the rights of the persons suspected or accused of wrongdoing. Interpretation of the *Charter* has brought an important change to these views. The courts have recognized that complainants, witnesses, and other third parties might have constitutional rights under the *Charter* that could be invoked and enforced in the course of criminal proceedings. Thus, for example, the right to a reasonable expectation of privacy has been identified as a reason not to disclose the personal records of complainants in the prosecution of sexual offences.[98] Similarly, freedom of expression has been invoked as a reason to allow a broadcaster the right to publish an account of some proceedings.[99] Further, in interpreting the right to a trial within a reasonable time, the Court's analysis has taken into account the societal interest in trials occurring promptly.[100]

The extent to which a person other than the accused may claim and enforce a right under the *Charter* during proceedings against the accused remains to be developed. It is of great significance, however, that this has already become an important part of the constitutional aspects of criminal procedure. This is not only apparent in decisions that would give third parties standing to assert their rights in court. Concern for the rights and interests of third parties has also had a powerful influence on the development of legislation in criminal procedure.[101]

---

96 See *R. v. Hebert*, [1990] 2 S.C.R. 151 and *R. v. Liew*, [1999] 3 S.C.R. 227. More recently, see the Court's discussion of this right in *R. v. Singh*, 2007 SCC 48.

97 See, for example, *R. v. Stinchcombe*, [1991] 3 S.C.R. 326 and *R. v. Dixon*, [1998] 1 S.C.R. 244. See also the discussion in Chapter 8.

98 *O'Connor*, above note 6 and *Mills*, above note 95.

99 See, for example, *Dagenais v. Canadian Broadcasting Corporation*, [1994] 3 S.C.R. 835; *Canadian Broadcasting Corporation v. New Brunswick (Attorney General)*, [1996] 3 S.C.R. 480; *R. v. Mentuck* , [2001] 3 S.C.R. 442; and *Re Vancouver Sun*, [2004] 2 S.C.R. 332.

100 See *R. v. Morin*, [1992] 1 S.C.R. 771.

101 See the discussion of this issue in Kent Roach, *Due Process and Victims' Rights* (Toronto: University of Toronto Press, 1999).

2) Statute

The essential elements of criminal procedure are found in the *Criminal Code*. This is not the sole statutory source of rules and principles of criminal procedure, however, because there are many additional elements scattered throughout federal legislation.[102] Specific police powers, for example, can be found in dozens of statutes dealing with different matters within federal jurisdiction. This is especially clear in relation to search and seizure. Many statutes also contain specific provisions that affect procedural aspects for the enforcement of criminal offences. There are also statutes that stand apart from the *Criminal Code*, but contain important elements of criminal procedure, such as the *Identification of Criminals Act*[103] and the *Criminal Records Act*.[104]

The presentation of the rules and principles of criminal procedure in the *Code* has become increasingly prolix with successive amendments. There are important features in the introductory Part, including some definitions applicable throughout (though other definitions are also found within particular parts) and provisions concerning the liability of persons who exercise powers under the *Code*. There are also important aspects of procedure that are found among parts of the *Code* that comprise substantive offences. Illustrations of this include the provisions on electronic surveillance,[105] the application for disclosure of personal records,[106] and the procedure for taking breath or blood samples in suspected cases of impaired driving.[107]

The *Criminal Code* contains twenty-eight parts and most of the provisions concerning procedure are found beginning in Part XIV. The general organizing principle is the chronological sequence of a criminal prosecution. This organizing principle is more approximate than rigorous, but it remains the only discernible principle for the order of these parts of the *Code*. Each individual part comprises clusters of provisions

---

102 See, for example, *Controlled Drugs and Substances Act*, above note 22; *Customs Act*, above note 28; *Firearms Act*, above note 30; *Fisheries Act*, R.S.C. 1985, c. F-14; *Competition Act*, R.S.C. 1985, c. C-34; *Food and Drugs Act*, R.S.C. 1985, c. F-27; *Income Tax Act*, R.S.C. 1985 (5th Supp.), c. 1; *Proceeds of Crime (Money Laundering) and Terrorist Financing Act*, S.C. 2000, c. 17; *Security of Information Act*, R.S.C. 1985, c. O-5; *Crimes Against Humanity and War Crimes Act*, S.C. 2000, c. 24; *Youth Criminal Justice Act*, S.C. 2002, c. 1; *Excise Act*, R.S.C. 1985, c. E-14; *Bankruptcy and Insolvency Act*, R.S.C. 1985, c. B-3.

103 Above note 19.

104 R.S.C. 1985, c. C-47.

105 Section 184.

106 Sections 278.1*ff*.

107 Sections 254*ff*.

that are thematically linked, though the thematic coherence of some parts is less apparent than others. The major procedural themes in Part XIV and the following are jurisdiction, search and seizure, compelling appearance, preliminary inquiry, trial procedure for summary-conviction offences and for indictable offences tried with or without a jury, sentencing, judicial review, and appeal.

It should also be noted that there are many cross-references among the various parts, with the result that the rules governing one set of procedures are found in whole or in part in an entirely different place. Somewhat oddly, much of Canadian criminal trial procedure derives from procedure in jury trials, the rules for which are found in Part XX of the *Code*. As a matter of fact, very few criminal trials are conducted with a jury, and, indeed, most occur in provincial courts that cannot have juries. However, the rules in Part XX are incorporated by reference in other parts, and they therefore have general application.[108]

3) Common Law

The *Criminal Code* is not, strictly speaking, a code. It is not a single, comprehensive statement of Canadian criminal law because, as already noted, there are many other statutes that deal with aspects of criminal law in Canada. The *Code* prohibits the prosecution of common law offences, with the exception of criminal contempt, but it expressly preserves the power of the courts to develop new common law defences.[109] It contains no complete General Part. Hence, the *Code* is more accurately defined as a consolidation of the principal elements of Canadian criminal law.[110]

This description is particularly apt as regards procedure. The *Code* establishes the architectural elements of criminal procedure and provides, in addition, many of the details. But, as noted, it is not a comprehensive statement of positive rules. To fill in the gaps, two sources may be called in aid. The first, which is not properly described as the common law, is the judicial interpretation of statutory provisions. This is not the common law at work because it is no more than judicial in-

---

108 Sections 572 and 795.

109 Sections 9 and 8(3), respectively.

110 For further discussion, see Alan Mewett, "The Criminal Law, 1867–1967" (1967) 45 Can. Bar Rev. 726; Josiah Wood & Richard Peck, eds., *One Hundred Years of the* Criminal Code *in Canada* (Ottawa: Canadian Bar Association, 1993). See also Gerry Ferguson, "From Jeremy Bentham to Anne McLellan: Lessons on Criminal Law Codification" in D. Stuart, R. Delisle, & A. Manson, *Towards a Clear and Just Criminal Law* (Toronto: Carswell, 1999) 192.

terpretation of what the legislature has said. Nevertheless, the common law is often useful in this exercise because it is an important historical source of analogies and other guidance.

The second source is the common law itself. In some instances, where the *Code* is incomplete, the common law might provide a source for the resolution of ambiguity. Indeed, the *Code* occasionally makes reference to principles of the common law without any further development or elaboration. For example, the *Code* expressly recognizes the power of the courts to punish for contempt (this is, substantively, the only common law crime that still exists in Canada, preserved in section 9). However, because it is a common law crime, there is no definition of the offence and no procedure for such cases. In effect, therefore, the *Code* incorporates the common law by reference, as it relates to contempt for a substantive definition and for procedure.[111]

Similarly, in instances where the *Code* is silent the common law might afford a solution of its own. Many illustrations might be given, but two will suffice. The doctrine of abuse of process leading to a stay of proceedings is a creation of the courts in Canada and, accordingly, until it was partly merged with the principles of fundamental justice in section 7 of the *Charter*, it was a creature of the common law.[112] The rule against multiple convictions is also a development of the courts at common law that extends the principle of protection against double jeopardy.[113]

4) Rules of Court

Section 482 of the *Criminal Code* allows for the creation of rules of court by the various courts of criminal jurisdiction. These rules and practice directions are administrative in nature and their purpose is the effective and efficient administration of the criminal law within the jurisdiction to which they apply. It is self-evident that rules of court may not alter the rights and liabilities of any party as they stand within the Constitution, statute, or common law. In brief, rules of court may not be inconsistent with the law.[114]

---

111 See *United Nurses of Alberta v. Alberta (Attorney General)*, [1992] 1 S.C.R. 901 and *R. v. Arradi*, 2003 SCC 23.
112 See, for example, *R. v. Jewitt*, [1985] 2 S.C.R. 128 and *O'Connor*, above note 6.
113 See *R. v. Kienapple*, [1975] 1 S.C.R. 729 and *R. v. Prince*, [1986] 2 S.C.R. 480.
114 See *R. v. Spencer (No. 2)* (1974), 16 C.C.C. (2d) 514 (N.S.C.A.); *R. v. Stokes and Stevenson* (1966), 49 C.R. 97 (Man. C.A.); and *R. v. Ashton* (1948), 92 C.C.C. 137 (Ont. C.A.).

Of growing importance in the administration of the courts, especially in large urban areas where, consequently, the courts have a large volume of cases, are procedures for the management of cases. Section 482.1 provides that trial and appellate courts may make rules for this purpose. The courts have discretion to determine whether there should be such rules and, if so, what the purpose and content should be. Once made, however, they are mandatory.

5) Judicial Independence

Though not strictly a separate source of criminal procedure, the Supreme Court has described judicial independence as the "the lifeblood of constitutionalism in democratic societies."[115] This principle is referred to in sections 96–100 of the *Constitution Act, 1867* and in section 11(d) of the *Canadian Charter of Rights and Freedoms*, but it also extends beyond the limited situations covered by those provisions.

Judicial independence requires both individual independence (that of individual judges) and institutional independence (that of the court of which the judge is a member). It depends on objective guarantees of the judiciary's freedom from influence or any interference by others in security of tenure, financial security, and administrative independence. The historic rationale for judicial independence was to ensure that judges were able to decide individual cases without governmental interference. More recently, it has also come to be seen as important to the courts' role of ensuring protection of the rule of law and of acting as a shield against unwarranted deprivations by the state of the rights and freedoms of individuals.

Concerns about judicial independence have recently led provinces to amend their processes for appointing justices of the peace to ensure that these officials will be capable of acting in a proper judicial manner when dealing with applications by police to obtain warrants, lay charges, and so on.[116]

FURTHER READINGS

CAMPBELL, MARY, "A Most Vexatious Burden": Jurisdiction in Canadian Correctional Law (LL.M. thesis, McGill University, 1997) [unpublished]

---

115 *R. v. Beauregard*, [1986] 2 S.C.R. 56 at 70.
116 *Ell v. Alberta*, [2003] 1 S.C.R. 857, 11 C.R. (6th) 207.

COUGHLAN, STEVE, "Common Law Police Powers and the Rule of Law" (2007) 47 C.R. (6th) 266

COUGHLAN, STEVE, "Police Detention for Questioning: A Proposal—Part I" (1985) 28 Crim. L.Q. 64

FERGUSON, GERRY, "From Jeremy Bentham to Anne McLellan: Lessons on Criminal Law Codification" in D. Stuart, R. Delisle, & A. Manson, *Towards a Clear and Just Criminal Law* (Toronto: Carswell, 1999) 192–218

FRIEDLAND, MARTIN, *A Century of Criminal Justice* (Toronto: Carswell, 1984)

HEALY, PATRICK, "Investigative Detention in Canada" [2005] Crim. L. Rev. 98

HOGG, PETER, *Constitutional Law of Canada*, 5th ed., looseleaf (Toronto: Carswell, 2007), c. 19

MITCHELL, GRAEME G., "*R. v. Godoy*: Constitutional Accommodation of Public Service Programs" (1999) 21 C.R. (5th) 217

MEWETT, ALAN, "The Criminal Law, 1867–1967" (1967) 45 Can. Bar Rev. 726

NEEDHAM, H.G., "Historical Perspectives on the Federal-Provincial Split in Jurisdiction in Corrections" (1980) 22 Can. J. Crim. 298

PRINGLE, HEATHER, "The Smoke and Mirrors of *Godoy*: Creating Common Law Authority While Making *Feeney* Disappear" (1999) 21 C.R. (5th) 227

ROACH, KENT, Due Process and Victims' Rights (Toronto: University of Toronto Press, 1999)

STRIBOPOULOS, JAMES, "In Search of Dialogue: The Supreme Court, Police Powers and the *Charter*" (2005) 31 Queen's L.J. 1

STUART, DON, "*Godoy*: The Supreme Court Reverts to the Ancillary Powers Doctrine to Fill a Gap in Police Power" (1999) 21 C.R. (5th) 225

WOOD, JOSIAH & RICHARD PECK, eds., *One Hundred Years of the Criminal Code in Canada* (Ottawa: Canadian Bar Association, 1993)

CHAPTER 3

ELEMENTS OF CRIMINAL PROCEDURE

A. CLASSIFICATION OF OFFENCES AND MODE OF TRIAL

1) Introduction

Over a number of years, and with increasing amendments to the *Criminal Code*, the procedures for deciding the mode of trial have become needlessly complex. The current scheme is "based more on the accidents of history than on any rational plan."[1] As a practical matter, it is easiest to understand the current system first by imagining the very simple system that, at least conceptually, underlies it and then by looking at the variety of exceptions that serve to effectively conceal that model.

Imagine a system of prosecuting crimes that has only two types of offences and two methods of prosecution: less serious offences that are prosecuted in lower courts, and more serious offences that are prosecuted in superior courts. That seems to be the underlying theory of our classification and mode of trial system, but it is subject to amendments, exceptions, and sub-exceptions relating to the number of types of offences, the number of modes of trial, and the provision to the accused of a choice of mode of trial in some cases and then the removal of that choice in others. We shall pursue each of these issues in more de-

---

1   Law Reform Commission of Canada, *Classification of Offences* (Ottawa: Law Reform Commission of Canada, 1986) at 1 [*Classification of Offences*].

tail below, but an overview of how these exceptions overlay the simple model will be a useful starting point.

First, in one sense our system has only two types of offences: summary conviction offences and indictable offences. However, the model is made more complex because the *Code* provides for a great number of offences that can be prosecuted in either fashion: these are referred to as "hybrid offences."

Second, there are not really only two modes of trial, but three. One mode of trial is in front of the "court of criminal jurisdiction," and the other mode of trial is in front of the "superior court of criminal jurisdiction." However, the superior court can hear matters in two ways: either without a jury (a 'judge alone' trial) or with a jury.

Third, we do not automatically send all less serious offences to the lower court and all more serious matters to the superior court. For summary conviction offences that equation does hold, and the only mode of trial for them is in the court of criminal jurisdiction. In the case of indictable offences, however, the accused is not forced to choose the "top of the line" mode of trial, and can instead choose whether to have a trial by superior court judge and jury, by superior court judge alone, or by provincial court judge. This choice is referred to as an "election."

Fourth, having given that election to the accused, the *Code* then takes it away again in a number of situations. For example, section 469 lists a series of offences that must be tried by a judge and jury, so the accused is given no election. Further, section 553 lists a number of offences that will be tried in provincial court, and so again the accused is given no election. In principle, the rationale for these two lists is that since section 469 contains such serious offences—for example murder—the public interest demands a jury trial. In contrast, section 553 lists offences that are less serious than most indictable offences (though not so much less serious as to be summary conviction offences, it seems), and so there is no justification to offer the accused any choice beyond provincial court.

Fifth, if the trial will eventually take place in a superior court (either a judge alone, or a judge and jury) the matter does not go immediately to trial, but can first be referred to a preliminary inquiry in front of the provincial court. Only if this proceeding concludes that there is sufficient evidence will a trial actually take place.

Finally, there are various other exceptions to exceptions, such as the ability of the Crown, in some cases, to compel a jury trial, regardless of the accused's election, or the ability of the accused to re-elect having made one election, and so on.

One might also note that the way in which the *Code* is drafted does not contribute to an easy understanding of this structure. Section 471, for example, states that trial by jury is compulsory for all indictable offences, unless some other *Code* provision creates an exception to that requirement. Other *Code* provisions then create exceptions for literally *every* offence. One could easily gain the impression that trial by jury is the norm when, in fact, it is a rarity.

2) Types of Offences

Criminal offences are classified as indictable or offences punishable on summary conviction. These are the only two classifications in Canadian criminal procedure. In every statutory provision that creates an offence Parliament designates the offence by one classification or the other.[2] However, for many offences Parliament has applied a hybrid classification to allow the prosecutor discretion as to whether to proceed by indictable-offence procedure or summary-conviction procedure. That is, the offence is designated to fall into either category. Offences thus designated are typically called hybrid or dual-procedure offences. These should not be viewed as a third classification of offences, however, because they represent no more than a legislative decision to allow the prosecution the right to elect to proceed by one form of procedure or the other.[3] Once that election is made, the procedure for that type of offence will be followed.

In broad terms, indictable offences are more serious than summary conviction offences but, unfortunately, the classification of the offence is not always a reliable indication of its relative seriousness. It is cer-

---

2   *The Contraventions Act*, S.C. 1992, c. 47 creates another category of offence called a "contravention," which means, according to s. 2, "an offence that is created by an enactment and is designated as a contravention by regulation." Section 8 prohibits the designation of an indictable offence. Section 4 states that the purposes of the Act are to provide a procedure for the prosecution that distinguishes between criminal and regulatory offences and to abolish the legal consequences of conviction. Section 63 specifically provides that there shall be no criminal record upon conviction. In sum, a contravention is not properly classified as a criminal offence, even though Parliament might have originally enacted the offence under the authority of s. 91(27) of the *Constitution Act, 1867* (U.K.), 30 & 31 Vict., c. 3.

3   Until the prosecutor elects otherwise, hybrid offences are treated as indictable offences: see the *Interpretation Act*, R.S.C. 1985, c. I-21, s. 34. *See R. v. Gougeon; R. v. Haesler; R. v. Gray* (1980), 55 C.C.C. (2d) 218 (Ont. C.A.); *R. v. Parsons* (1984), 14 C.C.C. (3d) 490 (Nfld. C.A.). This principle extends to the classification of offences for the exercise of police powers: see, for example, *Collins v. Brantford Police Services Board* (2001), 158 C.C.C. (3d) 405 (Ont. C.A.).

tainly true that indictable offences carry a higher maximum penalty than summary conviction offences but this, by itself, is not a sound or sophisticated gauge of the seriousness of crimes. Some serious offences of violence may be prosecuted by way of summary-conviction procedure while many non-violent, property offences must be prosecuted by indictable procedure. Neither the severity of the maximum penalty, nor the perceived seriousness of violence provides a sound basis to explain why offences have been designated as they have. Indeed, the existence of hybrid offences, and the growing numbers of them, seems only to provide acknowledgement that the classification of offences is not something that can easily be rationalized by reference to their seriousness.

Nevertheless, the classification of offences is one of the most important organizing principles in the law of criminal procedure. The most obvious is perhaps the jurisdiction of the courts over offences, but some other ramifications of the classification might be noted briefly. The scope of police powers is affected by the classification of offences. The power of the police to arrest, for example, is defined differently for summary conviction and indictable offences.[4] Similarly, the power of search and seizure under the *Criminal Code* varies to some degree with the classification of offences.[5] Procedures for compelling appearance and interim release, whether by authority of the police or a judge, are also affected by the classification of the offence with which the accused will be charged or already has been charged.[6]

The classification of offences, of course, has a profound effect on the manner in which proceedings are conducted in court. Another major difference between summary conviction and indictable offences is that there is no "statute of limitations" for the latter, but there is for the former. Summary conviction offences are time-barred six months after the completion of the offence.[7] In a case where the only available charge is a summary conviction offence, the classification might therefore determine whether there can be any proceedings at all. If a hybrid offence could be charged in relation to conduct that was completed more than six months previously, the prosecutor is not generally time-barred against proceeding by way of indictment.[8]

The classification of offences has important consequences with regard to the mode of procedure and the jurisdiction of the courts. Virtually all prosecutions begin with a charge document that is called an

---

4   Section 495.
5   Sections 487*ff.*
6   See Part XVI.
7   Section 786(2).
8   *R v. Phelps* (1993), 79 C.C.C. (3d) 550 (Ont. C.A.).

information.[9] In all summary conviction matters, and some indictable matters, the information remains the document of charge throughout the proceedings. In such cases the proceedings at trial are conducted in the provincial court.[10] For most other indictable offences, however, the usual procedure is to begin with a preliminary inquiry on the information before a provincial court judge (preliminary inquiries will be the subject of Chapter 9). The inquiry provides an opportunity for the parties to test the evidence of selected witnesses on specific issues. If the accused is committed for trial upon completion of the inquiry, the prosecutor may file a new document of charge, called the indictment, in the court where the accused will be tried. In most provinces the trial court will be the superior court, but in Quebec the provincial court has jurisdiction to try all offences except those in which there is trial by judge and jury.[11] Thus, the classification of the offence as a summary conviction matter or an indictable matter has a controlling effect on most elementary matters of jurisdiction.

Another important aspect of whether an offence is classified as summary conviction or indictable concerns sentencing. Indictable offences are typically defined to allow a maximum term of imprisonment that exceeds two years. This does not mean, of course, that all indictable offences are punished with imprisonment exceeding two years. Nonetheless, the point is significant because summary conviction offences allow a maximum of six months or a fine of two thousand dollars, or both, unless Parliament prescribes a higher maximum. In recent years there have been a few provisions where Parliament has attached penalties greater than six months, but Parliament has never attached a maximum of more than eighteen months to a summary conviction offence.[12] As previously noted, offenders sentenced to terms of less than two years are incarcerated in provincial jails, whereas offenders sentenced to more than two years are incarcerated in federal penitentiaries. Provincial jails, therefore, house offenders serving sentences for offences that might be summary conviction or indictable, provided that the actual term in the warrant of committal is less than two years. Inmates in federal penitentiaries are necessarily there to serve sentences for indictable offences. These factors are relevant in important ways,

---

9   Part XXVIII, Form 2.

10 Offences within the absolute jurisdiction of the provincial court, by virtue of s. 553, are classified as indictable, but they are tried on an information.

11 Section 552.

12 Offences punishable by eighteen months summary conviction have been called "super summaries": see, for example, ss. 264.1 and 271.

including the prosecutor's exercise of discretion with regard to hybrid offences and plea discussions.

Finally, the *Criminal Code* provides different arrangements for appeal in summary conviction and indictable matters.[13] The former are heard by the superior court of the province and the latter are heard in the court of appeal. There are also provisions in the *Code*[14] and the *Supreme Court Act*[15] dealing with appeals to the highest court in criminal matters. These matters are further discussed in Chapter 12.

Much criticism has been made of the current classification of offences.[16] Some form of classification is obviously necessary, but the thrust of most critiques has been that the system of classification in current Canadian law is irrationally complex because it no longer has any prescriptive coherence. Dividing offences into the approximate categories of "more serious" and "less serious" through the distinction between indictable and summary conviction offences has some intuitive attraction, but we now have the oddities that some indictable offences are treated, effectively for all purposes but sentencing, as summary, while some summary convictions offences are treated as much closer to indictable, solely for the purpose of sentencing. The distinctions are becoming so porous that it is difficult to see principle operating at a very strong level. Instead, the system reflects the anomalous accretion of particular rules and practices as Canadian law emerged from its origins in English law, and was progressively adapted to accommodate Canadian needs. The Law Reform Commission of Canada and others have argued that the current classification of offences is a profound impediment to needed reform of Canadian criminal procedure in all areas, but especially as regards the jurisdiction of the courts over offences.[17]

3) Mode of Trial

The *Constitution Act, 1867* gives provinces the authority to establish courts within their territorial jurisdiction.[18] In the *Criminal Code*, Parliament allocates jurisdiction over offences to the courts thus created

---

13 Sections 675 and 813.

14 See, in particular, s. 677 and ss. 691–696.

15 R.S.C. 1985, c. S-26.

16 See, for example, Tim Quigley, *Procedure in Canadian Criminal Law*, 2d ed., loose-leaf (Toronto: Thomson Carswell, 2005) c.3. See also *Classification of Offences*, above note 1.

17 Law Reform Commission of Canada, *Our Criminal Procedure* (Ottawa: Law Reform Commission of Canada, 1988).

18 Above note 2, s. 92(15).

by the provinces.[19] This section looks at some of the devices Parliament uses in defining the jurisdiction of the courts for trial, appeal, and other purposes.

For trial, the *Code* allocates jurisdiction over summary conviction offences to the provincial court. Indictable offences, on the other hand, may be tried either in a "superior court of criminal jurisdiction" or a "court of criminal jurisdiction." According to section 468, the superior court of the province is competent to try any indictable offence, but, in practice, the allocation of jurisdiction is more complex. Section 468 is broad, but it must be seen in the light of section 469, which provides that a court of criminal jurisdiction is also competent to try all indictable offences except for fourteen listed offences. For practical purposes, then, it is the "court of criminal jurisdiction" that has general competence to try indictable offences other than those offences that are specifically enumerated as being within the "exclusive jurisdiction" of the superior court. For further complexity, however, section 553 of the *Code* reserves to the provincial court the "absolute jurisdiction" to try a variety of offences listed there, almost all of them property offences. The "exclusive" jurisdiction of a court means that an offence can be prosecuted in that court alone and that no other court, even in principle, will have jurisdiction. Thus, any offence listed in section 469 can be tried only in the superior court. By virtue of section 468, jurisdiction over all other indictable offences is concurrent between the provincial and superior court, subject only to the definition of a "court of criminal jurisdiction" in section 552. The attribution of "absolute" jurisdiction in section 553 means that, despite this concurrency, the provincial court will be the only court that *in fact* can exercise jurisdiction with regard to the offences listed in that section.

There is little difficulty in identifying the superior court of criminal jurisdiction or the provincial court. What is the "court of criminal jurisdiction" that has general competence to try indictable offences not reserved to either the superior court of criminal jurisdiction or the provincial court judge? A partial definition is provided in section 2 of the *Code*, but a more useful guide to practice is the definition of "judge" in section 552. When read with others, this provision states that in all provinces, except Quebec, a judge of the superior court has jurisdiction to try any indictable offence except those reserved to the exclusive jurisdiction of the superior court or those reserved to the provincial court by section 553. The Cour du Québec has jurisdiction to try all

---

19   See Patrick Healy, "Constitutional Limits on the Allocation of Trial Jurisdiction to the Superior or Provincial Court in Criminal Matters" (2003) 48 Crim. L.Q. 31.

indictable cases except those reserved to the superior court of criminal jurisdiction.[20]

The terms "superior court of criminal jurisdiction" and "court of criminal jurisdiction" are neither clear nor essential. To minimize the difficulty it is advisable to bear two points in mind with regard to indictable offences. The exclusive jurisdiction of the superior court is defined in section 469. The absolute jurisdiction of the provincial court is defined in section 553. For the rest, the court of criminal jurisdiction as defined in section 2 is (at least in theory) the court of trial, and for practical purposes the court is identified in section 552.

As noted above, however, there is yet another qualification. For all indictable offences, except those in the exclusive jurisdiction of the superior court or the absolute jurisdiction of the provincial court, the accused has a right of election as to the mode of trial. This means a right to choose among trial by jury, trial by judge alone, or trial by a judge of the provincial court.[21] Thus, although the *Code* stipulates that all of these offences may be tried by a court of criminal jurisdiction, the right of election allows the accused a choice of jurisdictions. Many factors influence this election, and most conspicuous among them is that by electing trial before the provincial court an accused waives the right to request a preliminary inquiry.

In addition to the right of election, the accused may be entitled to a re-election under certain conditions.[22] It is not appropriate to try to describe all the various rights of re-election here. In some circumstances the accused can re-elect as of right, but in other cases the consent of the prosecutor is needed. In broad terms, it is easier to re-elect down from trial by judge and jury to trial by judge alone or trial by provincial court. It is also easier to re-elect the earlier the decision is made. For example, an accused who elects trial by provincial court judge can re-elect "up" as of right until fourteen days before trial, but only with the prosecutor's consent thereafter.[23]

The right to re-elect is by no means absolute, however, and is considerably narrowed if the prosecutor refuses consent. The election of the accused may also be pre-empted by the prosecution if the attorney general prefers a direct indictment (which can require the matter to go

---

20 That is, the Cour du Québec will not hear trials of offences listed in s. 469 or of any offence where the accused elects trial by jury.
21 Section 536.
22 Sections 561*ff.*
23 Section 561(2).

to trial without a preliminary inquiry[24]) or requires trial by judge and jury for an offence punishable by more than five years.[25]

Apart from appeal and trial, the allocation of jurisdiction is important for a wide variety of functions, including the issuance of forms of process and the conduct of hearings, such as bail applications and preliminary inquiries. Many of these functions are identified and discussed throughout this text. Here, it is important to note a broader point. Only superior courts have general and inherent jurisdiction, which means, among other things, that the superior court is the court of first instance for any justiciable issue that is not otherwise allocated by statute.[26] Provincial courts only have the powers that are expressly given to them by legislation. This means, in principle, that they are subject to review by way of a prerogative writ unless such relief is specifically excluded by law. The most common among these is the writ of *certiorari*, which may be issued by a superior court to quash a decision of a judge in a lower court who has acted without jurisdiction.

B. JURISDICTION

Jurisdiction is a word used variously to mean power, authority, competence, or geographical space. It is used to describe the functions of police officers, judges, courts, legislative bodies, and others. It is also used to describe limitations upon them. In criminal procedure all of these various meanings are used in different contexts and, given the importance attached to several, this chapter introduces elementary notions of jurisdiction in criminal procedure.

1) Jurisdiction to Prosecute

Almost all criminal cases in Canada are public prosecutions conducted by agents of the attorney general. In principle, however, anyone may commence a prosecution by laying an information. If the information is sworn, a private prosecution may proceed unless the case is taken over by the attorney general.

---

24 Section 577.
25 Section 568.
26 *MacMillan Bloedel Ltd. v. Simpson*, [1995] 4 S.C.R. 725.

a) Public Prosecutions

The attorney general is the principal law officer of the Crown, which means that he or she is the chief barrister and solicitor for the government.[27] There is an attorney general in the federal government and in each of the provincial governments.

Prosecutions are almost never conducted personally by the attorney general, but by persons who are legally authorized to act in his name.[28] Section 2 of the *Code* specifies that the attorney general may be represented by his deputy.[29] With regard to public prosecutions, the definition of "prosecutor" in section 2 includes counsel appearing for the attorney general with regard to indictable offences. Some provinces have adopted a model in which routine responsibility for the conduct of criminal prosecutions is confided to a senior person called the director of public prosecutions. This model does not change the constitutional position of the attorney general as chief law officer of the Crown, but it does ensure a measure of professional independence for purposes of prosecution. It also helps guarantee greater openness and accountability around decisions to lay or withdraw charges, at least where the attorney general is directly involved. Counsel may include not only professional prosecutors but also private counsel who are appointed *ad hoc* to act on behalf of the attorney general.[30] With regard to summary conviction matters, the definition of prosecutor in section 785 allows prosecution by the attorney general, counsel appearing for him, or an "agent." In some instances, a summary conviction prosecution may also be conducted by a peace officer.[31]

Apart from general principles governing the authority to prosecute, Parliament occasionally imposes a requirement that the attorney general consent to the prosecution of some offences. This requirement is found in section 2 of the *Code*, or in the provision that creates the offence, and it is a condition that must be met before a prosecution may be commenced.[32] In most instances where consent is required it refers to

---

27 See John Edwards, *The Law Officers of the Crown* (London: Sweet & Maxwell, 1964); John Edwards, *The Attorney General, Politics and the Public Interest* (London: Sweet & Maxwell, 1984).

28 *R. v. Harrison*, [1977] 1 S.C.R. 238. Unless the personal intervention of the attorney general is required by law, the agent may exercise the powers of the attorney general: see, for example, *R. v. Light* (1993), 78 C.C.C. (3d) 221 at 253 (B.C.C.A.).

29 Section 2. See also *Interpretation Act*, above note 3, s. 24.

30 *R. v. Moscuzza* (2003), 63 O.R. (3d) 636 (C.A.).

31 See the definition of "prosecutor" in s. 785, which includes an agent. However, an agent may not prosecute an indictable offence, even if the trial is in provincial court: see *R. v. Edmunds*, [1981] 1 S.C.R. 233.

32 *R. v. Sunila* (1987), 35 C.C.C. (3d) 289 (N.S.S.C.A.D.).

the attorney general of the province, but there numerous exceptions.[33] Where this requirement exists, it virtually guarantees that a private prosecution could not be commenced because the likelihood that the attorney general would give consent in such cases is theoretically real but practically nil.

The requirement for the consent of the attorney general is intended to ensure a critical examination of cases before charges are laid. The requirement typically exists in relation to offences that are likely to be highly sensitive to the public or that otherwise require rigorous consideration of the public interest in prosecution. Wherever the requirement exists, the authenticity of the attorney general's consent will be placed before the court and presumed valid unless the prosecutor is required to prove it. There are several ways in which the requirement for consent is expressed in the *Criminal Code* and other statutes.[34] Despite these variations, the essential distinction to retain is between cases in which the personal consent of the attorney general is required[35] and the majority of instances in which the statute demands only the "consent of the attorney general." In the latter case, there is some scope for ambiguity as to precisely what is required. Something less than the personal consent of the attorney general would be sufficient, but anything less than the consent of prosecuting counsel in the instant case might be inadequate. Accordingly, such authorization might be sought from senior prosecuting counsel within the territorial jurisdiction in which the case arises. This might include senior counsel responsible for the direction of prosecutions in a province or region. In any case, where some form of consent is required, it should be given in writing and placed before the court.

The attorney general and her agents have a large measure of discretion in the conduct of prosecutions. The requirement of consent is one among many, and many of the others have a much greater importance in the routine practice of criminal law. The prosecutor exercises various statutory powers, such as deciding whether an accused must have a jury trial, whether to proceed by direct indictment, whether to assume carriage of a private prosecution, or, in any case, whether to enter a stay of proceedings.[36] The prosecution also exercises discretion over many other decisions, such as whether to proceed by indictable or summary conviction procedure in the case of a hybrid offence, whether to with-

---

33 Sections 7(4.3), 83.24, 136, 166, 172, 318, 319, 754, and 803 for the former, and ss. 7(2.3), 54, 119, and 447.2 for the latter.
34 See, for example, ss. 7, 54, 119, 174, and 385.
35 For example, s. 485.1.
36 Sections 568, 577, and 579.

draw a charge, and whether to consent to an adjournment, launch an appeal, and so on.[37] In some provinces the prosecution has a role in charging decisions and therefore has input into whether to charge an offence and, if so, what charges.[38]

As the prosecution's discretion is derived from the royal prerogative, the courts will rarely interfere with the manner in which it is exercised. In the absence of gross abuse or ill-will, the courts will not contradict or challenge discretionary decisions that are reserved to the prosecution.[39]

b) Private Prosecutions

As previously noted, any person may commence a criminal prosecution by swearing an information before a competent judicial authority. The concept of a private prosecution is ancient in the common law and it reflects the right of every person subject to the sovereign to invoke the protection of the law by making a complaint of a breach of the King's Peace. In modern terms, a private prosecutor is any prosecutor under the *Code* who is not an agent of the attorney general. It should not be thought, however, that a private prosecution of alleged crime is in any way a private action between the parties. The private prosecutor is not a plaintiff but is allowed under the criminal law to prosecute in the place of the attorney general.

Although the right to commence a private prosecution is ancient, the growth and development of the role of the attorney general as the public prosecutor has diminished the frequency and the significance of private prosecutions. Indeed, virtually the only reason that motivates people today to commence a private prosecution is that a public prosecutor has decided not to proceed, either because there is insufficient evidence to sustain the case or because prosecution of the alleged offence is otherwise not in the public interest. Thus private prosecutions now tend to occur only when the attorney general or her agent has refused to lay charges.

The formal procedure for the commencement of a private prosecution is the same whether the offence alleged is indictable or summary, but the position is not the same for purposes of trial. Assuming that a judge receives and endorses the information, the informant becomes

---

37 *R. v. Beare*, [1988] 2 S.C.R. 387 at 410.

38 *R. v. Lafrance*, [1975] 2 S.C.R. 201. See the discussion in *R. v. Regan*, [2002] 1 S.C.R. 297 [*Regan*], of the ways in which the institutional arrangements between police and the Crown differ from province to province with regard to authority over charging decisions.

39 *R. v. T.(V.)*, [1992] 1 S.C.R. 749; *Regan*, ibid.

the prosecutor. The prosecutor has carriage of the case from that point and must conform to all of the obligations that prosecutors are obliged to fulfil. A private prosecutor, for example, would be no less bound by the obligation to make full disclosure to the defence than an agent of the attorney general.

A private prosecutor may appear personally or be represented by counsel.[40] If the offence is indictable and the accused is entitled to a preliminary inquiry, a private prosecution may proceed to the conclusion of the preliminary inquiry. At this point, however, the *Criminal Code* erects barriers to the continuation of the prosecution at trial. If the accused is ordered to stand trial after a preliminary inquiry, a private prosecutor may not prefer an indictment against that person without the written authorization of a judge in the court of trial. Similarly, in the event that there was no preliminary inquiry, or there was a preliminary inquiry at which the accused was discharged, the private prosecutor may not prefer a direct indictment without the written order of a judge.[41]

In all cases, indictable or summary, the attorney general may intervene in a private prosecution for the purpose of assuming the carriage of the prosecution or for the purpose of entering a stay of proceedings. With respect to indictable offences, this power is recognized expressly in section 579 of the *Code*. A similar power is given in section 579.1 to the Attorney General of Canada with respect to private prosecutions concerning federal offences outside the *Criminal Code* in which no provincial attorney general has intervened. With respect to summary conviction offences, the definition of "prosecutor" refers to instances in which the attorney general has not intervened, but there is no express provision in Part XXVII of the *Code* that is comparable to sections 579 or 579.1. It is arguable that express provision is not necessary because the power of an attorney general to intervene is well established at common law.

The *Criminal Code* includes procedural steps that must be observed at the commencement of a private prosecution. These were enacted to simplify and expedite proceedings. Section 507.1 requires that any information laid under section 504 by a private informant must be referred to a judge of the provincial court or, in Quebec, a judge of the Cour du Quebec. It is also possible to refer the matter to a justice designated specifically for this purpose if there is one in the jurisdic-

---

40   Section 785.
41   Section 577. See also *Johnson v. Inglis* (1980), 52 C.C.C. (2d) 385 (Ont. H.C.J.); *Garton v. Whelan* (1984), 14 C.C.C. (3d) 449 (Ont. H.C.J.), discussing the circumstances in which a judge should consent.

tion. This judicial officer will decide whether a charge will be laid and whether to compel the appearance of the accused to answer that charge by summons or by arrest warrant. No such decision can be made unless the judge or designated justice has heard and considered the allegations of the informant and the evidence of any witnesses. Further, he must be satisfied that the attorney general has already received a copy of the information, with reasonable notice of the date for hearing the informant and witnesses, and been given the opportunity to appear at the hearing to cross-examine witnesses and call any other relevant evidence.

If neither a summons nor a warrant is issued at the conclusion of the hearing the presiding judge or designated justice will endorse the information to that effect. If the informant does not seek to compel the issuance of process within six months of this endorsement, the matter is closed. If such proceedings are taken but no process is issued, the information is deemed never to have been laid.

Finally, there are several provisions of the *Code* that allow for a privately laid information to be received and, if endorsed, to lead to the issuance of an order for the respondent to be bound over. There are several instances in which orders of this kind can be sought and authorized. The model is found in section 810. Any person who has reason to believe that an indictable offence will be committed upon her, or upon a third party, may swear an information to this effect and, if it is received, seek an order for the respondent to be bound over upon conditions. These forms of procedure have become increasingly important in daily practice.

2) Territorial Jurisdiction

As a general rule, a person can only be held liable under Canadian criminal law for an offence that he commits within Canadian territorial limits. This principle of limitation is based upon the historical rationale that a violation of the criminal law is a violation of the sovereign's peace. Accordingly, the scope of the criminal law is normally coextensive with the territorial sovereignty of the state. This principle is expressed in section 6(2) of the *Criminal Code*.

Similar to almost every rule of criminal procedure, this general principle is subject to exceptions. For example, the *Code* specifically includes within Canada any offence committed within the territorial seas off Canadian shores.[42] Further, the Supreme Court of Canada has held that if an offence is committed abroad but has a "real and substantial"

---

42   See, for example, ss. 7, 57, 58, 74, 75, and 465.

connection to Canada, it falls within the class of offences committed in Canada.[43]

Further, in a variety of provisions the *Code* and other statutes explicitly create exceptions giving Canadian courts jurisdiction over offences committed outside Canadian territorial limits. Generally speaking, these provisions reflect obligations or agreements contracted by Canada in treaties with other states. However, the extraterritorial jurisdiction created in the *Code* does not, in every case, map onto pre-existing international agreements. Some reflect a deliberate decision in policy to extend the reach of Canadian jurisdiction to address specific Canadian interests abroad.[44]

In addition to issues of when behaviour abroad can attract criminal liability in Canada, there are also issues relating to police investigative techniques abroad that relate to prosecutions in Canada. In particular, suspects are sometimes interrogated while outside Canada, most often by foreign police but sometimes by Canadians. Canadian police might also be involved in searches conducted in other countries. A question has arisen, therefore, as to the extent to which an accused can complain of a failure to comply with *Charter* standards when the alleged failure occurred outside of Canada.

As a generalization, it is safe to say that the *Charter* is unlikely to have much influence on investigative techniques employed abroad. Foreign officials cannot be expected to comply with *Charter* standards and their failure to do so will not give rise to a *Charter* violation. The fact that U.S. police do not give a warning in accordance with section 10(b) requirements, for example, cannot give rise to a section 10(b) claim. However, if the conditions in which a statement was obtained are particularly egregious, it is possible that attempting to introduce that evidence at a trial in Canada might constitute a section 7 violation.[45] The *Charter* was found to apply in *R. v. Cook*, where two Canadian police officers went to the United States and interrogated an accused after having given him a section10(b) warning that was clearly deficient.[46] However, *Cook*'s authority is overshadowed by the Supreme Court's more recent decision in *Hape*, which (while not calling *Cook* wrong on

---

43 *Libman v. The Queen*, [1985] 2 S.C.R. 178.

44 See above note 42. For a review of the underlying theory behind extraterritoriality in criminal law, see Robert J. Currie & Steve Coughlan, "Extraterritorial Criminal Jurisdiction: Bigger Picture or Smaller Frame?" (2007) 11 Can. Crim. L. Rev. 141.

45 See the discussion in *R. v. Harrer*, [1995] 3 S.C.R. 562; *R. v. Terry*, [1996] 2 S.C.R. 207.

46 *R. v. Cook*, [1998] 2 S.C.R. 597 [*Cook*].

its own facts) concluded that the approach to extraterritorial application of the *Charter* in *Cook* was wrong.[47]

In *Hape*, Canadian police participated in several warrantless searches in the Turks and Caicos islands that, if conducted in Canada, would have violated section 8. There was no evidence in the case as to whether the searches complied with Turks and Caicos law. The Court held, though, that the accused could not claim a *Charter* violation. The general approach laid out in that case requires courts to answer two questions. The first, for the *Charter* to have any prospect of applying, is whether section 32 is met, which makes the *Charter* applicable only to Canadian state actors. Although, even if a Canadian state actor is involved, the principle of sovereignty will normally mean that the *Charter* still does not apply to that person's activities abroad. The *Charter* will only apply if there is an exception to sovereignty, such as evidence that the foreign state consented to the application of *Charter* standards: the Court observed that "[i]n most cases, there will be no such exception and the *Charter* will not apply."[48] In that event, the second question is whether admitting evidence obtained through the foreign investigation renders the trial unfair, thus giving rise to a section 7 violation. In most cases, however, neither part of the test will be met. Thus, the *Charter* has a minimal impact on investigations conducted outside Canada.

Proof that a Canadian court has jurisdiction over an offence committed within or without Canada is a necessary condition of criminal liability: jurisdiction over the locus of an offence is a condition of criminal liability but it is not the end of the analysis. The court must be satisfied that it has jurisdiction over the offence, whether that offence was allegedly committed outside Canada or within its territorial limits. Having jurisdiction requires more than just that the offence occurred in Canada, however.

In keeping with the adage that all crime is local, a criminal prosecution will typically be conducted in the judicial district within which an offence is alleged to have been committed. Precisely where this is will depend upon the manner in which a province or territory has organized its courts. Although it is now largely unnecessary, the *Code* provides that if the offence is alleged to have occurred in an unorganized area it may be prosecuted in the nearest judicial district.[49]

Not all offences are committed in a single place, of course. As a result, there can be jurisdiction in more than one country, more than one

---

47   *R. v. Hape*, 2007 SCC 26 [*Hape*].
48   *Hape, ibid.* at para 113.
49   Section 480.

province or territory, or more than one judicial district within a province or territory.[50] While no province or territory may assert jurisdiction over an offence wholly committed in another, a prosecution may be conducted in any province or territory in which an element of the alleged offence occurred. This principle therefore allows for concurrent jurisdiction. Territorial jurisdiction in a province will be found when there is a link between the judicial district of the court and the offence in the sense that some part of the *actus reus* of the offence occurred in that district.

In *R. v. Bigelow*,[51] for example, the accused was charged with detaining a child with the intent to deprive the mother of lawful custody. He had picked up the child for an access visit in Ontario and then flown to Alberta before the scheduled time to return the child. His argument was that the offence of "detaining" had not occurred in Ontario but in Alberta, and, therefore, that the Ontario trial court did not have jurisdiction.

The Ontario Court of Appeal acknowledged that section 478 would prevent an Ontario court from trying an offence "committed entirely in another province." However, the Court noted that offences could have elements that mean they were committed in more than one province, and identified three such grounds: continuity of operation, commission of an overt act, and the generation of effects. These three grounds are not entirely distinct and can overlap with each other. This would be the case, for example, where a telemarketing scheme that originates in one province causes the victim to make a decision to her detriment in another province, and leads to the deposit of funds to the offender's credit in a third province. In such a case all three of the grounds identified in *Bigelow* would operate. In *Bigelow* itself the commission of the overt act of boarding a plane with the child in Ontario, that this act was part of a pre-planned scheme, and that the mother was deprived of her custody rights in Ontario because of this act, was sufficient to give Ontario courts jurisdiction.[52]

People alleged to have committed an offence do not always stay in the judicial district that would have territorial jurisdiction. The *Code* provides that such persons may be transferred to the judicial district in which the offence is alleged to have been committed.[53] Following arrest, a judge may issue a warrant that, in effect, authorizes the forced

---

50 *R. v. L.(D.A.)* (1996), 107 C.C.C. (3d) 178 (B.C.C.A.).
51 (1982), 69 C.C.C. (2d) 204 (Ont. C.A.) [*Bigelow*].
52 See also *R. v. Trudel, ex p. Horbas & Myhaluk*, [1969] 3 C.C.C. 95 (Man. C.A.).
53 See, for example, s. 543, permitting a justice conducting a preliminary inquiry to have the inquiry and the accused transferred to the jurisdiction where the offence is alleged to have occurred.

removal of the accused to the jurisdiction in which the prosecution will take place.[54] Further, although a court cannot *try* an offence committed wholly in another jurisdiction, it is permitted to accept a guilty plea from an accused and impose sentence, provided the attorney general consents.[55] The *Code* does not allow the accused to be tried on the merits in the place where he is found because the evidence is not there. The consent of the attorney general ensures that a disposition of the case upon a guilty plea is consistent with the public interest.

A trial that is scheduled within the judicial district of the alleged offence may be moved to another district within the same province. Section 599 provides that a change of venue may be ordered if it is "expedient to the ends of justice."[56] This would appear to confer a broad discretion upon the court, but, in practice, a change of venue has always been exceptional. It may be sought by the prosecutor or the accused and the applicant must show cause as to why a change of venue is necessary. Clearly the application will be granted if there are grounds to believe that a jury in that venue could not try the accused impartially but applications for a change of venue are not restricted to a lack of impartiality in a jury trial. Further, questions of jury partiality in a particular location, at least where they arise out of extensive pre-trial publicity, might be better resolved through the challenge for cause procedures in the *Code* rather than through a change of venue. Whether the trial is by jury or judge alone, a change of venue may be ordered if the applicant can identify a cogent reason to suggest that the trial would be unfair or prejudicial to either party if it continued where it began.[57] The potential unfairness must relate to the location of the trial: where it relates to the evidence to be heard, moving the trial to a different location will not solve matters.[58]

3) Jurisdiction over the Accused

Apart from jurisdiction over the subject-matter of an offence, no court can adjudicate in respect of a particular person unless it also has jurisdiction over the accused. The central question is thus whether the accused is properly before the court. The court will have jurisdiction over the person of the accused if she is within the territorial limits of the

---

54   Sections 503(3) and 528.
55   Section 478(3).
56   In addition, s. 599(1)(b) permits a change of venue to be ordered if there is no jury panel in the district where the prosecution has begun.
57   *R. v. Charest* (1990), 57 C.C.C. (3d) 312 (Que. C.A.).
58   *R. v. Suzack* (2000), 30 C.R. (5th) 346 (Ont. C.A.).

court's jurisdiction or the accused has otherwise been lawfully ordered to appear before that court.[59]

For practical purposes the question has arisen chiefly in relation to the exercise of jurisdiction by provincial courts. As their authority to adjudicate is statutory, it may be questioned whether courts lose their jurisdiction over the accused by an error or omission relating to the process by which the accused is required to appear in court, such as appearances, adjournments, or the conduct of proceedings in the absence of the accused. A secondary question is whether jurisdiction that is lost can be regained. At one point these issues caused some concern, but section 485 now excuses most errors relating to the appearance of the accused. Because of that section, jurisdiction over an offence is not lost simply because a judge fails to exercise jurisdiction at any particular time or fails to comply with any of the *Code* provisions respecting adjournments or remands. Generally speaking, jurisdiction over an accused is not lost because of non-appearance.[60] Moreover, the courts have broad authority to issue process, such as a bench warrant for arrest, that allows jurisdiction over the person to be regained in the event that it is lost.[61] In addition, some authorities suggest that a court obtains jurisdiction over the person so long as the person is present in court, no matter what process has brought that person there.[62]

Apart from loss of jurisdiction over the accused, there are some persons over whom the courts have no jurisdiction. These include persons under the age of twelve, who are presumed by section 13 of the *Code* to be incapable of crime, and persons who are immune from prosecution for reasons of policy. The most obvious example of immunity is that extended to diplomats, but there was also an ancient principle that the Crown was immune from liability, based on the fiction that the sovereign can do no wrong.[63] It is noteworthy, though, that various amendments to the *Code*, intended to expand the circumstances in which organizations can be held criminally liable, include "public body" in the definition of "organization."[64] This could have the effect, in some cases, of extending the liability of the Crown.

---

59 Section 470.

60 Section 485(1.1).

61 Section 485(2).

62 *R. v. Lindsay* (2006), 207 C.C.C. (3d) 296 (B.C.C.A.).

63 See *Interpretation Act*, above note 3, s. 17 and *R. v. Eldorado Nuclear Ltd; Uranium Canada Ltd.*, [1983] 2 S.C.R. 551.

64 Section 2 and *An Act to Amend the Criminal Code (Criminal Liability of Organizations)*, S.C. 2003, c. 21.

4) Jurisdiction in Time

Indictable offences are generally not barred by a period of limitation or prescription. This means that offences committed many years previously might still be prosecuted, subject of course to considerations about the quality of evidence.[65] Summary conviction matters, however, are barred six months following the completion of the offence. These matters will influence the decision of prosecutors of whether to proceed by indictment in the prosecution of hybrid offences.[66] Some difficulty can arise in determining when the time limit for prosecuting an alleged summary conviction offence has passed.[67]

It is an elementary feature of the principle of legality that criminal offences do not have retrospective application, from which it follows that a court has no jurisdiction to try a charge of conduct that was not an offence when it occurred. This principle is confirmed in the *Criminal Code* and in section 11(g) of the *Charter*. In *R. v. Finta*, the Supreme Court stated that there is a partial exception to this principle for war crimes allegedly committed in Europe during the Second World War. The Court qualified the retroactive application of provisions of the *Criminal Code* concerning such crimes as a partial exception because the alleged crimes took place before they were declared offences in Canada; but the Court was satisfied that such offences were recognized as crimes in international law at the time of their commission.[68]

Note that the rule against retrospective application applies to substantive criminal law whereas procedural rules are ordinarily presumed to have immediate effect, and therefore will apply retrospectively. However, it will not always be straightforward to decide whether a provision is substantive or procedural. In general, a law will be classified as procedural in this analysis only if it is exclusively so, and will be classified as substantive if it creates or impinges on vested rights.[69]

The right to trial within a reasonable time, guaranteed by section 11(b) of the *Charter*, is not typically seen as an aspect of jurisdiction. Nevertheless, it should be mentioned because unreasonable delay can cause a *Charter* violation and the remedy for it is a stay of proceedings. When granted, the net effect is that the state has run out of the time within

---

65   The most common instances of this are the prosecutions of what are known widely as "historical sexual offences."

66   *R. v. Belair* (1988), 41 C.C.C. (3d) 329 (Ont. C.A.); *R. v. Kalkhorany* (1994), 89 C.C.C. (3d) 184 (Ont. C.A.).

67   *R. v. Belgal Holdings Ltd.*, [1967] 3 C.C.C. 34 (Ont. H.C.J.).

68   [1994] 1 S.C.R. 701.

69   *Re Application under Section 83.28 of the Criminal Code*, [2004] SCC 42.

which it can prosecute the accused. Technically, this does not mean that there is a loss of jurisdiction arising from unreasonable delay. But the effect of the stay is a judicial order that there is no jurisdiction to proceed.

Obviously, trial within a reasonable time is a principle of procedural fairness and for that reason it finds a place in the Constitution, among the principles of fundamental justice. Unreasonable delay has two possible causes, essentially. First, it may be attributed to one of the parties, or conceivably the court, but if the responsible party is the accused there will be no remedy under section 24 of the *Charter*. The second is institutional delay that is attributable to the absence of adequate resources for the administration of justice in a timely manner. Delay of this nature is most likely to be found in large, urban jurisdictions that have a high volume of cases. This was the case in *R. v. Askov*,[70] and, as a result, measures were taken to rectify the systemic difficulties identified by the Supreme Court in that instance. The Court's subsequent decision in *R. v. Morin*,[71] which placed a much greater emphasis on the need for the accused to demonstrate that actual prejudice arose from the delay, dramatically reduced the number of applications brought under this section. Recently, however, in Ontario in particular, institutional delay has increased and there has been a resurgence in section 11(b) applications.[72] Further, as various courts of appeal are interpreting the Supreme Court's guidelines from *Askov* and *Morin* in different fashions, it may be that the matter needs to be addressed once again by the highest court.[73]

5) Jurisdiction under the *Charter*

Section 24 of the *Charter* allows a court of competent jurisdiction to grant a remedy for the breach of rights guaranteed by that part of Constitution. But what is a court of competent jurisdiction? Could the accused argue at a bail hearing that he had been arbitrarily detained or that his right to counsel had been breached? Could he argue that he did not have adequate disclosure from the prosecution? Could he seek the exclusion of evidence obtained in violation of a guaranteed right? Could he seek a remedy at the preliminary inquiry?

---

70 [1990] 2 S.C.R. 1199.
71 [1992] 1 S.C.R. 771.
72 A number of delay cases have reached the Ontario Court of Appeal in the past few years, with varied success. See, in particular, the comments of Hill J. in *R. v. Lof* (2005), 36 C.R. (6th) 393 (Ont. S.C.J.) concerning the ongoing problem of delay in Peel, the jurisdiction from which *Askov* arose.
73 See the discussion in Gerry Ferguson & Steve Coughlan, *Annual Review of Criminal Law 2005* (Toronto: Carswell, 2006) c. 2.

In *R. v. Mills*[74] the Supreme Court decided that a court of competent jurisdiction means, for most practical purposes in criminal matters, the court of trial. The majority observed that the *Charter* itself included no express allocation of jurisdiction. On this basis, then, it was appropriate to determine if a judge at a preliminary inquiry was a court of competent jurisdiction, by reference to the ordinary principles of jurisdiction in criminal matters. In this regard, the *Criminal Code* certainly included no express attribution of jurisdiction over constitutional issues to provincial courts presiding over preliminary inquiries. However, neither the *Charter* nor the *Code* allocate jurisdiction over constitutional issues to the provincial court at trial, for that matter.

The Court's decision that a judge conducting a preliminary inquiry is not a court of competent jurisdiction to decide issues under the *Charter* was affirmed in *R. v. Hynes*.[75] While the proposition concerning a lack of statutory jurisdiction is weak in principle, it has been reinforced by other considerations. One such consideration is that this position avoids the possibility of contradictory decisions at the preliminary inquiry and trial. Another is that it avoids the likelihood of interlocutory appeals that would arise if constitutional remedies were granted at the preliminary inquiry. In short, there are arguments based upon the efficient administration of cases that support the decisions in *Mills* and *Hynes*. However, there is some awkwardness about this position too. It effectively requires a judge to ignore a possible *Charter* breach, no matter how glaring it might be. In any event, with recent amendments that radically trim the scope of preliminary inquiries, the significance of these issues is diminished.

For procedural purposes, however, there remains a question about which court a *Charter* application may be addressed to when there is no pending trial. In these instances the court of competent jurisdiction is the superior court. This is undoubtedly consistent with orthodox principles of jurisdiction, the most basic of which is that the superior court is a court of general and inherent jurisdiction that can hear any justiciable issue that is not otherwise expressly assigned to another court.

C. STATUTORY OVERVIEW OF PROCEDURE FROM CHARGING DECISION TO TRIAL

One of the major obstacles to getting a real sense of how criminal procedure works at the trial stage is the fact that the relevant sections are

---

74   [1986] 1 S.C.R. 863.
75   [2001] 3 S.C.R. 623.

found in widely disparate parts of the *Code*. As noted above, the *Code* is arranged in a roughly chronological fashion, but there are exceptions to this rule. For example, the procedures for summary conviction offences are set out nearly at the end, in Part XXVII, but nonetheless incorporate many earlier provisions by reference. Liberal use of the *Code*'s index is necessary simply to find where to look for the right rules. Therefore, it might be useful to lay out a brief road map showing the various routes that might be followed, from the commencement of proceedings to an eventual trial, and the relevant *Code* sections.

Under section 504, anyone can lay an information alleging the commission of an offence in front of a justice of the peace. This information will, according to section 506, be in Form 2, which is found in section 849. Under section 788, this is the document under which a summary conviction trial will take place.

The justice of the peace decides, under section 507, whether to issue a summons or a warrant, where "a case for doing so is made out,"[76] to require the accused to attend court. Note that these are two distinct steps: whether to do anything, and if so whether to proceed by warrant or summons. Under section 507(3), the evidence is taken on oath.

Alternatively, rather than initially seeking process under section 504, a peace officer might have arrested a person without a warrant. That person may still be in custody or may have already been released at some stage on an appearance notice.[77] In that event, section 505 creates an obligation to present whatever process was issued to a justice of the peace. Section 508 then imposes an obligation on the justice to perform a screening process similar to that in section 507.

Presuming the matter goes further, the accused will be arrested or will receive the summons that was issued. If the accused was arrested, he or she will (under section 503) be taken in front of a justice of the peace who will decide whether to hold or release the accused. This bail hearing will be conducted in accordance with the procedures in section 515. Frequently, as a practical matter, bail hearings are by a judge rather than a justice of the peace.

Following any issues concerning the release of the accused will be the "arraignment" — the accused's initial appearance in court to answer the charge. If the offence is hybrid, the Crown should elect whether to proceed by indictment or summary conviction at this stage. If the matter is a summary conviction, automatically or by election, the accused enters a plea and will be tried on the information in Form 2. However,

---

76   Section 507(1)(b).
77   See the discussion in Chapter 6.

it is possible at this stage for that information to be withdrawn and a different information laid. The procedures in Part XXVII apply to summary conviction trials, and under section 798 a summary conviction court judge has jurisdiction. If the matter is indictable, section 471 says the trial must be by judge and jury unless some other part of the *Code* specifies otherwise. In fact, exceptions of some sort are then made for every offence, and the vast majority of criminal trials occur without a jury. Most indictable offences can be tried in any court.

Section 469 gives a superior court of criminal jurisdiction (defined in section 2 for each province) the ability to try any offence. Section 468 gives a court of criminal jurisdiction (also defined in section 2 for each province) the ability to try any offence other than those listed in section 469. Section 554 gives a provincial court the ability to try any offence other than those listed in section 469. "Provincial court" is also defined in this section of the *Code* and in some provinces that definition overlaps with the definition of "court of criminal jurisdiction."

Although section 471 mandates jury trials as the putative norm, section 558 says that an accused can elect not to have a jury, except for the offences listed in section 469. Further, section 473 states that an accused can elect not to have a jury, even for the offences listed in section 469, with the attorney general's consent.

Normally, therefore, a choice of mode of trial exists and, under section 536(2), the accused is asked to elect a mode of trial. However, if the offence is listed as in the absolute jurisdiction of a magistrate, then the accused does not elect and is tried in provincial court.[78] Similarly, if the offence is listed in section 469, the accused does not elect and is sent to a trial by judge and jury (subject to the attorney general's consent, as in section 473).

If the accused refuses to elect, then according to section 565(1)(c) the trial will be by judge and jury. The same is also true, under section 567, if there is more than one co-accused and they elect differently from one another. Further, even if the accused does not want a jury, the attorney general can compel a jury trial if the offence is punishable by more than five years, under section 568.

If the accused elects trial by a provincial court judge, the accused can then enter a plea and the trial can take place at any point.

If the accused elects trial by judge alone or trial by judge and jury, then under section 535 there might be a preliminary inquiry if the accused or the Crown request one. Preliminary inquiries are governed by the procedures in Part XVII of the *Code* (see Chapter 9). Note that an

---

78   Section 553.

accused does not enter a plea at the preliminary inquiry stage: that is done in front of the court where the trial will take place.

A provincial court judge has the ability to convert a trial into a preliminary inquiry under section 555(1) where this seems appropriate "for any reason." Similarly, under section 555(2), where the value of a stolen item turns out to be high enough that the offence was not one of absolute jurisdiction, the accused is offered an election and the trial might become a preliminary inquiry. Conversely, where, under section 561(1)(a), an accused re-elects "down" to trial by provincial court judge during the preliminary inquiry, that preliminary can be turned into a trial under section 562.

The accused has various rights of re-election set out in section 561. Depending on whether the accused is re-electing up or down, and to what point the proceedings have advanced, re-election is either as of right or requires consent from the prosecutor.

If an accused elects trial by judge and jury but then fails to appear, then, under section 598, the later trial will not be in front of a judge and jury unless the accused shows a legitimate excuse.

Following the preliminary inquiry, the judge will either discharge the accused or order the accused to stand trial on some offence in respect of the transaction charged. These powers are set out in section 548(1), but neither result is quite what it sounds like. First, "ordering the accused to stand trial" has no independent effect. It is simply a precondition to further action, normally by the Crown. For an indictable offence trial to take place, a new document, an "indictment" (hence "indictable offence") must be "preferred" (that is, laid in front of the trial court to commence trial). According to section 566, the indictment may be in Form 4 (also found in section 849). Section 576 dictates that an indictment can only be preferred on a basis set out in the *Criminal Code*. Some of those bases are set out in section 574, which permits an indictment to be preferred: (a) on a charge for which the preliminary inquiry judge ordered the person to stand trial, or (b) on any charge founded on the facts disclosed at the preliminary. This latter provision means that the indictment may charge a different offence than the one charged in the information.

Where no preliminary inquiry is requested, section 574(1.1) permits an indictment to be preferred on any charge set out in an information after the accused has made an election on it.

Normally these powers to prefer an indictment would be relied upon by a Crown prosecutor, but section 574(3) permits a private prosecutor to prefer an indictment with leave of the intended trial court.

Note that discharging the accused does not guarantee that the accused will not stand trial. Under section 577 an indictment can also be preferred where no preliminary inquiry was held, a preliminary inquiry was commenced but not concluded or, most notably, a preliminary inquiry was held and *the accused was discharged*. An indictment under these circumstances, usually referred to as a "direct indictment," requires the written consent of the attorney general, or, in the case of a private prosecution, an order of a judge of the court where the information is preferred.

The various discretionary powers of the Crown prosecutor mentioned above do not violate the *Charter*, provided they are not used abusively. The Crown also has other powers, including staying the proceedings with the ability to recommence them within one year, under section 579, and intervening to take over a private prosecution, under sections 579.01 and 579.1.

FURTHER READINGS

CURRIE, ROBERT J. & STEVE COUGHLAN, "Extraterritorial Criminal Jurisdiction: Bigger Picture or Smaller Frame?" (2007) 11 Can. Crim. L. Rev. 141

EDWARDS, JOHN, *The Attorney General, Politics and the Public Interest* (London: Sweet & Maxwell, 1984)

EDWARDS, JOHN, *The Law Officers of the Crown* (London: Sweet & Maxwell, 1964)

HEALY, PATRICK, "Constitutional Limits on the Allocation of Trial Jurisdiction to the Superior or Provincial Court in Criminal Matters" (2003) 48 Crim. L.Q. 31

LAW REFORM COMMISSION OF CANADA, *Controlling Criminal Prosecutions: The Attorney General and the Crown Prosecutor* (Ottawa: Law Reform Commission of Canada, 1990)

LAW REFORM COMMISSION OF CANADA, *Our Criminal Procedure* (Ottawa: Law Reform Commission of Canada, 1988)

LAW REFORM COMMISSION OF CANADA, *The Classification of Offences*, (Ottawa: Law Reform Commission of Canada, 1986)

QUIGLEY, TIM, *Procedure in Canadian Criminal Law*, 2d ed. (Toronto: Thomson Carswell, 2005) c. 3

CHAPTER 4

SEARCH AND SEIZURE

A. INTRODUCTION

Other than in powers of arrest, the ability of police to interfere with the liberty of individuals is most evident in powers of search and seizure. Powers to search exist within the *Criminal Code* and other statutes and are also found at common law. Powers to seize are typically associated with search powers, though there are occasional exceptions to that rule.

Rules relating to search and seizure reflect competing concerns, as do all rules of criminal procedure. The Supreme Court noted in *Baron v. Canada* that "the decision to grant or withhold the warrant requires the balancing of two interests: that of the individual to be free of intrusions of the state and that of the state to intrude on the privacy of the individual for the purpose of law enforcement."[1] Early pronouncements by the Court fully recognize that the interests of individuals are entrenched in section 8 of the *Charter* as a guarantee against unreasonable search and seizure. Thus, for example, in the leading case of *Hunter v. Southam*, the Court noted that the question was "whether in a particular situation the public's interest in being left alone by government must give way to the government's interest in intruding on the individual's privacy in

---

1 *Baron v. Canada*, [1993] 1 S.C.R. 416 at para. 24 [*Baron*]. See also *R. v. S.A.B.*, 2003 SCC 60 at para. 43 [*S.A.B.*], where the Court noted that the issue in considering search powers is the balance between "the truth-seeking interests of law enforcement and the equally essential respect for individual rights."

order to advance its goals, notably those of law enforcement."[2] That is, priority was to be given to the individual interest.

More recently, this high respect for the individual right to be free from intrusions of the state has been less evident. Where, for many years, the *Code* contained a power to search places for evidence of crimes—a power with reasonably well-understood limits—a number of additional provisions have been added in the past few years. As will be discussed below, these provisions create warrants allowing police to obtain and bank DNA samples,[3] take impressions of feet, hands, teeth, and other parts of the body,[4] record telephone numbers,[5] track vehicles,[6] perform video surveillance,[7] and, indeed, to "use any device or investigative technique or procedure *or do any thing*" that would be an unreasonable search without a warrant.[8] Therefore, the state's statutory ability to intrude on the individual has become much greater.[9]

It appears that the Supreme Court might also have become less firm in their earlier view, expressed in *Hunter*, that one should prefer "the right of the individual to be free from state interference to the interests of the state in advancing its purposes through such interference."[10] In *CanadianOxy Chemicals Ltd.*, the Court held that

---

2   *Hunter v. Southam*, [1984] 2 S.C.R. 145 at 159 [*Hunter*].
3   Sections 487.04–487.091.
4   Section 487.092.
5   Section 492.2.
6   Section 492.1.
7   Section 487.01(4).
8   Section 487.01 [emphasis added]. These last two particular provisions will be discussed in Chapter 5. It should be noted that all of these methods of infringing on an individual's privacy fall within the meaning of "search." The question in deciding whether something is a search relates to whether a privacy interest is interfered with — see the discussion of "reasonable expectation of privacy" at Section D(1), below in this chapter. The Court has generally given "search" a broad interpretation. In *R. v. Silveira*, [1995] 2 S.C.R. 297 [*Silveira*], for example, the police forced entry into a dwelling house in order to secure the premises, but then waited until a search warrant arrived in order to actually inspect the premises. The Crown argued that this was an illegal entry followed by a lawful search, but the Court held that no artificial line could be drawn between the two actions.
9   See Stanley A. Cohen, "The Paradoxical Nature of Privacy in the Context of Criminal Law and the *Canadian Charter of Rights and Freedoms*" (2002) 7 Can. Crim. L. Rev. 125, where he argues that, although privacy has been given a central role in the analysis of "unreasonable search and seizure" in s. 8, the effect has been a narrowing of privacy by *Charter* cases.
10 *Hunter*, above note 2 at 160. The Court makes this observation in noting the intention of the *Charter*, but the guarantees in s. 8 are minimum guarantees, not the ideal. As a matter of fact, search and seizure law generally is so intimately bound up with the interpretation of s. 8, and, in particular, with the minimum

The purpose of s. 487(1) is to allow the investigators to unearth and preserve as much relevant evidence as possible. To ensure that the authorities are able to perform their appointed functions properly they should be able to locate, examine and preserve all the evidence relevant to events which may have given rise to criminal liability . . . . The function of the police, and other peace officers, is to investigate incidents which might be criminal, make a conscientious and informed decision as to whether charges should be laid, and then present the full and unadulterated facts to the prosecutorial authorities. To that end an unnecessary and restrictive interpretation of s. 487(1) defeats its purpose.[11]

There is little evidence of priority being given to the individual's interest in this approach.

Still, the point remains that search and seizure powers must respect individual interests, particularly given the protection from unreasonable search and seizure guaranteed in section 8 of the *Charter*. This balancing is reflected in a variety of ways in statutory and non-statutory search powers. The need for restraint manifests itself in various specific requirements such as accountability, openness, or, more simply, as an acknowledgment of the right to privacy.

Though search and seizure issues extend beyond *Charter*-related questions, important principles concerning search and seizure generally were laid down by the Supreme Court of Canada in the early section 8 case of *Hunter v. Southam*. Even though many search powers predated the *Charter*, today all are required, at a minimum, to comply with its terms. Most significant for immediate purposes were two findings in the case: the minimum constitutional requirements for a search with a warrant, and that a warrantless search is *prima facie* illegal. It is therefore most convenient to discuss search powers under two separate headings: searches with a warrant and searches without a warrant.[12]

requirements for searches laid down in *Hunter*, that it is neither desirable nor practical to separate *Charter* and non-*Charter* cases on the issue. This purpose must be taken to apply to searches and the interpretation of search powers generally, whether a *Charter* claim is specifically at issue or not.

11 *CanadianOxy Chemicals Ltd. v. Canada (Attorney General)*, [1999] 1 S.C.R. 743 at para. 22 [*CanadianOxy*].

12 It is worth noting that the distinction between searches with a warrant and searches without a warrant does not map perfectly onto the distinction between statutory search powers and common law search powers. Although searches with a warrant are statutory, warrantless searches can be created by statute as well as by common law. Indeed, in *R. v. Feeney*, [1997] 2 S.C.R. 13 [*Feeney*] the Supreme Court created, for a short time, a warrant requirement that was not in the *Code*, though a roughly corresponding provision has since been incorporated into the statute.

Logically prior to either issue, however, is the question of what constitutes a search in the first place.

B. WHAT IS A "SEARCH"?

The Court has adopted a purposive approach to defining "search" that is based on the goal of section 8 of the *Charter*.[13] The intent of that section, the Court has held, is to protect individuals from unjustified state intrusions upon their privacy. Accordingly, a state investigative technique is or is not a search depending on whether it infringes on a person's reasonable expectation of privacy.[14]

By this standard, of course, frisking suspects, having them turn out their pockets, and so on are searches, but so is the passive technique of conducting a "bedpan vigil."[15] Both the physical act of installing a tracking device in a car and the subsequent electronic monitoring of that car's movements constitute searches.[16] An inspection of a workplace is a search.[17] A wiretap is a search,[18] as is video surveillance and all existing or future technology allowing the state to intrude electronically on privacy.[19] Executing a search warrant on the interior of a building is, of course, a search, but so is inspecting the perimeter of the building.[20] Indeed, since it intrudes on a person's reasonable expectation of privacy, it is also a search when the police knock on a door to see if they will be able to smell marijuana when it is opened.[21]

An investigative technique will not count as a search only where it does not intrude on a reasonable expectation of privacy. For example, the Court has held that a request for various documents by Canadian officials to a foreign government does not intrude on a person's reasonable expectation of privacy: the foreign government's actions might, but the request from the Canadian government does not. Accordingly, that request is not a search.[22]

---

13   *CanadianOxy*, above note 11.
14   As will be discussed at Section C(2), below in this chapter, the Court has analyzed s. 8 with regard to an interest other than privacy once, but it did not suggest that a different definition of "search" was required.
15   *R. v. Monney*, [1999] 1 S.C.R. 652.
16   *R. v. Wise*, [1992] 1 S.C.R. 527 [*Wise*].
17   *Amax Potash Ltd. v. Saskatchewan*, [1977] 2 S.C.R. 576 [*Potash*].
18   *R. v. Duarte*, [1990] 1 S.C.R. 30 [*Duarte*].
19   *R. v. Wong*, [1990] 3 S.C.R. 36 at 43–44 [*Wong*].
20   *R. v. Kokesch*, [1990] 3 S.C.R. 3 [*Kokesch*].
21   *R. v. Evans*, [1996] 1 S.C.R. 8 [*Evans*].
22   *Schreiber v. Canada (Attorney General)*, [1998] 1 S.C.R. 841.

The Court has taken the same approach to deciding whether a "seizure" has occurred. The issue is not whether some measure of compulsion or deprivation was involved, but whether the accused's reasonable expectation of privacy was infringed. Thus, for example, making copies of a company's documents constitutes a seizure.[23] Further, even if a doctor willingly hands over a blood sample to the police, this will still be considered a seizure if the doctor was only authorized to have the blood sample for limited purposes.[24] Nonetheless, there is a distinction to be drawn between evidence that is "seized" and evidence that is merely "found." Thus, if the police take a sample of blood from a car seat at the scene of an accident such action will not infringe the accused's reasonable expectation of privacy and will not be a seizure.[25] For the same reason, no seizure is involved in gathering evidence, such as bodily samples, where it has been abandoned by an accused. However, the Court has tried to be careful to keep this exception under control. In *Stillman*, for example, they held:

> where an accused who is not in custody discards a kleenex or cigarette butt, the police may ordinarily collect and test these items without any concern about consent. A different situation is presented when an accused in custody discards items containing bodily fluids.[26]

In that case, they held that the accused had not abandoned a tissue, since he was in custody for many days and could not possibly avoid creating bodily samples at some point. Similarly, in *Nguyen* the Ontario Court of Appeal found a seizure, and a section 8 violation, when police officers offered an accused a piece of gum while transporting him from detention to court, knowing that he would need to discard the gum before he entered the courtroom.[27]

C. SEARCHES WITH A WARRANT

Historically, search warrants only authorized police to search a place, not a person.[28] Search of the person was only allowed, if at all, subsequent to some common law authority, or under the rare statutory

---

23   *Potash*, above note 17.
24   *R. v. Dyment*, [1988] 2 S.C.R. 417 [*Dyment*].
25   *R. v. Leblanc* (1981), 64 C.C.C. (2d) 31 (N.B.C.A.), cited in *Dyment*, *ibid.*
26   *R. v. Stillman*, [1997] 1 S.C.R. 607 at para. 62 [*Stillman*].
27   *R. v. Nguyen* (2002), 48 C.R. (5th) 338 (Ont. C.A.) [*Nguyen*].
28   *Re Laporte and the Queen* (1972), 29 D.L.R. (3d) 651 (Que. Q.B.) [*Laporte*]; *R. v. Légère*, [1988] N.B.J. No. 712 (C.A.) [*Légère*].

provision allowing it.[29] However, more recently the *Code* has added statutory provisions expanding the circumstances in which searches of the person can take place, and so it is worth discussing warrants to search places and warrants to search the person separately. Finally, a few miscellaneous search provisions are also worth noting.

1) Searching Places: Section 487[30]

The general search warrant provision is found in section 487 of the *Criminal Code* and raises a number of issues worthy of note. That section allows the issuance of a warrant for the search of a "building, receptacle or place" if satisfied on oath of reasonable grounds that evidence falling into one of four categories will be found. Each element, which reflects various aspects of the need for restraint in the use of investigative powers, is worth considering in turn.

That a warrant must be issued by a justice is a requirement of the *Code* means that section 487 complies with one of the minimum constitutional requirements laid down in *Hunter v. Southam*. In that case, the Court insisted that prior authorization for a search should come from someone "entirely neutral and impartial";[31] not necessarily from a judge, but at the least someone capable of acting judicially. An impartial decision-maker is required because "the decision to grant or withhold the warrant requires the balancing of two interests: that of the individual to be free of intrusions of the state and that of the state to intrude on the privacy of the individual for the purpose of law enforcement."[32] In *Hunter v. Southam* itself, members of the Restrictive Trade Practices Commission were authorized to issue the warrants in question. The Court found that the role of the commission was partly as an investigator and partly as an adjudicator, and that members were therefore not impartial enough to issue warrants. Similarly, in *Baron v. Canada* a warrant provision that did not leave any residual discretion

---

29 See, for example, s. 11(5) of the *Controlled Drugs and Substances Act*, S.C. 1996, c. 19 [*CDSA*].

30 Section 11(1) of the *CDSA*, *ibid.*, though not identical in wording, is closely modeled on s. 487 of the *Code*, and any analysis of the latter is likely to apply equally to the former.

31 *Hunter*, above note 2 at 162. In *Hunter*, the Court decided that for any warrant provision to pass scrutiny under s. 8, certain requirements must be met. In particular, they held that the prior authorization must come from someone capable of acting judicially, and that there must be reasonable and probable grounds established on oath to believe that an offence has been committed, and that evidence will be found at the place of the search.

32 *Baron*, above note 1 at 417.

with the issuing judge was struck down.[33] However, barring special circumstances,[34] a justice within the meaning of the *Code* — a justice of the peace or a provincial court judge — is impartial.[35]

It is also worth noting in this context to whom the warrant must be issued. A justice must be sure that some particular person is charged with responsibility for the search. This does not require that only one officer be named, that no-one not named in the warrant can participate in the search, or that everyone named in the warrant must participate. However, "there must be some person responsible for the way the search is carried out."[36] This issue of accountability is a reflection of the need for restraint in the use of state power. In the context of warrants issued under the previous *Narcotics Control Act*,[37] the Court characterized a warrant that did not describe the officer who was to conduct the search, limit the times during which the search could be conducted, or list the items being searched for as "a fishing license, not a search warrant."[38]

The power to search is limited to a "building, receptacle or place." This authority does not allow a warrant to be issued to search a person[39] or to take hair samples.[40] This latter finding has become of little importance since the passage of section 487.05 of the *Code*, which allows for warrants to take bodily samples in order to obtain DNA. "Place" includes the area surrounding a building, which has two main consequences. First, it means that a warrant is available to search the exterior of buildings and the surrounding area. This leads to the result that, since it would be possible to obtain a warrant to search the area around a house in principle, a search of that area without a warrant is *prima facie* unreasonable, in accordance with the rule laid down in *Hunter v. Southam*.[41] Second, when coupled with the need for specificity

---

33   *Ibid.*

34   See *R. v. Baylis*, [1988] S.J. No. 414 (C.A.).

35   The Supreme Court has not explicitly approved s. 487, though it was found by the Ontario Court of Appeal to be in compliance with the requirements of *Hunter*, above note 2: see *R. v. Times Square Book Store* (1985), 48 C.R. (3d) 132 (Ont. C.A.) [*Times Square*].

36   *R. v. Strachan*, [1988] 2 S.C.R. 980 at para. 30. The Court observes that "the warrant should make it clear who is in charge of, and responsible for, the search . . . Listing an entire drug squad by name in a warrant may undermine the effectiveness of the naming requirement just as much as a failure to name anyone at all."

37   *Narcotic Control Act*, R.S.C. 1985, c. N-1, repealed 1996, c. 19, s. 94 [*NCA*].

38   *R. v. Genest*, [1989] 1 S.C.R. 59 [*Genest*].

39   *Laporte*, above note 28.

40   *Légère*, above note 28.

41   *R. v. Debot*, [1989] 2 S.C.R. 1140, aff'g (1986), 30 C.C.C. (3d) 207 (Ont. C.A.) [*Debot*]; *R. v. Kokesch*, above note 20; *R. v. Plant*, [1993] 3 S.C.R. 281 [*Plant*]. However, see *R. v. Grant*, [1993] 3 S.C.R. 223 [*Grant*], where the Court held that

in warrants, this also means that a warrant to search the area around a house (the curtilage) does not include the ability to seize items found inside the house, while a warrant to search a house might not include the ability to search the area around the house.

The justice must be satisfied of more than the possibility that evidence will be found, otherwise intrusions based only on suspicion would be too readily permitted.[42] Further, the justice must be given facts that show the basis for the reasonable and probable grounds and not simply be satisfied that the police officer in fact has such a belief.[43] The Court has noted that the affidavit supporting a warrant need not be:

> as lengthy as À la recherche du temps perdu, as lively as the Kama Sutra, or as detailed as an automotive repair manual. All that it must do is set out the facts fully and frankly for the authorizing judge in order that he or she can make an assessment of whether these rise to the standard required in the legal test for the authorization. Ideally, an affidavit should be not only full and frank but also clear and concise.[44]

In this context, the Court has discouraged the use of "boiler plate" language in applications, on the basis that it adds little and can imply meaning that is not there. The Court has also recommended using affidavits directly from those with firsthand knowledge of the facts therein, such as the officers conducting the investigation.[45]

Beyond that, the requirement that the justice be satisfied on oath of reasonable grounds is interesting primarily for the issues of what will constitute reasonable grounds and how they may be obtained. For entirely understandable reasons, warrants are issued on an *ex parte* basis: the need for effective law enforcement certainly justifies not informing a suspect in advance of a search that will take place.[46] However,

---

although the power in s. 10 of the NCA, above note 37, to conduct warrantless searches of a place other than a dwelling house violated s. 8, the section did not need to be struck down completely, but rather could be read down to apply only in exigent circumstances.

42 *Hunter*, above note 2 at 167.

43 R. v. Pastro (1988), 42 C.C.C. (3d) 485 at 511 (Sask. C.A.).

44 R. v. Araujo, [2000] 2 S.C.R. 992 at para. 46 [Araujo].

45 Ibid. at para. 48.

46 See the discussion of this issue in R. v. B.(S.A.) (2001), 157 C.C.C. (3d) 510 (Alta.C.A.), holding that *ex parte* applications for warrants generally do not violate the *Charter*, whether the *Code* provision specifies that approach or not. In particular, the Alberta Court of Appeal held in B.(S.A.) that *ex parte* applications for DNA warrants are acceptable because, although a suspect's DNA cannot be changed despite notice of the application, the suspect might flee if given notice. The Supreme Court of Canada upheld this result (S.A.B., above note 1) without

in accordance with the principle of restraint, it is open to an accused to argue after the fact that, even though the warrant was issued by an independent decision-maker based on sworn information, the warrant nonetheless ought not to have been issued.[47]

Cases have held that the information justifying the issuing of a warrant can be hearsay, and need not be admissible in court. Similarly, the information might be privileged, because the police obtained the information from a confidential informer, for example. The Court has held that the identity of an informer need not be disclosed, either on an application to quash or at trial, unless the accused shows that disclosure of the identity of the informer "is necessary to establish the innocence of the accused" (known as the "innocence at stake" exception).[48] In any other circumstance, the legitimate needs of law enforcement to protect the identity of informers outweigh the interests of the accused to openness and disclosure.

There are some limits on the type of information that can justify a warrant. In particular, the information must have been legally gathered, and therefore a warrant based solely on information gained through a *Charter* violation will be quashed. In *Kokesch*,[49] for example, the police conducted a search of the exterior of the accused's residence. They found a metal vent covered with plywood, heard machines humming inside, and smelled marijuana from the edge of the plywood. Based on this information, the police obtained a search warrant for the premises that was subsequently quashed. Since the officers had no reasonable grounds to inspect the perimeter of the accused's residence initially, and since that inspection was itself a search, their observations — and therefore the evidence that was the basis for the search warrant — violated the *Charter*.[50] Accordingly, those observations could not be used as a basis for the warrant, and the evidence obtained through use of the warrant itself was excluded.[51]

---

making specific reference to the possibility of flight. The Court also noted that s. 487.05(1) does not prevent a judge from requiring that an application be *inter partes* in particular cases: see para. 56.

47   See the discussion at Section C(4), below in this chapter.

48   *R. v. Leipert*, [1997] 1 S.C.R. 281.

49   *Kokesch*, above note 20.

50   See, in contrast, *R. v. Wiley*, [1993] 3 S.C.R 263 [*Wiley*], where, although in fact the police relied on evidence obtained from a perimeter search to obtain a search warrant, there was still enough information to justify the warrant even without those observations, and the warrant was allowed to stand.

51   Of course, it is not the case that evidence obtained in violation of s. 8 or any other section of the *Charter* will be immediately excluded. Rather, that is a question that must be decided under s. 24(2) of the *Charter*. It has been sug-

The Court has also upheld the individual right to privacy in less clear circumstances, such as where police knock on a suspect's door in order to gain reasonable grounds for a search by, for example, smelling marijuana inside.[52] Although home-owners can sometimes be taken to have issued an implied invitation to anyone to knock on the door, that invitation is for limited purposes. When the police approach the residence and knock on the door for other purposes, their behaviour constitutes a warrantless search, which is *prima facie* unreasonable. On the other hand if the police approach for other legitimate reasons, but then discover evidence giving them reasonable grounds to search, there will be no *Charter* violation.[53]

Where a warrant is based only partly on illegally obtained information, a reviewing court is required to decide whether the untainted evidence would, on its own, have justified issuing the warrant, and either quash or uphold the warrant based on that determination.[54]

Finally, the types of things for which search warrants may be issued must be noted. The *Code* sets out four categories: i) anything on or in respect of which an offence has been committed; ii) anything that will provide evidence regarding an offence or the location of a person suspected of committing an offence; iii) anything reasonably believed to be intended to be used to commit an offence for which the person could be arrested without warrant; or iv) offence related property.[55] Offence related property is a recent addition to the section, and is defined

---

gested that, in drug cases, the Court is generally quite reluctant to exclude drugs found as a result of an unconstitutional search: see Don Stuart, "Eight Plus Twenty-Four Two Equals Zero" (1998) 13 C.R. (5th) 50. See also Nathan J.S. Gorham, "Eight Plus Twenty-Four Two Equals Zero-Point-Five" (2003) 6 C.R. (6th) 257.

52   *Evans*, above note 21.

53   See for example *R. v. Duong* (2002), 49 C.R. (5th) 165 (B.C.C.A.), leave to appeal to S.C.C. refused, [2002] S.C.C.A. No. 112, where the police approached the accused's door while looking for witnesses to a home invasion in the area, but then formed reasonable and probable grounds to believe he was committing a narcotics offence based on the accused's demeanour and a smell of burning and growing marijuana coming from the house. On the facts of that case, the trial judge held that the police officer's observations gave him grounds to arrest the accused, and to enter the residence in accordance with s. 529.3 in order to do so. Once he had entered the residence, the officer was entitled to conduct a limited search incident to the arrest, and the observations made during that limited search were properly relied on to obtain a warrant for a more complete search.

54   *Evans*, above note 21. However, see the discussion in Section C(4), below in this chapter.

55   Sections 487(1)(a)–(c.1).

in section 2 of the *Code* to mean, essentially, property that has been or will be used in committing an indictable offence.

These purposes for a search are broad, but they are not unlimited. They allow warrants to search not just for evidence of an offence, but also for evidence allowing the Crown to determine whether an accused will be able to put forward a successful defence, such as due diligence.[56] The Court has noted that:

> The words "in respect of" are, in my opinion, words of the widest possible scope. They import such meanings as "in relation to," "with reference to" or "in connection with." The phrase "in respect of" is probably the widest of any expression intended to convey some connection between two related subject matters.[57]

However, although the purpose for the search is broad, there are some limits. In particular, the purposes have been interpreted as limiting the power to a search for physical items, and therefore do not allow the seizure of the contents of a bank account.[58]

More important as a limit on the search warrant power is the need for specificity in advance. It is not sufficient for police simply to say that they believe evidence will be found if a search occurs. Rather, they must inform the issuing justice, with some reasonable degree of precision, what evidence will be found. Thus, for example, an application for a warrant that specified one publication by name, but otherwise only indicated that "other obscene materials" would be found was quashed with respect to all but the one, named magazine.[59] Nonetheless, it has been held that the degree of specificity required varies with the type of offence: it will be more difficult for investigators to specify in advance precisely what evidence they will find of tax evasion or fraud, for ex-

---

56 See *CanadianOxy*, above note 11.

57 *Ibid.* at para. 16, quoting from *Nowegijick v. The Queen*, [1983] 1 S.C.R. 29 at 39.

58 See *Re Banque Royale Du Canada and the Queen* (1985), 44 C.R. 3d 387 at 389 (Que. C.A). The Court quotes with approval the Law Reform Commission of Canada:

> 196. Another anachronism is the restriction of most search and seizure powers to "things", particularly in the case of those powers concerned with the recovery of the fruits of crime. The original common law search warrant developed by Hale was for stolen "goods". This focus on tangible objects was carried into subsequent provisions for search and seizure covering crimes of theft, including the present subsection 443(1) [now s. 487] of the *Criminal Code*. This focus, however, excludes from coverage forms of property such as funds in financial accounts, or information from computers, which may also represent the fruits of a crime.

59 *Times Square*, above note 35.

ample, and so more latitude must be shown in such cases.[60] The warrant must be specific so that the person whose property is searched is sufficiently informed of the reason for that search.[61]

Once again what is reflected here is the balancing of the legitimate interests of the individual and the state. The purpose of prior authorization, whether considering the search as a possible *Charter* violation or not, is to prevent a search from occurring unless it is genuinely shown to be necessary. Where the police cannot say, in advance and with some degree of precision, what evidence they think will be found, the warrant begins to look more like "a fishing license."[62]

However, the legitimate interests of law enforcement are not sacrificed. The *Code* also contains section 489, which allows the police who are searching under a warrant to seize items not mentioned in the warrant if they believe on reasonable grounds that they were obtained by, were used in, or afford evidence concerning an offence. In other words, as long as the warrant was validly issued, then the intrusion on the suspect's privacy has been justified. If, in the course of that search, different evidence is found, then new considerations arise justifying the seizure of that unanticipated material. Provided that the reviewing courts are vigilant not to engage in *post facto* justification of warrants simply because evidence was found, rather than judging them based on the information provided to the issuing justice, this is a workable compromise.

The balance of rights between the state's interests in investigating crime and the interests of individuals is reflected in a slightly different way with regard to the issue of sealing orders. The public can have an interest in seeing the information used by police to obtain search warrants or the search warrants themselves, but the police might see an ongoing need to keep that information confidential. The Court has held that the appropriate balance of interests in this situation favours openness, and that "[o]nce a search warrant is executed, the warrant and the information upon which it is issued must be made available to the public unless an applicant seeking a sealing order can demonstrate that public access would subvert the ends of justice."[63] In reaching this

---

60   R. v. *Church of Scientology* (No. 6), (1986) 27 C.C.C. (3d) 193 (Ont. H.C.J.).

61   *Alder v. Alberta (Attorney General)* (1977), 37 C.C.C. (2d) 234 (Alta. S.C.T.D.).

62   *Genest*, above note 38.

63   *Toronto Star Newspapers Ltd. v. Ontario* (2005), 29 C.R. (6th) 251 (S.C.C.), relying on *Attorney General of Nova Scotia v. MacIntyre*, [1982] 1 S.C.R. 175.

conclusion, the Court applied the same standard that it created in the case of publication bans to search warrants.[64]

Finally, note should be taken of section 488 of the *Code*, which requires that a warrant shall be executed by day unless reasonable grounds for executing it by night are provided to the issuing justice, and the warrant itself authorizes its execution by night.

2) Search of the Person: DNA warrants

It was noted above that statutory search powers have, traditionally, not allowed search of the person, a feature incorporated into the general warrant provision by the requirement that a search cannot affect a person's bodily integrity. However, recent amendments to the *Criminal Code* have authorized searches that have exactly that effect, allowing the taking of bodily samples for DNA analysis. In particular, warrants can be issued allowing the police to obtain hair, buccal swabs, or blood samples from a suspect. In a general outline, the rules surrounding DNA warrants are similar to those surrounding search warrants. As is appropriate, however, the greater intrusiveness of allowing a search directly affecting bodily integrity is balanced by greater protections for privacy. The Court has held that these provisions do not violate section 8 of the *Charter*.[65]

The basic requirements for a DNA warrant necessitate that a provincial court judge be satisfied by information on oath that a bodily substance connected with an offence[66] has been found, that a person was a party to the offence, and that DNA analysis of the substance will provide evidence about whether the bodily substance was from that person. These conditions more or less parallel the corresponding requirements for a search warrant; although note that, as with general warrants, the application cannot be made to a justice of the peace. There is also an explicit statement of the rule, implicit for search war-

---

64   See *Dagenais v. Canadian Broadcasting Corp.*, [1994] 3 S.C.R. 835, as well as
      Vancouver Sun (Re), [2004] 2 S.C.R. 332. See also *Ottawa Citizen Group Inc. v.
      Ontario* (2005), 31 C.R. (6th) 144 (Ont. C.A.), concerning the search warrants
      in the Maher Arar case. Discussion on this subject continues in Chapter 11.
65   *S.A.B.*, above note 1.
66   The *Code* specifies that the substance could have been found at the place the
      offence was committed, on or within the body of the victim, on anything worn
      or carried by the victim, or on or within the body of any person or thing "at any
      place associated with the commission of the offence": s. 487.01(4)(b).

rants, that conditions can be imposed to make the taking of the sample reasonable in the circumstances.[67]

Other requirements act to limit the availability of DNA warrants. They are only available in the case of "designated offences," for example, which consists of a list of offences in section 487.04. This list consists predominantly of sexual offences and offences causing death or bodily harm, with a number of other serious offences, such as hijacking, robbery, and arson, included. In addition, as with video surveillance warrants, the judge is required to believe that issuing the warrant is in "the best interests of the administration of justice." The Ontario Court of Appeal has held that the presence of a *Charter* violation in the course of obtaining grounds for a DNA warrant is not alone sufficient to prevent the warrant being issued, though the court reserved judgment on whether a "pattern of wilful and flagrant misconduct on the part of the police could lead a judge to deny a DNA warrant on the ground that it would be contrary to the best interests of justice to do so."[68] It is arguable that this is a lower standard, not a higher one, than the ordinary rule for search warrants, which only allows legally obtained evidence to be used in support of the application for the warrant.[69] Section 487.05(2) also requires the judge to have regard to "all relevant matters," which will include the nature of the offence, the circumstances of its commission, and whether a qualified peace officer or other person is available to take the sample.

Other provisions also aim at counterbalancing the intrusiveness of DNA warrants. A peace officer executing the warrant is required to inform the suspect of its contents, the nature of the procedures for taking samples, the purpose for taking them, and the police officer's authorization to use force.[70] In taking the sample, the officer is also required to respect the accused's privacy in a manner that is reasonable under the circumstances. Further, the *Code* requires that the samples taken and the results of analysis should not be used for any other purpose than the investigation of a designated offence meeting the warrant requirements.[71] Failure to comply with this obligation is actually an offence.[72] In addition, in many circumstances there is an obligation to destroy the samples taken and the results obtained. This is the case where: the

---

67   Section 487.06(2).
68   *Nguyen*, above note 27.
69   See the discussion of *Kokesch*, above note 20; *Evans*, above note 21; *Duong*, above note 53.
70   Section 487.07(1).
71   Sections 487.08(1) & (2).
72   Section 487.08(3).

analysis shows that the sample does not come from the person, the person is acquitted, or (unless new proceedings are commenced) one year has passed after a discharge at a preliminary inquiry, a withdrawal of charges, or a stay of proceedings.

In addition to these requirements, additional rules exist when the DNA warrant concerns a young person. In that event, the young person is to be informed of the right to a reasonable opportunity to consult with and have the warrant executed in the presence of counsel, a parent, or other adult. This requirement is similar to the rules concerning statements by young persons.[73]

The Court found the DNA warrant provisions to survive *Charter* scrutiny in *S.A.B.* In particular, it was argued that the provisions were unconstitutional on the grounds that such searches should only be available as a last resort (similar to wiretaps), that a higher standard than reasonable grounds should be required for such a warrant, and that a DNA warrant should not be issued *ex parte*. The Court rejected these arguments, holding, in essence, that the differences between DNA warrants and search warrants did not justify these higher standards. The Court noted that, although DNA warrants are quite intrusive in an informational sense, they are also more focused than wiretaps and would not intrude on the privacy of third parties. The state's interest in the evidence was also quite high, since it could be virtually conclusive either to prove an accused's guilt or to prevent a wrongful conviction. A judge issuing a DNA warrant would consider whether it was necessary in the interests of justice, which might act as a type of "last resort" rule where necessary, and would permit a judge to allow an *inter partes* application where appropriate.[74]

The Court also considered whether the principle against self-incrimination was violated by the provisions, but held that, given the absence of reliability concerns about DNA evidence and the additional safeguards built into the DNA warrant application process, this principle was not violated.[75]

A further aspect of DNA warrants that should be noted, at least briefly, is the portion of the *Code* creating a DNA databank. Those provisions allow gathering DNA samples, not in the context of investigating a particular crime, but rather to create a bank of information, similar

---

73 *Youth Criminal Justice Act*, S.C. 2002, c. 1, ss.146(2)(c) & (d).

74 *S.A.B.*, above note 1 at paras. 44–56.

75 See the discussion of this aspect of the case, which is more directly relevant to potential s. 7 claims, in David Stratas, "*R. v. B.(S.A.)* and the Right Against Self-Incrimination: A Confusing Change of Direction" (2003) 14 C.R. (6th) 227 [Stratas]; and Don Stuart, "*R. v. S.A.B.*: Annotation" (2003) 14 C.R. (6th) 208.

to books of mugshots or collections of fingerprints, to be used in the future. The offences for which DNA warrants are available are divided into "primary designated offences" (nearly all of which involve sexual assault or homicide) and "secondary designated offences." Where an accused is convicted of a primary designated offence, the court shall order a DNA sample to be taken for the DNA databank. In the case of a secondary designated offence, the court may make such an order if satisfied it is in the best interests of the administration of justice to do so.[76] In practical terms, this means that orders are quite likely to be made in this latter case as well. It has been held that the "best interests of the administration of justice" does not simply refer to detecting further crimes committed by the offender in question. Rather, it also includes deterring potential repeat offenders, promoting the safety of the community, detecting when a serial offender is at work, assisting in the solving of cold crimes, streamlining investigations, and assisting the innocent through early exclusion from suspicion or by exonerating the wrongfully convicted.[77]

The only circumstance in which an order will not be made is where the convicted person establishes that the impact of the order on his privacy would be grossly disproportionate to the public interest in the protection of society and proper administration of justice. It will be rare for such a challenge to succeed. The convicted person will be required to prove not only that the circumstances depart markedly from the cases Parliament is likely to have had in mind in drafting the provisions, but also that no terms or conditions imposed on taking the order could adequately restore the proper balance.[78]

The DNA databank provisions were not before the Court in *S.A.B.*, but they have since been upheld by the Court.[79] In rejecting challenges to the legislation, based on both section 8 and section 11 of the *Charter*, the Court held:

> Society's interest in using this powerful new technology to assist law enforcement agencies in the identification of offenders is beyond dis-

---

76   Note that special provisions allow the taking of such samples even if the conviction is for an offence committed before the DNA databank provisions came into force: s. 487.052. In the case of dangerous offenders, those convicted of more than one murder committed at different times, or those convicted of more than one sexual offence and serving a sentence of at least two years, an application can be made even though the declaration or convictions predate the DNA databank legislation: s. 487.055.

77   *R. v. P.R.F.* (2001), 57 O.R. (3d) 475 (C.A.).

78   *R. v. Jordan*, 2002 NSCA 11. See also *R. v. Isbister*, [2002] A.J. No. 246 (C.A.).

79   *R. v. Rodgers*, [2006] 1 S.C.R. 554.

pute. The resulting impact on the physical integrity of the targeted offenders is minimal. The potential invasive impact on the right to privacy has carefully been circumscribed by legislative safeguards that restrict the use of the DNA data bank as an identification tool only. As convicted offenders still under sentence, the persons targeted by s. 487.055 have a much reduced expectation of privacy. Further, by reason of their crimes, they have lost any reasonable expectation that their identity will remain secret from law enforcement authorities. Having regard to the interests at stake and the procedural safeguards afforded by the legislative scheme, I have also concluded that the *ex parte* nature of the proceedings meets the dictates of procedural fairness afforded under s. 7 of the *Charter*. Finally, ss. 11(h) and 11(i) of the *Charter* are inapplicable. The taking of DNA samples does not constitute a punishment within the meaning of s. 11 anymore than the taking of fingerprints or other identification measures.[80]

In addition to DNA warrants, the *Code* also contains a provision creating an "impression warrant" that allows a peace officer to obtain a handprint, footprint, tooth impression, or impression of any part of the body. Seemingly, Parliament's assumption is that such procedures will necessarily be less invasive of a person's bodily integrity and privacy than obtaining DNA samples, since few limitations surround such warrants. There is room to question this assumption: an impression of "any part of the body" has the potential to invade privacy quite significantly. Further, in *Stillman* the Court described taking dental impressions as "a lengthy and highly intrusive process" that, in the particular context of that case, amounted to "the abusive exercise of raw physical authority by the police."[81]

Impression warrants may be issued by a justice in respect of any offence, based on reasonable grounds to believe that the print will provide information concerning the offence. This wording does not seem to require that the person from whom the impression is taken be a suspect. There are requirements that conditions that make the search and seizure reasonable in the circumstances can be imposed, and that the warrant is in the best interests of the administration of justice.

3) Other Statutory Search Warrant Provisions

In addition to these warrants, other statutory provisions contain more specific search warrants. These generally, but not uniformly, share the

---

80   *Ibid.* at para. 5.
81   *Stillman*, above note 26 at para. 46.

basic characteristic of section 487 that a warrant can only be issued if a justice is satisfied by information on oath that there are reasonable grounds to authorize the particular intervention sought. Some of these warrant provisions are for purely investigative purposes. For example, section 256 provides for warrants to obtain a blood sample from a person suspected of driving while impaired. Other sections allow police to seek warrants to attach a tracking device to a vehicle or any other thing,[82] or to install a number recorder on a telephone,[83] and, of course, there are extensive provisions dealing with wiretaps.[84] Each of these latter three provisions shows the need to balance the interests of the individual and the state. Wiretaps are a particularly intrusive form of search, therefore, more restrictions are built into their availability than into ordinary search warrants. Warrants for tracking devices or number recorders, on the other hand, are more easily available than other warrants, since each only requires the issuing justice to be satisfied "that there are reasonable grounds *to suspect* that an offence . . . has been or will be committed."[85] Arguably, this lower standard is justified because of the relatively minor nature of the search. The Court held in *Wise* that a tracking device, which only determines the location of the item to which it is attached, is a minimal intrusion on privacy.[86] A number recorder, which indicates to where telephone calls have been placed and received from, but does not record the content of the communication, might also be minimally intrusive. Both provisions also contain the limitation that the warrant expires after sixty days.[87] However, the Court has yet to pronounce on the constitutionality of these two provisions.[88]

---

82   Section 492.1.

83   Section 492.2.

84   See Part VI of the *Code*.

85   See, however, the criticism of the way in which the "reasonable suspicion" standard has been elaborated in Peter Sankoff & Stéphane Perrault, "Suspicious Searches: What's So Reasonable about Them?" (1999) 24 C.R. (5th) 123.

86   *Wise*, above note 16. The reasoning in the case could be seen to apply to the particular tracking device in issue, rather than a blanket statement about tracking devices in general.

87   Sections 492.1(2) and 492.2(3).

88   The standard of reasonable suspicion might be hard to reconcile with the conclusion in *Hunter*, above note 2 at 167, that "[t]he purpose of an objective criterion for granting prior authorization to conduct a search or seizure is to provide a consistent standard for identifying the point at which the interests of the state in such intrusions come to prevail over the interests of the individual in resisting them. To associate it with an applicant's reasonable belief that relevant evidence may be uncovered by the search, would be to define the proper standard as the possibility of finding evidence. This is a very low standard which would validate intrusion on the basis of suspicion, and authorize fishing expeditions

Other warrant provisions are in whole or in part motivated by the nature of the item searched for. That is, the goal of the seizure is not simply to obtain evidence concerning a crime, it also has a preventive aspect. This motive seems to help explain the separate warrant provisions dealing with common gaming houses,[89] hate propaganda,[90] valuable minerals,[91] the search power in section 11 of the *Controlled Drugs and Substances Act*,[92] and the power to seize explosives.[93] Although it does not explicitly create a search power, this also appears to be the motive behind section 164, which permits a justice to issue a warrant for the seizure of obscene publications, crime comics, or child pornography. Indeed, the preventive concern can be dominant over the investigative one. For example, section 117.04 allows the police to seek a warrant to search for and seize a weapon on the grounds that it is not in the interests of safety for the person to have it.[94] Similar forfeiture concerns motivate provisions that allow warrants to search for property that can be forfeited under proceeds of crime legislation.[95] It is worth noting that the Ontario Court of Appeal has struck down section 117.04 for failing to comply with the standards in *Hunter v. Southam*.[96] Although the section requires the justice to be satisfied that it is not desirable for a named person to possess a firearm or other weapon, it does not require the justice to be satisfied that the person is in fact in possession of such items. The court found that, without that requirement, the provision permits too sweeping a search power, which could not be saved under section 1 of the *Charter*.

---

of considerable latitude. It would tip the balance strongly in favour of the state and limit the right of the individual to resist to only the most egregious intrusions. I do not believe that this is a proper standard for securing the right to be free from unreasonable search and seizure."

In *R. v. Nguyen*, 2004 BCSC 76, the number recorder warrant provisions in the *Code* were found to violate s. 8 of the *Charter* because of the "reasonable suspicion" standard. Other courts have disagreed with this conclusion: see *Cody c. R.*, 2007 QCCA 1276.

89 Section 199. That section also authorizes taking into custody anyone found in the common gaming house or common bawdy house.
90 Section 320.
91 Section 395.
92 *CDSA*, above note 29.
93 Section 492.
94 This section, unlike the others discussed here, does not explicitly require that the information be provided on oath. In *R. v. Hurrell* (2002), 4 C.R. (6th) 169 (Ont. C.A.) [*Hurrell*], the Ontario Court of Appeal held that the word "application" in the section should be read as a term of art, requiring that it be under oath.
95 Section 462.32(1).
96 *Hurrell*, above note 94.

4) Reviewing Warrants

The *Code* contains no provisions that allow for an appeal from the decision to issue a warrant. In the absence of such a statutory provision, there is no appeal from the issuance of a warrant.[97] This is true even if there is an issue as to whether the search violated section 8 of the *Charter* because the *Charter* does not create new appeal procedures.[98]

Nonetheless, it is possible to challenge the issuance of a warrant. *Certiorari* is available to review the process by which the warrant was issued, though this approach has been called an "idle exercise" since it does not result in either the return of the items seized or their exclusion as evidence.[99] The effect of quashing a warrant is to render the search warrantless, which means that it was *prima facie* unreasonable and in violation of section 8. However, it will still need to be determined whether the evidence should be excluded under section 24(2), a determination that depends on considerations broader than just those that relate to the warrant. As a result, that decision can only be made at trial. For this reason, courts have concluded that, generally, it will be preferable to leave challenges to the warrant to the trial stage, when the overlapping questions of violation and remedy can be dealt with together.[100] A pre-trial challenge to the warrant is possible, but is only appropriate where issues such as preventing a search arise.[101]

The central issue in reviewing a warrant is whether the requirements for its issuance under the *Code* have been met. Thus, for example, if the warrant fails to adequately describe the premises to be searched or the offence under investigation, the warrant can be quashed.[102] Similarly, inaccurate information about the suspect, which could contribute to the reasonable grounds for the search, can affect the decision.[103] However, the reviewing judge does not decide whether the warrant *should* have been issued. Rather, the question is whether there was evidence

---

97 *Knox Contracting Ltd. v. Canada*, [1990] 2 S.C.R. 338; *Kourtessis v. M.N.R.*, [1993] 2 S.C.R. 53.

98 *R. v. Meltzer*, [1989] 1 S.C.R. 1764.

99 *R. v. Zevallos* (1987), 59 C.R. (3d) 153 at 158 (Ont. C.A.) [*Zevallos*].

100 *Zevallos*, ibid.; *R. v. Tanner* (1989), 46 C.C.C. (3d) 513 (Alta C.A.); *R. v. Williams* (1987), 38 C.C.C. (3d) 319 (Y.T.C.A.).

101 *Zevallos*, ibid.

102 *Bergeron v. Deschamps*, [1978] 1 S.C.R. 243.

103 *R. v. Sismey* (1990), 55 C.C.C. (3d) 281 (B.C.C.A.) [*Sismey*].

upon which the issuing judge could have decided to issue the warrant.[104] The actual result of the search is not relevant on review.[105]

Review of the issuance of a search warrant can take place both on a facial and a sub-facial basis. That is, by determining whether the affidavit presented to obtain the search warrant actually contains sufficient information to justify the warrant, and whether, by going behind the form of the affidavit, it is possible to attack the reliability of its content.[106] Nonetheless, cross-examination on the affidavit to perform a sub-facial challenge is not automatically available. Some early cases suggested that the applicant must show on a *prima facie* basis that there was deliberate falsehood, omission, or a reckless disregard for the truth by the person swearing the affidavit before cross-examination would be permitted.[107] In *Garofoli*, however, the Court held that although cross-examination should not be the general rule and that leave of the reviewing judge was required, the standard of a *prima facie* case was too high. Rather, all that is necessary is a basis for the view that "the cross-examination will elicit testimony tending to discredit the existence of one of the preconditions to the authorization, as for example the existence of reasonable and probable grounds."[108] Cross-examination should normally be limited to questions aimed at showing there was no basis for issuing the warrant.[109]

On review, evidence that was used in support of the warrant may be excised from the application. Information that was misleading[110] or that the police should have known was not true[111] may be removed from the material that potentially justified the issuance of the warrant. Equally, if evidence used to justify the warrant was obtained through a *Charter* breach, that evidence will also be excluded.[112] The question then becomes whether the remaining evidence could have been sufficient to justify issuing the warrant.

It may be possible for the Crown to amplify the grounds that justified the issuance of the warrant if evidence is excised at the review

---

104 *R. v. Garofoli*, [1990] 2 S.C.R. 1421, 60 C.C.C. (3d) 161 at 188 (S.C.C.) [*Garofoli*].
    Garofoli actually concerns a wiretap authorization, but the same standard is applicable to search warrants: see *R. v. Breton* (1994), 93 C.C.C. (3d) 171 (Ont. C.A.).
105 *Descoteaux v. Mierzwinski*, [1982] 1 S.C.R. 860.
106 *Araujo*, above note 44 at para. 50.
107 *R. v. Collins* (1989), 69 C.R. (3d) 235 (Ont. C.A.).
108 *Garofoli*, above note 104 at 1465 (S.C.R.). The Court has subsequently reaffirmed this standard: *R. v. Pires*, [2005] 3 S.C.R. 343.
109 *Garofoli*, *ibid.*
110 *Sismey*, above note 103.
111 *Garofoli*, above note 104.
112 *Evans*, above note 21; *Grant*, above note 41; *Wiley*, above note 50.

hearing. However, this possibility only exists where the error leading to the excision occurred despite good faith on the part of the police.[113] The Court has noted that amplification requires a delicate balance. To never permit it would sometimes mean that a warrant was overturned due to some technical error, although in fact the police had valid grounds to obtain that warrant. Conversely, if amplification were too readily allowed, it could circumvent the *Charter* requirement of prior authorization for the warrant.[114]

Some earlier cases suggested that the basis upon which evidence was excised was of little importance in the reviewing process. In *Bisson*, for example, the Court held that

> errors in the information presented to the authorizing judge, whether advertent or even fraudulent, are only factors to be considered in deciding to set aside the authorization and do not by themselves lead to automatic vitiation of the wiretap authorization.[115]

The issue, the Court suggested, was whether, after the fraudulent information had been removed, the remaining information was sufficient to justify issuance of the warrant. More recently, however, the Court has recognized a basis for review beyond whether sufficient evidence remains. While in agreement that fraud does not automatically lead to quashing a warrant, the Court held that

> [t]his does not mean that errors, particularly deliberate ones, are irrelevant in the review process. While not leading to automatic vitiation of the warrant, there remains the need to protect the prior authorization process. The cases just referred to do not foreclose a reviewing judge, in appropriate circumstances, from concluding on the totality of the circumstances that the conduct of the police in seeking prior authorization was so subversive of that process that the resulting warrant must be set aside to protect the process and the preventive function it serves.[116]

Accordingly, it now seems clear that reviewing courts can quash a warrant based either on the inadequacy of the material remaining after some information is excised, or based on behaviour of the police that

---

113 *Araujo*, above note 44 at para. 58.
114 *Ibid.* at para. 59.
115 *R. v. Bisson*, [1994] 3 S.C.R. 1097 at para. 2.
116 *Araujo*, above note 44 at para. 54, cited from *R. v. Morris* (1998), 134 C.C.C. (3d) 539 at para. 43 (N.S.C.A.).

intentionally misled or otherwise subverted the process of prior authorization.[117]

Where a warrant is quashed, the search that ensued is determined to have been conducted on a warrantless basis. It is to the issue of warrantless searches that we now turn.

D. SEARCHES WITHOUT A WARRANT

Warrantless search powers are inextricably connected with the *Charter*. First, *Hunter v. Southam* found that a warrantless search is *prima facie* unreasonable under section 8. As a result, every warrantless search power, whether statutory or common law, must be made consistent with minimum *Charter* standards. Next, *R. v. Collins* set out the framework indicating what those minimum *Charter* standards were.[118] The result is that a discussion of warrantless search powers, even though non-*Charter* issues arise, is most sensibly framed around the caselaw on section 8 of the *Charter*. The two primary issues to be addressed are whether a reasonable expectation of privacy exists in order to invoke section 8 and whether the *Collins* criteria are met.

1) Reasonable Expectation of Privacy[119]

Trying to define the role that a reasonable expectation of privacy has with relation to searches and section 8 is like trying to hit a moving target. Early on in *Charter* jurisprudence the existence of a reasonable expectation of privacy was little more than a sorting mechanism — a method of determining that section 8 was the relevant right, but not a difficult threshold to cross. Since that time the Court has created exceptions to the circumstances in which an accused can be said to have a

---

117 See, generally, Robert W. Hubbard & Scott K. Fenton, "Supreme Court of Canada Wiretap Update — February 2001," in Osgoode Hall Law School, Professional Development Program, *Search and Seizure Law in Canada* (Toronto: Osgoode Hall Law School, 3 November 2001).

118 *R. v. Collins*, [1987] 1 S.C.R. 265 [*Collins*].

119 Whether an accused has a reasonable expectation of privacy is not, in principle, a question exclusively related to warrantless searches. Indeed, as discussed above, the concept is central to deciding whether a search or seizure has taken place at all. However, where a warrant provision exists, the very fact that police must persuade a third party capable of acting judicially that a search is justified demonstrates that the subject of the search does have a reasonable expectation of privacy. Therefore, a discussion of the limits of a reasonable expectation of privacy only becomes important in the warrantless search context.

reasonable expectation of privacy and thus has given other roles to that concept. The Court has also created two approaches to determining when a reasonable expectation of privacy exists that are not entirely reconcilable with one another. Finally, a recently created approach has been interpreted by lower courts in a way that has the potential to dramatically limit when an accused will be found to have a section 8 right at all though the Supreme Court seems to be attempting to stop that trend.

Some general observations about the concept should be made first. In *Hunter*, the Supreme Court made clear that section 8 of the *Charter* was intended to be a "broad and general right to be secure from unreasonable search and seizure."[120] They specifically rejected the notion that the intent was to protect property rights, and instead said that the important issue was privacy: the section 8 right "might protect interests beyond the right of privacy, but . . . its protections go at least that far."[121] Therefore, warrantless searches are inextricably intertwined with privacy concerns. As noted above, the definitions of both "search" and "seizure" amount to asking whether there has been an infringement of a reasonable expectation of privacy.

It is important to recognize that "reasonable" in this context is intended to be an assessment of *entitlement* to privacy, not a measure of whether a person, as a matter of fact, *has* privacy. In *Wong*, the Court rejected the notion that reasonable expectation of privacy should be judged based on a "risk analysis." Speaking in the particular context of video surveillance, the Court noted that "we can only be sure of being free from surveillance today if we retire to our basements, cloak our windows, turn out the lights and remain absolutely quiet."[122] The correct question is to ask about "the standards of privacy that persons can *expect* to enjoy in a free and democratic society."[123] Thus, for example, a person whose property is stolen still has a reasonable expectation of privacy in that property, despite the obvious fact that the thief has, at least temporarily, rendered that interest ineffective in any practical sense.[124] In contrast, if a person has genuinely abandoned an item then

---

120 *Hunter*, above note 2 at 158.
121 *Ibid.* at 159. Stratas, above note 75 at 231, in his comment on *S.A.B.*, above note 1, observes that, "while the Court opened the door to s. 8 covering interests other than privacy back in *Hunter v. Southam* in 1984, it has never gone through that door in any later case." *S.A.B.* was the first instance in which the Court considered the extent to which s. 8 protected an accused against self-incrimination.
122 *Wong*, above note 19 at para. 11.
123 *Ibid.* at para. 12 [emphasis added].
124 *R. v. Law*, [2002] 1 S.C.R. 227 [*Law*].

she can no longer expect to assert any privacy interest over it, and so the reasonable expectation is lost.[125]

Although the Court has been clear that it is entitlement, not risk, that settles whether an expectation of privacy is reasonable, the risk analysis approach is easy to slip into. In its brief decision in *R. v. Boersma*, for example, the Court upheld a British Columbia Court of Appeal decision, which held that an accused growing marijuana on Crown land had no reasonable expectation of privacy based on the question of "whether they were susceptible to being seen by other people."[126] This consideration seems to be a risk analysis, not a question of entitlement.

It is also important to see that reasonable expectation of privacy plays several distinct roles in the section 8 analysis. On the one hand it is a threshold step to decide whether section 8 is relevant at all — that is, whether what occurred constituted a search or a seizure. Beyond that, though, the nature of the accused's reasonable expectation of privacy is an important consideration in deciding how reasonable that search or seizure may have been. As the Court said in *R. v. Edwards*, for example,

> [t]here are two distinct questions which must be answered in any section 8 challenge. The first is whether the accused had a reasonable expectation of privacy. The second is whether the search was an unreasonable intrusion on that right to privacy.[127]

That is, a reasonable expectation of privacy settles whether a section 8 analysis is necessary and is also part of that analysis.

When treated as a threshold step, a reasonable expectation of privacy should be an easy margin to cross. To say that there is no reasonable expectation of privacy in this context is to say that *any* search would be reasonable (essentially, that police could search at will).[128] This is a finding that courts should be reluctant to make since it eliminates any balancing of competing interests. Until recently, one would have said

---

125 *Stillman*, above note 26.

126 [1994] 2 S.C.R. 488, aff'g [1993] B.C.J. No. 2748 at para. 11 (C.A.). See also the discussion of this issue in James Stribopoulos, "Reasonable Expectation of Privacy and 'Open Fields' — Taking the American 'Risk Analysis' Head On" (1999) 25 C.R. (5th) 351.

127 [1996] 1 S.C.R. 128 at para 33 [*Edwards*].

128 See, for example, *R. v. M.(M.R.)*, [1998] 3 S.C.R. 393 at para. 31 [*M.(M.R.)*]: "if there is no reasonable expectation of privacy held by an accused with respect to the relevant place, there *can be no* violation of s. 8" [emphasis added]. Another way to put the same point is that, in the absence of a reasonable expectation of privacy, any action undertaken by the police would not constitute a "search": see the discussion at Section B, above in this chapter.

that courts were, in general, reluctant to reach this conclusion but, as will be discussed below, that situation seems to be changing.

When treated as part of the analysis of how reasonable an intrusion was, reasonable expectation of privacy enters into balancing individual and state interests (in reality, it *is* the individual interest to be balanced). Therefore, part of the necessary analysis is to determine how significant an interest in privacy an accused may have in particular contexts. It has been held that this interest can be reduced in some circumstances but enhanced in others, depending on the specific issues at stake. The factors relevant to this analysis will be discussed at greater length in a moment, but, broadly speaking, courts look both to factors relating to the accused and to factors relating to society. On the individual side, a person has a greater privacy interest when the search involves a body cavity as opposed to the trunk of one's car.[129] On the state interest side, a person should reasonably expect less privacy while crossing an international border,[130] or when placing items in a school locker where school officials are required to provide a safe environment and to maintain order and discipline.[131] Similarly, where an item has been stolen, the owner has not lost all privacy interests, but does have a reduced expectation of privacy because it is reasonable to expect the police might need to examine the property in the course of investigating the offence.[132]

The nature of the state interest is relevant to the reasonableness of the accused's expectation of privacy, and can it also be seen as a competing interest in its own right in deciding whether a search is

---

129 On the intrusive nature of body cavity searches, see R. v. Simmons, [1988] 2 S.C.R. 495 [Simmons]. On the reduced expectation of privacy in a vehicle generally, see Wise, above note 16; R. v. Belnavis, [1997] 3 S.C.R. 341 [Belnavis]; R. v. Fliss, [2002] 1 S.C.R. 535 [Fliss].

130 Simmons, ibid. Note that courts of appeal have disagreed over the extent to which the fact that a person is travelling through an airport affects the reasonable expectation of privacy. In R. v. Lewis (1998), 13 C.R. (5th) 34 (Ont. C.A.) [Lewis] the Ontario Court of Appeal held that travellers must expect that their luggage will be subject to scrutiny for security purposes, and that therefore the expectation of privacy is generally lowered. The British Columbia Court of Appeal has taken issue with this suggestion in R. v. Truong, 2002 BCCA 315 at para. 16 [Truong]. There Donald J.A. held for the majority that "I respectfully disagree with the suggestion that for purposes of privacy it does not matter why state authorities may go through a passenger's luggage in an airport and I would not want to take the decision in Lewis that far. The statutory power to search for air safety reasons does not eliminate the right against intrusions for criminal investigation purposes."

131 M.(M.R.), above note 128.

132 Law, above note 124.

reasonable. That is, reducing the individual's privacy interest can affect the balance, but so equally can finding a greater than usual state interest. Search incident to arrest, for example,[133] is justified not because a person arrested has a lesser expectation of privacy, but because the immediate interest of the state in protecting the security of the arresting officer and others increases at the point of arrest.[134] Similarly, the state's interest in DNA evidence is significant, since it is a particularly powerful tool either to show an accused's guilt or prevent wrongful convictions.[135]

Of course, these two different approaches of treating a reasonable expectation of privacy sometimes as a threshold step and sometimes as a factor in the analysis are perfectly reconcilable with one another. The task in assessing a warrantless search is to balance the privacy interest of the accused against the investigative interests of the state. Both approaches reflect that balancing process. It is important to keep the two steps conceptually separate, however. Where an accused has no reasonable expectation of privacy, any state investigative interest will outweigh the accused's interests, and we need go no further in deciding how the balance is to be struck—any search will be reasonable. Where the accused has some, albeit reduced, reasonable expectation of privacy, there will be limits on the state's ability to search. Nonetheless, a less compelling interest than usual could justify a search.[136]

Reasonable expectation of privacy can also enter into the *Charter* analysis at stages other than section 8. For example, in determining whether a *Charter* violation ought to result in the remedy of exclusion of evidence under section 24(2), one factor courts look to is the seriousness of the breach. A particular section 8 violation might be seen as more serious, or less serious, depending on how much of an expectation of privacy the

---

133 See discussion at Section D(2)(a)(ii)(b), below in this chapter.

134 *R. v. Caslake*, [1998] 1 S.C.R. 51 at para. 17 [*Caslake*].

135 *S.A.B.*, above note 1 at para. 51.

136 *Plant*, above note 41, illustrates the wisdom of keeping a clear distinction between these two possible approaches. Police relied on the accused's electricity consumption records in seeking a warrant to search his residence for marijuana, but they obtained those records without a warrant, initially. The Court suggests at times that Plant had "no reasonable expectation of privacy with respect to the computerized electricity records" (at 295), at other times that he "cannot be said to have held a reasonable expectation of privacy in relation to the computerized electricity records *which outweighs* the state interest in enforcing the laws relating to narcotics offences" (at 296, emphasis added). If the latter characterization is the correct one, the Court really ought to have engaged in more analysis concerning the reasonableness of the search, not just Plant's expectation of privacy.

accused had. An illegal search of a vehicle in which there is said to be a reduced expectation of privacy is a less serious violation.[137]

Further, it is worth noting that "reasonable expectation of privacy" is not an all-or-nothing issue. It is possible to give up the interest in part, while retaining it in other ways. For example, the reasonable expectation of privacy in one's home might be given up to the extent that visitors are given an implied license to knock on the door to communicate with the resident. However, that implied license does not give police the right to knock on the door if their real purpose is to conduct a warrantless "olfactory search."[138] Implied consent allowing a doctor to take a blood sample for medical purposes does not eliminate the reasonable expectation that the sample will not be used for other purposes.[139] A person speaking in the presence of others has accepted the risk of being seen and heard by those present, but that does not imply any agreement to a permanent electronic record of the remarks being made.[140]

Other findings have been made concerning the reasonable expectation of privacy. The privacy interest alleged must be that of the accused person; one cannot object to an unreasonable invasion of another's privacy.[141] However, a person with no privacy interest in a place may nonetheless have a reasonable expectation of privacy regarding a search of items found in that place.[142]

If this is the type of role that a reasonable expectation of privacy plays, then it is important to consider what factors should be taken into account in determining whether a person has a reasonable expectation of privacy at all, and, if so, how substantial it is. The Court's first serious attempt to articulate these factors came in *Edwards*, in a context where the result was to find that the accused had no reasonable expectation of privacy at all, and therefore could not rely on section 8.

---

137 See, for example, *Belnavis*, above note 129; *Fliss*, above note 129; and *Wise*, above note 16.

138 *Evans*, above note 21.

139 *Dyment*, above note 24.

140 *Wong*, above note 19 at para. 22; *Duarte*, above note 18; and *Fliss*, above note 129.

141 *Edwards*, above note 127, *Belnavis*, above note 129.

142 *Edwards*, *ibid.*; *Belnavis*, *ibid.*; and *Plant*, above note 41 all raise this possibility, though, in fact, none of the accused succeeded with the claim. In *Belnavis*, for example, the Court allowed the possibility that a passenger who had no reasonable expectation of privacy in the vehicle in which she was found might, nonetheless, have had a reasonable expectation of privacy in the bags next to her, making a search of those bags unreasonable. However, as she did not assert ownership of the bag, and as it was a garbage bag and not a monogrammed piece of luggage, the Court held that she did not, in fact, have a reasonable expectation of privacy in the bag either.

In *Edwards*, police searched an apartment rented by the accused's girlfriend. They did not have a warrant for the search, and did not believe they had reasonable grounds to obtain a warrant. Normally, a warrantless search, especially without grounds for a warrant, would violate section 8 of the *Charter*. That result, though, would depend on the accused having a section 8 right at all. That is, a reasonable expectation of privacy in his girlfriend's apartment. The latter issue was said to be determined by "the totality of the circumstances," which consisted of a number of particular factors. Specifically, the Court referred to: presence at the time of the search; possession or control of the property or place searched; ownership of the property or place; historical use of the property or item; the ability to regulate access, including the right to admit or exclude others from the place; the existence of a subjective expectation of privacy; and the objective reasonableness of the expectation.[143]

Based on this test, Edwards was found not to have a section 8 right, primarily for the reason that he was only a "privileged guest" in the apartment, lacking the ability to regulate access to it by others. In *Belnavis*, the Court applied this same reasoning to conclude in that case that a passenger in a vehicle had no reasonable expectation of privacy.[144] Once again, that meant that there was no section 8 violation, despite a warrantless search that the trial judge found to have taken place without reasonable and probable grounds. Both *Edwards* and *Belnavis* saw vigorous dissenting judgments from Justice LaForest, decrying the dilution of section 8 protection that was inherent in the decisions. Nonetheless, the list of factors from *Edwards* has become a standard method of analysis of whether a reasonable expectation of privacy exists.

An important factor in that list is the accused's subjective expectation. This is a potentially complex point. Put simply, if I close my blinds, does that indicate that I do reasonably expect privacy or that I do not? The Court has recently observed:

> The subjective expectation of privacy is important but its absence should not be used too quickly to undermine the protection afforded by s. 8 to the values of a free and democratic society. In an age of expanding means for snooping readily available on the retail market, ordinary people may come to fear (with or without justification) that their telephones are wiretapped or their private correspondence is being read . . . . Suggestions that a diminished subjective expectation of privacy should automatically result in a lowering of constitutional

---

143 *Edwards*, above note 127 at para. 45.
144 *Belnavis*, above note 129.

protection should therefore be opposed. It is one thing to say that a person who puts out the garbage has no reasonable expectation of privacy in it. It is quite another to say that someone who fears their telephone is bugged no longer has a subjective expectation of privacy and thereby forfeits the protection of s. 8. Expectation of privacy is a normative rather than a descriptive standard.[145]

Although the list of factors in *Edwards* is an important method of analysis, it is not the only approach that the Court has established. In *R. v. Arp*, for example, the Court found that when the accused voluntarily provided a blood sample to the police, he ceased to have any reasonable expectation of privacy in it.[146] However, note that when a blood sample has been taken for a particular purpose an accused retains privacy interests in the sample.[147]

More importantly, the Court has also concluded that a reasonable expectation of privacy includes at least three separate types of interest that ought to be distinguished: personal privacy, territorial privacy, and informational privacy.[148] Personal privacy (whether one can be strip-searched, for example) generally attracts the highest level of protection. Territorial privacy relates to searches of places and is contingent on the particular place being searched (a person typically has the greatest degree of privacy in a home, less in a motor vehicle, and less still in a prison, for example). Informational privacy is based on the notion that

> In fostering the underlying values of dignity, integrity and autonomy, it is fitting that s. 8 of the *Charter* should seek to protect a biographical core of personal information which individuals in a free and democratic society would wish to maintain and control from dissemination to the state. This would include information which tends to reveal intimate details of the lifestyle and personal choices of the individual.[149]

---

145 *R. v. Tessling*, [2004] 3 S.C.R. 432 at para. 42 [*Tessling*].
146 [1998] 3 S.C.R. 339 [*Arp*]. See also *R. v. Lauda* (1998), 122 C.C.C. (3d) 74 at para. 34 (Ont. C.A.), where the court concluded, in two lines, that a trespasser growing marijuana in an abandoned field had no reasonable expectation of privacy, based on *Edwards*, above note 127 and *Belnavis*, above note 129.
147 *Dyment*, above note 24.
148 *Tessling*, above note 145 at para. 20. See also *S.A.B.*, above note 1 at para. 40, relying on *Dyment*, above note 24: "privacy may include territorial or spacial aspects, aspects related to the person, and aspects that arise in the informational context."
149 *Tessling*, *ibid.* at para. 25, quoting *Plant*, above note 41.

In *Tessling*, the Court emphasized that informational privacy was not limited to intimate details, but also that not all information an accused may wish to keep confidential is protected by section 8.

Two things are worth noting about the Court's decision in *Tessling* and about the division of privacy into three separate interests. First, although courts continue to try to use the *Edwards* factors to decide the question, in reality those considerations (possession, ability to regulate access, etc.) were set out with only territorial privacy in mind. Despite the fact that some of these considerations can be applied in other contexts, it is not clear that they are actually relevant. Consider "presence at the time of the search," for example. In the case of a search of a person, that person will necessarily be present, while, in the case of a search for information, it is hard to see why it should make a difference. The Court needs to address this discontinuity. Second, creating the category of "informational privacy" has had the effect of entirely removing section 8 rights in a number of cases. It may be that informational privacy is frequently less important than personal privacy—though not necessarily, since there is obviously some extremely private information. However, granting that information is often less private, this should mean that a lower expectation of privacy would be a relevant factor at the stage of determining whether a search was reasonable—it should not mean that there was no search at all. That has sometimes, unfortunately, been the unintended impact of *Tessling*.

The fact that informational privacy is one of the three protected categories, by itself, shows that personal information presumptively falls into the private sphere, and therefore that anyone arguing that this is not the case for some particular piece of data should have the burden of proof. Some post-*Tessling* Court of Appeal decisions, however, have effectively reversed this burden by classifying the privacy interest in question as an informational one, and then requiring the accused to demonstrate that the particular information was part of the "biographical core of personal information" entitled to protection. In *Tessling* the pattern and amount of heat being emitted by the accused's home was taken not to be a territorial privacy issue but one of information. Specifically the Court was considering whether a warrantless overflight by the police, in which they trained a Forward Looking Infrared camera (FLIR) on his house following a tip that he was conducting a marijuana grow operation, violated the accused's section 8 rights. Since he had no reasonable expectation of privacy, he had no section 8 *Charter* right. The Court held that on the current state of FLIR technology the accused's territorial privacy was not really invaded—all that was in issue was the informational privacy of the heat emanating from his house. This information on its own, the Court held, was meaningless, and therefore did not attract informational privacy.[150]

Subsequently, other courts have held observations, such as an accused's behaviour while in an ambulance or the undetectable-by-human-senses odours coming from belongings, to be mere information.[151] In each case the result was that there was no reasonable expectation of privacy at all, therefore no search in the meaning of section 8, and, consequently, no section 8 violation. These cases have been the subject of critical comment.[152]

Reducing protection for anything that can be recast as "informational" has the potential to significantly limit the scope of section 8. As noted earlier, the standard for finding that an accused has no reasonable expectation of privacy should remain high, precisely because when treated as an initial step it removes any need to engage in a balancing of interests. To say that an accused has a reasonable expectation of pri-

---

150 *Tessling*'s analysis on this point follows the Court's approach in *Plant*, above note 41, where it concluded that an accused's electrical consumption records were not subject to a reasonable expectation of privacy. Stuart criticized this reasoning, pointing out that the claim that the records reveal no personal information is hard to reconcile with the Court's conclusion that the records help give reasonable grounds for issuing a search warrant: Don Stuart, *Charter Justice in Canadian Criminal Law*, 4th ed. (Toronto: Thomson Carswell, 2005) at 252. In *Tessling*, the Court tried to address the issue of how meaningless information could help justify a search warrant, though not necessarily convincingly: see Steve Coughlan & Marc S. Gorbet, "Nothing Plus Nothing Equals . . . Something?: A Proposal for FLIR Warrants on Reasonable Suspicion" (2004) 23 C. R. (6th) 239. On *Tessling*, see also Renee Pomerance, "Shedding Light on the Nature of Heat: Defining Privacy in the Wake of *R. v. Tessling*" (2005) 23 C. R. (6th) 229 and James A. Stringham, "Reasonable Expectations Reconsidered: A Return to the Search for a Normative Core for Section 8?" (2005) 23 C. R. (6th) 245.

151 See, for example, *R. v. LaChappelle*, 2007 ONCA 655; *R. v. Taylor*, 2006 NLCA 41 [*Taylor*]; *R. v. Brown*, 2006 ABCA 199 [*Brown*]. *Brown* has since been reversed by the Supreme Court of Canada: *R. v. Kang-Brown*, 2008 SCC 18 [*Kang-Brown*]. The decision is complex because there are four opinions and no clear majority on any single approach. However, all nine judges agreed that there was a reasonable expectation of privacy and that the dog sniff was a search. Indeed, only one judgment even discusses that question, with the other seven judges taking it as simply unquestioned that the dog sniff was a search. In the companion case, *R. v. A.M.*, 2008 SCC 19 [*A.M.*] Justice Binnie did suggest that a dog sniff was "through the wall" technology, and that, unlike a FLIR, it permitted precise inferences about the concealed interior.

152 See Don Stuart, "Police Use of Sniffer Dogs Ought To Be Subject to *Charter* Standards: Dangers of *Tessling* Come to Roost" (2005) 31 C.R. (6th) 255; Steve Coughlan, "Privacy Goes to the Dogs" (2006) 40 C.R. (6th) 31; Jonathan Shapiro, "Narcotics Dogs and the Search for Illegality: American Law in Canadian Courts" (2007) 43 C.R. (6th) 299.

vacy is not to say that that accused is immune from search; it is simply to say that the accused's interests must be weighed against those of the state in deciding whether a particular search is reasonable. It may mean that some limits should be attached to the timing or techniques of the search, or that a warrant might be necessary, for example. The Court has recently warned against using *Tessling* to create too narrow an approach to protecting informational privacy:

> In *Dyment*, *Plant* and *Tessling*, the various categories of "information" (including "biographical core of personal information") were used as a useful analytical tool, not a classification intended to be conclusive of the analysis of information privacy. Not all information that fails to meet the "biographical core of personal information" test is thereby open to the police.[153]

The difficulty arises from the *post facto* nature of the determination.[154] Although, in advance one might easily be able to say "a warrant should be obtained in these circumstances," courts are more often confronted after the fact with situations where the police did not obtain a warrant and a finding that they needed one will mean there was a section 8 violation. In such circumstances, to find that the accused had no reasonable expectation of privacy could seem an attractive way to avoid the determination that there was a *Charter* violation, which would otherwise arise.[155]

---

153 A.M., above note 151 at para 68.

154 The Court has warned elsewhere about the danger of applying *post facto* reasoning to determining whether an accused has a reasonable expectation of privacy. In *Wong*, above note 19, the Court disagreed with the Ontario Court of Appeal's conclusion that a person who rents a hotel room in order to conduct illegal gambling has no reasonable expectation of privacy. The question that must be asked, the Court held, was whether someone renting a hotel room had a reasonable expectation of privacy — the nature of the activity to be carried on should not be relevant to the determination. Otherwise, if a search found illegal activity and the reasonable expectation of privacy was thereby eliminated, "the result would inevitably be to adopt a system of subsequent validation for searches. Yet it was precisely to guard against this possibility that this Court in *Hunter v. Southam Inc.*, *supra*, at p. 160, stressed that prior authorization, wherever feasible, was a necessary pre-condition for a valid search and seizure": *Wong*, above note 19 at para 19.

155 A violation of s. 8 will not automatically lead to the exclusion of the evidence. Evidence would only be excluded under s. 24(2) following an analysis based on the factors set out in *Collins*, above note 118 and *Stillman*, above note 26. Given that those factors tend to make real evidence more difficult to exclude than statements, and that searches are more likely to produce real evidence than statements, this is a context in which the state's interests are likely to be fully considered.

This situation is exacerbated by the fact that some lower courts have taken the Supreme Court's direction to rely on the totality of the circumstances, particularly in light of *Tessling*, as an indication that there are no rules at all. This is a large part of what makes the definition of a reasonable expectation of privacy a moving target at present.

That is, lower courts have sometimes concluded that it is no longer permissible to lay down rules in advance regarding whether particular search techniques will be allowed and that every case must be judged on a *post facto* basis. This approach, of course, provides no guidance to the police, who would like to know what search powers they have, nor to citizens who have an interest in knowing whether they can object to or refuse to cooperate in particular methods of investigation. Indeed, it is hard to see how such an approach can be reconciled with the rule of law and the requirement that criminal law be "fixed, pre-determined and accessible and understandable by the public."[156] It also seems impossible to reconcile with the fundamental approach laid down by the Supreme Court in the seminal section 8 case, *Hunter v. Southam*. In that case the Court held:

> . . . a *post facto* analysis would, however, be seriously at odds with the purpose of s. 8. That purpose is, as I have said, to protect individuals from unjustified state intrusions upon their privacy. That purpose requires a means of *preventing* unjustified searches before they happen, not simply of determining, after the fact, whether they ought to have occurred in the first place.[157]

Nonetheless this is the approach that is in fact taken by some courts.[158] It has resulted, for example, in courts finding that police officers who use their own sense of smell to deliberately check whether they can detect an incriminating odour are not conducting a search.[159] This result directly contradicts the Supreme Court's ruling in *Evans* concerning olfactory searches (or, at least, would contradict it in a rule-based system). If the lower courts are correct that there is a new approach to a reasonable expectation of privacy that insists on *post facto* determinations in every case, with no obligation to cohere with previous decisions, then (rather worryingly) the concept of contradiction largely disappears. This is a matter that requires strong clarifica-

---

156 *United Nurses of Alberta v. Alberta (Attorney General)*, [1992] 1 S.C.R. 901 at para. 48.
157 *Hunter*, above note 2 at 160 [emphasis in original].
158 *Brown*, above note 151, *Taylor*, above note 151.
159 *R. v. Rajaratnam* (2006), 43 C.R. (6th) 280 (Alta.C.A.).

tion by the Supreme Court, and it is unfortunate that it did not do so when deciding *Kang-Brown*.[160]

2) Are the *Collins* Criteria Met?

Once it has been determined that an individual has a reasonable expectation of privacy, the issue becomes whether the search itself is reasonable. Following the finding in *Hunter v. Southam* that warrantless searches are *prima facie* unreasonable, the Court developed a three-part test for answering that question in *Collins*: Is the search authorized by law? Is the law itself reasonable? Was the manner in which the search was carried out reasonable?

a)   Is the Warrantless Search Authorized by Law?

It was noted previously[161] that the police derive authority from three sources: statute, common law, and consent. All three sources are relevant to determining whether a warrantless search is reasonable. Various statutory provisions, some of which are contained in the *Code* but most in other statutes, allow warrantless searches in certain circumstances. *Charter* decisions have made the circumstances in which such statutory provisions will be upheld fairly clear, and have led to changes in some of those provisions. Some existing common law rules allow for warrantless searches, the most important of which is search incident to arrest. In principle, the ancillary power doctrine would allow the creation of new, common law, warrantless search powers. But, also in principle, that ought to be unlikely. *Hunter v. Southam* points out that the role of the *Charter* is to determine the limits on police power, not create new search powers. The Court has observed on a number of occasions that it is Parliament's role, not that of the Court, to determine whether new search powers are necessary:

> it does not sit well for the courts, as the protectors of our fundamental rights, to widen the possibility of encroachments on these personal liberties. It falls to Parliament to make incursions on fundamental rights if it is of the view that they are needed for the protection of the public in a properly balanced system of criminal justice.[162]

---

160 *Kang-Brown*, above note 151, overturned the Alberta Court of Appeal's decision that had adopted this approach, but without commenting on the approach in any way.

161 See Chapter 2.

162 *Wong*, above note 19 at para. 35. See also R. v. *Landry*, [1986] 1 S.C.R. 145 at 187, and R. v. *Bernard*, [1988] 2 S.C.R. 833 at 891.

Indeed, the Court has held that the common law should not be interpreted to allow searches in situations where there is a statutory scheme that applies to determine whether searches are permitted.[163] However, the possibility of creating new common law search powers remains open.[164] Finally, there are also circumstances in which warrantless searches have been permitted because the accused was taken to have consented to the search.

i)   Authorization by Statute

Warrantless searches are provided for in the criminal law context and in various administrative schemes. In the criminal law context, warrantless powers to search can be found in both the *Code* and the *CDSA*.[165] Each of these powers has been recently amended to conform to *Charter* decisions concerning predecessor sections. The need for this step was not surprising, since warrantless searches are *prima facie* unreasonable. Therefore, these statutory powers depend on the existence of some fact that creates an out-of-the-ordinary situation. In each case, there is an attempt to limit the warrantless power to circumstances where it can be said that the state interest takes priority over individual privacy interests.

Section 11 of the *CDSA* allows a peace officer to obtain a warrant to search a place for a controlled substance, for anything in which a controlled substance is concealed, for offence related property, or for evidence in respect of an offence under the *CDSA*. While executing that search warrant, however, under section 11(5) a peace officer is entitled to search any person found in the place, if the officer has reasonable grounds to believe that the person has the controlled substance or thing set out in the warrant. This is a broader power than the normal search warrant provision in section 487 of the *Code*, which does not permit searches of the person. However, it is more limited than the

---

163 *Evans*, above note 21 at para. 24. See also *R. v. Polashek* (1999), 25 C.R. (5th) 183 at para. 23 (Ont. C.A.) [*Polashek*], where the Ontario Court of Appeal implies that particular statutory change is relevant to determining how common law powers should be interpreted. Note, as well, that only existing common law powers and the ancillary doctrine are relevant sources of authority in this context. It was noted in Chapter 2 that police effectively have the power to adopt any practice that will not result in the exclusion of evidence. Although that point remains true, it is clear that it is not what the Court has in mind when speaking of a search being "authorized by law." Although many s. 8 violations may not lead to the exclusion of evidence, that does not mean that they are not s. 8 violations.

164 Discussed at Section D(2)(a)(ii)(c), below in this chapter.

165 *CDSA*, above note 29.

predecessor provision in the *NCA*.[166] That provision permitted police officers to search any person found in a place being searched for narcotics, based on nothing more than their presence in the location. In *Debot*, the Ontario Court of Appeal held that a similar provision in the *Food and Drugs Act*[167] would not be reasonable, and read it down to situations where the officer also had reasonable grounds to search the person.[168] Section 11(5) involves a slight broadening of police power, since the *NCA* search power was limited to a search for narcotics, while the *CDSA* warrant allows a search for other things, such as evidence of an offence, as well. This difference is unlikely to lead any court to conclude that the appropriate balance found in *Debot* has been upset.[169]

A further warrantless search power is found in section 11(7) of the *CDSA*, permitting an officer to conduct a warrantless search when the grounds for a warrant exist but exigent circumstances make it impracticable to obtain a warrant. Once again this is in accordance with *Charter* cases on the predecessor section, which had not been limited to exigent circumstances, but was read down in that way.[170] Equivalent provisions allowing warrantless searches in exigent circumstances are found in section 487.11 of the *Criminal Code*, in relation to the search warrant provision in section 487, and in sections 117.02 and 117.04(2). Again, these provisions intend to balance the potentially competing interests of individuals and law enforcement. Courts have held, for example, that warrantless searches of a vehicle may be more readily

---

166 *NCA*, above note 37.

167 R.S.C. 1985, c. F-27.

168 *Debot*, above note 41 (Ont. C.A.).

169 This change in wording also resolves another difficulty that had confronted the Crown in *Grant*, above note 41. In that case, police had conducted a warrantless perimeter search of the accused's property, looking for information based upon which they could obtain a search warrant. The Court noted that under the statutory provision in question, police could only conduct warrantless searches when looking for a narcotic. Therefore, the warrantless perimeter search could only fall under the power granted by the statute if the police thought they would find narcotics in the perimeter, which, of course, was not their expectation. By allowing searches for evidence of an offence as well as for controlled substances themselves, s. 11(7) of the *CDSA*, above note 29, removes that difficulty.

A superficially similar power, found in s. 199(2) of the *Code*, permits an officer to take any person into custody and to seize any evidence found while in a common gaming house. However, the provision does not explicitly confer a power to search the persons found and amounts to an arrest power. Although a power to search incident to arrest may thereby arise, it is not a statutory power.

170 *R. v. Rao* (1984), 40 C.R. (3d) 1 (Ont. C.A.) [*Rao*]. See also *Grant*, above note 41. Note that in *Grant* the Crown conceded that the provision as written violated the *Charter*.

allowed, since there could be a danger of a vehicle leaving the scene, but have refused to create a blanket exemption for vehicle searches in general.[171] What matters is the impracticability of obtaining a warrant in the particular case: "exigent circumstances will generally be held to exist if there is an imminent danger of the loss, removal, destruction or disappearance of the evidence if the search or seizure is delayed."[172]

In addition, a great variety of individual provisions in various federal and provincial statutes allow for investigative techniques that meet the definition of a search. Various cases have dealt with provisions of the *Food and Drugs Act*,[173] the *Customs Act*,[174] the Nova Scotia *Education Act*,[175] and various administrative schemes.[176] Indeed, the leading case, *Hunter v. Southam*, is itself based on a provision in the *Combines Investigation Act*.[177] Finally, there are occasional warrantless seizure powers in the *Code*, such as those authorizing the seizure of a weapon from a person who cannot produce a license for it,[178] of cocks from a cockpit,[179] or of counterfeit money.[180]

ii)   *Authorization by Common Law*

a.   General
The goal of search and seizure law is to protect a reasonable expectation of privacy, primarily by preventing unreasonable searches before they take place. Generally, greater privacy should be expected with regards to one's person rather than place. Therefore, it is ironic that although searches of a place generally require a warrant, searches of the person are more often authorized on a warrantless, common law basis. On the one hand, no common law powers to search property exist, other than as part of a search incident to arrest.[181] On the other hand, searches of the person, with few exceptions, such as warrants to obtain a blood or DNA sample, are not authorized by warrant provisions. Searches of

---

171   *Grant*, *ibid.*, R. v. *D.(I.D.)* (1987), 61 C.R. (3d) 292 (Sask. C.A.)[*D.(I.D.)*].
172   *Grant*, *ibid.* at 243.
173   *Debot*, above note 41.
174   *Simmons*, above note 129.
175   *M.(M.R.)*, above note 128.
176   *Rao*, above note 170, for example attaches an appendix listing twelve statutes outside the criminal law sphere containing warrantless search powers. See the separate discussion of administrative searches at Section E(1), below in this chapter.
177   *Hunter*, above note 2.
178   Section 117.03.
179   Section 447(2).
180   Section 462(2).
181   *Wong*, above note 19 at para. 29.

the person are not typically subject to judicial oversight beforehand, but instead are assessed for validity after the fact. The most important of these common law powers to discuss is search incident to arrest, though other issues are also worth consideration.

b. Search Incident to Arrest

When the police have validly arrested a person they are entitled, within some limits, to search that person. A form of this rule has existed for centuries, and in 1990, with *Cloutier v. Langlois*, the Court decided that a properly delimited power was consistent with *Charter* protections. However, deciding what counts as proper delimitation has not been absolutely straightforward in the years since this rule with "nebulous parameters"[182] was upheld. Nonetheless, it is particularly important to do so. Although in principle warrantless searches are intended to be the exception rather than the rule, as a matter of fact searches incident to arrest are generally taken to constitute the majority of searches actually conducted by police.[183] Therefore the limits on this power need to be clear and accepted.[184]

Search incident to arrest does not require that the police have reasonable grounds for the search. It simply flows from the fact that the accused has been arrested.[185] The search is not justified because of a reduced expectation of privacy on the part of the arrested person, but rather because the police have an increased need to gain control of things or information following an arrest, which outweighs the individual's interest in privacy.[186] Accordingly, although the accused has been arrested or detained and so is entitled to be told of the right to counsel, the search does need to wait on the accused actually exercising that right.[187]

In *Cloutier*, the Court held that the search can extend not only to the accused personally but also to the surrounding area.[188] As a result, a search made incident to arrest may include searching the building or vehicle in which the accused is arrested. However, much depends on the particular circumstances of the case. For example, the police cannot contrive to arrest a person in a particular location as a pretext for

---

182 *R. v. Golden*, [2001] 3 S.C.R. 679 at para. 23 [*Golden*].
183 *Ibid.* at para. 84; Stanley A. Cohen, "Search Incident to Arrest: How Broad an Exception to the Warrant Requirement?" (1988) 63 C.R. (3d) 182.
184 *Stillman*, above note 26 at 27.
185 *Debot*, above note 41 at para. 3 (S.C.C.); *Caslake*, above note 134 at para. 20.
186 *Caslake*, *ibid.* at para. 17.
187 *Debot*, above note 41 at para. 3 (S.C.C.).
188 *Cloutier v. Langlois*, [1990] 1 S.C.R. 158 [*Cloutier*].

performing a warrantless search of that location.[189] Further, searches of vehicles and of homes have tended to be treated differently. Courts have found it relatively easy to approve of vehicle searches, accepting, for example, that removing a loose door panel might be part of a search incident to an arrest.[190] Searches of the home, in contrast, raise greater privacy issues for the accused. The Supreme Court of Canada has yet to pronounce on the issue, but the Ontario Court of Appeal has decided that searches of a home incident to arrest are not allowed, other than in exceptional circumstances. Exceptional circumstances are situations in which a particularly compelling state interest arises. A risk of physical harm to those at the scene, for example, is likely to justify a warrantless entry into an arrestee's home where the simple interest in obtaining evidence would not do so.[191] Thus, the police may be permitted to search an accused's house incident to an arrest if there is reason to suspect that an injured person or an armed accomplice might be there. As with search incident to arrest generally, this power does not depend on the existence of reasonable and probable grounds, but it will be limited to the search that is necessary to fulfill the particular purpose.

The Court has been reluctant to impose strict temporal limits on search incident to arrest. A search can be incidental to an arrest even if it precedes the formal arrest. However, the grounds for the arrest must have already existed — evidence found during the search cannot then help justify the arrest.[192] There is also no strict time limit on how long after the arrest the search can take place. For example, a search of a vehicle six hours later could still be incidental to the arrest depending on the factors affecting the timing. The further in time from the arrest, the less likely the inference that the search is incidental to that arrest; but there is no absolute rule. What matters is the actual purpose motivating the search.[193]

Although the Court has phrased the requirements in a variety of ways, the power to search incident to arrest depends essentially on three questions: Was the arrest lawful? Was the search truly incidental to that arrest? Was the search conducted in a reasonable manner?[194] Of

---

189 *R. v. Lim (No. 2)* (1990), 1 C.R.R. (2d) 136 (Ont. H.C.J.), as cited in *R. v. Smellie*, [1994] B.C.J. No. 2850 at para. 49 (C.A.) [*Smellie*].

190 *Smellie, ibid.* See also the discussion contrasting searches of vehicles to searches of the person.

191 *R. v. Golub* (1997), 9 C.R. (5th) 98 (Ont. C.A.) [*Golub*].

192 *Polashek*, above note 163; *Debot*, above note 41 (Ont. C.A.).

193 *Caslake*, above note 134 at para. 18.

194 See, for example, *Stillman*, above note 26 at para. 27. In *Cloutier*, above note 188, the three factors listed by the Court were: the power did not impose a duty; the

these, it is the second factor that is in dispute most frequently and is the most important limit,[195] though each can be an issue.[196]

Whether a search is truly incidental to an arrest depends on the purpose behind that search. That is, it must be undertaken to achieve some valid purpose connected to the arrest. Accordingly, the police officer's motives and purposes for the search are a central issue. If the search was done to intimidate or put pressure on the accused, for example, then it was not incidental.[197] Further, if a search is conducted because of a policy to search everyone arrested, that will not be sufficiently incidental. Rather, the Court has held, the search must be incidental on both objective and subjective criteria.[198] That is, not only must a valid purpose objectively exist, but subjectively the officer must have made an individualized decision to conduct the search for that purpose. Thus in *Cloutier*, for example, although the police force in question maintained a general directive to search everyone arrested, the Court noted that the officers in the case had actually exercised their discretion in choosing to search the accused.[199] In *Caslake*, though, the officer testified that he conducted the search only because of an RCMP (Royal Canadian Mounted Police) policy to inventory the contents of an impounded car.[200] Thus, although objectively a search incident to the accused's arrest would have been justifiable, the actual search conducted was not in fact incidental to the arrest. The Court has adopted this approach to be more consistent with the goal of preventing the occurrence of unjustified searches, rather than remedying them after the fact.[201]

In general, the Court has held that for the search to be an incident of the arrest, the officer must have had one of several particular

---

search must be for a valid objective; and the search must not be conducted in an abusive fashion. The stipulation that the power does not impose a duty is not really a limit (it would be difficult for an accused to object to the fact that the police exercised their discretion to search unless there were also facts showing the search was not for a valid objective), though whether the arrest was lawful can function as a limit.

195 *Caslake*, above note 134 at para. 25.

196 See, for example, *R. v. Klimchuk* (1991), 67 C.C.C. (3d) 385 (B.C.C.A.) [*Klimchuk*], where the search was not incident to arrest because the arrest was not lawful.

197 *Cloutier*, above note 188, and *Caslake*, above note 134.

198 *Caslake*, ibid.

199 *Cloutier*, above note 188.

200 *Caslake*, above note 134.

201 *Caslake*, ibid. at para. 27. See also *Golub*, above note 191, where the Ontario Court of Appeal makes note that the search of the accused's house was not based on a pre-set protocol, but on a decision made at the scene by the officer in charge based on the available information.

purposes. The Court has not always been perfectly consistent on what those three purposes are, but in *Caslake* they were stated to be ensuring the safety of the police and the public, protecting evidence from destruction at the hands of the arrestee or others, and discovering evidence that can be used at the arrestee's trial.[202] There remains some ambiguity in the caselaw over whether this third purpose relates to *any* evidence or is restricted to evidence that may go out of existence if the search was delayed.

The original purposes of this search power were related to short term goals: to find items that might allow the arrested person to harm the officer or to escape and to prevent evidence under the control of the arrestee from being destroyed. In *Stillman*, the Court noted that after *Cloutier* some courts of appeal had extended the search power beyond preventing evidence from being destroyed, to the broader purpose of finding evidence relevant to the guilt or innocence of the accused.[203] The Court rejected that broader goal on the facts of *Stillman*, which concerned taking various bodily samples from the accused (including scalp and pubic hair, as well as dental impressions) because there was "no likelihood that the appellant's teeth impressions would change, nor that his hair follicles would present a different DNA profile with the passage of time."[204] Therefore, the search could not be justified as an incident of the arrest. Similarly, in *Golden*, dealing with the more intrusive issue of strip searches, the Court focused on the risk of disposal of evidence in assessing the reasonableness of the search power.[205]

However, in *Stillman* the Court left open the question of whether the broader purpose might be acceptable when the search involved a vehicle rather than the accused's person. In *Caslake*, a case actually dealing with a vehicle, it adopted a broader formulation of the type of evidence for which police can search. The Court listed both preventing the destruction of evidence and finding evidence that could be used at the accused's trial as legitimate purposes for the search.[206] Thus, although it did not explicitly acknowledge that it had done so, the Court followed the line of authorities that expanded the search incident to arrest power in the case of vehicles. The final result appears to be that there are two separate tests. In every case, it is permissible to

---

202 *Caslake*, above note 134. See the discussion of this issue in Stephen G. Coughlan, "Developments in Criminal Procedure: The 1997–98 Term" (1999) 10 Sup. Ct. L. Rev. 273 at 319.

203 *Stillman*, above note 26.

204 *Ibid.* at para. 49.

205 *Golden*, above note 182 at para. 93.

206 *Caslake*, above note 134 at para. 19.

search an accused for the purpose of protecting the officer or preventing escape, and, in every case, it is permissible to search for evidence that is in danger of being destroyed or disposed of. However, it is only permissible to search for the more general purpose of finding evidence not in danger of destruction where the search concerns a vehicle (or presumably other location). When the accused's body is involved, there is a heightened expectation of privacy that makes the search unreasonable.[207] Since evidence, such as an accused's DNA, is not in danger of being destroyed or altered, bodily samples cannot be seized as an incident of an arrest.

In the same vein, the Court has attached particular restrictions to strip searches. Most searches incident to arrest are justified because the police have a heightened interest in searching the accused that outweighs the accused's reasonable expectation of privacy. However, the accused's expectation of privacy becomes higher in the case of a strip search. Accordingly, the Court has held, strip searches cannot routinely follow on arrest. A routine strip search conducted in good faith, without violence, will violate section 8 if there are no compelling reasons for the search in the particular circumstances. The police must be able to point to reasonable grounds to believe that a strip search, rather than the more usual pat-down, is required in the particular circumstances.[208] The Court has also identified body cavity searches as a type of search even more intrusive than strip searches. Though the Court has yet to decide the point, its reasoning in *Golden* seems to clearly indicate that a body cavity search could not proceed without, at least, the same level of justification as needed for a strip search. Indeed, given the greater intrusiveness of the search, the Court may well decide that greater justification is required for a warrantless bodily cavity search, or that no such search should be permitted without a warrant.[209]

Similar considerations concerning an enhanced interest in privacy led the Ontario Court of Appeal to hold that searches of a home as an incident to an arrest are "generally prohibited subject to exceptional

---

207 *Stillman*, above note 26 at para. 42: "the invasive nature of body searches demands higher standards of justification." This is consistent generally with the Court's view, for example in *Simmons*, above note 129, that the greater the intrusion, the greater the need for justification for the search.

208 *Golden*, above note 182.

209 In *Feeney*, above note 12, for example, the Court held that warrantless entry into a dwelling house to effect an arrest would violate the *Charter*, and read in a warrant requirement to the *Code*.

circumstances where the law enforcement interest is so compelling that it overrides the individual's right to privacy within the home."[210]

The Supreme Court has also imposed other limitations on search incident to arrest. For example, the search must be related to the actual arrest made. That is, if the search is made for more than safety reasons, there must be some prospect of finding evidence relevant to the arrest made. Where an accused is arrested for traffic violations, therefore, a search incident to the arrest does not justify looking in the trunk of the car (once the officer's safety has been secured, nothing more is justified).[211] Similarly, an accused that is known to have a history of drug offences cannot be searched for drugs if the actual arrest is for a traffic violation.[212] Although reasonable grounds for the search are not required, the officer must be able to explain the valid purpose for the search related to the reason for the arrest.[213] This approach is intended to be consistent with the goal of preventing unreasonable searches before they happen rather than remedying them after the fact.[214]

c.   Search During an Investigative Detention

In *R. v. Mann*, the Court created a common law power to search during an investigative detention.[215] While superficially similar to search incident to arrest, this search power has some noteworthy differences. Specifically, it cannot accurately be described as a search "incident to" investigative detention (though that is in fact the Court's phrasing in *Mann*). When a suspect has been arrested, no independent reasonable grounds for a search need to exist because the arrest itself would have been illegal without such grounds (that is what is meant by describing the search as "incidental to" that arrest). An investigative detention, however, is defined precisely by the absence of reasonable grounds for an arrest. As a result, the Court has held that a search cannot automatically be conducted in such circumstances. Rather, there must be independent reasonable grounds specifically justifying the search.

Further, the scope of a search incident to investigative detention is more limited than a search incident to arrest because it is limited to concerns of officer or public safety. A search incident to arrest can be conducted on those grounds, or to protect evidence from destruction

---

210 *Golub*, above note 191 at para. 41.
211 *Caslake*, above note 134 at para. 22.
212 *Golden*, above note 182 at para. 92.
213 *Caslake*, above note 134 at para. 25.
214 *Hunter*, above note 2.
215 *R. v. Mann*, 2004 SCC 52 [*Mann*]. In this case Court also first approved the existence of a police power to detain for investigative purposes at all. See the discussion of that power in Chapter 7.

at the hands of the arrestee or others, and to discover evidence to be used at trial.[216]

Further, the Court notes that in accordance with *Collins*, the search must be conducted in a reasonable manner. In this context, that translates into a requirement that the search must be limited to a pat-down of the accused. Only if that pat-down gives rise to reasonable grounds to believe that a more intrusive search is necessary will an officer be enabled to proceed further, and, for example, reach into a suspect's pocket. In addition, the search must be both objectively and subjectively justified. Ultimately the Court concluded:

> where a police officer has reasonable grounds to believe that his or her safety or that of others is at risk, the officer may engage in a protective pat-down search of the detained individual. Both the detention and the pat-down search must be conducted in a reasonable manner.[217]

On the facts of *Mann*, the Court concluded that the initial pat-down search was justified (Mann had been stopped in connection with a break and enter and so may have had tools that could be used as weapons, and was stopped after midnight in an area with no other people around).[218] However, there was no justification for going beyond the initial pat-down. On the initial pat-down the officer felt something soft in the accused's pocket, but that did not reasonably give rise to safety concerns, and so the officer was not justified in then reaching into the pocket to see what was there. Therefore, the search violated section 8. Indeed, the Court found the violation to be serious enough to justify the exclusion of the evidence under section 24(2).

d. Exigent Circumstances

Exigent circumstances can be relevant to whether a warrantless search is permitted. However, exigent circumstances are not the justification for the search itself, but rather for proceeding without a warrant.

---

216 *Caslake*, above note 134. It has been argued that lower courts have begun to expand the search power relating to investigative detentions: see Scott Latimer, "The Expanded Scope of Search Incident to Investigative Detention" (2007) 48 C.R. (6th) 201.

217 *Mann*, above note 215 at para. 45.

218 *Ibid.* at para. 47. The absence of other people is a curious rationale. The only purpose for which such searches are permitted is to protect the safety of the officer *or others*. That would suggest that the presence of other people would increase the justification for a search, which in turn suggests that their absence would reduce the need. The presence of others and their absence cannot both add to the justification for the search.

Grounds for the search must exist independently. That is, the role of exigent circumstances is to justify conducting the search without risking the delay involved in getting judicial pre-authorization. As the Court said in *Colarusso*, "absent exigent circumstances, there is a requirement of prior authorization by a judicial officer as a precondition to a valid seizure for the criminal law purposes."[219]

The Court first adopted this approach in interpreting various statutory powers that create warrantless searches. The *NCA*,[220] for example, allowed police officers to search a place other than a dwelling house if they had reasonable grounds to believe narcotics were present. It was held that to comply with section 8, this and similar provisions needed to be read down to allow a warrantless search only where exigent circumstances made it impracticable to obtain a warrant.[221] Subsequent legislative change has enacted this principle uniformly.[222]

"Exigent circumstances" in the search and seizure context[223] has been defined in a manner consistent with its role: "an imminent danger of the loss, removal, destruction or disappearance of the evidence if the search or seizure is delayed."[224] The decision is to be made on a case-by-case basis. It had, for example, been argued that a warrantless search exemption for vehicles should exist, on the basis that they are mobile and can quickly leave the scene.[225] The Court rejected this argument, holding that

> While the fact that the evidence sought is believed to be present on a motor vehicle, water vessel, aircraft or other fast moving vehicle will often create exigent circumstances, no blanket exception exists for such conveyances.[226]

In addition to justifying the failure to obtain a warrant for a search, exigent circumstances can be relevant in other ways. In *Golden*, for

---

219 *R. v. Colarusso*, [1994] 1 S.C.R. 20 at para. 70 [*Colarusso*].
220 Above note 37.
221 *Grant*, above note 41; *Wiley*, above note 50; *Rao*, above note 170; *D.(I.D.)*, above note 171.
222 See s. 487.11 of the *Code* and s. 11(7) of the *CDSA*, above note 29. To similar effect, see also ss.117.02 and 117.04(2) of the *Code*, dealing with warrantless seizures of weapons.
223 For a criticism of recent jurisprudence suggesting that "exigent circumstances" has been broadened unacceptably, primarily in the warrantless entry context, see Heather Pringle, "Kicking in the Castle Doors: The Evolution of Exigent Circumstances" (2000) 43 Crim. L.Q. 86.
224 *Grant*, above note 41.
225 *D.(I.D.)*, above note 171, *Grant*, ibid., *Klimchuk*, above note 196.
226 *Grant*, ibid. at para. 32.

example, the Court held that strip searches should ordinarily be held at a police station, and could only take place in the field in exigent circumstances. In that context, such circumstances would include an urgency to search for weapons that might pose an immediate threat and it would be unsafe to wait and conduct the strip search at the police station.[227] Similarly, exigent circumstances can be relevant to the exclusion of evidence. A court might find that, although a search was illegal, exigent circumstances made the violation less serious, thus affecting the analysis under the *Stillman* test.[228]

iii) Authorization by Consent

A warrantless search will be authorized if the suspect consented to the search. The central questions to be asked in such cases concern whether the consent was valid and the extent of the consent.

The Court has recognized that an apparent consent must be taken with a grain of salt. In *Dedman*, dealing with a random stop by police officers of a vehicle, it observed:

> because of the intimidating nature of police action and uncertainty as to the extent of police powers, compliance in such circumstances cannot be regarded as voluntary in any meaningful sense . . . . A person should not be penalized for compliance with a signal to stop by having it treated as a waiver or renunciation of rights, or as supplying a want of authority for the stop.[229]

As the Ontario Court of Appeal has noted, "acquiescence and compliance signal only a failure to object; they do not constitute consent."[230] Therefore, a certain balance must be struck in considering consent. On the one hand it is reasonable in some situations for police officers to ask a person, in the absence of reasonable grounds, whether she will consent to a search. On the other hand such a search will be warrantless and therefore *prima facie* unreasonable. Further, the consent will have acted as a waiver of *Charter* rights, and the standard for finding waiver has appropriately been set high.[231]

In some circumstances, police with suspicions but without reasonable grounds will try to create a situation in which they can obtain the suspect's consent to a search.[232] Such a search may be permissible, but

---

227 *Golden*, above note 182.
228 *Silveira*, above note 8; *Klimchuk*, above note 196.
229 *R. v. Dedman*, [1985] 2 S.C.R. 2 at para. 59.
230 *R. v. Wills* (1992), 12 C.R. (4th) 58 at para. 44 (Ont. C.A.) [*Wills*].
231 *R. v. Clarkson*, [1986] 1 S.C.R. 383.
232 See for example *R. v. Truong*, above note 130; *R. v. Jones*, 2002 NSSC 101.

sometimes a suspect will feel no option but to consent to the search. It is important, therefore, to determine when consent is valid. The Court has noted that a valid waiver requires that the accused have at least "sufficient available information to make the preference meaningful."[233] The Ontario Court of Appeal in *R. v. Wills* held that several conditions need to be satisfied:

> In order for consent to operate as a waiver of section 8 rights, the Crown must establish on balance that i) there was a consent, express or implied; ii) the giver of the consent had the authority to give the consent in question; iii) the consent was voluntary and was not the product of police oppression, coercion or other external conduct which negated the freedom to choose whether to not to allow the police to pursue the course of conduct requested; iv) the giver of the consent was aware of the nature of the police conduct to which he or she was being asked to give consent; v) the giver of the consent was aware of his or her right to refuse to permit the police to engage in the conduct requested, and; vi) the giver of the consent was aware of the potential consequences of giving the consent.[234]

Therefore, although there is no constitutional obligation to inform a suspect of the right to refuse a search, failure to do so will likely result in the search being found involuntary.[235]

There is not always an obligation to inform an accused of the right to counsel prior to a consented search.[236] In some circumstances, the accused will have been detained prior to the search, and so is entitled to be informed under section 10(b). In that event, the failure to inform the accused of the right to counsel could lead to violations under both section 10(b) and section 8.[237] Further, when the search is nominally conducted with the suspect's consent, the police are required to suspend the search until the suspect has had the opportunity to consult with counsel.[238] However, if there is no *Charter* right to counsel, the important question is whether the suspect's consent was informed, a standard that may be achieved without access to counsel.

A further issue arises around the actual scope of consent given by a suspect. In some situations, evidence that is obtained from an ac-

---

233 *R. v. Borden*, [1994] 3 S.C.R. 145 at para. 34 [*Borden*], quoting *Wills*, above note 230.
234 *Wills, ibid.*
235 *Lewis*, above note 130.
236 *Wills*, above note 230.
237 *R. v. France*, 2002 NWTSC 32.
238 *Debot*, above note 41.

cused can only be used for limited purposes.[239] Further, an accused can sometimes attach limits to the extent of the consent given.[240] It can be difficult in practice, however, to tell whether this has occurred or what limits apply.

In *Borden*,[241] police were investigating an accused in connection with two sexual assaults. A DNA sample was left at the scene of the first offence, but not the second. The accused was arrested for the second assault, and as part of their investigation the police asked him whether he would supply hair samples and a blood sample. Their primary motive was in fact to see whether the sample would connect Borden to the first offence. They did not specifically disclose that fact to him, though the consent form he signed was deliberately worded to use the plural: "investigations."

The Court held that Borden had not consented to the use of his bodily samples in connection with the first investigation. Since there was also no statutory or common law authority allowing police to use them, the seizure was not authorized by law and his section 8 right was violated. It concluded:

> It was incumbent on the police, at a minimum, to make it clear to the respondent that they were treating his consent as a blanket consent to the use of the sample in relation to other offences in which he might be a suspect . . . it will not be necessary for the accused to have a detailed comprehension of every possible outcome of his or her consent. However, his or her understanding should include the fact that the police are also planning to use the product of the seizure in a different investigation from the one for which he or she is detained.[242]

This broad proposition has been narrowed by the Court's later decision in *Arp*. The police must disclose any specific uses they intend at the time they take the sample. However, if further possible uses arise later, there is no bar to using the sample. In *Arp*, the accused had consented to provide hair samples in connection with a murder investigation. He was informed that any evidence arising from the samples would be used against him. In fact, he was discharged at the preliminary inquiry for that offence, but three years after providing the hair

---

239 See *Dyment*, above note 24, where the Court held that blood samples taken by a doctor for medical purposes cannot simply be handed over to the police for use in a criminal investigation.
240 *Colarusso*, above note 219.
241 *Borden*, above note 233.
242 *Ibid.* at paras. 39 & 40.

samples he was investigated for a second murder. Police used a warrant to obtain the hair samples, and DNA testing linked him to the second murder. Relying on *Borden*, the accused objected to use of the sample provided for one investigation in a different investigation, but the Court dismissed his appeal. The Court re-affirmed that any consent must be an informed one, but also held that

> if neither the police nor the consenting person limit the use which may be made of the evidence then, as a general rule no limitation or restriction should be placed on the use of that evidence . . . the obligation imposed on the police in obtaining a valid consent extends only to the disclosure of those anticipated purposes known to the police at the time the consent was given.[243]

On the facts of *Arp*, the Court held that the original seizure by consent was valid because the police did not know that Arp would later be the suspect in another homicide, and they did inform him that any evidence gathered would be used in court. In the absence of a specific limitation to his consent, the Court held that the accused had given up any expectation of privacy in the hair sample. Accordingly, his section 8 right was not violated.

Even where consent is not valid, it can still have some relevance. In deciding under section 24(2) whether evidence should be excluded, some courts have held that an officer's mistaken belief that the accused had consented to the search made the section 8 breach a less serious one.[244]

b)   Is the Law Itself Reasonable?

Although *Collins* sets out this question as the second one to be addressed in determining whether a warrantless search is reasonable, little work is done at this stage. In practice, the question of whether the law is reasonable tends to be subsumed into the prior question of whether the search is authorized by law.

Where a statutory warrantless search power exists, courts tend to read down the power in a way that makes it coincide with constitutional minimum standards. Thus, for example, in *Grant* the Court found that the search power in section 10 of the *NCA* had to be read down only to apply in exigent circumstances.[245] When the law is interpreted in this way there is no real scope to then ask separately whether the law is reasonable.[246]

---

243   *Arp*, above note 146 at paras. 87–88.
244   See *Lewis*, above note 130; *R. v. Daley*, 2001 ABCA 155.
245   *Grant*, above note 41.
246   To similar effect see *R. v. Jacques*, [1996] 3 S.C.R. 312; *Garofoli*, above note 104.

If the power in question is a common law one, asking whether the search is authorized by law requires the court to decide the extent of the common law power. Since the common law is to be developed in a way that is consistent with the *Charter*, the result, once again, will be to settle the question of whether the law is reasonable. Thus, for example, in *Golden* the Court considered a strip search as an incident to an arrest, and articulated the new requirement that they could be conducted only if there were reasonable and probable grounds to believe a strip search was necessary. Then, turning to this second phase of the *Collins* test, they held that "as interpreted above, the common law power to search incident to arrest conforms with the constitutional protection against unreasonable search and seizure."[247] Similarly, in *Mann* the Court noted (though in a slightly different context) that the *Collins* test and the *Waterfield* test overlap on the issue of reasonableness.[248] The effect of this approach is to render redundant the separate step of asking "is the law itself reasonable? This is so not because the question is unimportant, but because it will already have been answered.

c)   Is the Manner in Which the Search Is Carried Out Reasonable?

Even if a search power exists, a court can find that the actual search in question was unreasonable because of the manner in which it was conducted. The "manner" refers specifically to the physical way in which the search is carried out. That a search was accompanied by a violation of section 10(b), for example, is not relevant to the manner in which the search was carried out.[249]

In *Collins*, the accused was searched for drugs by an officer who grabbed her by the throat at the first moment. The Court agreed that a search power may have existed, but noted that "without very specific information, a seizure by the throat, as in this case, would be un-

---

247   *Golden*, above note 182 at para. 104. To similar effect see also *Caslake*, above note 134. In *Stillman*, above note 26 at para. 49, the Court paid lip service to the notion of having two steps:

> The common law power of search incidental to arrest cannot be so broad as to encompass the seizure without valid statutory authority of bodily samples in the face of a refusal to provide them. If it is, then the common law rule itself is unreasonable, since it is too broad and fails to properly balance the competing rights involved.

248   *Mann*, above note 215 at para. 44. The most extreme example of this approach is in *R. v. Clayton*, 2007 SCC 32 where (as the minority noted) the creation of the common law power is substituted entirely for the *Charter* analysis: see paras. 58–63. However, it is a power to detain, not a search power, that is the central issue in that case.

249   *Debot*, above note 41 at para. 6.

reasonable."[250] In general, the more intrusive the nature of the search, the greater the constraints on the way in which they can reasonably be performed.[251] Thus, for example, in *Golden*, beyond deciding the circumstances in which strip searches incident to arrest were permitted at all, the Court went on to suggest guidelines for the manner in which such searches could be conducted. These guidelines raise issues such as the number and gender of the officers conducting the search, the location of the search, how quickly the search is conducted, and so on.[252]

A *Charter* breach can only be asserted by the person whose *Charter* rights were violated.[253] Nonetheless, the *Charter* rights of others can be relevant to the manner in which a search is conducted. In *R. v. Thompson*, for example, a wiretap authorization allowed the police to tap not only the accused's telephone, but also other telephones to which he might resort, including payphones. The Court acknowledged that it was permissible for authorizations to permit tapping of public phones, and that, therefore, the search was authorized by law. However, no restrictions had been placed on the wiretap, such as only allowing interception when there were reasonable grounds to believe the accused was using the public telephone in question at the time. In some cases the police simply installed listening devices and left them activated in case the accused came along, an approach that likely resulted in the interception of hundreds of unrelated private calls. On those facts, "given the extent of the invasion of privacy authorized in this case, a total absence of any protection for the public created a potential for the carrying out of searches and seizures that were unreasonable."[254]

As *Thompson* elucidates, there could be some difficulty reconciling the notion that the *Charter* rights of other persons are relevant to the manner of the search when, according to the facts in *Debot*,[255] the accused's own *Charter* rights are not relevant to that determination. In any event, in *Edwards*[256] the Court appears to limit the relevance of third party rights to cases where there is a "potentially massive invasion of . . . privacy."

---

250 *Collins*, above note 118 at para. 24.
251 *Golden*, above note 182 at para. 87.
252 *Ibid.* at para. 101.
253 *Edwards*, above note 127 at para. 34.
254 *R. v. Thompson*, [1990] 2 S.C.R. 1111 at 1145 [*Thompson*].
255 *Debot*, above note 41.
256 *Edwards*, above note 127.

E. VARIATIONS ON THE *HUNTER v. SOUTHAM* STANDARD

Although *Hunter* is the leading authority on search and seizure, both for setting out the minimum requirements for search with a warrant, and the rule that a search without a warrant is *prima facie* unconstitutional, it is not the governing authority in every circumstance. Slight variations of the rules, in two contexts, must be discussed: i) searches under an administrative scheme and ii) searches of press offices.

1) Administrative or Regulatory Searches

The Court has held on many occasions that *Charter* rights must be interpreted in a way consistent with the context in which they arise. This equally true in the case of section 8, where the Court has held that the approach to section 8 rights as described in *Hunter* does not apply outside the criminal law context. On some occasions, the state's primary interest in conducting a search will not be to prosecute a criminal offence, but rather to enforce the rules of some regulated activity. In that event, the state may well have an interest in "the restaurateur's compliance with public health regulations, the employer's compliance with employment standards and safety legislation . . . the developer's or homeowner's compliance with building codes or zoning regulations [or] compliance with minimum wage, employment equity and human rights legislation."[257] Effective regulation of these areas may require surprise inspections or the examination of records, and, therefore, the court has held that people engaged in these activities have a lower expectation of privacy in relation to those activities. Accordingly, searches and seizures that do not comply with the *Hunter* standards may nonetheless be reasonable under section 8.

On this basis, the Court has concluded that compelling a person to testify regarding predatory pricing procedures under the *Combines Investigation Act*,[258] or to produce various documents under the *Income Tax Act*[259] or the British Columbia *Securities Act*,[260] does not constitute unreasonable search or seizure. Although possible prosecution could

---

257 *Thomson Newspapers Ltd. v. Canada (Director of Investigation and Research, Restrictive Trade Practices Commission)*, [1990] 1 S.C.R. 425.

258 *Ibid.*

259 *R. v. McKinlay Transport Ltd.*, [1990] 1 S.C.R. 627; *R. v. Jarvis*, [2002] 3 S.C.R. 757 [*Jarvis*]; *R. v. Ling*, [2002] 3 S.C.R. 814.

260 *British Columbia Securities Commission v. Branch*, [1995] 2 S.C.R. 3. See also *Comité paritaire de l'industrie de la chemise v. Potash*; *Comité paritaire de l'indus-*

follow from engaging in the behaviour being investigated, the investigations and the offences are not criminal offences. Accordingly, a search can sometimes be reasonable, even if the *Hunter* protections are not in place.

The Court has at times recognized the importance of keeping this exception in its proper, limited place, so that it does not undermine the *Hunter* standards. In *Colarusso*,[261] for example, the coroner seized blood samples after a fatal traffic accident under provisions of the Ontario *Coroners Act*.[262] No judicial pre-authorization was needed for such a seizure. On the facts, it was clear that the seizure was just as much for the purposes of the police investigation into criminal charges as it was for the legitimate purpose of an inquest (the police transported the samples to the analyst, gave up their previous efforts to obtain a sample from the accused, and so on). The Court held that the evidence was not admissible in the criminal proceedings. Although no difficulty would arise in using the evidence in the context of an inquest "once the evidence has been appropriated by the criminal law enforcement arm of the state for use in criminal proceedings, there is no foundation on which to argue that the coroner's seizure continues to be reasonable."[263]

More recently, in *Jarvis* the Court has attempted to distinguish more clearly when the different levels of *Charter* protection apply. In that case the accused was required to produce various information under the *Income Tax Act*,[264] a statute that the Court notes depends on self-reporting and, therefore, is especially dependent on the honesty of taxpayers. As a result, broad inspection and audit powers are necessary to maintain the integrity of the tax system. At a certain point, however, investigation as to whether a taxpayer has remitted sufficient funds to the government can become an investigation into whether that taxpayer should be prosecuted for an offence. Accordingly, the Court said, differing levels of *Charter* protection might be found within the same statute. As a general guideline, administrative officials must cease to use their broader investigative powers, such as mandatory inspection

---

trie de la chemise c. Sélection Milton, [1994] 2 S.C.R. 406, regarding inspection of documents relating to work arrangements.

261 Above note 219.

262 R.S.O. 1990, c. C.37.

263 *Colarusso*, above note 219. See the similar point in *R. v. White*, [1999] 2 S.C.R. 417, where an accused was obliged under the British Columbia *Motor Vehicle Act*, R.S.B.C. 1996, c. 318, to report an accident to the police. Although that provision did not violate the principle against self-incrimination inherent in s. 7, if the statement was confined to the context in which it was taken it would violate s. 7 to let the statement be used in criminal proceedings.

264 R.S.C. 1985 (5th Supp.), c. 1.

or production of documents, "where the predominant purpose of a particular inquiry is the determination of penal liability," or put another way where there has been a "crystallization of the adversarial relationship."[265] Determining when officials have "crossed the Rubicon," as the Court puts it, depends on consideration of various factors, none of which is conclusive on its own. These include, in the income tax context, whether there are reasonable grounds to lay charges, whether the general conduct of the authorities was consistent with a criminal investigation, whether an auditor's files have been transferred to investigators, whether an auditor effectively acted as an agent for investigators and whether the investigators intended that, whether the evidence concerns liability to taxation or prosecution, and other circumstances.[266]

The general justification for departing from the *Hunter* standards in regulatory contexts is the principle that *Charter* rights must be interpreted in context. That principle is well-established, but its application does create a potential slippery slope around section 8 protection. In *Jarvis*, for example, the Court specifically notes that nothing prevents an auditor from passing files to investigators or stops investigators from using that evidence. This stance seems inconsistent with the approach in *Colarusso*.[267] Further, there is surely some irony in the fact that *Hunter*, the case that first delineated the high standards to which searches are generally to be held under section 8, itself concerned a search in a regulatory context. The Court suggests in *Jarvis* that the search in *Hunter* was a greater violation of privacy expectations because it authorized entry onto private premises.[268] Still, it must be said that, despite the steps taken in *Jarvis* to help clarify when different levels of *Charter* protection apply, there remains considerable scope for difference of opinion. Therefore, in many cases the decision as to whether a search was reasonable will only be made after the fact. That is a departure from the goal of section 8, which is to prevent unreasonable searches before they occur.

2) Searches of Media Offices

Special concerns come into play when warrants are issued for the search of media offices. In that event, the guarantee of freedom of the press in section 2(b) of the *Charter* becomes relevant. However, the Court has

---

265 *Jarvis*, above note 259 at paras. 88 and 102 respectively.
266 *Ibid.* at para. 94.
267 *Colarusso*, above note 219. See also David Stratas, "'Crossing the Rubicon': The Supreme Court and Regulatory Investigations" (2003) 6 C.R. (6th) 74.
268 *Jarvis*, above note 259 at para. 61.

held that there are no additional formal requirements. These special considerations should affect the way in which a justice of peace decides whether to issue a warrant, but only because they

> provide a backdrop against which the reasonableness of the search may be evaluated. It requires that careful consideration be given not only to whether a warrant should issue but also to the conditions which might properly be imposed upon any search of media premises.[269]

It had been argued that search warrants should not be issued in relation to media offices unless it was specifically shown that no reasonable alternative source of obtaining the information was available, or that reasonable steps had been taken to obtain the information from that alternative source. The Court agreed that the media play a vital role in a democracy and that they would generally be innocent third parties in relation to any criminal proceedings. Nonetheless, they refused to impose any absolute preconditions on such warrants. Alternative sources of information are a relevant factor for a justice of peace to consider in deciding whether to issue a warrant, and the Court noted that information in that regard should normally be disclosed in the warrant application. But other factors would also be relevant to the decision, including whether the search would unduly impede the gathering or dissemination of news, or whether the information had already been broadcast or published. Thus, for example, in *Canadian Broadcasting Corporation v. Lessard*[270] the warrant application did not disclose anything about alternative sources of information. The Court agreed that disclosure of such information would have been preferable. However, the search was conducted reasonably and there was no interference with the operation of the television station. Further, the news in question had already been broadcast, leading the court to conclude that seizure of the tapes would not have a chilling effect on sources for the media. On balance, despite the omission of information about alternative sources, the Court held the warrant was properly issued.

---

269 *Canadian Broadcasting Corp. v. New Brunswick (Attorney General)*, [1991] 3 S.C.R. 459 at para. 32.
270 *Canadian Broadcasting Corp. v. Lessard*, [1991] 3 S.C.R. 421.

FURTHER READINGS

COHEN, STANLEY A., "The Paradoxical Nature of Privacy in the Context of Criminal Law and the *Canadian Charter of Rights and Freedoms*" (2002) 7 Can. Crim. L. Rev. 125

COHEN, STANLEY A., "Search Incident to Arrest: How Broad an Exception to the Warrant Requirement?" (1988) 63 C.R. (3d) 182

COUGHLAN, STEVE, "Privacy Goes to the Dogs" (2006) 40 C.R. (6th) 31

COUGHLAN, STEVE & MARC S. GORBET, "Nothing Plus Nothing Equals . . . Something?: A Proposal for FLIR Warrants on Reasonable Suspicion" (2004) 23 C.R. (6th) 239

GORHAM, NATHAN J.S., "Eight Plus Twenty-Four Two Equals Zero-Point-Five" (2003) 6 C.R. (6th) 257

HUBBARD, ROBERT W. & SCOTT K. FENTON, "Supreme Court of Canada Wiretap Update — February 2001" in Osgoode Hall Law School, Professional Development Program, *Search and Seizure Law in Canada* (Toronto: Osgoode Hall Law School, 3 November 2001)

HUTCHISON, SCOTT C. & JAMES C. MORTON, *Search and Seizure Law in Canada*, looseleaf (Toronto: Carswell, 1991)

LATIMER, SCOTT, "The Expanded Scope of Search Incident to Investigative Detention" (2007) 48 C.R. (6th) 201

LAW REFORM COMMISSION OF CANADA, *Search and Seizure* (Ottawa: Law Reform Commission of Canada, 1984)

POMERANCE, RENEE, "Shedding Light on the Nature of Heat: Defining Privacy in the wake of *R. v. Tessling*" (2005) 23 C. R. (6th) 229

PRINGLE, HEATHER, "Kicking in the Castle Doors: The Evolution of Exigent Circumstances" (2000) 43 Crim. L.Q. 86

QUIGLEY, TIM, *Procedure in Canadian Criminal Law*, 2d ed., looseleaf (Toronto: Thomson Carswell, 2005), c. 8

SANKOFF, PETER & STÉPHANE PERRAULT, "Suspicious Searches: What's So Reasonable about Them?" (1999) 24 C.R. (5th) 123

SHAPIRO, JONATHAN, "Narcotics Dogs and the Search for Illegality: American Law in Canadian Courts" (2007) 43 C.R. (6th) 299

STRATAS, DAVID, "'Crossing the Rubicon': The Supreme Court and Regulatory Investigations" (2003) 6 C.R. (6th) 74

STRATAS, DAVID, "R. v. B.(S.A.) and the Right Against Self-Incrimination: A Confusing Change of Direction" (2003) 14 C.R. (6th) 227

STRIBOPOULOS, JAMES, "Reasonable Expectation of Privacy and 'Open Fields'—Taking the American 'Risk Analysis' Head On" (1999) 25 C.R. (5th) 351

STRINGHAM, JAMES A.Q., "Reasonable Expectations Reconsidered: A Return to the Search for a Normative Core for Section 8?" (2005) 23 C. R. (6th) 245

STUART, DON, "Police Use of Sniffer Dogs Ought To Be Subject to Charter Standards: Dangers of Tessling Come to Roost" (2005) 31 C.R. (6th) 255

STUART, DON, Charter Justice in Canadian Criminal Law, 4th ed. (Toronto: Thomson Carswell, 2005) c. 3

STUART, DON, "Eight Plus Twenty-Four Two Equals Zero" (1998) 13 C.R. (5th) 50

CHAPTER 5

OTHER INVESTIGATIVE POWERS

A. INTRODUCTION

This chapter deals with police investigative techniques other than searches with and without a warrant that were discussed in Chapter 4. There are a number of such techniques—indeed, as the discussion below will show there is in principle no necessary limit to their number—but the discussion here will focus on three specific areas. All three areas, this discussion suggests, show a recent and significant expansion in police powers.

First, section 487.01 of the *Code*, which creates "general warrants," will be examined. Most of the principles relating to the review of the issuance of search warrants discussed in the previous chapter apply equally to these warrants, and they also authorize techniques that infringe on a reasonable expectation of privacy. As a result, it would have been possible to discuss them in the Chapter 4. However, general warrants can authorize techniques going well beyond anything that one would traditionally think of as a search—in the terms of the statute they are available to authorize police to "do any thing"—and so they are worth singling out for particular discussion.

Second, police powers of detention will be considered. There are statutory powers of detention, some of which occur in the investigative process (breathalyzer tests, for example, involve a power to detain). What will be of most interest, however, are recent developments in caselaw that expand the powers of detention given to the police at common law, and, indeed, expand the notion of "common law powers" themselves.

Finally section 25.1 of the *Code*, which authorizes designated officers to break the law, will be discussed. It is perhaps obvious without elaboration that this provision might be a cause for concern about the expansion of police powers.

B. GENERAL WARRANTS: SECTION 487.01

Section 487.01 of the *Code* contains what is normally referred to as the general warrant provision. It is a relatively recent provision, intended to provide for warrants to perform investigative techniques that are not covered by other *Criminal Code* provisions. It is sometimes described as filling the gap left by section 487 and other warrant provisions in the *Code*, though it is a question for debate as to whether there could properly have been said to be a gap.

In *Wong*, the police had placed a small video camera in a hotel room to record activities within.[1] Had they wanted to audiotape the room, they would have had to comply with the *Code* provisions dealing with wiretaps. However, those provisions make no mention of video cameras, so the police argued that they needed no special permission. That is, in the absence of specific limitations on their powers, they were free to use whatever investigative means they chose. That approach, the Court decided,

> wholly misunderstands *Duarte*. It is the *Charter*, specifically s. 8, that protected the appellant there and it is the *Charter* that protects the present appellant . . . s. 8 was designed to provide continuing protection against unreasonable search and seizure and to keep pace with emerging technological development.[2]

In other words, the Court relied on the principle that individuals are to be free from state interference unless such interference is specifically authorized. The Court noted that, in the absence of authorization, video surveillance fell into the general category of warrantless searches, which are *prima facie* unreasonable. The Court also held that it was not their role to create authorization for video surveillance — that was a decision for Parliament to make:

---

1   *R. v. Wong*, [1990] 3 S.C.R. 36 at para. 28 [*Wong*].
2   *Ibid.*

Until such time as Parliament, in its wisdom, specifically provides for a code of conduct for a particular invasive technology, the courts should forebear from crafting procedures authorizing the deployment of the technology in question. The role of the courts should be limited to assessing the constitutionality of any legislation passed by Parliament which bears on the matter.[3]

One would most naturally read *Wong*, which refers to George Orwell's "classic dystopian novel" *1984*[4] in its reasoning, as a recognition of the right of individuals to be generally free from state interference:

> The notion that the agencies of the state should be at liberty to train hidden cameras on members of society wherever and whenever they wish is fundamentally irreconcilable with what we perceive to be acceptable behaviour on the part of government.[5]

However, Parliament appears to have read the decision to make precisely the opposite invitation. Section 487.01, although it does not quite allow agents of the state to search "wherever and whenever" they wish, verges dangerously close to that direction.[6]

Put broadly, the problem facing the police in *Wong* was that no warrant was available for placement of a video camera, but without a warrant the search was *prima facie* unreasonable. Parliament's response to the decision was to enact section 487.01, which is aimed at avoiding loss of evidence in cases of video surveillance, and in essentially any other case as well. Section 487.01 creates warrants to "use any device or investigative technique or procedure *or do any thing* described in the warrant that would, if not authorized, constitute an unreasonable search and seizure."[7] In other words, Parliament took a decision that relied on the assumption that there need to be limits to police investigative techniques and used it to justify a provision creating an unlimited range of potential police investigative techniques. It is hard to reconcile this approach with the conclusion in *Hunter v. Southam* that

---

3   *Ibid.* at para. 36.
4   *Ibid.* at para. 15, referring to George Orwell, *1984* (New York: Harcourt, Brace, 1947).
5   *Wong, ibid.*
6   One would, of course, comply with the letter of the principle, "the police only have the powers explicitly given to them," if one explicitly gave the police the power to do anything, but that would clearly violate the notion of restraint that is the spirit of the principle. A similar approach can be seen in the government's approach to the rule of law reflected in s. 25.1 of the *Code*, discussed in Section D, below in this chapter.
7   Section 487.01(1) [emphasis added].

an assessment of the constitutionality of a search and seizure, or of a statute authorizing a search and seizure, must focus on its "reasonable" or "unreasonable" impact on the subject of the search or the seizure, and not simply on its rationality in furthering some valid government objective.[8]

Section 487.01 seems to be justified only for the purpose of furthering a government objective.

Section 487.01 can be thought of as containing two investigative techniques: i) the very general power noted above, and ii) the power to engage in video surveillance. As additional requirements are imposed on video surveillance, it is sensible to discuss the more general power first.[9]

It is most useful to examine the general warrant in terms of the similarities and differences that arise from a comparison with section 487. Some features are common to the two provisions. A warrant in each depends on reasonable grounds being established by an information provided on oath, for example. A section 487.01 warrant also does not permit interference with bodily integrity, and can be subject to conditions. Both of these requirements are specifically stated in section 487.01, though they were only implicit in section 487.[10]

Of the requirements that are unique to section 487.01, some make the provision wider than the standard search warrant provision, while others are intended to attach greater restrictions. This, of course, is as it should be in a provision intended to balance competing interests, though it is questionable whether the balance has been adequately achieved.

The general warrant provision is obviously more broad not only because it allows a search for physical evidence, but also because it allows the police to use any device, technique, procedure or "do any thing." The Ontario Court of Appeal has held that "do any thing" is to be read literally and broadly and is not limited to things like the use of devices.[11] In particular, that means that section 487.01 can be used to issue a warrant to search a location, as section 487 potentially authorizes. This is significant primarily because of another way in which section 487.01 is more broad than section 487. That is, it allows an application

---

8   *Hunter v. Southam*, [1984] 2 S.C.R. 145 at 160 [*Hunter*].
9   See also Steve Coughlan, "General Warrants at the Crossroads: Limit or License?" (2003) 10 C.R. (6th) 269.
10 See *Re Laporte and the Queen* (1972), 29 D.L.R. (3d) 651 (Que. Q.B.) and *Descoteaux v. Mierzwinski*, [1982] 1 S.C.R. 860.
11 *R. v. Noseworthy* (1997), 33 O.R. (3d) 641 (C.A.).

based not just on reasonable grounds to believe that an offence has been committed, but on the basis that an offence "will be committed."[12] In combination, these interpretations mean that the general warrant provision creates an "anticipatory search warrant." In that context, it is worth noting that the general warrant provision is also broader in that (although it cannot interfere with bodily integrity) such a search is not limited to a building, receptacle, or place, as section 487 is.

An additional requirement in section 487.01(1)(c) is that no other statutory provision can authorize the procedure in question. It is primarily worth noting what this provision does *not* mean. This section is not the equivalent of the section 186(1)(b) limitation on wiretaps that no other technique is likely to succeed. That provision is intended to act as a limit on the use of wiretaps, by showing that they are, if not precisely a last resort, something similar to that.[13] The intention behind section 487.01(1)(c) is not to provide a limit but to show that there are no limits on the techniques potentially authorizable. If no other *Code* section or statute authorizes the procedures, then section 487.01 can authorize it.

For example, courts have considered applications under section 487.01: to install a digital recording ammeter for the purpose of recording the cycling pattern of electricity usage in a residence,[14] to make electronic copies of data in a computer system,[15] to perform phallometric testing,[16] to use a forensic fluorescent light to illuminate the inside of a vehicle to look for bloodstains,[17] and to record the sender and addressee information on mail delivered to a post office box.[18] General warrants have also been issued: to stop a drug courier's vehicle on the pretext of a traffic stop in order for police to appear to accidentally dis-

---

12   Section 487.01(1)(a). Ordinary search warrants do have a small anticipatory component in s. 487(1)(c) that permits the seizure of anything "intended to be used for the purpose of committing any offence against the person for which a person may be arrested without warrant."

13   Note that s.186 is incorporated into s. 487.01 when a warrant for video surveillance is sought. In *R. v. Araujo*, [2000] 2 S.C.R. 992 at para. 29, the Court held that there was no requirement for all other techniques to have been unsuccessfully attempted, but that there should be "practically speaking, no other reasonable alternative method of investigation."

14   *R. v. Christensen*, 2001 ABPC 227.

15   *Keating v. Nova Scotia (Attorney General)*, 2001 NSSC 85.

16   *R. v. Rayworth*, [1999] O.J. No. 5289 (S.C.J.), aff'd without reference to this issue, [2001] O.J. No. 4111 (C.A.).

17   *Criminal Code of Canada (Re)*, [2002] S.J. No. 54), 2002 SKPC 11.

18   *Canada Post Corp. v. Canada (Attorney General)* (1995), 95 C.C.C. (3d) 568 (Ont. Ct. Gen. Div.).

cover the narcotics in the trunk, and to do damage to a vehicle in the course of seizing narcotics from the trunk in order to make the seizure seem like a theft.[19] In these latter two cases the purpose of the particular investigative technique was to permit the police to seize a single drug shipment without exposing the fact that the conspiracy was under investigation. Note that the first of the two, the "pretext stop," amounts to the police being given a warrant to violate section 10(a) of the *Charter*, the right to be informed of the reason for one's detention, as well as other *Charter* rights such as the right to disclosure. In the "pretext theft" case, the warrant was struck down on review because one of the potential consequences was that the Hell's Angels, to whom the narcotics were being delivered, were likely to suspect the courier himself of having taken them. This would increase the likelihood of useful information being exposed on the wiretaps in place, as well as placing the courier in danger of injury or death. The warrant was overturned not because of the latter possibility *per se*, but because the police had not informed the issuing judge about it.

On the one hand, if police are going to engage in particular investigative techniques, it is preferable for them only to do so when authorized in advance. On the other hand, the unlimited breadth of techniques allowed under the general warrant provision fails to consider whether there are particular techniques that simply should not be used at all, rather than only used with prior authorization. The Supreme Court noted in *R. v. Kokesch* that "the unavailability of other, constitutionally permissible, investigative techniques is neither an excuse nor a justification for constitutionally impermissible investigative techniques,"[20] and also held (and recently reiterated in *Buhay*) that where the police have suspicions but "no legal way to obtain other evidence, it follows that they must leave the suspect alone."[21] Although this is not precisely the same issue, the essence of the reasoning is the same. The fact that a technique is not already authorized by the *Code* does not by itself lead to the conclusion that there should be a *Code* provision authorizing it. However, that is the effect of section 487.01. Put simply, is it not *1984*,[22] provided a judge authorizes the hidden cameras wherever and whenever the state wishes? The issue, in reality, is whether the portions of the general warrant provision which make it more restrictive than the search warrant provisions adequately counter-balance the broader powers provided.

---

19   See *R. v. H.H.N.*, 2000 ABPC 173 and *R. v. Knight*, 2006 NLTD 186 respectively.
20   [1990] 3 S.C.R. 3 at para. 45 [*Kokesch*].
21   *Ibid.* at para. 46, quoted with approval in *R. v. Buhay*, 2003 SCC 30 [*Buhay*].
22   Above note 4.

A few requirements of section 487.01 differ from section 487 in ways that are intended to make it more restrictive. First, the warrant can only be issued by a judge or justice, not by a justice of the peace.[23] Second, the judge can attach conditions "to ensure that any search or seizure authorized by the warrant is reasonable in the circumstances."[24] Finally, there is a specific requirement that the judge be satisfied that "it is in the best interests of the administration of justice to issue the warrant."[25]

Difficulties have been noted at times with the procedures used by justices of the peace in issuing warrants,[26] so requiring that a general warrant can only be issued by a judge does show a commitment to greater formality. However, *Hunter v. Southam* had already required that whoever issued a warrant, whether under the *Code* or any other statute, had to be capable of acting judicially. Perhaps the terms of section 487.01 give greater grounds for confidence that this standard will consistently be met, though it is arguable that, inferentially, the heightened requirement suggests that the minimum constitutional standard is not consistently met in the case of other warrants.[27]

The ability to attach conditions has the potential to provide for sufficient balancing of individual freedom against the investigative needs of the state, but it does not guarantee such balancing. Only the conditions that "the judge considers advisable" need to be imposed, and so a great deal will depend upon which judges the police choose to approach when seeking a general warrant.

More work might be done by the separately imposed requirement that issuing the warrant is in the best interests of the administration of justice. This additional requirement holds the greatest hope of actually

---

23   The Court noted in *R. v. S.A.B.*, 2003 SCC 60 at para. 38 that the similar requirement in the case of DNA warrants showed that Parliament was attentive to the seriousness of the interests at stake.

24   Section 487.01(3).

25   Section 487.01(1)(b).

26   It was noted, for example, in *Criminal Code of Canada (Re)*, above note 17 at para. 11, that the relative lack of formality in having warrants issued by justices of the peace is efficient but

the J.P. has in many instances become involved in a manner which has raised questions about the requisite judicial neutrality . . . see for example, *R. v. Gray* (1993), 22 C.R. (4th) 114 (Man. C.A.); *R. v. Hallman*, [2001] B.C.J. No. 1966 (B.C.S.C.); *R. v. Howe*, [1994] B.C.J. No. 2731 (B.C.C.A.); *R. v. McCluskie*, [1995] B.C.J. No. 1075 (B.C.S.C.); *R. v. Clarkson*, [1999] B.C.J. No. 559 (B.C.S.C.); *R. v. Kelly*, [1995] B.C.J. No. 1369 (B.C.C.A.); *R. v. Baker*, [1997] 7 WWR 713 (Sask. Q.B.); and *R. v. Paulson*, [1993] B.C.J. No. 1944 (B.C.S.C.).

27   See, generally, the discussion of this issue and protocol for applying for s. 487.01 warrants set out in *Criminal Code of Canada (Re)*, ibid.

providing a reasonable limit on the search power, and balancing the greater intrusiveness of the rest of the section. What do these words mean? To date, no court of appeal has pronounced on the words in this context, so there is no authority to cite. At a minimum, however, it would seem that they must mean that there is *some* additional requirement beyond those necessary to obtain a search warrant in section 487. If there is not, then the general warrant power does "further some valid government objective" without considering "its 'reasonable' or 'unreasonable' impact on the subject of the search or the seizure."[28] Where the potential intrusion into liberty and privacy is greater than in *Hunter*, one would expect the protections of liberty and privacy to also be greater.

Initial indications in this regard are not especially hopeful. Although the words have not been considered in the context of section 487.01, the same phrase appears in section 186(1)(a) of the *Code*, in dealing with authorizations for wiretaps.[29] One lower court case that considered the relationship between section 487.01 and section 186(1)(a) noted that this prerequisite

> imports as a minimum requirement that the [authorizing court] must be satisfied that there are reasonable and probable grounds to believe that an offence has been, or is being, committed and that the authorization sought will afford evidence of that offence": see *R. v. Duarte*, *ibid*. The result is that the statutory requirements of [s. 186(1)(a)] are identical to the constitutional requirements: see *R. v. Garofoli* (1990), 60 C.C.C. (3d) 161 at 182 (S.C.C.).[30]

If this approach is taken, then the requirement of section 487.01(2) is reduced to the existence of reasonable and probable grounds—it would provide no additional protection.[31]

---

28   *Hunter*, above note 8 at 157.
29   See also Chapter 4, Section C(2) for interpretation of the phrase in the context of DNA warrants.
30   *R. v. Gatfield*, [2002] O.J. No. 166 at para. 60 (S.C.J.).
31   Note as well, in this regard, s. 487.01(4), which requires a judge issuing a warrant for video surveillance, when the subject of surveillance has a reasonable expectation of privacy, to impose "such terms and conditions as the judge considers advisable to ensure that the privacy of the person or any other person is respected as much as possible." One ought to view this in the context of *Wong*, above note 1, where the question of whether the accused had a reasonable expectation of privacy in a hotel room was one of the central issues in dispute. However, there is the danger that judges interpreting the section will take the explicit mention of respecting privacy in the context of video surveillance as an indication that respect for privacy is *not* a consideration when the warrant deals with techniques

In fact, however, no *Charter* challenges to the general warrant provision seem to have reached any court of appeal,[32] and so this broad power to search or perform any other investigative technique remains in the *Code*.

The video surveillance provisions of section 487.01 incorporate all of the other general warrant requirements, and additional ones as well. Section 487.01(4) imposes the particular obligation that a warrant for video surveillance in circumstances where a suspect has a reasonable expectation of privacy[33] shall contain conditions that respect the privacy of the individual as much as possible. It is not immediately apparent how one should read this section in comparison with section 487.01(3), which simply allowed a judge issuing a general warrant to attach conditions to make the search or seizure "reasonable in the circumstances." One potential reading, though an unfortunate one, would be that respect for privacy is not necessarily a concern that judges need take into account in issuing a general warrant. Individuals must hope that the courts will consider the requirement in section 487.01(4) as imposing an enhanced degree of concern for privacy when video surveillance is in issue, rather than diluting the protection offered by section 487.01(3).

However, the real limits on video surveillance are not found directly in section 487.01, but rather in its incorporation of the essential rules concerning electronic surveillance.[34] It is not appropriate to consider those rules in detail here, but they include the limit on the use of videotaping to investigate the offences listed in section 183, the rules for audiotaping with consent, and the application procedures for a warrant. This has the effect that, unlike other procedures potentially authorized under section 487.01, videotaping can only be used when other techniques have failed or are doubtful to succeed. The requirement of presenting an annual report concerning authorizations is also incorporated.

---

or devices other than video surveillance. *R. v. Lauda* (1998), 122 C.C.C. (3d) 74 (Ont. C.A.) refers to this requirement in a way that suggests it is relevant to more than just video surveillance, though it is not very clear on the point.

32   The issue has been raised in trial level courts. See, for example, *R. v. Kuitenen*, [2001] B.C.J. No.1292 (S.C.).

33   Strictly speaking, s. 487.01(4) only refers to an authorization to "observe" by means of television cameras, though it has been held to include recording by that means as well: *R. v. McCreery*, [1996] B.C.J. No. 2405 (S.C.).

34   It has been suggested that the reference to a suspect's reasonable expectation of privacy in s. 487.01(4) is a "limiting feature" on the accused's right, which is not present in the case of audiotaping. In other words, in some circumstances a suspect might be protected against audiotaping but not be protected against videotaping. See *R. v. Hangman*, [2000] M.J. No. 300 at para. 27 (Q.B.).

C. POWERS OF DETENTION

1) Definition of Detention

Detention can have more than one meaning, and so could deal, for example, with long term interferences with liberty such as those involved in being placed in a psychiatric facility following a not criminally responsible by reason of mental disorder finding[35] or being declared a dangerous offender.[36] In this context, however, it is detention at the investigative stage that is relevant (those detentions most similar to arrests in their purpose and duration). Essentially, that amounts to considering detentions where rights may arise under section 10 of the *Charter*. Section 10 gives various rights on arrest or detention, including the right to counsel. Much of the discussion of those issues is contained in Chapter 7 and will also be relevant here, although there can be an issue over precisely when the section 10(b) right "kicks in" where a detention, rather than an arrest, is at issue.

The Court has delineated the types of detentions in which those rights arise with reasonable clarity. In *R. v. Thomsen*, the Court held:

1. In its use of the word "detention", s. 10 of the *Charter* is directed to a restraint of liberty other than arrest in which a person may reasonably require the assistance of counsel but might be prevented or impeded from retaining and instructing counsel without delay but for the constitutional guarantee.

2. In addition to the case of deprivation of liberty by physical constraint, there is a detention within s. 10 of the *Charter*, when a police officer or other agent of the state assumes control over the movement of a person by a demand or direction which may have significant legal consequence and which prevents or impedes access to counsel.

3. The necessary element of compulsion or coercion to constitute a detention may arise from criminal liability for refusal to comply with a demand or direction, or from a reasonable belief that one does not have a choice as to whether or not to comply.

4. Section 10 of the *Charter* applies to a great variety of detentions of varying duration and is not confined to those of such duration as to make the effective use of *habeas corpus* possible.[37]

---

35   *R. v. Owen*, 2003 SCC 33.
36   *R. v. Johnson*, 2003 SCC 46.
37   [1988] 1 S.C.R. 640 at 649 [*Thomsen*].

In other words, "detention" can include not only those situations where the police have an actual legal power to compel a person to remain, but also some situations of "psychological detention" in which no such power exists, yet the person complies with the police demand nonetheless.[38] Detentions include not only breathalyzer demands at the side of the road, but also demands for breath samples for a roadside screening device[39] or a breathalyzer demand made at an accused's home after the accused has been initially questioned by consent without being detained.[40]

An accused can be detained despite an absence of a physical restraint and despite the fact that he was not physically prevented from making a telephone call to counsel.[41] Similarly, the fact that a person has complied with a police request to stop is not sufficient to make the stop voluntary and therefore not a detention.[42]

The primary purpose of granting *Charter* rights on detention, and in particular the right to contact counsel, is to protect the detainee from possible self-incrimination.[43] It is designed to deal with interactions between the individual and the state, normally, though not exclusively, in the context of the investigation of a criminal offence. A demand by a school's vice-principal that a student comes to the office is not a detention in the relevant sense.[44] Similarly, routine questioning of everyone entering the country by customs officials is not a detention, though singling out a particular person for a strip search is.[45]

Although there is a particular focus on the right to obtain legal advice, the Court has been resistant to arguments that the right should be reduced in situations where legal advice would have been of limited value to the accused. That counsel would likely have informed a detainee of the obligation to comply with a breathalyzer demand, for example, does not affect the content of the section 10(b) right or the likelihood of the evidence being excluded under section 24(2).[46] Similarly, the fact that there was a statutory power to conduct a search,

---

38   *R. v. Therens*, [1985] 1 S.C.R. 613 [*Therens*].
39   *Thomsen*, above note 37.
40   *R. v. Schmautz*, [1990] 1 S.C.R. 398 [*Schmautz*].
41   *Ibid.*
42   *Dedman v. The Queen*, [1985] 2 S.C.R. 2 [*Dedman*].
43   *R. v. Bartle*, [1994] 3 S.C.R. 173.
44   *R. v. M.(M.R.)*, [1998] 3 S.C.R. 393. For criticism of the Nova Scotia Court of Appeal decision to the same effect, see A. Wayne MacKay, "Don't Mind Me, I'm From the R.C.M.P.: *R. v. M.(M.R.)* — Another Brick in the Wall between Students and Their Rights" (1997) 7 C.R. (5th) 1.
45   *R. v. Simmons*, [1988] 2 S.C.R. 495 [*Simmons*].
46   *Therens*, above note 38.

whether the detainee consented or not, does not mean that the detainee would not have benefited from the advice of counsel.[47]

One quite significant area in which the question of whether a person has been detained remains unsettled is in the context of police questioning. A wide range of potential interactions can arise. In some cases, police investigate a particular crime and interview a person who may or may not be a suspect from the start. Questioning will be aimed at gathering information about a particular offence and can occur at the police station, the accused's residence, or some other location. In other cases, police simply question random persons they meet on the street or whom they drive by. Such questioning often begins with simply asking the person her name, or purpose, or asking to see identification. Sometimes the questioning may not be entirely random, and police might, for example, question a person who partly meets the description of a person wanted for an offence. In other cases factors such as the time, location, or race of the person questioned may factor into an officer's decision to ask questions.[48] Some persons that are questioned should be considered detained, others should not. These situations generally fall to be analyzed within the context of psychological detention, but exactly how to decide which people fall into which category has not been authoritatively determined.[49]

---

47   *Simmons*, above note 45. See also *R. v. Strachan*, [1988] 2 S.C.R. 980 at para. 44, where the Court rejected an approach that "would result in treating violations of s. 10(b) differently depending on the role counsel could have performed and would invite idle speculation on what might have happened if the accused had exercised the right to counsel."

48   On the issue of race as a factor in these decisions, see David Tanovich, "*R. v. Griffiths*: Race and Arbitrary Detention" (2003) 11 C.R. (6th) 149 [Tanovich 2003] and David Tanovich, "Using the *Charter* to Stop Racial Profiling: The Development of an Equality-Based Conception of Arbitrary Detention" (2002) 40 Osgoode Hall L. J. 145 [Tanovich 2002]. See also David Tanovich, *The Colour of Justice* (Toronto: Irwin Law, 2006).

49   For discussion of detention in the context of questioning at a police station, see: *R. v. D.E.M.* (2001), 156 Man. R. (2d) 231 (C.A.); *R. v. Johns* (1998), 14 C.R. (5th) 302 (Ont. C.A.); *R. v. Hawkins*, [1993] 2 S.C.R. 157 [*Hawkins*]; *R. v. Moran* (1987), 36 C.C.C. (3d) 225 (Ont. C.A.) [*Moran*]. For cases dealing with questioning on the street, see: *R. v. H.(C.R.)*, 2003 MBCA 38 [*H.(C.R.)*]; *R. v. Tammie*, 2001 BCSC 366 [*Tammie*]; *R. v. T.A.V.* (2001), 48 C.R. (5th) 366 (Alta. C.A.); *R. v. Powell* (2000), 35 C.R. (5th) 89 (Ont. Ct. J.) [*Powell*]; *R. v. Ramdeen*, [2000] O.J. No. 5350 (Ct. J.); *R. v. Hall* (1995), 22 O.R. (3d) 289 (C.A.); *R. v. Lawrence* (1990), 59 C.C.C. (3d) 55 (Ont. C.A.); *R. v. Grafe* (1987), 36 C.C.C. (3d) 267 (Ont. C.A.). Other circumstances, such as questioning an individual at home or in a hospital, have also arisen: see *R. v. Samuels*, [2001] O.J. No. 3966 (S.C.J.); *R. v. H. (D.E.)*, 2000 BCCA 314.

The difficulty in this area arises from the fact that there are competing legitimate interests. Not every conversation between a police officer and an individual should automatically be considered a detention: police interviewing the witnesses to a traffic accident should not be obliged to warn each of them of the right to counsel. However, the Court has recognized the concept of psychological detention precisely because most people do not know whether they are in fact compelled to comply with police requests or not, and so cooperation cannot always be seen as truly voluntary.[50]

Further, the primary justification for the section 10(b) right is that people interacting with the police are entitled to be protected from potential self-incrimination. In situations where an actual offence is being investigated and the extent of a person's involvement is unclear, there is a benefit for police, and a corresponding detriment to the individual, to be able to characterize the individual as merely a witness, not a suspect, and therefore not advise that person of their right to counsel. The less likely it is that a situation will be classified as a detention the greater the risk that rights will not be adequately protected. Equally, where the police are nominally "randomly" asking questions on the street, the potential that the detention would be seen as arbitrary is that much greater. If it is not a detention at all, however, there is no potential for courts to engage in the balancing involved in deciding whether it was arbitrary or not. Among other issues, it becomes more difficult to determine whether the detention was actually random, or whether it was in reality based, in part, on improper motives, such as the race of the person.[51] The net effect is a potential expansion of police power; not by design, but in result. This expansion will, based on the caselaw, often arise in exactly those situations where the person questioned would have benefited from legal advice. An accused who gives his name, which the police then run through Canadian Police Information Computer (CPIC) while continuing to engage in conversation, may well have wanted to know that there was no obligation to remain or to answer questions, particularly when he is then arrested for violating curfew or on an outstanding warrant.[52]

The Court has achieved some balance between competing legitimate interests in other situations, but to date no clear test has emerged in this context. Indeed, some courts have expressed a preference for failing to articulate a clear test, holding that "bright-line rules" are inappropriate where a "fact-specific and context-sensitive inquiry" is

---

50   *Therens*, above note 38.
51   See the discussion in the articles by Tanovich, above note 48.
52   See, for example, *H.(C.R.)*, above note 49; *Tammie*, above note 49; *Powell*, above note 49.

needed.[53] This approach has been criticized on the persuasive basis that it benefits everyone, police as well as individuals, when there is some reasonable degree of consistency and advance knowledge with regards to what powers to detain police actually have.[54]

To the extent that any consensus has emerged, it has been criticised as inadequately protecting individual rights and as not reflecting the reality of many police/ individual interactions.[55] The Supreme Court has yet to address the issue in any serious way.[56] Courts of appeal have suggested that the decision is a contextual one and that a number of factors must be taken into account. These include: whether the language and tone of voice used by the police seemed more like a request or a direction; whether the person was told she did not have to answer or accompany the police; whether the person was given a choice about where to be questioned; whether (if the questioning was at a police station) the person was taken to the station or came there in response to a request; whether an actual investigation was underway and, if so, the stage it was at; the questions asked; personal characteristics such as the age, intelligence, and level of sophistication of the person questioned; and the subjective belief of the person questioned and whether that

---

53 *R. v. Grant* (2006), 209 C.C.C. (3d) 250 at paras. 13 and 15 (Ont. C.A.).

54 See, for example, James Stribopoulos, "The Limits of Judicially Created Police Powers: Investigative Detention after *Mann*" (2007) 52 Crim. L.Q. 299.

55 Regarding questioning of persons in connection with the investigation of a specific offence, see Don Stuart, *Charter Justice in Canadian Criminal Law*, 4th ed. (Toronto: Thomson Carswell, 2005) at 323–28. See also the contrary opinions on the Newfoundland Court of Appeal judgment in *R. v. Hawkins* (1992), 14 C.R. (4th) 286 (Nfld. C.A.) in David M. Tanovich "*R. v. Hawkins*: Annotation" (1992) 14 C.R. (4th) 286 (Nfld. C.A.) and Anthony Allman, "Detention—What Does It Mean? A Comment on *R. v. Hawkins*" (1993) 18 C.R. (4th) 17. Regarding street level encounters with the police, see Tanovich 2003, above note 48 at 149, where he observes that "[t]estimony from the police that they asked the individual 'to come over' or 'we want to speak to you' or 'where are you guys headed' or 'what are you doing here' or 'what's your name' too often gets characterized as a request rather than a demand."

56 The issue arose in *Hawkins*, above note 49 (S.C.C.), but the Court's decision was virtually a one-line rejection of the Newfoundland Court of Appeal decision, without any real explanation. Similarly, in *R. v. Chaisson*, 2006 SCC 11, the Court restored a trial judge's decision that an accused had been arbitrarily detained without offering anything by way of general principle. In *R. v. Elshaw*, [1991] 3 S.C.R. 24 the accused was stopped while walking away from a park, having jumped over a fence, and was placed in the back of a police car and questioned. Justice L'Heureux-Dubé in dissent argued, based in part on the Ontario Court of Appeal decision in *Moran*, above note 49, that the accused was not detained. The majority accepted the Crown's concession that the accused was detained without analyzing the issue.

belief was objectively justified.[57] A court should consider "the entire relationship between the questioner and the person being questioned."[58]

In practice, courts applying these factors most frequently seem to find that a person, whether stopped on the street or questioned at a police station, was not detained and so had no section 10(b) right. In street encounters this result is often reached because the police did not in fact have the power to detain the accused and testified that they would have allowed the person to leave had they tried to do so. In *H.(C.R.)*, for example, the Manitoba Court of Appeal found no detention after the police, with no basis for suspicion at all, requested the names of several youths who were walking along the street, ran their names through CPIC, then arrested one for violating a curfew term in a probation order. They relied in part on the facts that the police did not block the youths' path with their car, did not physically impede their progress, and testified that they would have let the youths leave had they refused to give their names. Other cases have found that no detention occurred based on similar police testimony that they would have let individuals leave had they not complied with the request to come over or to answer questions.[59] Paradoxically, the absence of any power authorizing the police to do the thing they were doing apparently makes it *less* likely there will be a *Charter* violation.

This approach is difficult to reconcile with the reasoning adopted in other cases dealing with the right to counsel, such as *R. v. Manninen*.[60] In that case, the court noted that answering questions could not be seen as a waiver of the right to counsel. Although in this context the issue is not one of waiver, a purposive analysis should lead one to the same conclusion. If those who comply with police requests to stop and answer questions are not detained, then there will be only two groups of people: those who "voluntarily" stop and so are not detained, and those who do not stop and are not detained. In either case the section 10(b) protections arising on detention would become largely irrelevant. It limits the protections arising from the *Charter* to those people who actually know of and act in reliance on their rights in advance, which is not generally the approach taken. Put another way, it would mean that only the uncooperative would have this *Charter* right. From the point

---

57 Many cases discuss the factors involved, but see in particular *Moran*, above note 49 at 258–59 and *H.(C.R.)*, above note 49 at paras. 27–30.

58 *H.(C.R.)*, *ibid.* at para. 30.

59 In *R. v. L.B.*, 2007 ONCA 596 the Ontario Court of Appeal overturned a lower court decision based on the legal error of failing to follow the approach in *H.(C.R.)*, above note 49. See also *Tammie*, above note 49.

60 [1987] 1 S.C.R. 1233 [*Manninen*].

of view of society, we prefer people in general to comply with police requests. This preference is not encouraged by removing *Charter* protections from those who do follow such requests.[61]

Further, this restrictive reading is difficult to reconcile with cases such as *Dedman*. The Court held there that

[a] person should not be prevented from invoking a lack of statutory or common law authority for a police demand or direction by reason of compliance with it in the absence of a clear indication from the police officer that the person is free to refuse to comply. Because of the intimidating nature of police action and uncertainty as to the extent of police powers, compliance in such circumstances cannot be regarded as voluntary in any meaningful sense . . . A person should not be penalized for compliance with a signal to stop by having it treated as a waiver or renunciation of rights, or as supplying a want of authority for the stop.[62]

In *Dedman* the Court was dealing with random stops of vehicles. Given the Court's view that there is a lower expectation of privacy in a vehicle than elsewhere,[63] one would expect *Charter* rights to be more strongly protected in the case of a person walking, not driving. Oddly, in *H.(C.R.)* the court concluded the opposite, deciding that when a vehicle is pulled over the police have more obviously assumed control over the movements of the individual and, therefore, the argument for detention is stronger. This approach allows the lack of actual authority to be relevant in different ways in the two situations, which amount to a "double-lowering" of rights. First, *Charter* rights are less well-protected for drivers than for pedestrians because of the lower expectation of privacy in a vehicle. Next, *Charter* rights are less well-protected for pedestrians than for drivers because the lower expectation of privacy actually authorizes investigative techniques that qualify as a detention of drivers, while pedestrians are simply taken to consent.[64]

---

61   Note, as well, that being uncooperative carries its own hazards for the accused. In *R. v. Griffiths* (2003), 11 C.R. (6th) 136 (Ont. Ct. J.) the police attempted to rely on the fact that the accused had walked away upon seeing them as a factor justifying stopping him. The argument did not succeed in that case.

62   *Dedman*, above note 42 at para 59.

63   See, for example, *R. v. Wise*, [1992] 1 S.C.R. 527; *R. v. Belnavis*, [1997] 3 S.C.R. 341.

64   See also Tim Quigley, "*R. v. H.(C.R.)*: Annotation" (2003) 11 C.R. (6th) 152 at 153 [Quigley (*H.(C.R.)*)], where he notes that, because of the court's rejection of the analogy between vehicle and pedestrian stops, psychological detention becomes difficult to establish. He suggests that, "had the accused testified that he felt under compulsion, the Court would then have rejected this claim on the ground that it was not a reasonable belief."

This is an area of law that would benefit from clarification by the Supreme Court.[65]

2) Common Law Powers of Detention

a) Introduction

Some powers of detention exist by statute. The ability to make breathalyzer demands and random routine traffic stops, and some aspects of customs searches, for example, are all legislatively created detentions.[66] Detentions that are only created by common law are more controversial. The Court has occasionally, and increasingly, used the *Waterfield* test to create new common law police powers.[67] In *Dedman* it authorized a program of random stops of vehicles. Most recently, it relied on *Waterfield* to create police powers of investigative detention short of arrest and to permit a police roadblock.[68]

In *Dedman*, the Court considered the R.I.D.E. program of randomly stopping vehicles with the goal of detecting impaired drivers. No statutory authority allowed the stops, so the question became whether they were authorized at common law. The majority of the Court, relying on *Waterfield*, held that they were.

The *Waterfield* test involves asking two questions of the conduct of the police: whether

> (a) such conduct falls within the general scope of any duty imposed by statute or recognized at common law and (b) whether such conduct, albeit within the general scope of such a duty, involved an unjustifiable use of powers associated with the duty.[69]

---

65 Alan D. Gold, relying on an analogy to searches, argues that police questioning should be presumed to be a detention unless the person concerned knew of the right to leave. He argues that matters could frequently be clarified in advance, and fewer judicial resources therefore used, if courts imposed the obligation on police to actually say to people being questioned "you're free to leave": see "Perspectives on Section 10(b) — The Right to Counsel Under the *Charter*" (1993) 22 C.R. (4th) 370. In reply, see Anthony Allman, "Further Perspectives on Section 10(b) of the *Charter*: A Reply to Gold" (1994) 25 C.R. (4th) 280.

66 See for example *Therens*, above note 38; *R. v. Ladouceur*, [1990] 1 S.C.R. 1257 [*Ladouceur*]; *R. v. Monney*, [1999] 1 S.C.R. 652; *Simmons*, above note 45. Note, in particular, *R. v. Orbanski*; *R. v. Elias*, 2005 SCC 37, holding that the power to conduct roadside sobriety tests was implicit in the general power to stop vehicles in s. 76.1(1) of Manitoba's *Highway Traffic Act*, S.M. 1985–86, c. 3.

67 See the discussion of the *Waterfield* test in Chapter 2.

68 See *R. v. Mann*, 2004 SCC 52 [*Mann*] and *R. v. Clayton*, 2007 SCC 32.

69 *R. v. Waterfield*, [1963] 3 All E.R. 659, quoted in *Dedman*, above note 42 at para. 66. More recently, see *R. v. Decorte*, [2005] 1 S.C.R. 133, which upheld the abil-

The Court held that the random stops satisfied both aspects of the test. Preventing crime and protecting life and property by controlling traffic, the goals of the R.I.D.E. program, were well within the scope of duties of the police. Given the seriousness of the problem of impaired driving, the need to deter it, the fact that driving is a licensed activity, the well-publicized nature of the program, and that the stop would be of a short duration and minimal inconvenience, the interference was deemed not unreasonable. Accordingly, the use of power was not unjustifiable and the police were authorized to make the stops at common law.

Random stops of vehicles such as in *Dedman*, or under a statutory scheme as in *Ladouceur*, do not violate the *Charter*. A power to stop, which lies in the absolute discretion of a police officer, does violate the prohibition against arbitrary detention in section 9. However, a majority of five judges concluded that concerns about highway safety meant that the violation was justified under section 1.[70] A detention will not be arbitrary in the meaning of section 9 if it is based on criteria that are reasonable and can be clearly expressed.[71]

Some instances of unreasonable criteria for stops can be found. In the Ontario Court of Appeal decision in *Calderon*,[72] for example, the court found a section 9 violation when the police had stopped a vehicle based on what they claimed a drug-interdiction course had taught them were indicators that the occupants were drug couriers. The "indicators" that the officers had relied upon were the presence of cell phones, a pager, a road map, some fast food wrappers, and two duffel bags, as well as the notion that the car being driven seemed too expensive "for what the driver and the passenger looked to me."[73] The last criterion was rejected outright as an inappropriate criterion, but so too were the preceding ones. All of those factors, the court held, were neutral and were unsurprising items to find in a car. Each of the officers acknowledged on cross-examination that they had stopped many cars based on these "indicators" and had never before found drugs. The stop based on these neutral and unreliable factors was therefore an arbitrary detention.

There is a developing jurisprudence on stops based on racial profiling, and a recognition that it leads to a finding of a section 9 violation. Clear guidelines have yet to be laid down by the Supreme Court of Canada, though lower courts have begun to grapple with the issue.

---

ity of First Nations constables to conduct R.I.D.E. stops just outside a reserve, though in that case, that ability was based on a statutory power.

70   *Ladouceur*, above note 66.

71   *R. v. Wilson*, [1990] 1 S.C.R. 1291.

72   *R. v. Calderon* (2004), 23 C.R. (6th) 1 (Ont. C.A.) [*Calderon*].

73   *Ibid.* at para. 61.

In *Brown*, for example, the Ontario Court of Appeal acknowledged the possibility that in some cases police stops might be improperly motivated by the race of the accused, leading to a section 9 violation. Such cases, they held, are unlikely to be proven by direct evidence, and so must be inferred from the circumstances:

> where the evidence shows that the circumstances relating to a detention correspond to the phenomenon of racial profiling and provide a basis for the court to infer that the police officer is lying about why he or she singled out the accused person for attention, the record is then capable of supporting a finding that the stop was based on racial profiling.[74]

Successful racial profiling claims have been few, but have begun to arise.[75]

The *Dedman* decision has been properly criticized for its use of *Waterfield*, which was actually intended as a way of understanding the limits on existing police powers, not as a method of creating new powers.[76] Nonetheless, as discussed in Chapter 2, its use to expand police powers is well-entrenched in Canadian law. In *Mann*, the Court has again relied on *Waterfield* to decide that police officers who do not have reasonable grounds to arrest a person have the power to stop that person for investigative purposes nonetheless, if they have "reasonable grounds to detain."[77] The Court has also relied on *Waterfield* in *Clayton*.[78] It might be said that the Court did so to create a police power to set up roadblocks, but that may not be accurate. As will be seen when that case is discussed, the approach taken to *Waterfield* in *Clayton* is extremely expansive, and potentially does far more than simply authorize the particular power used in that case.

However, it is best to begin by discussing the "investigative detention" power created in *Mann*. That power is more controversial, more likely to be used, and more susceptible to misuse than the roadblock power.

---

74   *R. v. Brown* (2003), 173 C.C.C. (3d) 23 at para. 45 (Ont. C.A.).

75   See, for example, *R. v. Khan* (2004), 24 C.R. (6th) 48 (Ont. S.C.J.). See also David Tanovich, "Operation Pipeline and Racial Profiling" (2002) 1 C.R. (6th) 52 and Tanovich 2002, above note 48.

76   See, for example, James Stribopoulos, "A Failed Experiment? Investigative Detention: Ten Years Later" (2003) 41 Alta.L. Rev. 335 at 348–52 [Stribopoulos]; Don Stuart, "*R. v. Dedman*: Annotation" (1985) 46 C.R. (3d) 194 at 195. See also the discussion of *Waterfield* in Chapter 2, Section A(3)(b).

77   *Mann*, above note 68.

78   Above note 68.

b)   Investigative Detention

The first suggestion that there was a power of investigative detention in Canada came in the Ontario Court of Appeal decision in *Simpson*. That decision suggested that such a power existed on some occasions, though not on the facts of that case itself. There was no general power to detain, the Court noted, but they held that a person could be briefly detained for questioning "if the detaining officer has some 'articulable cause' for the detention."[79] Articulable cause was said to be a necessary but not sufficient condition for the detention, and the detention was meant to be brief. This approach was adopted by a number of other courts of appeal, though later courts largely ignored the notion that articulable cause was only the first step and turned that concept into the test for detention.[80] Further, the notion that articulable cause should normally support only a brief detention to ask for identification was largely lost, as many courts added an automatic ability to search the person as an incident to the detention or even to use reasonable force in effecting the detention.[81]

Although investigative detention based on articulable cause proved popular with lower courts, it was unpopular with commentators, who generally saw it as an expansion of police powers and a diminution of individual liberty created with too little attention to principle.[82] At least

---

79   *R. v. Simpson* (1993), 20 C.R. (4th) 1 at para 58 (Ont. C.A.).

80   A very incomplete list of cases applying the doctrine includes *R. v. Burke* (1997), 118 C.C.C. (3d) 59 (Nfld. C.A.); *R. v. Chabot* (1993), 86 C.C.C. (3d) 309 (N.S.S.C.A.D.); *R. v. Boudreau* (2001), 196 D.L.R. (4th) 53 (N.B.C.A.); *R. v. Lewis*, (1998), 38 O.R. (3d) 540 (C.A.); *R. v. Lake*, (1997), 113 C.C.C. (3d) 208 (Sask. C.A.) [*Lake*]; *R. v. Dupuis* (1994), 162 A.R. 197 (C.A.) [*Dupuis*]; *R. v. Yum*, 2001 ABCA 80 [*Yum*]; *R. v. V.(T.A.)* (2001), 48 C.R. (5th) 366 (Alta. C.A.) [*V.(T.A.)*]; and *R. v. Ferris* (1998), 16 C.R. (5th) 287 (B.C.C.A.), leave to appeal to S.C.C. refused, [1998] S.C.C.A. No. 424 [*Ferris*].

81   For incidental search powers, see *Ferris, ibid.*; *R. v. Lal* (1998), 56 C.R.R. (2d) 243 (B.C.C.A.), leave to appeal to S.C.C. refused, [1999] S.C.C.A. No. 28; *R. v. McAuley* (1998), 126 Man. R. (2d) 202 (C.A.); *Lake, ibid.*; and *R. v. Waniandy*, (1995) 162 A.R. 293 (C.A.). For the use of force, see *Yum, ibid.*

82   See, for example, Peter Sankoff, "Articulable Cause Based Searches Incident to Detention — This *Cooke* May Spoil the Broth" (2002) 2 C.R. (6th) 41; Steve Coughlan, "Search Based on Articulable Cause: Proceed with Caution or Full Stop?" (2002) 2 C.R. (6th) 49; Aman S. Patel, "Detention and Articulable Cause: Arbitrariness and Growing Judicial Deference to Police Judgment" (2000) 45 Crim. L.Q. 198; Lesley A. McCoy, "Liberty's Last Stand? Tracing the Limits of Investigative Detention" (2002) 46 Crim. L.Q. 319; Jason A. Nicol "'Stop in the Name of the Law': Investigative Detention" (2002) 7 Can. Crim. L. Rev. 223, Stribopoulos, above note 76; Quigley (H.(C.R.), above note 64; and Steve Coughlan, "*R. v. Mann*: Annotation" (2003) 5 C.R. (6th) 306.

in part, however, the issue was settled by the Court's decision in *Mann*, although some issues remain unaddressed.[83]

In *Mann* the Court decided that police can sometimes detain individuals for investigative detention, though the decision is very cursory. In substance, the decision amounts to confirming that such a power *does* exist without explaining very fully *why* it should exist. The Court refers briefly to *Simpson*[84] and to one other court of appeal decision, devotes two short paragraphs to the nearly forty years of U.S. jurisprudence on this issue, and engages in essentially no analysis of the many arguments raised against the power by commentators.

On the one hand, the Court appears to take the question of whether an investigative detention power exists at all as settled by the lower court jurisprudence, though this is not explicitly stated. On the other hand, *Mann* clearly does not adopt or confirm the very broad approach to investigative detention reflected in those cases — it is a fresh starting point. The *Mann* investigative detention power itself is quite limited. Indeed, the Court specifically states that it is not creating a general power of detention for investigative purposes.[85] The Court describes the power in this way:

> The detention must be viewed as reasonably necessary on an object-ive view of the totality of the circumstances, informing the officer's suspicion that there is a clear nexus between the individual to be detained and a recent or on-going criminal offence. Reasonable grounds figures at the front-end of such an assessment, underlying the officer's reasonable suspicion that the particular individual is implicated in the criminal activity under investigation. The overall reasonableness of the decision to detain, however, must further be assessed against all of the circumstances, most notably the extent to which the interference with individual liberty is necessary to per-form the officer's duty, the liberty interfered with, and the nature and extent of that interference, in order to meet the second prong of the *Waterfield* test.[86]

---

83   Generally speaking, the decision in *Mann* was not well-received by commenta-tors either: see Benjamin L. Berger "Race and Erasure in *R. v. Mann*" (2004) 21 C.R. (6th) 58; Eric V. Gottardi, "*R. v. Mann*: Regulating State Intrusions in the Context of Investigative Detentions" (2004) 21 C.R. (6th) 27; Tim Quigley "*Mann*, It's a Disappointing Decision" (2004) 21 C.R. (6th) 41; David Tanovich "The Colourless World of *Mann*" (2004) 21 C.R. (6th) 47; and Joseph R. Marin, "*R. v. Mann*: Further Down the Slippery Slope" (2005) 42 Alta. L. Rev. 1123.

84   Above note 79.

85   *Mann*, above note 68 at para. 17.

86   *Ibid.*, at para. 34.

It is clear from this description that police cannot detain a person because they are suspicious in some general way. Rather, they must be suspicious of a particular person because of some suspected connection to a particular crime already known to them. This is an important point. There is a great difference between the police stopping a person who is leaving the scene of a reported break-in, and the police stopping a person walking along the street looking in some way "suspicious." Consistent with this approach, the Court specifically rejects as not relevant any consideration at this stage of whether an accused is in a "high crime area"; suspicions must be specific to the accused.

The reference to a "recent or on-going" criminal offence precludes using the power because of a suspicion that a person contemplated committing a criminal offence. In that event, the Canadian power of detention is more limited than its U.S. counterpart. The U.S. Supreme Court created their "stop and frisk" power in *Terry v. Ohio*, where a police officer became suspicious that several men were planning to rob a store.[87]

Despite the fact that *Mann* is fairly clear on these points, they have not always been recognized by lower courts. Although there is no consistent pattern, some lower courts seem to have taken *Mann* to simply affirm *Simpson*, rather than to have articulated a new test with particular requirements. As a result, the need for a clear nexus to a recent or ongoing offence and the prohibition on using the power for anticipated offences has not always been acknowledged.[88]

It is worth observing that the *Mann* test is narrower than just the test of a "clear nexus." That is, even when a clear nexus exists, the specific individual decision to detain must still be justified based on the circumstances. In effect, the Court has refrained from creating an investigative detention power under the *Waterfield* test. Instead, it has created a framework, based on the *Waterfield* test, to be applied to assess each specific decision to detain.

A further explicit change made from existing caselaw relates to terminology. Where lower courts had spoken about "articulable cause," the Supreme Court has substituted the phrase "reasonable grounds to detain," holding that this phrasing is more consistent with Canadian terminology. Justice Deschamps in dissent, (and surely correct on this point) suggests that this phrasing will lead to confusion:

---

87 *Terry v. Ohio*, 392 U.S. 1, 88 S.Ct. 1968.
88 See the discussion of this issue in Christina Skibinsky, "Regulating *Mann* in Canada" (2006) 69 Sask. L. Rev. 197.

"Reasonable grounds" has traditionally been employed to describe the standard which must be met in order to give rise to the power to *arrest* a suspect . . . the very purpose of the common law power to detain . . . is to provide police with a less extensive and intrusive means of carrying out their duties where they do not have sufficient grounds for arrest, i.e. where there are *no* "reasonable grounds."[89]

Left largely unsettled by the case are questions concerning sections 9 and 10 of the *Charter*. The Court held that because there was the common law power for the police to detain Mann, he was not arbitrarily detained. It also accepted the trial judge's decision that Mann had in fact been detained. Nonetheless it also stated:

the police cannot be said to "detain", within the meaning of ss. 9 and 10 of the *Charter*, every suspect they stop for purposes of identification, or even interview.[90]

This is a worrying finding. Many court of appeal decisions turned to investigative detention as a way of avoiding a finding that section 9 was violated where police had acted on less than reasonable grounds. That is, although an officer had no arrest power, there was no section 9 violation because of the power to detain short of arrest.[91] Indeed, it has even been specifically found that there was no section 9 violation despite an illegal arrest on this basis.[92] Thus, creating a power to detain for investigative purposes short of arrest dramatically weakens the protection in section 9 already. To raise in the same breath the suggestion that some people stopped for investigative purposes are not even detained in the first place is simply to slide further down the slope.

The Court was able to deal briefly with section 10 of the *Charter* on the facts of this case. It held that section 10(a) applied, and therefore that a person detained for investigative purposes should be informed of the reason. It left for another day, however, the question of how the right to counsel in section 10(b) should be applied in these circumstances.[93] To date, the Court has not dealt with that issue, but some

---

89　*Mann*, above note 68 at para. 64 [emphasis in original].

90　*Ibid.* at para. 19.

91　See, for example, *Dupuis*, above note 80; *Yum*, above note 80; *V.(T.A.)*, above note 80.

92　*R. v. Pimentel*, 2000 MBCA 35.

93　The situation seems similar to that of roadside screening devices, considered in *Thomsen*, above note 37. The police are assuming control of the suspect's movements, and the short duration does not remove it from the realm of "detention." In *Thomsen*, the Court found that there was a s. 10(b) violation but that it was justified under s. 1. The same result might follow here.

lower courts have suggested that section 10(b) rights do not necessarily arise in the investigative detention context.

In R. v. Suberu, for example, the Ontario Court of Appeal dealt with a case in which an accused had been subject to investigative detention but not told of the right to counsel, and who gave incriminating answers to questions before he was so informed.[94] In addition, evidence was found by the officer during this detention before the accused was given his section 10(b) rights. The Court of Appeal concluded that there was no section 10(b) violation on the basis that the words "without delay" in that section were not equivalent to "immediately." That meant that the police were not required to inform every suspect immediately of the right. Rather, they concluded, the police could wait a short period of time in order to determine whether anything but a very brief detention was necessary.

The court argued that there were two underlying purposes for the right in section 10(b): i) to allow the person to obtain legal advice about her rights while under police detention (particularly the rights against self-incrimination and to silence) and ii) to assist the person to regain her liberty as quickly as possible. It held that, in the context of an investigative detention, informing the person of the right to counsel would actually hinder the second of these purposes. Investigative detentions are only intended to be of brief duration, and informing the person of the right to counsel would necessarily lengthen that time.

One might challenge the approach in Suberu as inconsistent with the general approach to Charter rights. In essence, the reasoning amounts to saying that one cannot have both brief investigative detentions and section 10(b) rights, and therefore there will be no section 10(b) rights in this context. However, section 52 of the Constitution Act, 1982[95] states that laws that are inconsistent with the Charter are of no force and effect. That is, when a law and a Charter right conflict, it is the law that must give way and not the Charter right. Suberu is on appeal to the Supreme Court of Canada, where one expects this issue will be resolved.

The Court of Appeal did note that under their interpretation there would be no section 10(b) violation if incriminating evidence was found before the accused was informed of the right to counsel, which would limit the accused's opportunity to seek exclusion. However, they suggested that, depending on the facts, the accused might be able to

---

94   R. v. Suberu (2007), 45 C.R. (6th) 47 (Ont. C.A.) [Suberu].

95   The Constitution Act, 1982, being Schedule B to the Canada Act 1982 (U.K.), 1982, c. 11.

argue that admitting the evidence at trial would violate section 7 and gain a remedy in that way.[96]

c)   Police Roadblocks

Subsequent to *Mann*, the court relied on the *Waterfield* test to create another police power of detention. On the facts of the case the Court was simply approving the actions of the police in setting up a roadblock. However, the way in which the majority reasoned raises the possibility that other, much broader powers to detain also exist.

In *Clayton*[97] the police received a report of men with guns in a parking lot (and describing particular vehicles), and in response the police set up a roadblock. They stopped all vehicles leaving the parking lot, whether they matched the vehicle descriptions or not, and Clayton and Farmer, the occupants of one car, were both found to have handguns. A central issue was whether there was a violation of the section 9 right of both of the accused not to be arbitrarily detained. The majority held that there would be no violation if the police had acted lawfully, and so the real issue in the case became whether the police had a power to set up the roadblock. Since they had no statutory power to do so, the only possibility was that they were authorized at common law.

There was both a majority and a minority decision in the case. All nine judges concluded that the police did have the power to act as they had, but they reach that conclusion for different reasons. It is in these different approaches that the new and potentially enormous expansion to *Waterfield* can be seen.

The minority judges held that the proper method of analysis was first to ask whether the police acted lawfully in stopping the accused, which amounted to asking whether there was a common law power permitting them to do so. The second question was whether that common law power resulted in an arbitrary detention. If so, the next step was to ask whether that law was justified under section 1 of the *Charter*. Finally, in some cases it would be necessary to ask whether the power was exercised reasonably in the totality of the circumstances. Applying that approach, the minority concluded that no previously existing common law power (such as those in *Dedman*[98] or *Mann*[99]) authorized the stop but that (using the *Waterfield* test) a new common law power

---

96   The Court of Appeal relies on *R. v. Harrer*, [1995] 3 S.C.R. 562 and *R. v. Terry*, [1996] 2 S.C.R. 207, for this suggestion. See the discussion of those cases in Chapter 3.

97   Above note 68.

98   Above note 42.

99   Above note 68.

should be created. Specifically, a power should be created to set up a roadblock of all vehicles in response to a report of ongoing serious firearm offences. As a result, the detention was authorized by law. That law would create an arbitrary detention (since it would permit stops in the absence of individualized suspicion) but would be saved under section 1, much like the power in *Ladouceur*.

The majority agreed that the issue was whether the police had the power to act as they did, but did nothing further by way of *Charter* scrutiny. As the minority pointed out, the majority substituted the question of whether the *Waterfield* test was met for the *Charter* analysis. Further, their approach to *Waterfield* seems to broaden the scope of what powers police have—or, alternatively, to limit when police action will be found to violate the *Charter*, which, on the majority approach, will amount to the same thing. As noted above, the *Waterfield* test depends on two criteria: i) that the police were acting in the general course of their duties, and ii) that the actions they took were not an unjustifiable use of powers associated with those duties. The first criterion is rarely an issue, and so it is the second that really settles the point. In *Clayton*, the majority effectively reduced that question to whether, in the totality of the circumstances, "the detention of a particular individual is 'reasonably necessary.'"[100] But to say that the police can detain an individual whenever that is reasonably necessary is to make that ability available to police far more frequently.

Even in *Mann* the Court noted the fundamental principle that "the police . . . may act only to the extent that they are empowered to do so by law."[101] That amounts to saying that the norm is for the police to be unable to interfere with individual liberty, no matter how reasonable it might be to do so, unless they have been given a specific power. The approach in *Clayton*, in contrast, seems to amount to saying that the police have the power to do anything that is reasonable. In that event, the norm is that police are empowered to act, with an exception for cases where that can be shown to be unreasonable. If *Clayton* truly is meant to signal a new approach to powers of detention and is adopted in future cases, then police power, in this regard, will have been dramatically expanded.[102]

---

100 *Clayton*, above note 68 at para. 30.

101 *Mann*, above note 68 at para. 15.

102 For discussions of the hazards inherent in the *Clayton* decision, see Steve Coughlan, "Whither—or Wither—Section 9" (2008) 40 Sup. Ct. L. Rev. (2d) 147, and James Stribopoulos, "The Forgotten Right: Section 9 of the *Charter*, Its Purpose and Meaning" (2008) 40 Sup. Ct. L. Rev. (2d) 211.

D. THE ABILITY TO BREAK THE LAW: SECTION 25.1

A further set of provisions relating to police that needs to be examined is contained in sections 25.1–25.4 of the *Criminal Code*, which permit designated police officers to break the law. The sections are not explicitly phrased to create a power. Rather, these sections talk about such an officer being "justified" in doing particular things. That language is normally associated with defences, and the sections are found in the general part, under the heading "Protection of Persons Administering and Enforcing the Law." Nominally, all that these provisions do is protect particular officers from criminal liability in particular situations. From their nature and their genesis, however, it is clear that the provisions actually create what amounts to a new police power.

The provisions allow the federal or provincial minister responsible for police to designate certain officers. An officer so designated "is justified in committing an act or omission . . . that would otherwise constitute an offence" if two further conditions are met. The first condition is simply that the officer is investigating an offence or criminal activity. The second condition is that the officer:

> (c) believes on reasonable grounds that the commission of the act or omission, as compared to the nature of the offence or criminal activity being investigated, is reasonable and proportional in the circumstances, having regard to such matters as the nature of the act or omission, the nature of the investigation and the reasonable availability of other means for carrying out the public officer's law enforcement duties.

In other words, designated officers are permitted to break the law if, in their judgment, that is a reasonable choice.

Designations for this purpose are not made in relation to a particular investigation, but rather with regard to the particular officer.[103] The designation is to be made on the advice of a senior official, and there is provision for civilian oversight.[104] It is not explicitly stated in the section, but that this power is intended for officers performing undercover work is clear. It is also possible for other officers to be designated on an emergency basis by a senior official in exigent circumstances, but such a designation expires after a maximum of forty-eight hours.[105] Some-

---

103 Section 25.1(4).
104 Sections 25.1(4), (3.1), & (3.2) respectively.
105 Section 25.1(6).

what surprisingly, there is a statutory requirement to annually report the number of emergency designations made, but no similar obligation to report the number of "ordinary" designations.[106]

There are some limits on the ability of designated officers to break the law. Section 25.1(11) states that:

(11) Nothing in this section justifies

(a)   the intentional or criminally negligent causing of death or bodily harm to another person;

(b)   the wilful attempt in any manner to obstruct, pervert or defeat the course of justice; or

(c)   conduct that would violate the sexual integrity of an individual.

In addition, section 25.1(9) refers to actions "that would be likely to result in loss of or serious damage to property." Such actions are not forbidden, but alternative, additional conditions are attached to performing them. First, a designated officer can be authorized in writing by a senior official to commit the act. This senior official is to apply specified criteria in deciding—the section does not explicitly state "in advance," of the act, but that must be the intention.[107] That point is clear because the alternative, additional condition is that the officer believes on reasonable grounds that the grounds for obtaining written authorization exist, but the circumstances make it not feasible to obtain the authorization. The only specific circumstances that could justify an officer acting in this way are the need to

(i)   preserve the life or safety of any person,

(ii)   prevent the compromise of the identity of a public officer acting in an undercover capacity, of a confidential informant or of a person acting covertly under the direction and control of a public officer, or

(iii)   prevent the imminent loss or destruction of evidence of an indictable offence.[108]

There is again an annual reporting requirement as to how frequently these provisions are relied upon.[109]

This structure of designating officers, civilian oversight, emergency designations, authorizations in writing, and so on make clear that what

---

106   Section 25.3(a).
107   Section 25.1(9)(a).
108   Section 25.1(b).
109   Section 25.3.

is really at issue is a police power, not a defence. That point is also clear, though, from the way in which the provisions came about.

The provisions were a legislative response to a Supreme Court of Canada decision regarding police undercover work.[110] In a narcotics investigation, the police used what is referred to as a "reverse sting," which meant that they posed as the sellers of drugs rather than as buyers. The *Narcotic Control Act*,[111] the relevant statute at the time, did not specifically authorize the police to do this, and so they sought an opinion from the Department of Justice as to whether this technique would be legal. The real issue in the case was whether the accused were entitled to disclosure of that legal opinion. The argument of the accused, in seeking a stay of proceedings based on abuse of process, raised the issue of police good faith. In effect, it was agreed that if the police had acted in accordance with the legal advice that they had been given, then they had acted in good faith. The accused argued, though, that the police could not simply assert that they had followed the legal advice they were given. Rather, they had to either disclose that opinion or abandon their good faith claim. Disclosure, then, was really the central issue.

The Court concluded that the accused were entitled to disclosure of the opinion. In the course of reaching the decision, the Court did observe that "the conclusion that the RCMP acted in a manner facially prohibited by the Act is inescapable."[112] However, that was far from the central point of the analysis. The Court went on to observe that police illegality did not automatically lead to the conclusion that there had been an abuse of process, or to the conclusion that the accused were entitled to a remedy. The illegality in and of itself was a relatively small issue. To the extent that it was an issue at all, it was because of the question of whether the police had acted abusively in carrying out the investigation as they did, not whether the police were themselves at risk of prosecution and therefore in need of a defence.

As a police power, the provisions have been the subject of relatively little commentary, but that commentary has been critical. It has been firmly argued that the provisions are inconsistent with the rule of law, and therefore threatens fundamental principles. It has also been argued that this cost has been paid for, effectively, no benefit, since the actual need for the police to break the law in the course of their investigations is small to non-existent.[113]

---

110 *R. v. Campbell*, [1999] 1 S.C.R. 565 [*Campbell*].

111 R.S.C. 1985, c. N-1 [since repealed].

112 *Campbell*, above note 110 at para. 25.

113 See Marc S. Gorbet, "Bill C-24's Police Immunity Provisions: Parliament's Unnecessary Legislative Response to Police Illegality in Undercover Operations"

That there appears to be no caselaw discussing the sections is both unfortunate and unsurprising. It is unfortunate because the provisions raise fundamental issues about what powers can legitimately be given to the state to investigate crime, and these issues ought to be argued in court. It is unsurprising because the power has been presented in the *Code* as though it were really a defence. Prior to section 25.1 being introduced to the *Code*, the appropriate use of prosecutorial discretion meant that criminal charges were not laid against police for mere technical violations of the law in any event, and only in the event of egregious violations would they have been prosecuted. That fact alone makes section 25.1 largely redundant. More importantly, it also means that the circumstances in which the provisions might be pleaded, and therefore discussed in court, never actually come to court. As a result, the chance for judicial scrutiny has effectively been eliminated.

FURTHER READINGS

ALLMAN, ANTHONY, "Detention — What Does It Mean? A Comment on *R. v. Hawkins*" (1993) 18 C.R. (4th) 17

ALLMAN, ANTHONY, "Further Perspectives on Section 10(b) of the *Charter*: A Reply to Gold" (1994) 25 C.R. (4th) 280

BERGER, BENJAMIN L., "Race and Erasure in *R. v. Mann*" (2004) 21 C.R. (6th) 58

COUGHLAN, STEVE, "General Warrants at the Crossroads: Limit or License?" (2003) 10 C.R. (6th) 269

COUGHLAN, STEVE, "Search Based on Articulable Cause: Proceed with Caution or Full Stop?" (2002) 2 C.R. (6th) 49

COUGHLAN, STEVE, "Whither — or Wither — Section 9" (2008) 40 Sup. Ct. L. Rev. (2d) 147

GOLD, ALAN, "Perspectives on Section 10(b) — The Right to Counsel under the *Charter*" (1993) 22 C.R. (4th) 370

(2004) 9 Can. Crim. L. Rev. 35. It is worth noting that Gorbet is a former RCMP undercover officer. See, as well, Grégoire Charles N. Webber, "Legal Lawlessness and the Rule of Law: A Critique of Section 25.1 of the *Criminal Code*" (2005) 31 Queen's L.J. 121.

GORBET, MARC S., "Bill C-24's Police Immunity Provisions: Parliament's Unnecessary Legislative Response to Police Illegality in Undercover Operations" (2004) 9 Can. Crim. L. Rev. 35

GOTTARDI, ERIC V., "*R. v. Mann*: Regulating State Intrusions in the Context of Investigative Detentions" (2004) 21 C.R. (6th) 27

LAW REFORM COMMISSION OF CANADA, *Arrest* (Working Paper 41) (Ottawa: Law Reform Commission of Canada, 1985)

LAW REFORM COMMISSION OF CANADA, *Arrest* (Report 29) (Ottawa: Law Reform Commission of Canada, 1986)

MACKAY, A WAYNE, "Don't Mind Me, I'm From the R.C.M.P.: *R. v. M.(M.R.)* — Another Brick in the Wall between Students and Their Rights" (1997) 7 C.R. (5th) 1

MARIN, JOSEPH R., "*R. v. Mann*: Further Down the Slippery Slope" (2005) 42 Alta. L. Rev. 1123

MCCOY, LESLEY A., "Liberty's Last Stand? Tracing the Limits of Investigative Detention" (2002) 46 Crim. L.Q. 319

NICOL, JASON A., "'Stop in the Name of the Law': Investigative Detention" (2002) 7 Can. Crim. L. Rev. 223

PATEL, AMAN S., "Detention and Articulable Cause: Arbitrariness and Growing Judicial Deference to Police Judgment" (2002) 45 Crim. L.Q. 198

QUIGLEY, TIM, *Procedure in Canadian Criminal Law*, 2d ed., looseleaf (Toronto: Thomson Carswell, 2005), cc. 6 and 8

QUIGLEY, TIM, "*Mann*, It's a Disappointing Decision" (2004) 21 C.R. (6th) 41

SANKOFF, PETER, "Articulable Cause Based Searches Incident to Detention — This *Cooke* May Spoil the Broth" (2002) 2 C.R. (6th) 41

SKIBINSKY, CHRISTINA, "Regulating *Mann* in Canada" (2006) 69 Sask. L. Rev. 197

STRIBOPOULOS, JAMES, "A Failed Experiment? Investigative Detention: Ten Years Later" (2003) 41 Alta. L. Rev. 335

STRIBOPOULOS, JAMES, "The Limits of Judicially Created Police Powers: Investigative Detention after *Mann*" (2007) 52 Crim. L.Q. 299

STRIBOPOULOS, JAMES, "The Forgotten Right: Section 9 of the *Charter*, Its Purpose and Meaning" (2008) 40 Sup. Ct. L. Rev. (2d) 211

STUART, DON, *Charter Justice in Canadian Criminal Law*, 4th ed. (Toronto: Thomson Carswell, 2005) cc. 4 and 5

TANOVICH, DAVID, "*R. v. Griffiths*: Race and Arbitrary Detention" (2003) 11 C.R. (6th) 149

TANOVICH, DAVID, "Using the *Charter* to Stop Racial Profiling: The Development of an Equality-Based Conception of Arbitrary Detention" (2002) 40 Osgoode Hall L. Rev. 145

TANOVICH, DAVID, "The Colourless World of *Mann*" (2004) 21 C.R. (6th) 47

TANOVICH, DAVID, *The Colour of Justice* (Toronto: Irwin Law, 2006)

TANOVICH, DAVID, "Operation Pipeline and Racial Profiling" (2002) 1 C.R. (6th) 52

WEBBER, GRÉGOIRE CHARLES N., "Legal Lawlessness and the Rule of Law: A Critique of Section 25.1 of the *Criminal Code*" (2005) 31 Queen's L. J. 121

CHAPTER 6

COMPELLING APPEARANCE AND JUDICIAL INTERIM RELEASE

A. INTRODUCTION

Many aspects of criminal procedure are quite intricately linked. For example, laying of an information in front of a justice serves several distinct functions. It commences the prosecution and is the document upon which either a preliminary inquiry will be based or a summary conviction trial will be held. It is also the foundation for a variety of methods to compel an accused to appear and answer to the charges laid out in the information. Yet, that initial appearance will not actually be for a trial on the charges, so the question arises as to what will happen to the accused in the interim. Thus, the *Code* provisions that set out the methods to make an accused first appear and those that deal with releasing or holding the accused pending trial form a whole, and both appear in Part XVI, "Compelling Appearance of Accused Before a Justice and Interim Release."

The issues related to the content of charges and the preferring of charges for trial will be discussed in Chapter 11. This chapter deals only with the procedure by which those charges are first laid. The charge is the focal point for various forms of compelling the appearance of the accused in court, and determines issues of jurisdiction and many other features of pre-trial procedure.

Following the discussion of charges, we turn to the various mechanisms that may be used to compel the appearance of an accused person in court. The most obvious of those mechanisms is to arrest an accused, either with or without a warrant. Powers of arrest raise a host of issues of their own, particularly in light of section 10 of the *Charter*, which gives rights on arrest or detention. This chapter will not attempt to deal with all the issues surrounding powers of arrest—this will be the subject of the next chapter. However, enough must be said here about arrest, with and without a warrant, to situate it in relation to the other methods of compelling appearance. This will result in a certain amount of repetition between the two chapters, but not an excessive amount.

Finally, this chapter will turn to the topic of compelling an accused's appearance to answer to charges. In particular, the question of what to do with the person once she has appeared will be examined; namely, the principles governing judicial interim release.

B. LAYING CHARGES

It is easy to see the laying of an information as simply a technical requirement among so many other particular rules that must be followed in the course of criminal proceedings. In one sense that view is correct, but at the same time it is important to recognize the wider significance. The time when an information is laid before a justice marks a momentous occasion: it is the point at which some person passes from being a "suspect" to being an "accused." That transition has great consequences for the individual, for their family, for the victim of the offence, for the criminal justice system, and for society as a whole. It means, for the most part, that the system has stopped trying to discover who committed an offence, and will, from that point forward, be focused on proving the guilt of one particular person. Such a step should not be taken lightly.

The process of laying a charge consists of both a ministerial and a judicial function. Under section 504 of the *Code*, the justice will perform the essentially bureaucratic and non-discretionary function of receiving the information. That step alone is of no consequence, however, unless the judge then takes discretionary and judicial action under section 507. It is worth looking at the two steps separately and in detail.

With the exception of direct indictments, indictable offences are charged when an information is sworn, received, and approved by a judicial officer, in accordance with sections 504 and following of the *Criminal Code*.[1] This procedure applies equally to offences prosecuted

---

1   A direct indictment may be preferred at any time and may follow a charge that is first laid by way of an information.

by summary proceedings under Part XXVII.[2] When acting under section 504, the justice acts in a "ministerial" (administrative) fashion and has no discretion over whether to receive the information.

An information may be sworn by any person who has reasonable grounds to believe that an offence has been committed. No person may be considered an accused person in the absence of a charge and, correspondingly, no court can have jurisdiction over the prosecution of an accused person in the absence of a charge.[3] In Canada, public prosecutions begin when an information is laid by a public officer. In some Canadian jurisdictions, charges are laid by peace officers, while in others they are laid by prosecutors after they have reviewed reports from the police or other authorities.[4] But, whether the informant is a peace officer, prosecutor, or private prosecutor, section 504 of the *Code* states some elementary requirements that must be met before a justice may receive and consider an information:

> 504. Any one who, on reasonable grounds, believes that a person has committed an indictable offence may lay an information in writing and under oath before a justice, and the justice shall receive the information, where it is alleged
>
> (a) that the person has committed, anywhere, an indictable offence that may be tried in the province in which the justice resides, and that the person
> (i) is or is believed to be, or
> (ii) resides or is believed to reside,
>
> within the territorial jurisdiction of the justice;
>
> (b) that the person, wherever he may be, has committed an indictable offence within the territorial jurisdiction of the justice;
> (c) that the person has, anywhere, unlawfully received property that was unlawfully obtained within the territorial jurisdiction of the justice; or
> (d) that the person has in his possession stolen property within the territorial jurisdiction of the justice.

---

2   See s. 788 and following.
3   See definition of accused in s. 493.
4   See the discussion of pre-charge screening in R. v. *Regan*, 2002 SCC 12, as well as Law Reform Commission of Canada, *Controlling Criminal Prosecutions: The Attorney General and the Crown Prosecutor* (Ottawa: Law Reform Commission of Canada, 1990).

Thus, an information must be in writing and under oath and it must allege the commission of an offence by an identifiable person. It also must contain allegations that affirm the territorial jurisdiction of the justice before whom it is laid.

Section 506 provides that the information may be laid in the manner set out in Form 2. Although this is stated as a discretion, it is prudent for an information to be laid in this manner so that it complies with matters of form that are essential to jurisdiction, such as the date and place of the alleged offence, the date and place of the information, the identity of the informant, and the identity of the justice.

The informant must declare in the information that he has reasonable grounds to believe that an offence has been committed. Grounds for such a belief need not be based on the personal knowledge of the informant but may be based on reports that he has received. However, the person swearing the information must personally hold the necessary belief. It is not sufficient, for example, for a police officer to lay an information simply on the basis that she was instructed to do so by her superior: the officer must personally know enough to reasonably believe that the offence has been committed.[5]

Most prosecutions in Canada are public ones, but when the informant is not a peace officer or an agent of the attorney general the procedure undertaken is called a private prosecution. In such a case the informant must be prepared to carry forward the prosecution personally if the information is signed by a judicial officer. Private prosecutions are comparatively rare but they do occur, usually when public authorities have declined to commence a prosecution. However, the *Code* provides that the attorney general may intervene in any private prosecution that has been commenced, either to assume carriage of it or to stop it by means of a stay of proceedings.[6]

Once the information has been received, under section 504, the justice who received the information must consider the substance of the informant's allegations, under section 507. In this judicial function, the justice exercises discretion as to whether it is appropriate to take any action or to require the accused person to answer the charges.[7]

This function is performed *ex parte*, and so the justice will consider the allegations in the absence of the person or persons accused in the information. It also means that this hearing is generally not conducted in open court. Nevertheless, the justice must act judicially in the con-

---

5   *R. v. Pilcher* (1981), 58 C.C.C. (2d) 435 (Man. Prov. Ct.).

6   Sections 579.01 and 579.1.

7   *R. v. Allen* (1974), 20 C.C.C. (2d) 447 (Ont. C.A.) [*Allen*].

sideration of the information. He will examine the allegations of the informant and may ask questions of that person or any other witness where he considers such evidence necessary or desirable to ascertain the basis of the informant's belief that an offence was committed. Any evidence thus taken by the justice must be given under oath and recorded, but the justice is not obliged to observe the rules and principles governing the admissibility of evidence at a preliminary inquiry or trial.

Upon considering the information, the justice must decide whether to endorse it. The *Code* does not state explicitly the standard that the justice must apply in this decision, but it is clear that the justice must personally consider and agree that there are reasonable grounds to believe that an offence was committed by the person to be charged.[8] This does not require that the informant prove the allegations; nor does it require the justice to make any judgment concerning the sufficiency of the case for prosecution. The justice need only be satisfied that there are reasonable grounds, as disclosed in the information and any evidence adduced in support thereof, to believe that the offence was committed by the person named. If the justice is satisfied, she will sign the information. This endorsement marks the moment at which a charge is formally laid and a prosecution begins. At this point, the person named in the information is an accused person before the court.

The judge must refuse to issue process if he is not satisfied that it discloses reasonable grounds to believe that an offence has been committed. However, a refusal to issue any process by one justice does not prevent the informant from seeking a summons or warrant from a different justice based on the information.[9]

C. COMPELLING APPEARANCE

The compelling appearance and bail provisions in Part XVI of the *Code* operate by granting broad powers to police and judges to restrict the liberty of individuals but then attaching significant limitations on the use of those powers. The result is an attempt to satisfy the needs of the state to ensure that accused persons are present for their trials while, at the same time, using those powers with as much restraint as possible.

In general terms, the *Code* provides powers to police to require an accused to attend court through some type of written demand, or to

---

8   *R. v. Jeffrey* (1976), 34 C.R.N.S. 283 (Ont. Prov. Ct.).
9   *Allen*, above note 7.

arrest the person: preference is given to not arresting. If the person is arrested, the system requires various actors along the way to consider whether the accused can be released without being taken to a justice. If the accused is taken to a justice, the system is then designed to release the accused with as few restrictions as necessary. In short, the *Code* provides that, if possible, appearance should be sought without arrest and detention. The various ways in which arrest or continued detention are meant to be avoided to the extent possible are discussed further in the next chapter.

In addition, the *Code* provides that, where a person is released, preference should be given to the means of compelling appearance that is least onerous, especially as regards the imposition of a money debt as a form of security. Where Part XVI allows for continued detention before trial, it also includes mechanisms for review of that detention. These issues will be discussed in part D of this chapter.

A further demonstration of the restraint built in to Part XVI is seen in the fact that a police officer's decision that an accused should be made to attend court is never sufficient on its own: it is always necessary for some judicial officer to confirm that decision. In some cases, the officer's initial interaction is with the individual accused of committing a crime. In that event, a justice must later confirm the officer's actions and agree that charges should be laid. In other cases, the charges are laid in front of a justice first, and the police then seek out the individual. Although there are similarities between the two situations, it is convenient to consider them separately. Accordingly, we shall consider: (i) the process for compelling an accused to appear when charges have not yet been laid and (ii) the process that is used after charges have been laid.

1) Compelling Appearance Pre-charge

If a peace officer decides that a person should be prosecuted, there are various ways to compel that person to attend court before an information is laid and he is actually charged. The most obvious is to make an arrest without a warrant.[10] A central point to note is that an arrest is not necessarily the only way, or even the preferred way, to compel appearance, even if no charge has yet been laid. Other procedural mechanisms may be used, whether there has been an arrest without warrant or not. In effect, the *Code* provides that a person may be required to

---

10   The law with respect to arrest is explored at greater length in Chapter 7.

attend court by means of an appearance notice, a promise to appear, or a recognizance.

Section 495(2) of the *Code* makes a preference for less intrusive means explicit. A peace officer's power to arrest without warrant is created in section 495(1) and is quite broad. Section 495(2), however, suggests that, in the case of less serious offences, an officer should not necessarily use those arrest powers. "Less serious," in this context, is defined broadly to mean summary conviction offences, hybrid offences, or indictable offences listed in section 553 (those in the absolute jurisdiction of a provincial court judge).[11] In the case of those offences, the *Code* suggests that an officer should issue an appearance notice instead, unless there is a good reason to arrest.[12] A "good reason to arrest" is limited to the possibilities that the person will not show up in court unless arrested or that there is a need to:

(i) establish the identity of the person,
(ii) secure or preserve evidence of or relating to the offence, or
(iii) prevent the continuation or repetition of the offence or the commission of another offence.[13]

Section 495(2)[14] is phrased in a confusing way, but the principle underlying it is that, for less serious offences, police officers should not arrest simply because they have the power to do so. The section does not actually *remove* the power to arrest, though, and so in practice it often occurs that the peace officer does make an arrest and then determines whether to release that individual or take him into custody.

If the officer decides, under section 495(2), not to arrest, section 496 authorizes the officer to issue an appearance notice.[15] An appearance notice directs the person to whom it is issued to appear in court at a specified date, time, and place. Further, the appearance notice must inform the person of the consequences that flow from non-compliance with its terms. Those consequences are that failure to appear at the specified time is an offence under section 145 of the *Code*, and that an arrest warrant can be issued under section 508.

Even if a peace officer has arrested a person, it is not the end of the story. The officer can decide afterward, under section 497(1), to release that person with the intention to compel her appearance by means of a summons or an appearance notice. Here, the *Code* provisions closely

---

11 Subsections 495(2)(c), (b), & (a).
12 Section 496.
13 Subsections 495(2)(e) & (d).
14 See Chapter 7 for further discussion on this section of the *Code*.
15 See Form 9 at s. 849 of the *Code*.

parallel those relating to the original decision to arrest and they still reflect a preference for release in some cases. Specifically, in the same circumstances of summary conviction offences, hybrid offences, or indictable offences listed in section 553, the stated preference is for releasing the accused. The only exceptions to that preference are for the same grounds as found in section 495(2) (to ensure appearance in court, establish identity, secure evidence, or prevent further offences) with one addition. A peace officer might also decide not to release the accused after arrest in order to "ensure the safety and security of any victim of or witness to the offence."[16]

In the event that a person is arrested without warrant and taken into custody by the arresting peace officer, he will be brought before the officer in charge or another peace officer. Under section 498, the officer in charge can also decide to release the arrested person and, once again, is directed to prefer this course of action in many circumstances. Indeed, in section 498 the range of offences for which release is preferred is even broader than in previous sections: in addition to summary conviction, hybrid, or section 553 offences, the officer in charge is also to release a person arrested for any other offence punishable by imprisonment for a term of five years or less.

Corresponding to the fact that release is possible for more serious offences at this stage, the officer in charge is also permitted to impose more restrictive conditions on the accused in order to be released. Since the officer in charge is also a peace officer, she may of course decide either to release the person, with no intention that he should be charged, or she may release him upon issuing an appearance notice. Under section 498, the officer in charge is also entitled to release an accused with the intent to compel appearance by way of summons, as was the arresting officer under section 497. In addition, an officer in charge can release an arrested person on a "promise to appear" or on a recognizance. A promise to appear, set out in Form 10, is a written promise by the accused to attend court at a specified date and time. As with an appearance notice, failure to comply with the promise is an offence.[17] A recognizance, set out in Form 11, is a written acknowledgement of a debt, in an amount not exceeding five hundred dollars, which would be forfeited upon failure to appear in court. The officer in charge may fix the amount of the recognizance but may not require sureties to secure the debt. That is, only the accused can be asked to acknowledge the debt.

---

16   Section 497(1.1)(a)(iv).
17   Section 145(5).

Further, in cases where the accused is not ordinarily resident in the province, or resides more than two hundred kilometres from the place of custody, the officer may release the accused on a recognizance, or actually require the deposit of money or other security to ensure attendance. As with a promise to appear, failure to comply with the recognizance is an offence.

Across sections that deal with release (sections 495, 497, and 498), the language on its face appears to be mandatory: the officer in question "shall not arrest" or "shall release." However, in each case, further subsections qualify this obligation by stating that an officer who fails to comply with the section is still acting in the execution of duty. In effect, then, these provisions are more in the nature of advice or guidance rather than legal requirements.[18]

Apart from compelling appearance in court, an appearance notice, a promise to appear, or a recognizance may require the attendance of a person at some location (typically a police station) for the purpose of identification under the *Identification of Criminals Act*.[19] Failure to comply with this requirement is also punishable as an offence under section 145 of the *Code*.

All forms of release by a peace officer or officer in charge take place before an information has been laid and endorsed by a justice, except for cases in which the officer in charge is authorized to release a person arrested with warrant (discussed below). Nevertheless, all forms of process issued before charge contemplate that the person named in the appearance notice, promise to appear, or recognizance will attend court at the time and place stated. Before that first appearance, an information must be laid before a justice by the process outlined above.[20]

If the justice is not satisfied that there are reasonable grounds to believe that an offence has been committed, he will cancel any form or process that has been previously issued by a peace officer or officer to appear, and will direct that notice be given to the person who had been issued such process. If the justice endorses the information, however, he may either confirm the form of process that has already been issued or may cancel it and issue a summons or warrant for arrest.[21]

The scheme of process before charge requires that, following an accused's arrest and release, a charge be laid "as soon as practicable thereafter and in any event before the time stated," for appearing in court in

---

18   See the further discussion of this issue in the context of ss. 495(2) & 495(3) in Chapter 7.

19   R.S.C. 1985, c. I-1.

20   Section 504.

21   Section 507.

whatever document has been issued to the accused with her release.[22] A failure to lay a charge within that time means that the binding effect of the particular process that has been issued lapses. If no charge is laid in time, an accused cannot be charged with failing to appear on time. However, that is largely the extent of the effect of any such failure. First, the failure to lay an information in the prescribed time does not bar the police from laying a new information in order to have the person compelled to appear. Further, the "as soon as practicable" requirement has been held to be merely directory rather than mandatory. The requirement is meant to guarantee an opportunity for judicial intervention to cancel the process if it should not have been issued in the first place.[23] Therefore, the failure to meet that requirement does not render the information null, cause the court to lose jurisdiction, or confer any freestanding right on the accused. The same result has been held to follow even if the information has not been laid by the time the accused appears in court. To hold that a prosecution would be barred, it has been held, would amount to creating a time limit for the prosecution of an offence, which does not now exist in the case of indictable offences. The time requirements in the section

> are steps in the process designed to bring an accused before the court on a timely basis and without the necessity of prior detention. They are not pre-conditions to the jurisdiction of the court to try the offence . . . .[24]

If the person does appear at the required time, the court may assume jurisdiction over the offence and over the person.

2) Compelling Appearance Post-charge

The foregoing discussion was concerned with procedure where police interaction with the accused precedes the laying of charges (in large measure, arrests without warrant and issuing appearance notices). One might conceptualize those situations as ones where the police have been present at the crime itself, such as a fight outside a bar, and have acted immediately to intervene and arrest or otherwise deal with those involved. In such a case, it is of necessity that a justice will review any charging decision after the fact. In other cases, the police (i) investigate a crime, (ii) decide who they believe the guilty party is, and (iii) lay a charge before a justice in order to compel that person to

---

22   Section 505.
23   *R. v. Gougeon* (1980), 55 C.C.C. (2d) 218 (Ont. C.A.).
24   *R. v. Markovic* (2005), 200 C.C.C. (3d) 449 (Ont. C.A.).

appear. In such cases, the review by the justice will occur before the police interaction with the accused. In practice, the distinction is not nearly so clear-cut—police might be interviewing someone and decide during the interview that there are reasonable grounds for arrest, for example—but that, at least, provides a rough guide to the reason that different sets of procedures are necessary.[25]

In these latter cases, where interaction with the justice precedes interaction with the accused, the same process, discussed above, of laying an information before a justice is followed. The criteria in that regard are the same whether the police lay the charge before interacting with the accused or after. However, in these circumstances, the justice will issue process in the form of either a summons or a warrant for the arrest of the accused if the charge is endorsed.

A summons is a document issued by the court commanding the accused named therein to attend court at a specified time and place. It recites the offence or offences that the accused has been charged with and it contains the same particulars as other documents of process that concern jurisdiction. It is in Form 6, and specifies the date to appear in court, a date to appear for fingerprinting, and the consequences of non-appearance.[26] It is to be served in person, or left with an adult at the person's last known address.[27]

An arrest warrant includes substantially the same details as a summons, but adds a command to peace officers within the local jurisdiction to arrest the person charged and to bring her to court. The warrant is addressed to all peace officers in the jurisdiction and remains in effect until it is executed.

The choice between a summons or an arrest warrant lies in the discretion of the justice. However, section 507(4) directs a justice to issue a summons unless there are reasonable grounds to believe that a warrant is necessary in the public interest. At a policy level, this is parallel to section 495(2), directing police officers to prefer the use of an appearance notice to an arrest for some offences. Nonetheless, it is a

---

25 For example, that was the situation in *R. v. Evans*, [1991] 1 S.C.R. 869. Similarly, in *R. v. Stillman*, [1997] 1 S.C.R. 607, the police arrested the accused at an early stage but then released him. Months later, after further investigation, they arrested him again, essentially for the purpose of being able to conduct a search incident to arrest. In that case, the searches were found to be unconstitutional because they were not truly incident to the arrest.

26 Sections 509(1), (4), & (5).

27 Section 509(2).

much more vague direction than that detailed provision, and might be subject to a *Charter* challenge.[28]

A judge will decide to issue a warrant in order to "compel the accused to attend before him or some other justice for the same territorial division."[29] This phrasing is not meant to permit a judge to say "when this person is arrested take her in front of no-one but me." Rather, it simply intends that the person arrested is required to be brought before *some* judge.[30]

The *Code* allows the justice who issues an arrest warrant to endorse it for the specific purpose of authorizing the officer in charge of a station or lock-up to release an accused, pending her appearance in court.[31] Correspondingly, the officer in charge is then authorized to release the accused.[32] In part, this release power corresponds to that given to an officer in charge in the case of a warrantless arrest, which, it will be recalled, included attaching more restrictive conditions to the release, thus corresponding to the more serious range of offences for which release was available. In this circumstance, the officer is given an even more extensive power to attach conditions because the officer in charge has already been specifically authorized by a justice to release the accused. In such a case, the officer in charge can still release, under section 498, on a promise to appear, recognizance, or deposit (though not with intent to use a summons, since the person has already been arrested). In addition, the officer can release the person on an undertaking to do one or more of the following: remain within a specified territorial jurisdiction; notify the police of any change in address, employment, or occupation; abstain from communicating with specified people (typically victims, witnesses, or co-accused); abstain from going to specified places; deposit a passport; abstain from possessing a firearm; report as required; abstain from the use of drugs or alcohol; and comply with any other conditions necessary for the safety and security of victims or witnesses.[33]

As will be seen below, these optional conditions are very much like those that may be imposed by a judge at a bail hearing in accordance with section 515(4). For this reason the *Code* provides that a person who has been released on conditions or a prosecutor may apply to a justice for a modification of the conditions stipulated in the undertak-

---

28   See the discussion of this issue in Chapter 7.
29   Section 507(1)(b).
30   *R. v. Davidson* (2004), 26 C.R. (6th) 264 (Alta. C.A.).
31   Section 507(6).
32   Section 499.
33   Section 499(2).

ing — essentially as though the release had been on judicially ordered bail.[34]

If a person is arrested and the police decide not to release under any of the various powers to do so, outlined above, that person must be brought before a justice without unreasonable delay, and in any case within twenty-four hours.[35] These are independent deadlines: the section does not give the police the right to hold a person for twenty-four hours. Rather, the primary obligation is to take the person in front of a justice without unreasonable delay and twenty-four hours is the outer limit of what is reasonable.[36] Accordingly, a delay of twelve hours would be unreasonable if there was no good reason, on the facts of the particular case, not to have taken the accused in front of a justice in four hours. Each case will depend upon its particular facts.

Courts have been divided on whether a failure to comply with this twenty-four hour deadline results in an arbitrary detention, which violates section 9 of the *Charter*.[37] However, to date that discussion has taken place on the assumption that a detention could be illegal without necessarily being arbitrary in the meaning of section 9. The Supreme Court has recently stated that unlawful detentions will be considered to be arbitrary detentions under the *Charter*, so this analysis might change.[38]

In any case, the significance of this requirement is that the person is delivered from the custody of the police into the jurisdiction of the court to be dealt with according to law. At this point, therefore, it is necessary to turn to the final portion of this chapter, dealing with judicial interim release.

D. JUDICIAL INTERIM RELEASE

The general philosophical approach to judicial interim release defines the compelling appearance powers described so far in this chapter — a statutory preference for interfering with liberty as little as necessary. The provisions are structured on the general assumption that an ac-

---

34   Section 499(3).
35   Section 503.
36   *R. v. Storrey*, [1990] 1 S.C.R. 241.
37   See, for example, *R. v. Simpson* (1994), 29 C.R. (4th) 274 at para. 98 (Nfld. C.A.), rev'd [1995] 1 S.C.R. 449; *R. v. E.W.* (2002), 168 C.C.C. (3d) 38 (Nfld. C.A.); *R. v. Tam and Lai* (1995), 100 C.C.C. (3d) 196 (B.C.C.A.); *R. v. C.K.* (2005), 36 C.R. (6th) 153 (Ont. Ct. J.).
38   *R. v. Clayton*, 2007 SCC 32 at para. 19.

cused should be released pending trial and with as few restrictions as possible. Indeed, the *Code* creates what is usually referred to as a "ladder" approach to bail. This means that an accused is presumed to be entitled to release and the Crown must justify each increasing step of intrusiveness. There are exceptions for section 469 and other offences, and they will be discussed below, but this is the general approach.

It is worth noting a rule that is slightly inconsistent with this policy. As noted above, an accused must be brought to a justice without unreasonable delay, a rule that is meant to guarantee that person a speedy consideration of release. However, the justice that the accused is taken to can adjourn the bail hearing by up to three days without the consent of the accused. Longer delays are also possible, though in that case the consent of the accused would be required.[39]

Once the hearing is held, however, section 515 directs that the justice *shall* order that the accused is released on an undertaking without conditions, unless the Crown shows cause as to why something more restrictive is justified. For this reason, these are often referred to as "show cause" hearings. The *Code* permits these hearings to be conducted by a "justice," which includes a justice of the peace, but quite commonly they are in fact held in front of a provincial court judge.

Section 515(2) of the *Code* sets out the range of restrictions on liberty, short of detention, that can be imposed on an accused as conditions of release. They are

(a) an undertaking with conditions;

(b) a recognizance without sureties and without deposit—that is, the accused promises to pay a sum of money if she does not appear as required;

(c) a recognizance with sureties—that is, a third party also agrees to owe the debt if that accused does not appear;

(d) a recognizance without sureties but with a deposit of money "or other valuable security" —this condition can only be imposed with the consent of the prosecutor, and;

(e) a recognizance with or without sureties and with a deposit of money or other valuable security if the accused is not ordinarily resident in the province or within two hundred kilometres of the place in which he is in custody.

The *Code* specifies that a justice cannot make an order under any of paragraphs (b) to (e) unless the prosecutor shows cause as to why an or-

---

39   Section 516.

der under the immediately preceding paragraph would be inadequate.[40] Once again, this reflects the policy of Part XVI that, in general, restraint should be used in interfering with the liberty of an accused.

Sections 515(4) through 515(4.3) provide the various types of conditions that may, or must, be imposed when an order for release is made under section 515(2). All of these are related to the objectives of ensuring the accused attends court or ensuring the safety of the community while she is on release. They are similar to those (mentioned above) available to an officer in charge who is authorized by the arrest warrant to release the person arrested. Release conditions should be realistic and workable, rather than "set[ting] the accused up to fail."[41] Further, there must be some type of causal relationship between the crime charged and the particular conditions imposed. However, this connection need not be so specific that, for example, a curfew cannot be imposed even though the particular offence charge occurred during the day.[42]

The remaining possibility, beyond the various forms of release in section 515(2), is that the Crown might show cause as to why the accused should remain in custody until trial. Section 515(1) of the *Code* specifies that there are only three grounds on which continued detention of an accused may be ordered. The first two of these are relatively uncontroversial: (a) the detention is necessary to ensure the accused's attendance in court; or (b) the detention is necessary for the protection or safety of the public. In this context "public" includes victims and witnesses, and the justice is directed to consider "all the circumstances, including any substantial likelihood that the accused will, if released from custody, commit a criminal offence or interfere with the administration of justice." These are sometimes referred to as the primary and secondary grounds for detention, though that terminology is a holdover from a previous version of the section and no order of priority is actually intended today.

The third possible ground for detention is more controversial, and is worth quoting:

> (c) on any other just cause being shown and, without limiting the generality of the foregoing, where the detention is necessary in order to maintain confidence in the administration of justice, having regard to all the circumstances, including the apparent strength of the prosecution's case, the gravity of the nature of the offence, the

---

40   Section 515(3).
41   *R. v. Thomson* (2004), 21 C.R. (6th) 209 (Ont. S.C.J.).
42   *R. v. Patko* (2005), 197 C.C.C. (3d) 192 (B.C.C.A.).

circumstances surrounding its commission and the potential for a lengthy term of imprisonment.

This ground was enacted after an earlier version, which provided a residual ground for detention "in the public interest," was found to violate the guarantee to reasonable bail found in section 11(e) of the *Charter*. In particular, the Court held that denying bail based solely on the "public interest" was too vague and imprecise.[43] The amendment was designed to qualify the residual ground by reference to criteria that have been recognized in various decisions.

This new section, 515(10)(c), was itself challenged and was both upheld in part and struck down in part. The opening words of the section, "any other just cause" were struck out, on the ground of vagueness. The Court was divided over whether the same objection applied to the rest of the section, but, in a five–four split, upheld it.[44] The minority took the view that the enumerated considerations did not do enough to differentiate the new section from the old "public interest" criterion that had been found unacceptable. In contrast, the majority felt that the criteria delineated the risk-zone clearly enough that the vagueness claim was not made out.

The majority did note that this third ground should be used sparingly, and courts have noted that detention based solely on it would only be justified in rare cases.[45] On that basis there is some justification for thinking of it as literally a "tertiary" ground. However, it is not clear that all courts respect this rule in practice.[46]

Where the prosecutor justifies continued detention by showing cause, the justice must add a statement of the reasons for this decision to the warrant of committal.[47]

That is the general scheme for bail hearings, but, as noted above, there are some exceptions to this approach. The first one worth noting is created by section 515(6). That section lists a number of offences for which the onus is reversed. That is, for the offences listed in that section, the justice is directed to order that the accused *shall* be detained unless the accused shows cause not to do so. One of these cases is where the accused is not ordinarily resident in Canada. In such an event, if the accused does show cause as to why she should not be detained, a

---

43   *R. v. Morales*, [1992] 3 S.C.R. 711 [*Morales*].

44   *R. v. Hall*, 2002 SCC 64.

45   *R. v. LaFramboise* (2005), 203 C.C.C. (3d) 492 (Ont. C.A.).

46   See D. Stuart & J. Harris, "Is the Public Confidence Ground to Deny Bail Used Sparingly?" (2004) 21 C.R. (6th) 232.

47   Section 515(5).

judge can order her release on any of the bases applying to other bail hearings.[48] The other reverse onus offences in section 515(6) involve cases where: a) the offence charged was alleged to be committed while the accused was already out on bail; b) the offence charged was a criminal organization, terrorism, or national security offence; c) the offence related to failing to attend court as ordered by some previous process; or d) the offence was punishable by life imprisonment under the *Controlled Drugs and Substances Act*.[49] The first and last of these reverse onuses have been challenged under the *Charter* but upheld.[50] In these cases, the accused is not only given the onus of showing cause that detention is not justified but, if ordered released, he must also show why the conditions that can attach to his release should *not* be imposed.

The second exception to the general bail scheme applies to section 469 offences, the most common of which is murder. In this case, section 515(11) states that a justice has no authority to release the accused and must order her detained to be "dealt with according to law." That is not the end of the story, however. In this event, the accused will, in accordance with section 522, be taken before a judge of the superior court—no one else is authorized to release a person charged with a section 469 offence before trial. In this hearing, there is again a reverse onus, with the accused being required to justify release.[51] If the accused is ordered to be released, any of the ordinary conditions of release can be imposed.

A decision made by a justice concerning release or detention may be reviewed by a judge upon application of the accused or the prosecutor.[52] Applications of this kind are common and there is no limitation of such applications that may be made, except that following a review a further application cannot be brought for thirty days, unless the accused or the prosecutor has the leave of a judge. These reviews provide an opportunity to adjust or correct the order at the original bail hearing, and also provide an opportunity to reconsider the appropriateness of the order if circumstances have changed. Where interim release has

---

48   Section 515(8). Note, as well, that the determination of whether a person is ordinarily resident in Canada requires a case-by-case analysis. A refugee claimant, for example, might be ordinarily resident here, and therefore not subject to the reverse onus: see *R. v. Oladipo* (2004), 26 C.R. (6th) 393 (Ont. S.C.J.).

49   S.C. 1996, c.19.

50   See, respectively, *Morales*, above note 43 and *R. v. Pearson*, [1992] 3 S.C.R. 665.

51   Section 522(2).

52   Sections 520 & 521.

been denied, an accused person in custody is entitled to an automatic review if the trial has not commenced within a specified time frame.[53]

If not amended in some fashion, an order for judicial interim release lasts until the end of trial and, if an accused is found guilty of a non-section 469 offence, the term of the release will last until the time of sentencing. This remains the case even if for some reason a new information is laid in respect of an offence for which process has already been issued. However, a preliminary inquiry judge or trial judge can vacate any previous order (whether for detention or release) and substitute a different order where cause to do so is shown.[54]

The justice who conducts a bail hearing is not constrained by the rules and principles of admissibility that apply with respect to evidence at trial. Section 518, which sets out the principles of evidence at a bail hearing, concludes with a paragraph that allows the justice to "receive and base his decision on evidence considered credible or trustworthy by him in the circumstances of each case." This broad statement of admissibility is supplemented by more specific elements in section 518, such as the admissibility of wiretap evidence and evidence that relates both to the character and circumstances of the accused and the circumstances of the alleged offence. However, that section also specifies that a bail hearing may not be used to interrogate or examine the accused about the offence itself. Although the justice may conduct inquiries under oath of or about the accused, neither the justice nor the prosecutor may examine the accused about the circumstances of the alleged offence, unless she has elected to testify in the hearing at the invitation of her counsel or on her own decision. Of course, even at this stage the accused is entitled to protect herself against self-incrimination, and thus any questions put to the accused at the bail hearing should in principle be confined to matters that are relevant to a determination of the hearing. However, it must be said that this can be a difficult issue to control at a bail hearing, especially as the prosecutor is specifically entitled to produce evidence of the alleged offence and the probability of conviction.

Finally, it is worth noting that the forms of police process or judicial process that have been discussed here permit an accused person to remain at liberty, but these processes do so trusting that the accused will comply with any conditions imposed, including the requirement to appear in court. Unsurprisingly, not every accused persons turns out to have been deserving of this trust. The *Code* therefore provides that

---

53   Section 525.
54   Section 523.

an accused who has or is about to violate some condition of release can be arrested, with or without warrant.[55] A person thus arrested must be taken before a justice or, in the case of a person previously released or arrested for an offence listed in section 469, taken before a judge of the superior court.

FURTHER READINGS

LAW REFORM COMMISSION OF CANADA, *Compelling Appearance, Interim Release and Pre-trial Detention* (Ottawa: Law Reform Commission of Canada, 1988)

LAW REFORM COMMISSION OF CANADA, *Controlling Criminal Prosecutions: The Attorney General and the Crown Prosecutor* (Ottawa: Law Reform Commission of Canada, 1990)

QUIGLEY, TIM, *Procedure in Canadian Criminal Law*, 2d ed., looseleaf (Toronto: Thomson Carswell, 2005) cc. 5 and 9

STUART, D., & J. HARRIS, "Is the Public Confidence Ground to Deny Bail Used Sparingly?" (2004) 21 C.R. (6th) 232

STUART, DON, *Charter Justice in Canadian Criminal Law*, 4th ed. (Toronto: Thomson Carswell, 2005) c. 6

TROTTER, GARY, *The Law of Bail in Canada*, 2d ed. (Scarborough, ON: Carswell, 1999)

---

55   Section 524.

CHAPTER 7

ARREST

This chapter deals with powers of arrest, most, but not all, of which are exercised by police. There is some overlap between this chapter and others. Obviously, arrest is one of the methods of compelling a person's appearance in court, and so the procedures here must be seen in light of the discussion in Chapter 6. In addition, the *Charter* guarantees particular rights on arrest *or* detention. Detention was previously discussed in Chapter 5, but section 10(b) issues were not raised there. Accordingly, the discussion of those rights here is also relevant to that earlier chapter.

A. INTRODUCTION

This section deals with powers of arrest, both those given to police officers and those available more broadly. Arrest powers are most important in the context of apprehending a person believed to have committed a crime, and so the major focus of this chapter will be the arrest powers found in Part XVI of the *Code*, "Compelling Appearance." However, other arrest powers for various purposes are also found in the *Code* and will be outlined briefly.

Arrest is only one of the methods that can compel the appearance of an accused before a court. Part XVI also contains provisions that allow an accused to be brought to court by two other methods, a summons or an appearance notice. Those techniques were discussed at greater length in Chapter 6, but it is useful to review them here.

Similar to powers of search and seizure, Part XVI of the *Code* is aimed at balancing legitimate state interests in prosecuting crime against individual freedom. On the one hand, it is sometimes necessary to require a person to answer to a criminal charge, and therefore to appear in court to do so. On the other hand, our Western democratic principles hold that the state should not interfere with the liberty of individuals without good reason and no more than is necessary. In large part, therefore, while Part XVI of the *Code* creates coercive powers given to the police, it attempts to reflect the principle of restraint while doing so. It is an attempt to find the right balance between crime control and due process interests.[1]

Accordingly, in principle a police officer cannot unilaterally compel the appearance of an accused in court. That decision must, at some stage, be confirmed by a judicial officer, typically a justice of the peace. That confirmation can occur either before the officer deals directly with the accused person or afterward, but it must occur. Similarly, there are different levels of compulsion that can be directed toward the accused. The accused may receive a request[2] in writing to appear in court on a particular day and is trusted to do so, or could, in contrast, physically be taken into control by the police officer and given no choice but compliance.

These two variables—judicial confirmation before or after, and a request in writing versus physical control—create four possibilities, which conform to the four methods of compelling an accused's appearance created by Part XVI. At the least intrusive level, a police officer can show a justice that there are reasonable grounds to believe that a person has committed an offence and consequently obtain a summons requiring the accused to appear in court on a specified date.[3] Alternatively, the officer can first encounter a person on the street committing an offence and then require that person to appear in court by means of an appearance notice. This appearance notice must subsequently be confirmed by a justice.[4]

This chapter, however, deals with the more intrusive methods involved in taking physical control of the person, either after judicial authorization to do so has been issued or before (that is, arrest with or without a warrant). It is worth noting, however, that Part XVI has

---

1   See Herbert L. Packer, *The Limits of the Criminal Sanction* (Stanford: Stanford University Press, 1968) at 154–72 for a fuller discussion of these concepts.
2   The word "requested" is used here for convenience sake, though of course an accused who does not appear will be arrested: see s. 512(2).
3   Section 507(1)(b). See s. 509 for the contents of a summons.
4   Sections 501, 505, and 508(1)(b).

a number of rules aimed at having the state use the least intrusive, yet effective, means possible. Where a police officer seeks judicial authorization first, for example, the justice is to issue a summons, unless it is shown to be necessary in the public interest to issue a warrant.[5] Even if an accused has already been arrested with a warrant, the peace officer concerned is required to release that person as soon as practicable and use a summons or appearance notice instead.[6] If the arresting officer takes the accused into custody, the officer in charge (of the place of detention) is equally directed to release the person as soon as practicable and use a summons or appearance notice to compel appearance before the court.[7] These limitations reflect the principle of restraint in the use of police powers. It will be seen that this principle is also reflected, in various ways, in the arrest powers themselves.

This section deals first with arrest with a warrant, arrest without a warrant, and the various supporting provisions affecting those powers. It then briefly considers the arrest powers outside of Part XVI. Finally, the constitutional and other rights that arise on arrest are outlined. These constitutional rights are also relevant to detentions.

As a final preliminary point, however, it should be made clear exactly what constitutes an arrest. An arrest consists of words of arrest accompanied either by touching of the person with a view to detention, or by the person submitting to the arrest.[8] The word "arrest" need not actually be used, provided the accused can be reasonably supposed to have understood that she was under arrest.[9] Although reducing arrest to touching the accused can make it seem like "a children's game" and could appear to make the arrest an instantaneous thing, arrest is a continuing act, starting with the moment of custody and extending until the person is either released from custody or brought before a justice and detained.[10] The primary significance of this conclusion is that the powers available to make an arrest originally, such as the use of force, continue to be available.

---

5   Section 507(4).

6   Section 497(1).

7   Section 498.

8   *R. v. Whitfield*, [1970] S.C.R. 46 [*Whitfield*].

9   *R. v. Latimer*, [1997] 1 S.C.R. 217 [*Latimer*]. This rule is, in principle, a reasonable one, though its actual application in *Latimer* amounted to justifying a police action that was consciously intended not to be an arrest, as an arrest : see Stephen G. Coughlan, "Developments in Criminal Procedure: The 1996–97 Term" (1998) 9 Sup. Ct. L. Rev. (2d) 273 at 290–93.

10   *R. v. Asante-Mensah*, 2003 SCC 38 at paras. 33 and 43 [*Asante-Mensah*].

B. ARREST WITH A WARRANT

As discussed in Chapter 6, a warrant can only be issued after an information that sets out the reasonable grounds to believe that a person has committed an offence is laid before a justice. Section 504 creates this rule for indictable offences, and section 795 adopts the procedures of Part XVI for summary conviction offences. A personal appearance by the peace officer is not essential, and it is possible to lay an information electronically.[11] Where, having heard the allegations of the informant and the evidence under oath of any witnesses, a justice who is satisfied that a case for doing so is made out can issue either a summons or warrant requiring the accused to attend before a justice to answer the charge. A summons, rather than a warrant, must be issued unless the evidence discloses reasonable grounds to believe that it is "necessary in the public interest" to issue a warrant.[12]

This "necessary in the public interest" criterion was also formerly used in section 515 of the *Code* in considering bail for an accused pending trial. In *Morales*, it was struck down as unconstitutionally vague and therefore a violation of section 11(e) of the *Charter*.[13] That subsection has since been replaced by a new provision that specifies criteria to be used in deciding whether an accused's detention is necessary to maintain confidence in the administration of justice. The new provision was upheld by the Court in a five to four decision that has attracted some criticism.[14] In the context of section 507(4), the public interest criterion has received relatively little attention at all and has not been challenged under the *Charter*.[15]

This relative lack of attention may largely be due to the fact that, unlike a bail hearing, the application for an arrest warrant is made on an *ex parte* basis. The issue has occasionally arisen in complaints of a violation of the right to a trial within a reasonable time, and there is some lower court authority suggesting that if the police are going to claim that a warrant, rather than a summons, is necessary then they

---

11 Section 508.1.
12 Section 507.
13 *R. v. Morales*, [1992] 3 S.C.R. 711.
14 *R. v. Hall*, [2002] 3 S.C.R. 309. See the discussion of the decision in Don Stuart "*R. v. Hall*: Annotation" (2002) 4 C.R. (6th) 197 and Tim Quigley, "*R. v. Hall*: Annotation" (2002) 4 C.R. (6th) 197.
15 See, however, the discussion in *R. v. Fosseneuve* (1995), 43 C.R. (4th) 260 (Man. Q.B.) [*Fosseneuve*] at Section C(2), below in this chapter, regarding the use of the public interest criterion in warrantless arrests.

have an obligation to make reasonable efforts to effect the arrest.[16] Authorities conflict on whether issuing a warrant with respect to a person already in custody in order to preserve jurisdiction is in the public interest.[17] For the most part, however, little attention has been paid to the issue.

Warrants are directed only to peace officers, though that term has a relatively broad definition, including of course police officers, but also in some cases correctional officers, customs officers, fisheries officers, mayors, pilots in command of an aircraft, and others.[18] The peace officers to whom a warrant is directed must be within the territorial jurisdiction of the person who issues it.[19] In practical terms, however, there are few real obstacles to the use of an arrest warrant anywhere in the country. A warrant issued by any court other than a justice or a provincial court judge can automatically be executed anywhere in Canada.[20] A warrant from a justice or provincial court judge can be executed anywhere in the province in which it is issued.[21] In the case of fresh pursuit, however, a warrant can be executed anywhere in Canada, and in any event, a peace officer to whom a warrant is directed can execute that warrant even when not in the territory for which that person is a peace officer.[22] Finally, a warrant issued in one jurisdiction can be endorsed by a justice of another jurisdiction and become executable there if the accused is believed to be in that other jurisdiction.[23]

A warrant must name or describe the accused, set out briefly the offence that the accused is charged with, and order that the accused be brought before a justice to be dealt with according to law. Arrest warrants do not expire, but simply remain in force until executed.[24] Section 29 of the *Code* requires an officer executing a warrant to have it where it is feasible to do so, and to provide it where requested. It also requires anyone who arrests, with or without a warrant, to give notice to the

---

16   R. v. *Yellowhorse* (1990), 111 A.R. 20 (Prov. Ct.); R. v. *Heidecker*, [1992] A.J. No. 91 (Prov. Ct.).

17   Compare R. v. *Horton*, [2002] O.J. No. 1219 (S.C.J.) and *Re Inverarity and the Queen* (1984), 18 C.C.C. (3d) 74 (Sask. Q.B.). In any case, it is more difficult under current *Code* provisions for a court to lose jurisdiction than it was in the past: see the discussion in Chapter 11.

18   Section 2.

19   Section 513. Territorial division includes a province, a county, a town, or any other judicial division appropriate to the context: s. 2.

20   Section 703.

21   Section 703(2).

22   Section 514.

23   Section 528.

24   Section 511.

arrested person of "(a) the process or warrant under which he makes the arrest; or (b) the reason for the arrest."[25] One might naturally have read this section disjunctively, on the assumption that (a) applies to arrests with a warrant and (b) to arrests without a warrant. However, this was the not approach taken by the Court in *R. v. Gamracy*, a decision that removed much of the real force of the provision. In that case an officer made an arrest, but only told the accused that there was an outstanding warrant. The officer did not have the warrant itself nor did he know what offence the warrant dealt with. The Court held that this was sufficient compliance with section 29. The arrest was not an arrest with a warrant, but a warrantless arrest under section 495(1)(c), to be discussed below. In that event, "there is a warrant" was held to be sufficient notice of the reason for the arrest.[26]

Gamracy is a pre-*Charter* case, and section 10(a) now creates the constitutional right to be informed promptly on arrest of the reasons therefor. That right requires that an accused be given sufficient information to decide whether to submit to the arrest and to make an informed choice about whether to exercise the right to counsel. More frequently, the section has been considered in circumstances where the reason an accused is detained changes during the course of an investigation,[27] with the result that little attention has been paid to the content of the right at the time an accused is first arrested. It therefore remains unclear whether *Gamracy* still represents the state of the law.[28]

C. ARREST WITHOUT A WARRANT

Warrantless arrests are governed by sections 494 and 495 of the *Criminal Code*, which create a number of arrest powers available to three groups. Section 494(1) creates arrest powers available to anyone, section 494(2) creates a special arrest power relating to property owners, and section 495(1) creates arrest powers available only to peace officers. Section 494 is sometimes spoken of as providing power for a "citizen's arrest," although it can in fact be used by anyone, peace officers in-

---

25   Section 29.

26   *R v. Gamracy*, [1974] S.C.R. 640 [*Gamracy*].

27   See, for example, *R. v. Borden*, [1994] 3 S.C.R. 145 [*Borden*]; *R. v. Smith*, [1991] 1 S.C.R. 714 [*Smith* 1991]; *R. v. Evans*, [1991] 1 S.C.R. 869 [*Evans*]; and *R. v. Black*, [1989] 2 S.C.R. 138 [*Black*].

28   *Gamracy*, above note 26, has been followed post-*Charter* but has not been considered in connection with the s. 10(a) issue: see, for example, *R v. Kozoway* (1993), 142 A.R. 323 (Q.B.), aff'd (1994), 157 A.R. 79 (C.A.).

cluded. Historically, it is section 494 that descends more directly from the common law powers of arrest, while section 495 creates additional powers for peace officers, an office which did not exist when powers of arrest first developed.[29]

The different powers of arrest are defined largely by two variables: indictable offences vs. criminal offences, and "finds committing" powers vs. "reasonable belief" powers. In each case the former option is more limited than the latter.

Some arrest powers are limited to indictable offences (that is, ones that can be prosecuted by indictment, which in this context includes hybrid offences).[30] Other arrest powers apply to criminal offences in general, and therefore include summary conviction offences as well. Indeed, many provinces have incorporated the *Criminal Code* arrest powers into their provincial offence acts, so as a practical matter some *Code* arrest powers apply to non-*Code* offences.[31]

The "finds committing" standard requires that the person arresting have actually witnessed the commission of the offence. The requirement is read to mean "apparently" finds committing, in the sense that a subsequent acquittal of the accused on the charge for which she was arrested does not retroactively invalidate the arrest power. Thus in *R. v. Biron*, for example, the accused was properly arrested for causing a disturbance since an officer witnessed the behaviour constituting the disturbance. The fact that Biron was eventually acquitted of that charge (because there was no proof at trial of the specific allegation of shouting) did not mean that he was illegally arrested, and so he was still guilty of resisting a peace officer in the execution of duty.[32] *Biron* is a pre-*Charter* case and so it may now be possible to argue that an arrest

---

29   See *R. v. Lerke* (1986), 49 C.R. (3d) 324 at 330 (Alta. C.A.): "The power exercised by a citizen who arrests another is in direct descent over nearly a thousand years of the powers and duties of citizens in the age of Henry II in relation to the 'King's Peace.'" See also *Asante-Mensah*, above note 10 at para. 40: "The development of modern police forces brought about a transfer of law enforcement activities from private citizens to peace officers. But it is the peace officer's powers which are in a sense derivative from that of the citizen, not the other way around."

30   *Interpretation Act*, R.S.C. 1985, c. I-21, s. 34(1)(a).

31   In addition, other arrest powers exist in other statutes. See, for example, *Asante-Mensah*, above note 10, and its discussion of the arrest power given to private citizens (and therefore to private security firms) by Ontario's *Trespass to Property Act*, R.S.O. 1990, c. T.21 or the extensive review of federal non-*Criminal Code* and provincial arrest powers in Law Reform Commission of Canada, *Arrest* (Ottawa: Law Reform Commission of Canada, 1986) [Law Reform Commission].

32   *R. v. Biron*, [1976] 2 S.C.R. 56. There is a further complicating factor in *Biron*: the officer who arrested the accused was not the officer who witnessed the apparent offence, but that does not affect the main point.

made when the accused is ultimately found not to have committed an offence violates the right, in section 9, to be free from arbitrary detention. However, as the section 9 analysis stands now, though, the argument seems unlikely to succeed.[33]

"Reasonable grounds to believe" that an accused has committed an offence requires that the person performing the arrest subjectively believes that the person has committed the offence, and that the belief is objectively justifiable. That is, a reasonable person standing in the shoes of the arresting officer would have also believed that grounds for arrest existed. The objective standard for a warrantless arrest, therefore, is the same as that required for obtaining an arrest warrant.[34] Whether the standard is met in an individual case is not always easy to determine and depends on the particular facts. More than mere suspicion is necessary, but the police are not required to have a *prima facie* case before arresting. Accordingly, although police cannot arrest simply in order to investigate and obtain reasonable grounds, the fact that an investigation continues after an arrest does not automatically mean that the arrest was not based on reasonable grounds.[35]

Both the subjective and objective tests must be met. It is easy to see that an objectively unreasonable arrest should not be allowed simply because of the officer's personal belief. Equally, though, even if reasonable grounds for arrest exist on an objective basis, the arrest is improper if the officer does not have the necessary subjective belief. The issue is not simply whether grounds to arrest exist, but whether the officer *acts upon* such grounds.[36]

1) Section 494 Arrest Powers

The arrest powers in section 494(1) are given to anyone, and are the most limited powers. Anyone may arrest a person whom he finds committing an indictable offence. Alternatively, anyone may perform an arrest when she believes, on reasonable grounds, that some person has committed a criminal offence *and* is escaping and being freshly pursued by some other person with authority to arrest.

---

33 See the discussion of s. 9 at Section C(2), below in this chapter, in the context of s. 495(3) of the *Code*.
34 *R. v. Storrey*, [1990] 1 S.C.R. 241 [*Storrey*].
35 *Storrey*, ibid.; *R. v. Duguay, Murphy and Sevigny*, [1989] 1 S.C.R. 93 [*Duguay*].
36 *R. v. Coles*, 2003 PESCAD 3. Similarly see *R. v. Caslake*, [1998] 1 S.C.R. 51 where the Court held that a search that would have been objectively justifiable as an incident to an arrest was unreasonable because that was not the officer's subjective purpose.

Section 494(2) creates a slightly broader arrest power for property owners and their designates. Anyone who owns or is in lawful possession of property can arrest not only for indictable offences, but also for any criminal offence they find being committed on or in relation to their property. "Property" is defined in section 2 of the *Code* to include real or personal property.

Anyone other than a peace officer who makes an arrest is required to deliver the arrested person "forthwith," that is, as soon as reasonably possible or practicable under all the circumstances.[37]

2) Section 495 Arrest Powers

Peace officers' arrest powers are much broader. Sections 495(1)(a) and (b) effectively allow a peace officer to arrest in any situation but two: i) where the officer did not find the accused committing the offence, the offence is only a summary conviction one, and no arrest warrant has been issued, or ii) where the officer believes that a summary conviction offence is about to be committed.

Section 495(1a) permits a peace officer to arrest anyone who

> has committed an indictable offence or who, on reasonable grounds, he believes has committed or is about to commit an indictable offence.

Section 495(1)(b) permits a peace officer to arrest anyone he finds committing a criminal offence. Finally, section 495(1)(c) permits a peace officer to arrest a person if he reasonably believes that a warrant exists for the person's arrest.

Read in one fashion, the first clause of section 495(1)(a) would make the second clause redundant. If a peace officer could arrest anyone who has in fact committed an indictable offence, it would be unnecessary also to have a power to make such an arrest on reasonable grounds. In practice, the section has not been interpreted in such a broad way. Section 495(1)(a) is taken to require that the officer has personally witnessed the offence, believes on reasonable grounds that the offence has been committed, or believes on reasonable grounds that the offence is about to be committed.[38]

---

37   *R. v. Cunningham* (1979), 49 C.C.C. (2d) 390 (Man. Co. Ct.).

38   *R. v. Klimchuk* (1991), 8 C.R. (4th) 327 (B.C.C.A.). The court distinguishes witnessing the offence personally in s. 495(1)(a) from the "finds committing" power in s. 495(1)(b), on the basis that the former is restricted to situations where the officer witnessed the offence but could not prevent it before its completion, while "finds committing" requires that the arrested person still be in the process of committing the offence.

The arrest power in section 495(1)(b) authorizes an arrest at any time where the officer witnesses the actual commission of the offence. Section 495(1)(c) adds the power to arrest without warrant on the basis that a warrant exists. The Law Reform Commission of Canada noted that this latter provision could seem contradictory, but recommended its retention. They noted that although an officer who encounters a suspect at a traffic check or while on routine patrol typically could not, as a practical matter, actually obtain a copy of the warrant, the existence of the warrant amounts to "judicially certified" reasonable grounds.[39]

Although these arrest powers are quite broad, the principle of restraint is still reflected to some extent, specifically in section 495(2).[40] At first glance, the provision, beginning with the words "a peace officer shall not arrest," appears to put an actual limit on the powers of arrest in section 495(1)(a). In fact, given the effect of section 495(3), it does not actually do so, but it does provide some guidance to the way in which peace officers should exercise their discretion in the use of arrest powers. In effect, it is not a removal of the arrest power, but advice about when not to use it.

Section 495(2) is drafted in a very oblique fashion. It is structured as a triple, and sometimes a quadruple, negative. It applies only in the case of arrests for relatively less serious offences. That is, according to section 495(2)(a) through (c), it applies to indictable offences in the absolute jurisdiction of a provincial court judge, to hybrid offences, and to summary conviction offences. In those cases section 495(2) directs peace officers not to arrest simply because an arrest power exists, rather the section calls for some other factor to be present as well. First, the officer may arrest because she believes on reasonable grounds that an arrest is the only way to do one of three things:

(i)   establish the identity of the person,

(ii) secure or preserve evidence of or relating to the offence, or

(iii) prevent the continuation or repetition of the offence or the commission of another offence.[41]

---

39 Law Reform Commission, above note 31 at 23–24.

40 A further example of restraint is found in s. 6 of the *Youth Criminal Justice Act*, S.C. 2002, c. 1 [*YCJA*], which requires a peace officer, before taking any measures, to consider whether it would be sufficient simply to administer a caution or refer the young person to a community program or agency.

41 Section 495(2)(d). Strictly, the subsection only includes these factors among aspects of the public interest, and the criterion for not arresting is that the public interest can be satisfied without an arrest. It was held in *R. v. Fosseneuve*, above note 15, that the section had to be read down to only the three criteria listed on the grounds that, otherwise, the "public interest" criterion permitted an arrest

Alternatively, the officer may also arrest because he reasonably believes that the person will not attend court unless arrested. That is, under the circumstances it is evident to the officer that an appearance notice will not be sufficient.[42]

However, although section 495(2) sets out circumstances in which peace officers ought to use an appearance notice rather than arrest a person, section 495(3) makes it clear that the officer's power to arrest still exists (section 495(2) gives guidance but does not operate as a real limit). As noted above, a major goal of section 10(a) of the *Charter* is to allow an accused to know why he is being arrested, in order to decide whether to submit to the arrest. A peace officer who attempts to arrest a person without authority to do so is committing an assault, and the person would have the right not to submit and to resist the officer's actions. However, if the officer actually had the power to arrest, then a person resisting would be guilty of either resisting or assaulting an officer in the execution of duty.[43] The important issue, then, is whether an officer who ignores section 495(2) is still acting in the execution of duty. Section 495(3) states that an officer acting under section 495(1) is deemed to be in the execution of duty "notwithstanding subsection 495(2)."[44] In other words, as long as the power to arrest was created by subsection (1), subsection (2) did not remove it.[45]

---

on unconstitutionally vague grounds. It is important to realize, though, that s. 495(2) does not create an arrest power. That power must already exist from s. 495(1) or elsewhere. See, however, the discussion of *R. v. Moore*, [1979] 1 S.C.R. 195 [*Moore*] below at note 45.

42   Section 495(2)(e). Note as well s. 496, which authorizes the use of an appearance notice when an officer does not arrest by virtue of s. 495(2).

43   Sections 129(a) and s. 270(1)(a) respectively.

44   Section 495(3)(b) seems to permit the argument that an officer who fails to comply with s. 495(2) is not acting in the execution of duty in other contexts, such as a tort action for false arrest or wrongful imprisonment. However, as the subsection begins with the phrase "notwithstanding subsection (2)," but ends with the requirement that subsection (2) was not complied with, there is certainly scope for argument about the meaning of the provision.

45   A word must be said somewhere about the Court's curious decision in *Moore*, above note 41. Moore was a cyclist who went through a red light, in the sight of a police officer. The officer stopped him and requested identification, which Moore refused to provide. Moore was convicted of obstructing an officer in the execution of duty. The Court's rationale was that the officer was obliged under s. 495(2) not to arrest Moore if he could identify him, and therefore the officer had a duty to try to obtain identification. By refusing to provide such identification Moore was therefore obstructing the officer. This decision can be and has been criticized for confusing police duties with police powers, and for creating a duty on the part of Moore where none existed by statute or common law.

Even if an arrest that does not accord with section 495(2) is still legal, one might argue that an arrest made where the *Code* suggests it should not be is an arbitrary detention and therefore violates the right in section 9 of the *Charter*. On current caselaw, however, such an argument seems unlikely to succeed. Section 9 is relatively less developed than many other *Charter* rights. For example, it is not absolutely clear whether an illegal arrest is automatically an arbitrary detention, though the most recent pronouncements of the Court state that it is.[46] Of interest, however, is that the only definition of "arbitrary" offered by the Court so far requires a finding that the law provides no express or implied criteria to govern the exercise of the discretion to detain.[47] In this case, the arrest would not be illegal despite ignoring section 495(2)

The better approach would be that adopted by the Ontario Court of Appeal in analogous circumstances in *R. v. Hayes*, [2003] O.J. No. 2795. There, the accused was required by statute to hand over his motorcycle helmet for inspection but refused to do so, and was thus charged with obstruction. The court held that, by failing to hand over his helmet, Hayes made himself potentially liable to a $1000 fine. But issuing a written notice to Hayes creating such liability was the only enforcement mechanism open to the officer. Hayes was not guilty of obstructing the officer for his non-compliance. Similarly, one would think that a person in Moore's position becomes potentially liable to the more intrusive enforcement mechanism of arrest rather than receiving an appearance notice, but that the officer still has that option open and therefore is not obstructed.

Moore is a pre-*Charter* case and it is possible that on the same facts a different result would be found today.

46   The Ontario Court of Appeal held in *R. v. Duguay, Murphy and Sevigny* (1985), 45 C.R. (3d) 140 (Ont. C.A.) that not every unlawful arrest would be arbitrary, and, for example, that an arrest based on reasons falling just short of the "reasonable grounds" standard might not violate s. 9. This point was not at issue when the decision was affirmed in the Supreme Court of Canada: *Duguay*, above note 35, and was deliberately left open in other decisions: see, for example, *Latimer*, above note 9. However, most recently in *R. v. Clayton*, 2007 SCC 32 the Court stated at para. 19:

If the police conduct in detaining and searching Clayton and Farmer amounted to a lawful exercise of their common law powers, there was no violation of their *Charter* rights. *If, on the other hand, the conduct fell outside the scope of these powers, it represented an infringement of the right under the* Charter *not to be arbitrarily detained* or subjected to an unreasonable search or seizure. [emphasis added]

This affirms that an unlawful detention would be an arbitrary detention. However, the point was not actually crucial to the decision in *Clayton*, and so it is not clear how it will be applied in future cases. See the discussion of s. 9 in Steve Coughlan, "Whither—or Wither— Section 9" (2008) 40 Sup. Ct. L. Rev. (2d) 147, and James Stribopoulos, "The Forgotten Right: Section 9 of the *Charter*, Its Purpose and Meaning" (2008) 40 Sup. Ct. L. Rev. (2d) 211.

47   See *R. v. Hufsky*, [1988] 1 S.C.R. 621; *R. v. Ladouceur*, [1990] 1 S.C.R. 1257.

and, if in compliance with section 495(1), would be based on objective criteria. Unless the analysis of section 9 begins to equate arbitrariness with factors other than randomness, a challenge based on the failure to comply with section 495(2) is unlikely to succeed.

3) Other *Criminal Code* Arrest Powers

The *Code* contains many other arrest powers, mostly with a warrant, though occasionally other warrantless ones as well. The majority are arrest powers intended to provide a measure of compulsion to the judicial process. An accused who evades service of a summons, does not appear for fingerprinting, or violates a condition of the undertaking by which he was released may have an arrest warrant issued, for example.[48] In the last context, a person who has agreed to act as surety for an accused released pending trial can apply to be released from that obligation, and is then empowered to arrest the accused.[49] An accused may fail to appear for trial, resulting in the issuance of a bench warrant.[50] Proceedings may also be adjourned, stayed, and so on and need to be recommenced later, with the result that the appearance of the accused must be compelled again, and an arrest warrant is typically an option at these stages as well.[51] Similarly, arrest warrants can sometimes be used to compel the appearance of witnesses.[52] Arrest warrants can also be used to help preserve the jurisdiction of the Court.[53]

Not all the other arrest powers simply support the court process, however. Section 199(2) of the *Code* creates a particular warrantless arrest power for a peace officer who finds someone keeping a common gaming house or anyone found therein. In addition, section 31 allows a peace officer who witnesses a breach of the peace to arrest

> any person whom he finds committing the breach of the peace or who, on reasonable grounds, he believes is about to join in or renew the breach of the peace.

---

48   Sections 512(c), 510, and 524.
49   Section 796.
50   Section 597.
51   See, for example, ss. 485 and 578(1)(b), though many provisions of the *Code* serve the same general purpose. Note that these provisions frequently rely on the "public interest" as the deciding criterion concerning issuance of a warrant, and therefore may be subject to *Charter* challenge: see the discussion under Section B and in note 15, above in this chapter.
52   Sections 698, 704, and 705.
53   Section 498, and see the discussion in Chapter 11.

Note that a "breach of the peace" is not itself a criminal offence,[54] though of course much behaviour that would constitute a breach of the peace would equally meet the definition of some offence, such as causing a disturbance, rioting, unlawful assembly, or others.[55]

The power in section 31 is limited to breaches of the peace that have already occurred. There is some authority, however, suggesting that police also have a common law power to arrest for apprehended breaches of the peace.[56] This is a troublesome suggestion for several reasons. First, if it is confined to the finds committing standard, the section 31 power is, at most, a minimal extension over the power to arrest in section 495(1)(b), which lets an officer arrest on a finds committing basis for any criminal offence. To allow arrest for apprehended breaches of the peace, however, is in large part to extend the power to arrest to cover summary conviction offences that have not occurred, precisely an omission that was made from section 495. More troubling than the particular expansion of police powers in this circumstance, however, is the notion that common law arrest powers exist at all. It was noted in Chapter 2 that although the common law is a potential source of police power it is a controversial one. Particularly in areas such as arrest, where one may have taken Parliament to have consciously defined all the powers, allowing common law arrest to exist[57] (or to be created) also creates considerable scope for uncertainty.[58]

---

54 *Frey v. Fedoruk*, [1950] S.C.R. 517.

55 See Bruce P. Archibald, "*Hayes v. Thompson and Bell*: Annotation" (1985) 44 C.R. (3d) 316 [Archibald].

56 *Hayes v. Thompson* (1985), 44 C.R. (3d) 316 (B.C.C.A.) [*Hayes*]; *Brown v. Durham Regional Police Force* (1998), 21 C.R. (5th) 1 [*Brown*]. The Ontario Court of Appeal held in at para. 74 in *Brown* that:

> The apprehended breach must be imminent and the risk that the breach will occur must be substantial. The mere possibility of some unspecified breach at some unknown point in time will not suffice. These features of the power to arrest or detain to avoid a breach of the peace place that power on the same footing as the statutory power to arrest in anticipation of the commission of an indictable offence. That is not to say that the two powers are co-extensive. Many indictable offences do not involve a breach of the peace and, as indicated above, conduct resulting in an apprehended breach of the peace need not involve the commission of any offence.

57 *Hayes*, *ibid.*, speaks about this power as a pre-existing common law power, but *Brown*, *ibid.*, describes it as a manifestation of the ancillary power doctrine, which more usually is used as a way of describing newly created common law powers. See the discussion in Chapter 2.

58 See Archibald, above note 55.

D. SUPPORTING POWERS

A number of provisions in the *Code* provide additional power or protection to peace officers or others performing arrests. Anyone making a lawful arrest, for example, is justified in using as much force as necessary to do so, provided she is acting on reasonable grounds.[59] This power is set out in the *Criminal Code* for arrests under that Act, but the use of reasonable force is incidental to arrests in any case, such as those carried out under some provincial Act.[60] Latitude is permitted, since peace officers have a duty to act, sometimes in difficult and exigent circumstances.[61] Nonetheless, an officer is criminally responsible for using excessive force.[62]

A special rule applies to the use of force likely to cause death or grievous bodily harm to effect an arrest. Such action is only permitted when: even if there is a warrant, a warrantless arrest would be allowable; the person has taken flight to avoid arrest; the person using the force believes on reasonable grounds it is necessary for the purpose of protecting the officer or some other person from imminent or future death or grievous bodily harm; and finally that the flight of the person cannot be prevented in a less violent manner.[63]

Anyone arresting the wrong person under a warrant is not criminally responsible, provided he believed in good faith and on reasonable grounds that the correct person was being arrested. This same protection also applies to anyone called on to assist in the arrest.[64]

Police also have the power to search a person who has been arrested (this issue is discussed in Chapter 4).

Special rules apply when the police enter a dwelling house to make an arrest because of the increased privacy interest in that situation. At common law, relatively little additional protection was provided to a suspect in this situation, but the Court held in *R. v. Feeney* that some of the common law rules did not pass *Charter* scrutiny.[65] Therefore, some

---

59   Section 25(1). Section 25 is phrased in the language of justification, meaning that, in principle, it actually creates a defence to a criminal charge rather than a power. Practically speaking, the distinction is of little importance.

60   *Asante-Mensah*, above note 10.

61   *Ibid.*

62   Section 26.

63   Section 25(4).

64   Section 28.

65   In *R. v. Feeney*, [1997] 2 S.C.R. 13 [*Feeney*] the Court held that the common law requirements for entry into a dwelling house to effect an arrest were simply that the officer had reasonable grounds to believe that the person sought was within the premises; proper announcement was made; the officer believed reasonable

of those common law rules have now been overridden by statute.[66] In essence, the judicial pre-authorization requirement that applied to entry to conduct a search now also applies to entry to effect an arrest.

Peace officers are now required to obtain specific authorization on an arrest warrant if they wish to enter a dwelling house in order to effect the arrest. The person issuing the warrant must be satisfied on reasonable grounds that the person to be arrested will be present in the dwelling house. In addition, the officer executing the warrant must have grounds to believe that the person to be arrested is present immediately before entering the dwelling house.[67] Similarly, a separate warrant that simply authorizes peace officers to enter a dwelling house can be issued if an arrest warrant already exists, or the person can be arrested without warrant.[68] In either case, the warrant can include any conditions the judge or justice feels are advisable to ensure that the entry is reasonable under the circumstances.[69]

A peace officer can enter without a warrant in exigent circumstances, which include situations where the officer has reasonable grounds to believe the entry is necessary to prevent imminent harm or death to some person, or is necessary to prevent the imminent loss or destruction of evidence relating to an indictable offence. Even then, however, warrantless entry is only allowed where there are reasonable grounds to believe the person is in the house and the conditions for obtaining a warrant exist but the exigent circumstances make it impracticable actually to obtain a warrant.[70] In assessing the practicability of obtaining a warrant, courts will need to have regard for section 529.5,

---

grounds for the arrest existed; and reasonable grounds for the arrest did exist on an objective basis. These requirements amounted to little more than having grounds for arrest and reasonably believing the person was in the dwelling house, though the Court also suggested that, before forcing entry, police should have requested and been refused admission (paras. 24 and 26). The Court held that privacy interests, of increasing importance with the introduction of the *Charter*, were not adequately respected by these rules.

66 See Renee M. Pomerance, "Parliament's Response to *R. v. Feeney*: A New Regime for Entry and Arrest in Dwelling Houses" (1998) 13 C.R. (5th) 84 and Robert W. Fetterly & Daniel A. MacRury, "Arrest of Persons in Dwelling-House (Feeney Warrants—The First Three Years)" (2001) 45 Crim. L.Q. 101 (Part I) and (2001) 45 Crim. L.Q. 360 (Part II) for discussion of these provisions.

67 Section 529.

68 Section 529.1.

69 Section 529.2.

70 Section 529.3. See Heather Pringle, "Kicking in the Castle Doors: The Evolution of Exigent Circumstances" (2000) 43 Crim. L.Q. 86 for criticism of this provision. She argues, at 108, that it creates a "dangerous extension of the exigent circumstances doctrine as it has been generally understood in Canada." In par-

which permits applications for entry warrants to be made by telephone or other means of telecommunications.

Normally, a peace officer entering a dwelling house to effect an arrest must first announce her presence. However the *Code* does sometimes permit an officer who is lawfully entering, either with or without warrant, to omit the prior announcement. The justice issuing the warrant must be satisfied on reasonable grounds that prior announcement would expose the peace officer or some other person to imminent bodily harm or death, or that prior announcement would lead to the imminent loss or destruction of evidence of an indictable offence. Even then, the peace officer executing the warrant (or entering in exigent circumstances without a warrant) must also have reasonable grounds to believe those same things immediately before entering without announcement.[71]

Although the *Code* only explicitly permits warrantless entry in exigent circumstances, there is also a common law exception in the case of hot pursuit. This exception was specifically held in *Feeney* to be justified despite the new rules required by the *Charter*. "Hot pursuit" refers to situations where there is "continuous pursuit conducted with reasonable diligence, so that pursuit and capture along with the commission of the offence may be considered as forming part of a single transaction."[72] There is no strict requirement that the officers personally witnessed the offence, though clearly the definition requires a connection approaching that. In such cases, entry without a warrant is justified on a number of grounds, including that the offender should not be rewarded for having fled or be encouraged to do so, that a person who is in the process of fleeing the police will not have his "domestic tranquility" interrupted by the entry, and that it might not be possible to identify the offender later if she is not arrested immediately. The hot pursuit exception is not limited to indictable offences but applies more broadly, including to provincial offences.[73] It remains unsettled as to

---

ticular, she notes that s. 529.3 reverses *Feeney*, above note 65, on the question of whether potential loss of evidence can constitute exigent circumstances.

71   Section 529.4. Interestingly, although the judge or justice issuing the warrant is required to have reasonable grounds to believe, in relation to either ground, the officer is only required to have reasonable grounds to *suspect* imminent bodily harm or death, though the standard of reasonable belief applies to the loss of evidence. Normally, suspicion is taken to be a lower standard than belief, and this is perhaps intended to be justified here because of the greater consequences flowing from the risk of bodily harm than from the risk of lost evidence.

72   *R. v. Macooh*, [1993] 2 S.C.R. 802 at 817 [*Macooh*], quoting from Roger E. Salhany, *Canadian Criminal Procedure*, 5th ed. (Aurora, ON: Canada Law Book, 1989) at 44.

73   *Macooh, ibid.*

whether there is a requirement of prior announcement when an officer in hot pursuit enters to arrest.

E. RIGHTS ARISING ON ARREST

The word "rights" in this context is used broadly to include not only those rights guaranteed by the *Charter* on arrest, but also statutory provisions that apply once an arrest has occurred and that offer protection to an accused.

1) Statutory Protections

As noted above, the *Code* provisions that deal with compelling appearance try to balance state concerns with respect for the accused's liberty interest. The *Criminal Code* sets out several obligations on the part of police following an arrest. Generally speaking, these provisions are reflections of the principles of restraint and attempt to limit the use of coercive police powers to the extent possible. An example, though minor, is section 503(4), which requires an officer who has arrested a person to prevent the commission of an offence to release the accused unconditionally once that justification no longer exists.

Several of these provisions mirror section 495(2), discussed above, and its approach of creating an arrest power, but providing guidelines around when not to use it. As discussed in Chapter 6, section 497 calls upon an officer who has arrested a person for one of the offences listed in sections 495(2)(a), (b), or (c) to release that person on an appearance notice or summons unless grounds similar to those in section 495(2)(d) and (e) apply. Section 498 imposes a similar duty, with similar limitations on the officer in charge of the place where an arrested person is placed in custody.

When neither the arresting officer, nor officer in charge release the accused, section 503 comes into play. That section requires that an arrested person be taken in front of a justice of the peace to consider the issue of release.[74] In most circumstances this must occur without unreasonable delay and, in any event, within twenty-four hours. The Court has been clear that this provision does not mean the police have twenty-four hours to take an accused before a justice ("without unreasonable delay" is the important criterion and twenty-four hours is

---

74   See the much fuller discussion of judicial interim release in Chapter 6.

simply the outside limit on reasonableness).[75] Whether some period shorter than twenty-four hours was a reasonable time depends on the facts of the case. In *Storrey*, where a lineup was arranged involving witnesses who had to be brought in from outside the jurisdiction and may have resulted in the accused being released without charges, an eighteen hour delay was reasonable. That does not mean, however, that the police can always defer taking the accused in front of a justice because they are pursuing an investigation. A release within twenty-four hours might still have been unreasonably delayed.[76]

It is worth noting that the justice of the peace may decide that the accused should not be released. Similarly, the Crown may apply to the justice for a three day adjournment of the release hearing, during which time the accused will continue to be detained.[77] Neither of these possibilities, however, relieve the police of their obligation to take the accused to a justice.[78] Failure to comply with this obligation may constitute an arbitrary detention under section 9 of the *Charter*, but on current caselaw will not necessarily. Generally speaking, whether the detention is seen as arbitrary as well as in violation of section 503 will depend on whether there is an explanation, and if so what it is, for the delay.[79] Unreasonable delay of less than twenty-four hours for which there is no explanation is likely to be found both illegal and arbitrary. Rather oddly, however, given the approach that has been taken to section 9, it seems that a delay of more than twenty-four hours for which some explanation could be offered may be found illegal but not arbitrary.[80]

The twenty-four hour outside limit only applies where a justice is available in that time, otherwise the only requirement is that there be no unreasonable delay.[81] However, lack of availability cannot be argued on a simple administrative basis, such as that the courts do not sit on weekends. The provision is only intended to apply in remote areas and similar situations.[82] Even in such cases, the provisions of section 515(2.3)

---

75   *Storrey*, above note 34.
76   See, for example, *R. v. W.(E.)* (2002), 7 C.R. (6th) 343 (Nfld. C.A.) [*W.(E.)*]; *R. v. Koszulap* (1974), 27 C.R.N.S. 226 (Ont. C.A.).
77   Section 516.
78   See *W.(E.)*, above note 76; *R. v. Simpson* (1994), 29 C.R. (4th) 274 (Nfld. C.A.), rev'd on other grounds [1995] 1 S.C.R. 449; *R. v. MacPherson* (1995), 100 C.C.C. (3d) 216 (N.B.C.A.).
79   See *R. v. Tam* (1995), 100 C.C.C. (3d) 196 (B.C.C.A.); *R. v. Charles* (1987), 59 C.R. (3d) 94 (Sask. C.A.).
80   See the discussion of s. 9 at Section C, above in this chapter.
81   Section 503(1)(b).
82   *Simpson*, above note 78 (Nfld. C.A.).

that allow an accused to appear in front of a justice by telephone or other telecommunications device would need to be taken into account.

Other specific rights arise with respect to young persons who are arrested. Section 25 of the *Youth Criminal Justice Act*[83] gives a young person the right to counsel on arrest, which of course is already guaranteed by section 10(b) of the *Charter* (see the discussion below). In addition, the *YCJA* requires that notice of the arrest be given to a parent of the young person. Further, specific statutory rules about interrogations of a young person after arrest provide that any statement is not admissible where the young person was not given the chance to contact counsel and a parent, or was not given the opportunity to have either or both present.[84]

2) *Charter* Rights Arising on Arrest

Section 10 of the *Charter* creates specific guarantees arising on arrest (in fact, those rights arise on either arrest or detention, and so are relevant in that latter context as well). Unlike section 8, which has had significant impact on the rules regarding searches and how they are to be conducted, the impact of section 10 has largely been to add additional requirements to the information to be given to an accused at the time of an arrest. There has also been an impact on the procedures followed afterward to facilitate actual contact by the accused with counsel. Most of this caselaw developed fairly early under the *Charter*, and section 10 now has a relatively settled jurisprudence.[85]

Section 10(a) provides that an accused is to be informed promptly of the reasons for the arrest or detention. The Court held in *Evans* that this right "is founded most fundamentally on the notion that one is not obliged to submit to an arrest if one does not know the reasons for it."[86] This section has provided less protection than it might, however. The test focuses on what the accused can be reasonably supposed to

---

83   *YCJA*, above note 40.

84   *Ibid.*, ss. 146(2)(c) & (d).

85   One particular issue that remains unsettled is whether s. 10 applies in the case of arrests not made by peace officers. In *Lerke*, above note 29, the Alberta Court of Appeal held that when one private citizen arrests another, *Charter* rights arise. Specifically, in that case, the right against unreasonable search and seizure was at issue. In contrast, in *R. v. J.(A.M.)* (1999), 137 C.C.C. (3d) 213 the British Columbia Court of Appeal decided that *Charter* rights did not arise on a citizen's arrest. In *Asante-Mensah*, above note 10, the Supreme Court of Canada noted the issue, but found that they were not required to address it: see para. 77.

86   *Evans*, above note 27 at 886–87.

have understood, rather than on any precise words used.[87] In itself, that need not be objectionable, but it has been applied in a way with the potential to weaken the right. In *Latimer*, for example, the police decided not to arrest the accused and told him that he was being "detained for investigation" instead. That is, the police consciously purported to take the accused into custody on a basis that was not legally available, since no such power to detain for investigation existed, and offered that false explanation to the accused. The Court nonetheless relied on *Evans* to find that the accused knew he was in an extremely grave situation with regard to his daughter's death, and therefore there was no section 10(a) violation.[88]

Similarly, in *Smith* 1991 the practical impact of section 10(a) was reduced. In that case the accused was told that he was under arrest in connection with a shooting incident, but he was not told that the victim had died. The Crown conceded that section 10(a) had been violated, but relied on the accused's subsequent waiver of the right to counsel. The Court agreed, holding that, even if the accused was not aware of the specific charge, he had sufficient information to know the extent of his jeopardy, and therefore his waiver of counsel was valid despite the section 10(a) violation.[89]

Although allowing an accused to decide whether to submit to an arrest is described as the primary reason for section 10(a), from the start it has been acknowledged that a secondary reason is linked to the right to counsel in section 10(b): "[a]n individual can only exercise his section 10(b) right in a meaningful way if he knows the extent of his jeopardy."[90] This aspect of section 10(a) has received attention in cases where an accused is originally arrested for one reason but the reason for her continued detention then changes. The Court has held that it can be necessary to re-advise the accused so that he can consider again whether to seek legal advice.[91] It is to section 10(b) that we now turn.

Section 10(b) guarantees the right "to retain and instruct counsel without delay and to be informed of that right." The Court has noted that this protection is provided because the effective assistance of counsel is seen as crucial in our society, and, indeed, the right to it is a

---

87   *Ibid.* at 888.
88   *Latimer*, above note 9 at para. 31.
89   *Smith* 1991, above note 27.
90   *Black*, above note 27 at 152–53.
91   *Borden*, above note 27; *Smith* 1991, above note 27; *Evans*, above note 27; *Black*, above note 27.

principle of fundamental justice.[92] The purpose of the right, the Court has said, is to provide an accused with an opportunity to be informed of her rights and obligations and to obtain advice on exercising those rights and fulfilling those obligations. In particular, upon the arrest the accused has been deprived of liberty and may need legal assistance in regaining it. Equally, or more importantly, the accused is at risk of self-incrimination and is in need of legal advice, particularly advice about the right to silence and how to exercise it.[93]

Note that, like all *Charter* rights, the rights arising in section 10(b) are subject to the reasonable limits clause in section 1. In most cases, a failure to comply with one of the aspects of the right to counsel will not be saved under section 1, which makes *Charter* rights subject to "such reasonable limits *prescribed by law* as can be demonstrably justified in a free and democratic society" (emphasis added). The emphasized phrase requires that, if a *Charter* violation is to be saved, the police must have been given, either by statute or common law, the power to override the *Charter* right in question. Most commonly, if a police officer fails to give sufficient information to an accused about contacting counsel or some other aspect of section 10(b), that failure is not prescribed by law— it is simply an oversight. Therefore, section 1 analyses arise only infrequently with regards to the right to counsel, since they are typically settled at this relatively straightforward step, prior to getting into any difficult balancing of what sorts of limits are justifiable in a free and democratic society.

However, it is possible for a statute to prescribe a limit on section 10(b), like any other right, and in those cases the courts must consider whether the limit is justified. Accordingly, it has been determined that statutory limits that prevent an accused from having access to counsel prior to blowing into a roadside screening device or performing roadside sobriety tests can be justified.[94]

In a typical case where section 10(b) rights have not been limited by section 1, however, various obligations have been imposed on the police at the time of the arrest or detention. The Court has divided these into "informational" and "implementational" obligations,[95] and it is convenient to discuss them under those headings.

---

92 See *Lavallee, Rackel & Heintz v. Canada (Attorney General); White, Ottenheimer & Baker v. Canada (Attorney General); R. v. Fink*, [2002] 3 S.C.R. 209; *R. v. G.D.B.*, [2000] 1 S.C.R. 520.

93 *R. v. Bartle*, [1994] 3 S.C.R. 173 at 191 [*Bartle*]; *R. v. Manninen*, [1987] 1 S.C.R. 1233 at 1242–43 [*Manninen*].

94 *R. v. Thomsen*, [1988] 1 S.C.R. 640; *R. v. Orbanski; R. v. Elias*, 2005 SCC 37.

95 *Bartle*, above note 93.

a) Informational Duties

Most obviously, section 10(b) specifically sets out the requirement that an accused must be informed of the right to retain and instruct counsel without delay. This is normally done through a "standard caution" that is distributed to police officers, which they read to the accused. This caution is intended to be as instructive and clear as possible, but in most cases the police are not required to take any steps other than reading the caution to be sure that the accused has actually understood the right. However, where special circumstances do exist the police must take additional steps to be sure the accused comprehends the right. Such special circumstances could include language difficulties, a known or obvious mental disability, or any genuine inability to comprehend the right on the part of the accused.[96]

Other information must also be included in the standard caution. The police must give the accused information about access to counsel free-of-charge for persons who meet the financial criteria set by provincial Legal Aid plans. In addition, the accused should be given information about access to immediate temporary legal advice, irrespective of financial status.[97] In the latter case, the accused should also be told how to gain access to the service, for example by telling the accused that he will be given the telephone number for duty counsel if he so wishes.[98] However, police compliance with the duty to inform an arrested person of how to gain access is determined with regard to the circumstances of the case. In *Latimer*, for example, the Court held that there was no section 10(b) violation when the police did not give the accused the telephone numbers for either the duty counsel scheme in the province or the local legal aid office. They held that the former service was not available to the accused since it operated only outside normal business hours, and that the telephone number for the latter service was easily available by looking in the phone book.[99] The Court did stress, though, that more may be required of the police in other cases.

Although the police must inform an accused of any existing duty counsel scheme in the province, the Court held in *R. v. Prosper* that section 10(b) does not impose an obligation on provinces actually to have such a scheme.[100] Practically speaking, however, while formally refusing to create such a requirement, the Court left provinces with little realistic alternative. Relying on an implementational duty discussed

---

96 *Evans*, above note 27; *Bartle*, *ibid*.

97 *R. v. Brydges*, [1990] 1 S.C.R. 190.

98 *Bartle*, above note 93 at 195. See also *R. v. Pozniak*, [1994] 3 S.C.R. 310.

99 *Latimer*, above note 9.

100 [1994] 3 S.C.R. 236 [*Prosper*].

below, the Court held that, although there need not be a duty counsel scheme, police must hold-off from attempting to gain incriminatory evidence from an accused who expresses the wish to contact counsel.[101] This would mean, for example, that police frequently could not administer breathalyzer tests unless a duty counsel system was in place. As a matter of fact, Nova Scotia, the province from which *Prosper* arose and which at the time lacked a duty counsel scheme, implemented one in the wake of that decision.

Because the purpose of the right to counsel is to allow an accused to be protected against self-incrimination, an accused should be re-warned of the right if there is a substantial change in the circumstances affecting the accused's degree of jeopardy. That is, failure to re-warn in such situations might violate section 10(b), as well as section 10(a).[102] In addition, if an accused who initially indicates a desire to speak to counsel later indicates he has changed his mind, the police have an obligation to re-warn that person of his right to a reasonable opportunity, and also to inform him of their obligation to hold-off from eliciting evidence.[103]

The police also must not act to undermine the right, by making disparaging comments about counsel's loyalty, commitment, availability, or the amount of legal fees, for example.[104] Similarly, offering a one-time only plea bargain with a time limit that expires before an accused will be able to reach counsel is a section 10(b) violation. The Crown or police should offer any plea bargain to the accused's lawyer or to the accused with counsel present, unless there has been an express waiver of counsel. This is a requirement in all cases, not simply those where the offer has an expiration date.[105]

Finally, note that the informational aspects of the section 10(b) right arise in every arrest. In contrast to the implementational requirements discussed below, all accused, whether they have expressed an interest in learning more about duty counsel or any other aspect of the right, are to be given all the information noted above.[106]

---

101 *Manninen*, above note 93.
102 *R. v. Paternak*, [1996] 3 S.C.R. 607.
103 *Prosper*, above note 100. This is generally referred to as a "*Prosper* warning."
104 *R. v. Burlingham*, [1995] 2 S.C.R. 206 at 221 [*Burlingham*].
105 *Ibid.* at 230. One might think of these aspects of the right to counsel as implementational rather than informational, but the Court speaks of them as the latter. Classifying them as informational does, in the Court's analysis, make them less easily subject to waiver: see Section E(2)(b), below in this chapter.
106 *Bartle*, above note 93. See the discussion of waiver of s. 10(b) rights, below in this chapter.

b) Implementational Duties

In addition to informing an accused of the right to counsel, two further correlative duties can arise on arrest. First, where an arrested person has indicated a wish to speak to counsel, the police must provide that person with a reasonable opportunity to do so. In *Manninen*, for example, the accused was arrested at a private business and the court found there was no reason that the police could not have allowed him to use the telephone in that office, rather than wait until they returned to the police station. The accused was not required to ask to use the telephone; the obligation to facilitate contact with counsel meant that the police should have offered him its use. In situations of urgency this obligation may temporarily be postponed, but otherwise it should be complied with.[107] A reasonable opportunity to consult with counsel includes the right to do so in private, whether privacy is specifically requested or not.[108] Subject to the issue of reasonable diligence, discussed below, this right also includes the opportunity to contact the counsel of one's choice.[109]

Secondly, when an arrested person has requested counsel the police must hold off from questioning or otherwise seeking to elicit evidence from that person until she has had a reasonable opportunity to contact counsel. Thus, in *Manninen*, it was fairly clear that there was a section 10(b) violation when the police immediately questioned the accused and paid no attention to his expressed wish to speak to counsel. Equally, it meant there had been a violation in *R. v. Ross*, where the accused was required to participate in a lineup after having been unable to reach his counsel at 2:00 a.m. In that case, the Court held that it was unsurprising that counsel could not be reached at that hour, that there was no urgency or other compelling reason to conduct the lineup immediately, and therefore that the police were required to hold off.[110] As noted above, this duty to hold off also prevents the police from conducting breathalyzer tests without first giving the accused the reasonable opportunity to consult with counsel.[111]

These implementational duties differ in an important regard from the informational ones, however, in that they are not quite so firmly guaranteed. This is true in three separate but related ways: they do not arise for every accused, they can be waived, and they can be lost through a lack of reasonable diligence.

---

107 *Manninen*, above note 93.
108 *R. v. Playford* (1987), 61 C.R. (3d) 101 (Ont. C.A.).
109 *R. v. Ross*, [1989] 1 S.C.R. 3 at 10–11 [*Ross*].
110 *Ibid.*
111 *Prosper*, above note 100.

First, the implementational duties only arise when an accused has actually indicated a wish to speak to counsel. Unless there is evidence that suggests the accused did not understand the right to counsel, then the onus is on the accused to prove that he asked to speak to counsel but was denied the right, or that she was denied any opportunity even to ask to speak to counsel.[112] This is distinct from the informational components of the right, all of which must be told to all accused whether they request information about, for example, legal aid or not.[113]

Second, implementational duties can be waived, though informational ones virtually cannot be. A valid waiver requires that an accused have full knowledge of the right he is giving up. A person who has not yet received all the informational components of the right to counsel is therefore not in a position to waive the right.[114] Accordingly, even if an arrested person indicates that she does not want to hear the information in the standard caution, that will not normally be a valid waiver and the police have an obligation to inform her nonetheless. Before the police can choose to forgo the obligation, it would not only be necessary for the person to have said that she understands the right to counsel, but there would also need to be reasonable grounds to believe that the claim was correct.[115]

In contrast, implementational duties can be waived. Most simply, an arrested person could explicitly decline to contact counsel after being given the opportunity to do so. Implicit waivers are also possible, though the standard is very high and the waiver, though implicit, must be clear and unequivocal.[116] In particular, cooperating with the investigation by answering questions or participating in a lineup will not constitute a waiver.[117]

Finally, implementational duties can be lost. If an arrested person "is not being reasonably diligent in the exercise of his rights" then the correlative duties from *Manninen* are not a bar to the police continuing their investigation nonetheless.[118] This rule was laid down in *R. v. Tremblay*, a case where the trial judge found that the accused was ·.

---

112 *R. v. Baig*, [1987] 2 S.C.R. 537.

113 *Bartle*, above note 93.

114 *Ibid.* at 204.

115 *Ibid.* at 206. The Court offers the example of a person who, after having already spoken to duty counsel, is re-warned of the right to counsel because of a change in circumstances during questioning. In such a case, it might not be necessary to tell the person once again of the existence of duty counsel.

116 *Clarkson v. The Queen*, [1986] 1 S.C.R. 383 at 394–95 [*Clarkson*], quoting *Korponay v. Attorney General of Canada*, [1982] 1 S.C.R. 41.

117 *Manninen*, above note 93; *Ross*, above note 109.

118 *R. v. Tremblay*, [1987] 2 S.C.R. 435 [*Tremblay*].

actively obstructing the investigation, and the evidence suggested that he was using the right to counsel as a means of stalling a breathalyzer test. Even so, the Court actually found a section 10(b) violation in his case, though in *obiter* they created the "reasonable diligence rule" and did not exclude the breathalyzer evidence under section 24(2). Lack of reasonable diligence does not lead to a complete loss of section 10(b) rights. The arrested individual still has the right to speak to counsel. However, the police are no longer obliged to hold off their investigation until the arrested person has had a chance to do so. This is the case even if a person who has lost the right through lack of reasonable diligence subsequently reiterates the wish to speak to counsel.[119]

Given the particular facts of *Tremblay* it is unfortunate that the Court chose to describe the accused's obstructionist behaviour as a lack of reasonable diligence. The real complaint in *Tremblay* seemed to be that the accused was asserting his *Charter* right not because he had any real interest in it, but as an improper means of avoiding responsibility. That objection is consistent with a purposive approach to the *Charter* and to the approach taken to other rights.[120] But phrasing the concern, in an understated way, as a lack of reasonable diligence has led to an expansion of the standard; a change to the detriment of all arrested persons. The result is to make the argument against the existence of the *Charter* rights plausible in a much wider range of cases.[121] In *Smith*, for example, the accused was arrested at 7:00 p.m. and, after several stops en route, he asked to call counsel at 9:00 p.m. upon arriving at the police station. After being given a telephone book he decided not to call because only his lawyer's office number was listed and he did not expect that his lawyer would be in the office at that time. The

---

119 *R. v. Smith*, [1989] 2 S.C.R. 368 [*Smith* 1989].

120 In the context of disclosure, for example, the Court has required that an accused who is aware of undisclosed information must actively seek it out. An accused cannot choose to have her *Charter* right to disclosure violated so that she can then seek a remedy: see the discussion in Chapter 8. Similarly, in cases that deal with the right to a trial within a reasonable time, the Court's analysis has tried to prevent giving a remedy to an accused who does not genuinely want a prompt trial, but actually wants a *Charter* s. 11(d) violation and a remedy therefore: see *R. v. Morin*, [1992] 1 S.C.R. 771.

121 In *Prosper*, above note 100, it can hardly be surprising that the Court found the accused had been reasonably diligent when he made fifteen phone calls, all unsuccessful, to all twelve legal aid lawyers on the list given to him by the police. He was not also required "to call at random lawyers listed in the Yellow Pages late on a Saturday afternoon and plead for free or cut-rate legal advice": *Prosper* at para. 56. But, in making this decision, the Court rejected the argument that had succeeded in the Court of Appeal.

court split four to three as to whether the accused had complied with the reasonable diligence standard, with the majority finding that he had not. It is difficult not to think that a different decision would have been reached had the Court asked itself whether the accused was only pretending to assert his *Charter* rights as a way of obstructing the investigation.[122]

The rule that an implicit waiver of *Charter* rights must be clear and explicit is not, at a theoretical level, easily reconciled with the view that no implementational duties arise unless an accused requests counsel and that an accused must be reasonably diligent in exercising the right. All three are ways of deciding that the accused does not benefit from the implementational duties, but they set different standards for deciding the issue. Silence would not be a clear and explicit waiver, which leads to the conclusion that the arrested person was entitled to the implementational duties. But silence would be a failure to request counsel, or a failure of reasonable diligence, which leads to the conclusion that the arrested person was not entitled to the implementational duties. Silence, or other ambiguous behaviour on the part of an accused, allows courts to apply either of the conflicting lines of authority, with conflicting results.[123]

In conclusion, it is worth noting one particular point that is *not* an implementational duty. A person who has been arrested and has already spoken with counsel may then be questioned by the police. Even if that person indicates that he does not wish to speak with the police, it does not impose a duty on the police to stop their questioning. That is, there is nothing analogous to the obligation to hold off originally that arises at a later stage. The person is not required to answer questions, but that does not mean the police are not entitled to ask them.[124]

---

122 *Smith* 1989, above note 119.

123 See, for example, *R. v. Hollis* (1993), 17 C.R. (4th) 211 (B.C.C.A.). This situation is particularly odd when one considers that a waiver must be considered in light of all the circumstances. To say "I know my rights" is not a valid waiver of the informational components. If an accused says "I don't want a lawyer," that waiver cannot be taken at face value and courts must decide whether the arrested person had a true understanding of the consequences: *R. v. Clarkson*, above note 116. The anomalous result is that there is greater protection under s. 10(b) for an accused who expressly waives the right than for one who says nothing. See Stephen Coughlan, "When Silence Isn't Golden: Waiver and the Right to Counsel" (1990) 33 Crim. L.Q. 43.

124 *R. v. Singh*, 2007 SCC 48. The decision actually analyzes this question as an aspect of s. 7 and the right to silence, but the analogy to s. 10(b) is noted.

FURTHER READINGS

COUGHLAN, STEPHEN, "When Silence Isn't Golden: Waiver and the Right to Counsel" (1990) 33 Crim. L.Q. 43

COUGHLAN, STEVE, "Whither—or Wither—Section 9" (2008) 40 Sup. Ct. L. Rev. (2d) 147

FETTERLY, ROBERT W., AND DANIEL A. MACRURY, "Arrest of Persons in Dwelling-House (Feeney Warrants — The First Three Years) (Part I)" (2002) 45 Crim. L.Q. 101

FETTERLY, ROBERT W., AND DANIEL A. MACRURY, "Arrest of Persons in Dwelling-House (Feeney Warrants — The First Three Years) (Part II)" (2002) 45 Crim. L.Q. 360

LAW REFORM COMMISSION OF CANADA, *Arrest* (Ottawa: Law Reform Commission of Canada, 1986)

PACKER, HERBERT L., *The Limits of the Criminal Sanction* (Stanford: Stanford University Press, 1968)

POMERANCE, RENEE M., "Parliament's Response to *R. v. Feeney*: A New Regime for Entry and Arrest in Dwelling Houses" (1998) 13 C.R. (5th) 84

PRINGLE, HEATHER, "Kicking in the Castle Doors: The Evolution of Exigent Circumstances" (2000) 43 Crim. L.Q. 86

STRIBOPOULOS, JAMES, "The Forgotten Right: Section 9 of the *Charter*, Its Purpose and Meaning" (2008) 40 Sup. Ct. L. Rev. (2d) 211

CHAPTER 8

DISCLOSURE

A. INTRODUCTION

For many years, no effective right to disclosure of the Crown's case existed in Canada. Practice with regard to disclosure varied from court to court, and even from prosecutor to prosecutor. Despite calls for comprehensive disclosure schemes from the Law Reform Commission of Canada[1] no statutory scheme was introduced. The problems that could arise from non-disclosure were made dramatically clear in the investigation of the wrongful conviction of Donald Marshall, Jr., leading that Royal Commission to point to the need for consistent disclosure.[2] In general terms, that state of affairs changed with the Supreme Court of Canada decision in *R. v. Stinchcombe* in 1991, which concluded that an accused person had a right, under section 7 of the *Canadian Charter of Rights and Freedoms*, to disclosure of the Crown's case.[3] The exact contours of this right have continued to be developed in subsequent caselaw, although *Stinchcombe* remains the leading case establishing

---

1   Law Reform Commission of Canada, *Discovery in Criminal Cases* (Ottawa: Law Reform Commission of Canada, 1974), and *Disclosure by the Prosecution* (Ottawa: Law Reform Commission of Canada, 1984).

2   Royal Commission on the Donald Marshall, Jr. Prosecution, *Royal Commission on the Donald Marshall, Jr. Prosecution, Findings and Recommendations*, vol. 1 (Halifax: The Commission, 1989).

3   *R. v. Stinchcombe*, [1991] 3 S.C.R. 326 [*Stinchcombe*].

the general principle. The Court has summarized the current state of affairs with regard to disclosure:

> The Crown must disclose all relevant information to the accused, whether inculpatory or exculpatory, subject to the exercise of the Crown's discretion to refuse to disclose information that is privileged or plainly irrelevant. Relevance must be assessed in relation both to the charge itself and to the reasonably possible defences. The relevant information must be disclosed whether or not the Crown intends to introduce it in evidence, before election or plea. Moreover, all statements obtained from persons who have provided relevant information to the authorities should be produced notwithstanding that they are not proposed as Crown witnesses. This Court has also defined the concept of "relevance" broadly . . . .[4]

B. CONTENT OF THE RIGHT TO DISCLOSURE

1) Creation of the Right: *R. v. Stinchcombe*

In *Stinchcombe*, the Court found a duty on the part of the Crown to disclose its evidence to the accused. The Court rejected a number of arguments against disclosure. It pointed out that the Crown's role is not to obtain a conviction but to lay all relevant evidence before the court. Any information in the hands of the Crown is therefore not a tool to convict the accused, but the property of the public to be used to ensure that justice is done. The Court also rejected the suggestion that Crown workloads would be increased by an obligation to disclose. It noted, as the Law Reform Commission studies found, that increased disclosure actually leads to an increase in cases settled, guilty pleas entered, and charges withdrawn, thereby decreasing Crown and court workloads. The Court acknowledged that some risk to informers may come from disclosure, but determined that this only affects the manner and timing of disclosure, not the general principle. The Court also acknowledged that disclosure may allow an accused to tailor a defence to anticipate the prosecution's case, but held, nonetheless, that fairness to the accused requires that the accused see the evidence in advance.

This latter point is the most important in the Court's reasoning. Although policy arguments lead them to conclude that routine disclosure is a desirable feature of the criminal justice system, it is the *Charter*, and in particular the accused's right under section 7 to make full an-

---

4   *R. v. Taillefer*, 2003 SCC 70 at para. 59 (page references omitted) [*Taillefer*].

swer and defence, that is the mechanism by which that end is achieved. The Court concludes that "there is a general duty on the part of the Crown to disclose all material it proposes to use at trial and especially all evidence which may assist the accused even if the Crown does not propose to adduce it."[5] The fact that this right is guaranteed by the *Charter* has been significant in much of the Court's later reasoning.

2) Structure of the Right

First, the structure of the right as set out in *Stinchcombe* should be described. Whether evidence appears to be inculpatory or exculpatory is irrelevant to the obligation to disclose. The Crown is required to disclose on the request of the accused, made any time after a charge is laid. Disclosure ought to be made prior to election or plea, so that the accused can take the disclosed material into account in making a decision on those issues. The material to be disclosed includes all witness statements, whether the Crown intends to call the witness or not, and notes or "will say" statements where no actual statement exists. If there are no notes, the Crown should disclose the name, address, and occupation of a witness and any information the prosecution possesses concerning the evidence that person might give. In later cases the duty to disclose has been described as "triggered whenever there is a reasonable possibility of the information being useful to the accused in making full answer and defence."[6]

The obligation to disclose rests with the Crown in a broader sense—it includes both the Crown prosecutor and the police.[7] Further, the obligation to disclose is a continuing one, and the Crown must disclose any additional information it receives. Equally, the defence has a continuing obligation to seek disclosure, and is not entitled to assume that it has received all relevant information.[8] Where, following a review of disclosure by the trial judge, circumstances have changed, the appropriate approach for the Crown is to re-apply to the trial judge concerning the issue, rather than to fail to disclose and argue the issue on appeal.[9]

---

5   *Stinchcombe*, above note 3 at 338, quoting from *R. v. C.(M.H.)* (1988), 46 C.C.C. (3d) 142 (B.C.C.A.).

6   *R. v. Dixon*, [1998] 1 S.C.R. 244 at para. 21 [*Dixon*].

7   *R. v. Jack* (1992), 70 C.C.C. (3d) 67 (Man. C.A.), relying on *R. v. C. (M.H.)*, [1991] 1 S.C.R. 763 at para. 32, which in turn had adopted a passage from *R. v. Caccamo*, [1976] 1 S.C.R. 786.

8   *Dixon*, above note 6 at para. 55. These two rules are to a certain extent contradictory, and will no doubt give rise to disputes in practice: see the discussion of the need for due diligence by defence counsel in Section B(3)(b), below in this chapter.

9   *R. v. Khela*, [1995] 4 S.C.R. 201 at para. 10 [*Khela*].

The right to disclosure is not absolute. The Crown is obliged to err on the side of inclusion, but "it need not produce what is clearly irrelevant."[10] Similarly, the rules of privilege interact with the Crown's obligation to disclose. It may be necessary, for example, to protect the identity of informers— this does not permit the Crown to refuse disclosure, but gives them some discretion with regard to the timing and manner.[11] Further, the need to complete an investigation may justify the Crown in delaying some disclosure.[12] The obligation to disclose evidence does not include a requirement that the Crown make its witnesses available for oral discovery.[13]

In later cases, the Court has distinguished between evidence known to exist but which has not been disclosed, and evidence whose existence in dispute. In the former case, the burden clearly rests with the Crown to justify the non-disclosure of the evidence "by demonstrating either that the information sought is beyond its control, or that it is clearly irrelevant or privileged."[14] In the latter case, however, the Crown cannot be expected to justify the non-disclosure of evidence of which it is unaware or which it denies exists. In such circumstances, therefore, the defence is first required to show some basis that will allow the trial judge to conclude that potentially relevant further material exists.[15] The right to disclosure is not meant to allow fishing expeditions on the part of the defence, and so does not, for example, require the Crown to disclose whether the accused has been the subject of a wiretap unrelated to the charges actually laid.[16]

The rule of full disclosure, and its reliance on the accused's right to full answer and defence, has been applied in more specific contexts. In *R. v. Egger*,[17] for example, the Court was required to consider section 258(1)(d) of the *Code*, which allows the Crown to rely on a certificate of a qualified technician as proof of the concentration of alcohol in the accused's blood, as determined from an analysis of a blood sample. That section requires that the Crown have taken two samples of the accused's blood, one to be provided to the accused on request for analysis. How-

---

10   *Stinchcombe*, above note 3 at 339.
11   Where the level of disclosure has already been reviewed by a court and an order made, however, the Crown no longer has discretion over the issue: see *Khela*, above note 9 at para. 14, and the further discussion of this issue below.
12   *Stinchcombe*, above note 3 at 339.
13   *Khela*, above note 9 at para. 18.
14   *R. v. Chaplin*, [1995] 1 S.C.R. 727 at para. 25 [*Chaplin*].
15   *Ibid.* at 743.
16   *Ibid.*
17   *R. v. Egger*, [1993] 2 S.C.R. 451 [*Egger*].

ever, the section does not explicitly require that the accused be given notice of the existence of the sample. The Court noted that "one measure
of the relevance of information in the Crown's hands is its usefulness to
the defence: if it is of some use, it is relevant and should be disclosed."[18]
The various possible uses noted included "meeting the case for the
Crown, advancing a defence or otherwise in making a decision which
may affect the conduct of the defence such as, for example, whether to
call evidence."[19] Accordingly, it concluded that the Crown was required
to inform the accused of the existence of the sample, and to do so at a
time when the accused can usefully act on the information.

Similarly in *R. v. Durette*[20] the Court held that the same principles
apply in the context of wiretap applications:

> Apart from public interest concerns which may operate in a particu-
> lar case, I see no reason why an accused should not be entitled to
> see exactly what the judge saw who relied on the affidavits to issue
> the authorization. Disclosure of the full affidavit should be the start-
> ing premise. Anything less potentially impairs an accused's ability to
> make full answer and defence and must be justified by the Crown in
> accordance with established principles. Editing of these affidavits is
> best viewed as a necessary evil.[21]

The existence of the right to disclosure has also affected the Court's
analysis in other areas. In *R. v. Cook*,[22] for example, the Court concluded that the Crown had no obligation to call witnesses in order for
all material facts to be brought forward. Given the accused's right to
disclosure, the Crown's decision not to call a witness will not prejudice
an accused. If the Crown decides not to call a witness whose testimony
has changed from an earlier statement, for example, the accused will
have received the earlier statement and will be entitled to the later one,
due to the Crown's ongoing obligation to disclose.

3) Remedy for Breach of What Right: Disclosure or Full Answer and Defence?

The Court noted in *Stinchcombe* that the Crown's discretion with regard to disclosure can be reviewed by the trial judge if defence counsel
disagrees with the way in which it has been exercised. In such a review,

---

18   *Ibid.* at para. 20.
19   *Ibid.*
20   *R. v. Durette*, [1994] 1 S.C.R. 469 [*Durette*].
21   *Ibid.* at 495, quoting Doherty J.A. in the court below.
22   *R. v. Cook*, [1998] 2 S.C.R. 597 [*Cook*].

the onus would rest with the Crown to justify an exception to the rule of complete disclosure. Quite apart from issues of review by the trial judge, however, an issue which has frequently arisen is the effect of non-disclosure and the remedy that should flow from it. In *Stinchcombe* itself, the Court found that the accused might have conducted his defence differently by calling a particular witness, and that calling that witness could have affected the outcome of the trial. Accordingly, it ordered a new trial. Later cases have pursued the issue of remedy more fully, finding that in some circumstances a stay of proceedings is the appropriate remedy for non-disclosure. However, the caselaw has not been entirely consistent on this point, and may be regarded as still in transition. The most important cases since *Stinchcombe* to have discussed the issue of remedy are *Carosella*,[23] *La*,[24] and *Dixon*.

The Court has not been entirely consistent in its analysis of which *Charter* right is at issue when the Crown has failed to disclose relevant information. The earlier cases that considered this issue looked at whether disclosure was itself an independent *Charter* right or whether it was just an aspect of the right to full answer and defence. This seemed at first to matter on the assumption that one could proceed directly to the question of remedy once a breach of some *Charter* right had been found. As the Court's jurisprudence has developed, however, it has become apparent that although disclosure is said to be a *Charter* right in its own right, no remedy will be given for that breach unless it also amounts to a breach of the right to full answer and defence.

a)   The Original Position: Remedy for Non-disclosure

Carosella[25] dealt with an accused charged with gross indecency. Before contacting the police, the complainant had visited a rape crisis centre and been interviewed by a social worker, who took notes of the conversation. The accused later applied for production[26] of the records, but by that time they had been destroyed (the Centre had a policy of shredding

---

23   *R. v. Carosella*, [1997] 1 S.C.R. 80 [*Carosella*].

24   *R. v. La*, [1997] 2 S.C.R. 680 [*La*].

25   Above note 23.

26   An issue that will be pursued further is the distinction between disclosure, which involves the Crown giving the accused material that is in its possession, and production, which consists of the accused obtaining material which is in the hands of a third party. *Carosella*, *ibid.*, ought strictly to be a production case, and indeed Justice L'Heureux-Dubé argued in dissent that the rules around disclosure have nothing to do with the case since the files were never in the control of the Crown. The majority concluded that the disclosure rules apply since the complainant had agreed to production of the files and therefore they would have been disclosed to the Crown.

files where there was police involvement before they were served with any application for production). The Court therefore had to determine whether the non-production of the notes violated the accused's *Charter* rights, and, if it did, whether a stay was the appropriate remedy. [27]

The first issue the Court needed to address, therefore, was exactly what *Charter* right was in play. The issue was whether disclosure is, in itself, a right implicit in section 7, or whether section 7 protects the accused's right to full answer and defence, one aspect of which is the need for disclosure. The Ontario Court of Appeal had held that disclosure was simply an aspect of the right to full answer and defence, a conclusion that Justice L'Heureux Dubé, dissenting in the Supreme Court, agreed with. There was some justification for taking this view. In the earlier *R. v. O'Connor*[28] decision, a majority had supported a portion of Justice L'Heureux Dubé's judgment, in which she stated:

> the right of an accused to full disclosure by the Crown is an adjunct of the right to make full answer and defence. It is not itself a constitutionally protected right. What this means is that while the Crown has an obligation to disclose, and the accused has a right to all that which the Crown is obligated to disclose, a simple breach of the accused's right to such disclosure does not, in and of itself, constitute a violation of the *Charter* such as to entitle a remedy under s. 24(1).[29]

The difference between the two possibilities is most important because of the effect it will have on the need for an accused to show prejudice arising from the non-disclosure. If the right in question is the right to full answer and defence, then non-disclosure may not actually harm the accused in a particular case. For instance, the accused's ability to make full answer will not be affected by failure to disclose inculpatory information that does not form part of the Crown's case. However, if the accused has a *Charter* right to disclosure itself, then the non-disclosure of any information will automatically constitute a breach of that right. There will be no need to consider the actual effect of the

---

27   On this issue generally, see Paul Calarco, "What Happens When Evidence Has Not Been Recorded? Staying Charges to Ensure a Fair Trial" (2001) 44 Crim. L.Q. 514.

28   [1995] 4 S.C.R. 411 [*O'Connor*].

29   *Ibid.* at para. 74, citing the Court of Appeal decision (1994), 89 C.C.C. (3d) 109 at 148–49. Until *Carosella*, above note 23, was handed down, there was no reason to think that the majority in *O'Connor*, who agreed with the portion of Justice L'Heureux-Dubé's reasons in which this appeared, did not also ascribe to this particular passage. Courts of appeal had assumed it to be the majority position in the interim: see Graeme Mitchell, "*R. v. Carosella*: Difficult Cases Make Dangerous Law" (1997) 4 C.R. (5th) 209 [Mitchell].

non-disclosure on the accused. As Justice L'Heureux Dubé had further noted in *O'Connor*:

> . . . the non-disclosure of information which ought to have been disclosed because it was relevant, in the sense there was a reasonable possibility it could assist the accused in making full answer and defence, will not amount to a violation of the accused's section 7 right not to be deprived of liberty except in accordance with the principles of fundamental justice unless the accused establishes that the non-disclosure has probably prejudiced or had an adverse effect on his or her ability to make full answer and defence.[30]

However, the majority in *Carosella* reached the opposite conclusion on both issues. They concluded that breach of the obligation to disclose "is a breach of the accused's constitutional rights without the requirement of an additional showing of prejudice . . . the breach of this principle of fundamental justice is in itself prejudicial."[31] In the particular circumstances in *Carosella* it followed that "if the material which was destroyed meets the threshold test for disclosure or production, the appellant's *Charter* rights were breached without the requirement of showing additional prejudice."[32]

However, prejudice would remain relevant at the stage of determining remedy on this analysis. Remedies range, the court notes, from adjournments to a stay of proceedings.[33] In *Carosella*, while reaffirming the principle that a stay should only be granted in the clearest of cases, the majority concluded that it was the appropriate remedy. In general, stays can be justified on either of two bases: (i) where prejudice to the accused cannot be remedied, or (ii) where there would be irreparable prejudice to the integrity of the justice system if the prosecution were continued.[34] The majority concluded that both tests were met in this case. First, the Court noted the significance of the evidence destroyed, the trial judge's conclusion that it "would more than likely have assisted the accused in his defence,"[35] and the absence of any alternative remedy to cure this prejudice. Alternatively, the majority concluded, a stay could be justified because of the deliberate decision of an agency

---

30 *O'Connor, ibid.*
31 *Carosella*, above note 23 at para. 37.
32 *Ibid.* at para. 40.
33 *Ibid.* at para. 26. Other cases have found that costs can be an appropriate remedy: see for example *R. v. Lee*, [1996] O.J. No. 1276 (Gen. Div.); *R. v. S.V.L.*, [1995] O.J. No. 2867 (Prov. Div.); *R. v. Dix*, [1998] A.J. No. 419 (Q.B.).
34 *Carosella, ibid.* at para. 51, quoting from *O'Connor*, above note 28.
35 *Carosella, ibid.* at para. 53, quoting the trial judge.

that receives government funds to destroy documents ("conduct designed to defeat the processes of the court").[36]

Carosella was a much discussed decision and many people felt that the Court's obvious annoyance at the rape crisis centre's policy affected its reasoning too greatly.[37] It certainly is not clear that later decisions are easily reconciled with Carosella, but at the same time the Court has continued to frame the discussion in the terms set out there.

b) The Later Position: Remedy for Failure of Full Answer and Defence

La,[38] decided only shortly after Carosella, reaffirms the principle that disclosure is an independent right guaranteed by section 7, not merely an aspect of the right to full answer and defence. However, in its actual result, it diminishes the significance of that principle.

In La, a police officer tape recorded an interview with the complainant in a sexual assault case at a time prior to any charges being laid. The complainant was a thirteen year-old runaway, and the interview was conducted in connection with a secure treatment application. By the time the accused came to trial, the police officer had lost the forty-five minute tape, though he did testify that the complainant told a few lies on it. The trial judge held that the non-disclosure of the tape impaired the accused's ability to cross-examine the complainant and entered a stay of proceedings. On the face of it, the argument for a stay appears to be at least as strong as in Carosella. The accused did not receive disclosure, which alone constitutes a violation of section 7 without a showing of prejudice. The argument for prejudice is stronger here, in any case, since the evidence was actually a tape recording of the complainant herself, and it was known that she had lied in the interview. In Carosella, in contrast, the missing material was only another person's notes, and the complainant had consented to their production of the missing material and indeed was upset that they had been destroyed. There was less reason in Carosella to think that the missing material was actually of any use to the accused.

Nonetheless, what the majority actually found in La was that the accused's section 7 right was not violated at all. Despite best efforts on the part of the police, the Court found that evidence will sometimes be

---

36   Ibid. at para. 56.
37   See Mitchell, above note 29; David Paciocco, "In Defence of R. v. Carosella: The Continuing Need for Prejudice" (1997) 4 C.R. (5th) 199; Stephen G. Coughlan, "Developments in Criminal Procedure: the 1996–97 Term" (1998) 9 Sup. Ct. L. Rev. (2d) 273.
38   Above note 24.

lost. Where the Crown can show that the evidence was not lost due to unacceptable negligence, the majority stated, the duty to disclose is not breached. It will still be possible for the accused's right to full answer and defence to be breached. However, this will only be the case if the accused can establish actual prejudice.[39] In this particular case, the majority held that the tape was relevant enough to meet the standard for disclosure in *Stinchcombe*, but fell short of establishing a serious impairment of the right to make full answer and defence.[40]

In practical terms, this removes much of the effect of the finding in *Carosella* that disclosure is a right in itself. The major significance of that finding was that it removed the need for the accused to show prejudice in order to show a *Charter* breach. But if there is no breach of that right where the Crown can satisfactorily explain the failure to disclose, then breach of the right to disclosure itself becomes less important. In many cases, given *La*, the accused will have to show a breach of the right to full answer and defence, and so will need to show some prejudice from the non-disclosure.

This pulling away from the standard in *Carosella* can be seen clearly in *Dixon* and its companion cases.[41] Those cases arise from a set of complex facts, in which a number of accused were charged with assault in circumstances where there were many witnesses and many different accounts of what had occurred. None of the defence counsel had received copies of statements from four witnesses, though the pre-trial disclosure they had received included other information from which one could infer that these four people were potential witnesses. During the trial several of the defence counsel became aware of the undisclosed statements, but decided, based on summaries, not to request copies of the statements themselves. Only after the trial was over did the defence counsel review the statements. Although two of the statements contained nothing relevant, the other two contained information which, while not of enormous significance, met the *Stinchcombe* threshold and should have been disclosed. The Court was therefore faced with a slightly new twist from that of *Carosella* or *La*. In those cases, it was known during the trial that there was undisclosed information. In *Dixon*, the failure to disclose did not become apparent until after the trial. This difference in timing is relevant both to whether there is a *Charter* breach and to the remedy to be granted. The case is

---

39 *Ibid.* at para. 25.
40 *Ibid.* at para. 33.
41 *Dixon*, above note 6; *R. v. McQuaid*, [1998] 1 S.C.R. 285; *R. v. Robart*, [1998] 1 S.C.R. 279; *R. v. Smith*, [1998] 1 S.C.R. 291 [*Smith*]; *R. v. Skinner*, [1998] 1 S.C.R. 298 [*Skinner*].

therefore interesting both for how it shows the Court coping with the role of prejudice and for its approach to a remedy.

In *Carosella*, the Court held that disclosure was an independent right guaranteed by section 7, and that prejudice was not relevant to whether that right had been breached—prejudice was only relevant at the remedy stage. Thus, in *Carosella*, the Court moved directly to determining a remedy after deciding the right to disclosure was breached. In *Dixon* the Court, in large measure, undid the main effects of having made disclosure an independent right. The Court held that

> the right to disclosure is but one component of the right to make full answer and defence. Although the right to disclosure may be violated, the right to make full answer and defence may not be impaired as a result of that violation.[42]

Most recently in *Taillefer*, without adverting to the previous dispute over the issue, the Court held that

> Infringement of that right [disclosure] is not always an infringement of the right to make full answer and defence. There are situations in which the information not disclosed will meet the minimum test set out in *Stinchcombe* while having only marginal value to the issues at trial. To determine whether there is an infringement of the right to make full answer and defence, the accused will have to show that there was a reasonable possibility that the failure to disclose affected the outcome at trial or the overall fairness of the trial process.[43]

In each of these latter two cases, it was only after finding a breach of the right to full answer and defence that the Court considered remedy. Thus, the Court has changed the approach in *Carosella* to a three-part test: (1) Was the accused's right to disclosure breached? (2) If so, did that breach violate the accused's right to make full answer and defence? and (3) If so, what remedy should be granted? Given this approach, it remains literally true, as stated in *Carosella*, that disclosure is an independent right and that it is not necessary to show prejudice to establish a breach of that right. However, as no consequences will attach to a breach of the right to disclosure alone, then in this context the major consequences of those findings will have disappeared.

Dixon does not change the *Stinchcombe* standard for disclosure, and so the first question incorporates those rules. To decide whether the breach of disclosure affected full answer and defence, the Court said

---

42   *Dixon, ibid.* at para. 31.
43   *Taillefer*, above note 4 at para. 71 (references omitted).

that the accused must show that there is a reasonable possibility the non-disclosure affected the outcome at trial or the overall fairness of the trial process.[44] This standard will be met where there is either (1) a reasonable possibility that the evidence would have affected the decision to convict, or (2) a reasonable possibility that lines of inquiry with witnesses or opportunities to gather further evidence exist, which would have been available if the evidence had been disclosed.[45] This second set of factors is described as the "fairness of the trial process."

In assessing whether undisclosed evidence could have affected the decision to convict, a court must look at the evidence as a whole and not at each undisclosed piece of information individually.[46] In *Dixon*, the Court decided that although the statements were relevant, they contained only relatively insignificant inconsistencies that could not affect the decision to convict. In *Smith*, in contrast, there was a reasonable possibility that one of the statements could have affected the outcome, since the witness said that he did not see Smith hit anyone. The Court therefore ordered a new trial. Similarly, in *Taillefer* the defence could have used undisclosed evidence to challenge the credibility of important Crown witnesses, or to have presented an alternative theory about how the crime was committed.

With regard to the fairness of the trial process, the Court stressed in *Taillefer* that the standard is only that of "reasonable possibility." That is, a judge should not try to assess the evidence and decide whether it actually would have affected a jury's deliberations. It is sufficient that there be a reasonable possibility it would have done so for the fairness of the trial process to be affected.

The most significant factor discussed in *Dixon* and its companion cases is due diligence on the part of defence counsel.[47] Defence counsel knew or should have known, the Court said, of the possible undisclosed evidence. Upon becoming aware of the statements, the Court said, it is surprising that defence counsel did not request them. They conclude that

---

44   *Dixon*, above note 6 at para. 34. See also *Taillefer, ibid.*

45   *Dixon, ibid* at para. 36.

46   *Taillefer*, above note 4 at para. 92*ff.*

47   This is also an area in which the law surrounding disclosure is unsettled. On the one hand, as noted in *Smith*, above note 41, the Court took a statement in which the witness said he did not see the accused hit anyone to be relevant to the first test, whether the non-disclosure affected the outcome. On the other hand, in *Skinner*, above note 41, the Court took a similar non-disclosure to justify a new trial based on the second test, that the fairness of the trial process was affected.

defence counsel is not entitled to assume at any point that all relevant information has been disclosed to the defence. Just as the Crown's disclosure obligations are ongoing, and persist throughout the trial process, so too does defence counsel's obligation to be duly diligent in pursuing disclosure.[48]

More simply, at a certain point defence counsel was faced with a choice: "call for the statements or live without them."[49]

One must consider some aspects of the rules on disclosure to not have been authoritatively stated yet. *Carosella*, *La*, *Dixon*, and *Taillefer* are not entirely consistent with one another, though a general consensus appears by confining *Carosella* largely to its own facts. Still, there are significant factual differences between the cases. In *Carosella*, the undisclosed evidence was requested by defence counsel before the trial began and it was impossible to disclose it. In *Dixon*, on the other hand, the *Charter* claim was not advanced until the appeal and it concerned evidence that the Crown would readily have disclosed had it been requested earlier. In *Taillefer*, the non-disclosure was not discovered until years later, and not until after one accused had served eight years of a sentence following a guilty plea. *Dixon's* three-part test is stated as applying to situations where the non-disclosure is only raised after trial. Where the accused requests a remedy prior to that, an order for disclosure or an adjournment might be a sufficient remedy.[50] In that way, the right to a fair trial will be protected in advance, not remedied after the fact.

However, even in this context the differing cases leave room for dispute about the correct approach. In *Carosella* and *La* the complaint about non-disclosure arose at an early stage, but nonetheless the evidence could not be disclosed. The spirit of the reasoning in *Dixon* should be equally applicable to that situation, but it is inconsistent with the actual approach in *Carosella*. This situation will need to be resolved.

Further, *Dixon's* introduction of a duty of due diligence on the part of the accused in obtaining disclosure creates scope for much variation in individual cases. Whether a particular failure of disclosure is to be laid at the feet of the Crown or the defence is likely to be hotly disputed in many cases, the Court will need to clarify these rules further.[51]

---

48 *Dixon*, above note 6 at para. 55.
49 *Ibid.*
50 *Ibid.* at para. 31.
51 See also Graeme G. Mitchell, "*R. v. Dixon*: The Right to Crown Disclosure — A Roadmap for the Future" (1998) 13 C.R. (5th) 260.

C. CONFLICTING PROTECTIONS: DISCLOSURE AND PRIVILEGED INFORMATION

The final point worth discussing in relation to disclosure is its inter-action with the laws of privilege. Because the obligation to disclose is not absolute, "the Crown may justify non-disclosure in circumstances where 'the public interest in non-disclosure outweighs the accused's interest in disclosure.'"[52] Indeed, in *Stinchcombe* the Court stated that the right to disclosure was subject to the rules of privilege. In particular, noteworthy cases have considered informer privilege, solicitor client privilege, and privilege in counselling records.[53]

1) Informer Privilege

Informer privilege is a longstanding common law rule, reiterated by the Court in *Bisaillon v. Keable*.[54] The identity of police informers is entitled to the highest level of protection, not only to protect the individuals concerned, but also to preserve that investigative method. If those with confidential information about crimes were not confident that their identities would be protected, they would be far less likely to report that information to the police. This type of privilege was described as being unlike, for example, Crown privilege, in which the court could decide in the individual case whether it was more important to protect the privilege or the integrity of the trial. The rule gives a trial judge

> no power of weighing or evaluating various aspects of the public in-terest which are in conflict, since it has already resolved the con-flict itself. It has decided once and for all, subject to the law being changed, that information regarding police informers' identity will be, because of its content, a class of information which it is in the public interest to keep secret, and that this interest will prevail over the need to ensure the highest possible standard of justice.[55]

---

52   *Michaud v. Quebec (Attorney General)*, [1996] 3 S.C.R. 3 at para. 47, quoting from *Durette*, above note 20.

53   For a discussion of other potential claims of privilege and their possible impact on an accused's right to disclosure, see Ian Carter, "Chipping Away at *Stinchcombe*: The Expanding Privilege Exception to Disclosure" (2002) 50 C.R. (5th) 332.

54   *Bisaillon v. Keable*, [1983] 2 S.C.R. 60 [*Bisaillon*]. Most recently the Court has stated again the importance of this privilege in *Named Person v. Vancouver Sun*, 2007 SCC 43, in the context of discussing its interaction with the open court principle.

55   *Bisaillon*, *ibid.* at 98.

At common law, the only derogation from the rule of informer privilege was the "innocence at stake exception." Only if the evidence establishes a basis for this exception, such as that "the informer is a material witness to the crime, acted as an *agent provocateur*,"[56] or planted the material found under a search warrant,[57] will identifying information be revealed.[58]

In *Leipert*, the Court concluded that this "ancient and hallowed" common law rule was unchanged by the obligation of disclosure established in *Stinchcombe*.[59] *Stinchcombe* had held that disclosure was subject to privilege, and the Court found no inconsistency between that rule and the common law rule of informer privilege.[60]

Indeed, the Court reaffirmed the importance of the common law rule, stressing its particular application in the case of anonymous informers through programs such as Crimestoppers. The privilege extends not only to the name of the informer, but to any information that may enable identification. However, it is "virtually impossible for the court to know what details may reveal the identity of an anonymous informer."[61] As a result, judges should not attempt to edit a tip sheet and order the edited tip sheet disclosed. Rather, the judge should simply uphold informer privilege and not require any information to be disclosed. Only if the accused can establish some basis to conclude that without the disclosure the accused's innocence is at stake, should the trial judge review the tip sheet and potentially order the disclosure of some portion of it. Even then, the Crown has the choice of staying the proceedings rather than making the disclosure.[62]

2) Solicitor-Client Privilege

Solicitor-client privilege is an equally ancient and hallowed doctrine that has existed at common law for hundreds of years.[63] Protecting as it does the ability of an accused person to gain legal advice in confidence, it has been recognized as occupying a unique position of fundamental

---

56   *R. v. Leipert*, [1997] 1 S.C.R. 281 at para. 22 [*Leipert*].

57   *Ibid.* at para. 26.

58   See the further discussion of the innocence at stake exception in Section C(2), below in this chapter.

59   *Leipert*, above note 56 at para. 9.

60   *Ibid.* at para. 25.

61   *Ibid.* at para. 28.

62   *Ibid.* at para. 33.

63   See, for example, the discussion in *Descôteaux v. Mierzwinski*, [1982] 1 S.C.R. 860; *R. v. Solosky*, [1980] 1 S.C.R. 821.

importance. Indeed, it has been classified as a principle of fundamental justice.[64] However, an accused's right to full answer and defence, of which the right to disclosure is a part, is also a principle of fundamental justice. On occasion, it may be necessary for an accused to infringe another person's solicitor-client privilege in order to make full answer and defence. Neither principle will always prevail, and, therefore, in certain circumstances solicitor-client privilege will be required to give way.[65] Because of the importance of the privilege, though, that should only occur in limited, defined circumstances. The Court concluded in *McClure* that, just as with informer privilege, the obligation to disclose[66] arises only when the accused's innocence is at stake.

> The *McClure* test comprises a threshold question and a two-stage innocence at stake test, which proceed as follows:
>
> • To satisfy the threshold test, the accused must establish that:
>   – the information he seeks from the solicitor-client communication is not available from any other source; and
>   – he is otherwise unable to raise a reasonable doubt.
> • If the threshold has been satisfied, the judge should proceed to the innocence at stake test, which has two stages.
>   – Stage #1: The accused seeking production of the solicitor-client communication has to demonstrate an evidentiary basis to conclude that a communication exists that could raise a reasonable doubt as to his guilt.
>   – Stage #2: If such an evidentiary basis exists, the trial judge should examine the communication to determine whether, in fact, it is likely to raise a reasonable doubt as to the guilt of the accused.[67]

In dealing with the threshold test, the Court has generally adopted a stringent position, as is consistent with protecting solicitor-client privilege as much as possible. The initial question asks whether the information is available *in an admissible form* from some other source. If it is not, the test could effectively never be met (if the accused did not know in some fashion that potentially useful evidence existed in a solicitor's file, no application would ever be made).[68] However, it must

---

64   *R. v. McClure*, [2001] 1 S.C.R. 445 at para. 41 [*McClure*].
65   *Ibid*. at para. 38.
66   Strictly, this will be a question of *production* of evidence from a third party, not *disclosure* of evidence in the hands of the Crown.
67   *R. v. Brown*, 2002 SCC 32 at para. 4 [*Brown*].
68   Layton points out that in most instances the only people that are, in fact, likely to know of potentially exculpatory information protected by solicitor-client

be clear that the other sources of information are not merely potentially inadmissible but genuinely unavailable. Thus, for example, if there is an issue as to whether other evidence may not be available because it is hearsay, a trial judge should first determine whether that evidence falls into any of the hearsay exceptions. The *McClure* application should only be considered after it has been decided that the other evidence is definitely unavailable.[69] If there is a possibility that the third party has effectively waived solicitor client privilege, then that too should be decided first.[70] A *McClure* application is intended to be a last resort.

The accused must also be unable to prove innocence in any other way. Once again, this means that all sources of evidence against the accused must be decided first. A case based entirely on circumstantial evidence is the least likely to succeed, and so infringement of solicitor-client privilege is less likely to be needed. But, if the Crown might strengthen its case by calling a jailhouse informant to report an alleged confession by the accused, the privileged information might be more needed, and so the Crown should make that decision before the *McClure* application.[71]

Whether the accused can prove innocence in any other way also affects the appropriate timing for a *McClure* application. Usually a trial judge should postpone the application at least until the Crown has closed its case. If the Crown has not proven its case beyond a reasonable doubt at that stage, the *McClure* application is unnecessary. Even then the trial judge may postpone the application further until the defence has presented its case, to see whether a reasonable doubt has arisen in some other way. Further, a *McClure* application can be renewed at a later stage of the trial if the defence feels it is then clearer that the accused has no other way to prove innocence.[72]

The first step in the innocence at stake test only requires the accused to provide an evidentiary basis that a communication exists that *could* raise a reasonable doubt. Mere speculation that such evidence may exist will not suffice, since the test is not meant to authorize fishing expeditions. However, the standard cannot be too high, since the accused is unlikely to have very precise information about the com-

---

privilege are the other solicitor and client. See David Layton, "*R. v. Brown*: Protecting Legal-Professional Privilege" (2002) 50 C.R. (5th) 37 for a discussion of voluntary release of privileged information by a lawyer.

69   *Brown*, above note 67 at paras. 44–45.

70   *Ibid.* at para. 45.

71   *Ibid.* at para. 50.

72   *Ibid.* at paras. 52–54.

munication.[73] If the evidence suggested to exist merely challenges credibility or raises a collateral matter, it is unlikely to pass this part of the threshold test.

Where the first stage is passed, the trial judge should examine the record to determine whether there is useful evidence in it. At this stage, the higher standard, that the evidence *is likely to raise* a reasonable doubt about the accused's guilt, is applied:

> In most cases, this means that, unless the solicitor-client communication goes directly to one of the elements of the offence, it will not be sufficient to meet this requirement. Simply providing evidence that advances ancillary attacks on the Crown's case (e.g., by impugning the credibility of a Crown witness, or by providing evidence that suggests that some Crown evidence was obtained unconstitutionally) will very seldom be sufficient to meet this requirement.[74]

Nonetheless, the trial judge is not asking whether the evidence *will* raise a reasonable doubt, but merely whether it is likely to.[75]

In determining this question, the trial judge is not limited to the written materials in the file — the same principles govern solicitor-client communications whether they are oral or in writing. Accordingly, it is open to the trial judge to request that the solicitor providing the file also supply an affidavit stating that the file is a complete record or contains all other information necessary to complete the record.[76]

Evidence should not be disclosed from the file simply because it will strengthen the accused's case or it is more likely to be believed than other evidence. It cannot be released to corroborate other evidence the accused has led. The solicitor's file must be the *only way* for the accused to prove innocence.[77]

In deciding what information to disclose from the file, the trial judge should be similarly circumspect. The file should be edited to remove reference to any other offences or to other third parties, and only the information actually necessary to raise a reasonable doubt should

---

73 *McClure*, above note 64 at para. 52.

74 *Ibid.* at para. 58. Layton is critical of this aspect of the Court's decision, arguing that, although described as the "innocence at stake" exception, the real issue is whether reasonable doubt is at stake. Therefore, information going to a witness's credibility, to admissibility of evidence, or to a stay application could be regarded as equally worthy of disclosure. See David Layton, "*R. v. McClure*: The Privilege on the Pea" (2001) 40 C.R. (5th) 19 [Layton].

75 *McLure, ibid.* at para. 59.

76 *Brown*, above note 67 at para. 65.

77 *Ibid.* at para 72.

be released.[78] Further, the information is to be released only to the accused, not to the Crown.[79] Finally, the person whose privilege is being infringed will enjoy use and derivative use immunity concerning the information released.[80]

3) Counselling Records

The most controversial area in which the Court has dealt with disclosure is in the context of an accused's right to see psychiatric, medical, or other counselling records regarding a complainant, particularly complainants in a sexual assault trial.[81] This situation differs from disclosure of other privileged documents in several noteworthy ways.

First, the type of privilege concerned is not a "class privilege," as informer privilege and solicitor-client privilege are. Although a complainant has a privacy interest in counselling records, they are not automatically subject to the same kind of "blanket" protection. Rather, any claim of privilege was originally based on a case-by-case analysis according to the Wigmore test for privilege.[82] The right to disclosure automatically yields to a class privilege, while individual analysis and the weighing of interests is necessary when dealing with case-by-case privilege.

A second way in which this area differs from the previous is that it has been the subject of legislative action by Parliament—claims by an accused for access to such records are now governed by sections 278.1 to 278.91 of the *Criminal Code*.

---

78   *Ibid.* at para. 77.
79   *Ibid.* at para. 84.
80   *Ibid.* at para. 99.
81   A great deal has been written on the decisions handed down on this subject. See, for example, Lise Gotell, "The Ideal Victim, the Hysterical Complainant and the Disclosure of Confidential Records: A Case Study of the Implications of the *Charter* for Sexual Assault Law" (2002) 40 Osgoode Hall L.J. 251 [Gotell]; Jamie Cameron, "Dialogue and Hierarchy in *Charter* Interpretation: A Comment on *R. v. Mills*," (2001) 38 Alta. L. Rev. 1051; Lise Gotell, "Colonization Through Disclosure: Confidential Records, Sexual Assault Complainants and Canadian Law" (2001) 10 Soc. & Leg. Stud. 315; Karen Busby, "Third Party Records Cases Since *R. v. O'Connor*" (2000) 27 Man. L.J. 355; Peter Sankoff, "Crown Disclosure after *Mills*: Have the Rules Suddenly Changed?" (2000) 28 C.R. (5th) 285; Don Stuart, "*Mills*: Dialogue with Parliament and Equality by Assertion at What Cost?" (2000) 28 C.R. (5th) 275; Karen Busby, "Discriminatory Uses of Personal Records in Sexual Violence Cases" (1997) 9 C.J.W.L. 148; Heather Holmes, "An Analysis of Bill C-46, Production of Records in Sexual Offence Proceedings" (1997) 2 Can. Crim. L. Rev. 71; Bruce Feldthusen, "Access to the Private Therapeutic Records of Sexual Assault Complainants" (1996) 75 Can. Bar Rev. 537.
82   *McClure*, above note 64 at para. 29.

Finally, this area differs because most frequently the records will not be in the hands of the Crown, but will still rest with the psychiatrist, doctor, or counsellor. Most commonly, what will actually be at issue is "production," (the handing over of documents in a third party's hands), not "disclosure" (the handing over of documents in the hands of the Crown). Different considerations arise in cases of production, including the accused's greater interest of privacy, the fact that third parties have no obligation to assist the defence, and that the records are not part of the case the accused has to meet. All of these factors mean that the accused faces a higher burden than normal in obtaining access to this material, though not as high a burden as when a class privilege is in issue.[83]

The controversy over this area of law is reflected in the Court's decision in *O'Connor*, the legislative response to that decision, and *R. v. Mills*,[84] the Court's decision on a *Charter* challenge to the legislation. To properly understand the current situation, however, it is not sufficient to look merely at the "last word" — it is necessary to begin with *O'Connor*.

In *O'Connor*, the accused was charged with several counts of sexual assault. He obtained a pre-trial order for disclosure of the complainants' entire medical, counselling, and school records. When the accused was unsuccessful in obtaining all these records, the trial judge entered a stay, eventually leading the Supreme Court to consider the question of the procedure to be applied when an accused seeks documents such as counselling records in the hands of a third party.

The Court created a two stage process for deciding whether third-party records should be produced. At the first stage, the accused must persuade the judge to examine the record personally. At the second stage, having looked at the records, the judge is required to decide whether to release it or some portions of it to the accused. Most of the controversy has related to what factors should guide the decision at each stage.

A majority of five judges held that at the first stage, it was necessary to consider not just the accused's right to make full answer and defence, but also to weigh the third party's privacy interests in the

---

83   Layton observes that the number of standards applicable to third-party production is "ever-growing": simple materiality in many cases; the *O'Connor* test where constitutionally protected privacy interests are at stake; ss. 278.1–278.91 where those interests arise in the context of a sexual assault trial; and the "innocence at stake" standard of informer privilege and solicitor-client privilege. See Layton, above note 74.

84   [1999] 3 S.C.R. 668 [*Mills*].

balance.[85] The accused must show that the records are likely relevant. However, "likely relevance" is this context is a higher standard than the normal question of whether the information may be useful to the defence. Rather, the accused must satisfy the trial judge "that there is a reasonable possibility that the information is logically probative to *an issue at trial or the competence of a witness to testify*."[86] While this is a higher standard than normal, it is not to be interpreted as an onerous one, since the accused will have to make submissions to the judge without knowing what is in the record.[87] The majority suggested that evidence in counselling records may be relevant by containing information about the events underlying the charge, by revealing the use of a therapy influencing the complainant's memory of the events, or by bearing on the complainant's credibility.

The majority specifically rejected the minority's suggestion that at the first stage, in addition to showing likely relevance, the accused should also have to satisfy the trial judge that the salutary effects of producing the documents outweighs the deleterious effects. That question, according to the majority, is confined to the second stage.[88]

At the second stage, where the trial judge decides whether to order any portion of the record produced, all the judges agreed that a number of factors were relevant to the decision:

> (1) the extent to which the record is necessary for the accused to make full answer and defence; (2) the probative value of the record in question; (3) the nature and extent of the reasonable expectation of privacy vested in that record; (4) whether production of the record would be premised upon any discriminatory belief or bias [and] (5) the potential prejudice to the complainant's dignity, privacy or security of the person that would be occasioned by production of the record in question.[89]

Four of the nine judges, however, unsuccessfully argued that further factors should be considered:

> "the extent to which production of records of this nature would frustrate society's interest in encouraging the reporting of sexual offences and the acquisition of treatment by victims" as well as "the effect on

---

85 Provided the records were not already in the hands of the Crown. If that were the case, the majority held, the third party would no longer have a privacy interest.

86 *O'Connor*, above note 28 at para. 22 [emphasis in original].

87 *Ibid.* at para. 25.

88 *Ibid.* at para. 21.

89 *Ibid.* at para. 31.

the integrity of the trial process of producing, or failing to produce, the record, having in mind the need to maintain consideration in the outcome."[90]

The majority said that the former consideration was a relevant but not paramount consideration,[91] and that the second consideration was only relevant in deciding admissibility of the evidence, not in deciding whether the material should be produced for the accused.

In response to the *O'Connor* decision, Parliament enacted sections 278.1 to 278.91 of the *Criminal Code*. The exact details of that scheme will be detailed in a moment, but it is worth observing the somewhat complicated assortment of rules that now potentially apply because of this series of judicial and legislative decisions. Material in the hands of the Crown will be dealt with according to the *Stinchcombe* disclosure rules. *O'Connor* created rules for production of records in the hands of third parties, but those have been replaced by a statutory scheme in most but not all instances. As a result, all three sets of rules remain relevant (where records are in the hands of a third party but are not records of the sort listed in section 278.1, the *O'Connor* rules continue to apply).

In any event, it is necessary now to look in detail at the statutory scheme. In essence, those provisions enact the minority decision in *O'Connor*. That is, they follow the same general two-step approach adopted by the majority—indeed, by all judges—in that case, but require the trial judge also to take into account the factors the majority said did not arise. The provisions are broader than the majority decision in *O'Connor*, in the sense that they provide more protection to complainant's interests, in other ways as well.

The majority in *O'Connor*, for example, was primarily concerned with "therapeutic records," which are "intensely private."[92] Even the minority only suggested that other documents, such as school records or private diaries, may also attract a reasonable expectation of privacy,[93] and that this question "is inherently fact- and context-sensitive."[94] The statutory scheme, however, states that

> "record" means any form of record that contains personal information for which there is a reasonable expectation of privacy *and includes, without limiting the generality of the foregoing,* medical,

---

90   *Ibid.* at para. 32.
91   *Ibid.* at para. 33.
92   *Ibid.* at para. 7.
93   See the discussion of reasonable expectation of privacy in Chapter 4.
94   *O'Connor*, above note 28 at para. 99.

psychiatric, therapeutic, counselling, education, employment, child welfare, adoption and social services records, personal journals and diaries, and records containing personal information the production or disclosure of which is protected by any other Act of Parliament or a provincial legislature, but does not include records made by persons responsible for the investigation or prosecution of the offence.[95]

Therefore, the legislative provision appears, in one way, to apply to more records than the *O'Connor* rules would,[96] since *prima facie* any listed third-party record is covered by it, and not merely those found to attract a reasonable expectation of privacy after a fact- and case-sensitive analysis.

Further, the scheme in *O'Connor* was limited to records still in the hands of third parties. Those in the hands of the Crown no longer attracted a reasonable expectation of privacy, the majority said, and therefore were subject to the ordinary *Stinchcombe* rules. The minority expressed no opinion on this issue.[97] Section 278.2(2), however, makes the statutory scheme applicable even to records already in the hands of the Crown, unless the complainant or witness has "expressly waived the application of those sections."

In considering the first stage, section 278.5(2) requires the judge to balance the salutary and deleterious effects of producing the record for the judge's own inspection, as the minority in *O'Connor* wished. In particular, the accused is required not only to show that the record is likely relevant, but also that "the production of the record is necessary in the interests of justice."[98] Further, that section states that the decision at both the first and second stage should be based on the five factors the majority in *O'Connor* said should settle the issue, and that the trial judge "shall take . . . into account" the additional factors the minority held were relevant.

On the face of it, then, the statutory scheme departs from the *O'Connor* rules in a number of ways that were specifically considered and rejected by the majority of the Court. Given that the *O'Connor* rules

---

95   Section 278.1 [emphasis added].

96   Note, however, that s. 278.2 restricts the operation of this scheme to production in the context of prosecutions for various listed offences, all of which are sexual offences of one sort or another. In any other context, it appears that the *O'Connor* rules will still apply. As a practical matter, of course, it appears to have been primarily in the context of sexual offences that such applications have been made.

97   *O'Connor*, above note 28 at para. 98.

98   Section 278.5(1)(c).

were based on the accused's section 7 rights, it was therefore question-able as to whether the statutory scheme violated the *Charter*.

In *Mills*,[99] the trial judge found that the scheme violated an ac-cused's section 7 and section 11(d) rights and struck it down. When the issue reached the Supreme Court, the legislation was upheld. A proper understanding of the current state of the law, however, requires recog-nizing that in *Mills* the Court upheld the statutory scheme by reading it down (without referring to their approach as such[100]) to correspond as closely as possible to the majority decision in *O'Connor*.

In dealing with the statutory scheme's wider list of records cov-ered by the scheme, the Court adopted the position of a lower court.[101] Section 278.1, they conclude, does not mean that every type of record listed attracts a reasonable expectation. Rather, only records of the type listed in which there is *also* a reasonable expectation of privacy will be governed by the scheme. In effect, the fact- and case-sensitive decision from *O'Connor* will still be necessary.[102]

The statutory scheme is also broader than *O'Connor* because it ap-plies to records already in the hands of the Crown. But this will not be the case where the complainant has expressly waived these protections. That is, where a "fully informed complainant expressly waives the pro-tection of the legislation, by declaration or *by voluntarily providing her records to the Crown*."[103] The Court interprets the legislative scheme as simply filling a void left by the *O'Connor* rules (i.e., how to deal with third party records that come into the Crown's hands through a search warrant or similar means), but not as changing the *O'Connor* rules.[104]

The statutory scheme requires the accused, at the first stage, to show that production is necessary in the interests of justice, a consideration motivated by the desire to give greater weight to a complainant's pri-vacy interests. In *Mills*, the Court upheld this requirement by making it secondary to, and indeed in some ways converting it to, concern for the accused's right to make full answer and defence. A judge is required to protect that right of the accused. If it is necessary to examine the

---

99 *Mills*, above note 84.

100 The Court speaks of itself in *Mills*, *ibid.*, as deferring to Parliament, but in its actual approach it is not genuinely deferential: see Steve Coughlan, "Complain-ants' Records after *Mills*: Same As It Ever Was" (2000) 33 C.R. (5th) 300.

101 *R. v. Regan* (1998), 174 N.S.R. (2d) 230 (S.C.).

102 Gotell, above note 81 at 283, indicates that in a number of post-*Mills* cases, lower court judges have ordered production on the basis that the statutory scheme was not applicable to the particular records in question.

103 *Mills*, above note 84 at para. 106 [emphasis added].

104 *Ibid.* at para. 109.

documents to see whether they should be produced to the accused, then production to the judge is necessary in the interests of justice.[105] The accused must have access to all documents that might be constitutionally required: "a production regime that denied this would not be production 'necessary in the interests of justice.'"[106] "Read correctly," this requirement is constitutional.[107]

Finally, the legislative scheme requires that the judge shall take into account at both stages the factors that *O'Connor* said were not to be considered at all, or were only to be considered at the second stage. The Court minimizes the practical effect of these changes by finding that the addition of these factors to the legislative scheme does not necessarily make any difference:

> s. 278.5(2) does not require that the judge engage in a conclusive and in-depth evaluation of each of the factors. It rather requires the judge to "take them into account" — to the extent possible at this early stage of proceedings — in deciding whether to order a particular record produced to himself or herself for inspection. Section 278.5(2) serves as a check-list of the various factors that *may* come into play in making the decision regarding production to the judge.[108]

The Court makes clear that the accused's right to full answer and defence is not to be compromised by this change:

> Therefore, while the s. 278.5(2) factors are relevant, in the final analysis the judge is free to make whatever order is "necessary in the interests of justice" — a mandate that includes all of the applicable "principles of fundamental justice" at stake.[109]

In practical terms, it appears that *Mills* has resulted in some, but not dramatic, change. There are indications that because of the standard set in *Mills*, lower court judges decide less frequently that records meet the likely relevance standard, for example, and so do not examine the records personally.[110] However, this does not automatically mean that there is less production of records to accused in the end, rather it may simply be the case that records that would not ultimately have been disclosed are filtered out at an earlier stage. Further, the type of

---

105 *Ibid*. at para. 132.
106 *Ibid*. at para. 130. See Gotell, above note 81 at 286n: this aspect of the *Mills* reasoning has been frequently cited by lower courts as justification for production.
107 *Mills*, *ibid*. at para. 133.
108 *Ibid*. at para. 134 [emphasis added].
109 *Ibid*.
110 Gotell, above note 81.

analysis that is undertaken seems not to have changed dramatically. *Mills* itself asserts the relevance of the complainant's privacy *and* equality rights, and the legislative scheme includes factors intended to reflect broader societal interests.[111] However, very few later cases have considered any interests other than privacy.[112] Note as well that the statutory scheme has been held to apply even when third-party records are first sought as fresh evidence on appeal.[113]

The final word on production of third-party records, then, is found in *Mills'* upholding of the statutory scheme in sections 278.1 to 278.91. Proper understanding of that scheme, however, depends on understanding the prior decision in *O'Connor*, since *Mills* did *not* intend to "shift the balance away from the *primary* emphasis on the rights of the accused."[114]

FURTHER READINGS

BUSBY, KAREN, "Discriminatory Uses of Personal Records in Sexual Violence Cases" (1997) 9 C.J.W.L. 148

BUSBY, KAREN, "Third Party Records Cases Since *R. v. O'Connor*" (2000) 27 Man. L.J. 355

PAUL CALARCO, "WHAT HAPPENS WHEN EVIDENCE HAS NOT BEEN RECORDED? STAYING CHARGES TO ENSURE A FAIR TRIAL" (2001) 44 CRIM. L.Q. 514

CAMERON, JAMIE, "Dialogue and Hierarchy in *Charter* Interpretation: A Comment on *R. v. Mills*" (2001) 38 Alta. L. Rev. 1051

CARTER, IAN, "Chipping Away at *Stinchcombe*: The Expanding Privilege Exception to Disclosure" (2002) 50 C.R. (5th) 332

COUGHLAN, STEVE, "Complainants' Records after *Mills*: Same as It Ever Was" (2000) 33 C.R. (5th) 300

COUGHLAN, STEPHEN G., "Developments in Criminal Procedure: the 1996–97 Term" (1998) 9 Sup. Ct. L. Rev. (2d) 273

---

111 See, for example, s. 278.5(2) of the *Code*, including "society's interest in encouraging the reporting of sexual offences."
112 Gotell, above note 81.
113 *R. v. Rodgers* (2000), 144 C.C.C. (3d) 568 (Ont. C.A.).
114 *R. v. Shearing*, 2002 SCC 58 at para. 132 [emphasis in original].

FELDTHUSEN, BRUCE, "Access to the Private Therapeutic Records of Sexual Assault Complainants" (1996) 75 Can. Bar Rev. 537

GOTELL, LISE, "Colonization Through Disclosure: Confidential Records, Sexual Assault Complainants and Canadian Law" (2001) 10 Soc. & Leg. Stud. 315

GOTELL, LISE, "The Ideal Victim, the Hysterical Complainant and the Disclosure of Confidential Records: A Case Study of the Implications of the *Charter* for Sexual Assault Law" (2002) 40 Osgoode Hall L.J. 251

HOLMES, HEATHER, "An Analysis of *Bill C-46*, Production of Records in Sexual Offence Proceedings" (1997) 2 Can. Crim. L. Rev. 71

LAW REFORM COMMISSION OF CANADA, *Disclosure by the Prosecution* (Ottawa: Law Reform Commission of Canada, 1984)

LAYTON, DAVID, "*R. v. Brown*: Protecting Legal-Professional Privilege" (2002) 50 C.R. (5th) 37

LAYTON, DAVID, "*R. v. McClure*: The Privilege on the Pea" (2001) 40 C.R. (5th) 19

MITCHELL, GRAEME, "*R. v. Carosella*: Difficult Cases Make Dangerous Law" (1997) 4 C.R. (5th) 209

MITCHELL, GRAEME G., "*R. v. Dixon*: The Right to Crown Disclosure — A Roadmap for the Future" (1998) 13 C.R. (5th) 260

PACIOCCO, DAVID, "In Defence of *R. v. Carosella*: The Continuing Need for Prejudice" (1997) 4 C.R. (5th) 199

QUIGLEY, TIM, *Procedure in Canadian Criminal Law*, 2d ed., looseleaf (Toronto: Thomson Carswell, 2005) c. 12

SANKOFF, PETER, "Crown Disclosure after *Mills*: Have the Rules Suddenly Changed?" (2000) 28 C.R. (5th) 285

STUART, DON, *Charter Justice in Canadian Criminal Law*, 4th ed. (Toronto: Thomson Carswell, 2005) c. 2

STUART, DON, "*Mills*: Dialogue with Parliament and Equality by Assertion at What Cost?" (2000) 28 C.R. (5th) 285

CHAPTER 9

PRELIMINARY INQUIRY

A. INTRODUCTION

Before an accused is tried on an indictable offence, a preliminary inquiry may be conducted by a justice,[1] at the request of the prosecution or the accused, unless the offence within the absolute jurisdiction of the provincial court judge.[2] This entitlement can be overridden if the attorney general elects to proceed by way of a direct indictment, pursuant to section 577 of the *Criminal Code*, which has the effect of putting an indictment immediately before the court of trial.[3] There is no en-

---

1 A "justice" is defined in s. 2 of the *Code* to mean either a justice of the peace or a judge of the provincial court. In virtually all jurisdictions of Canada, a preliminary inquiry is held by a provincial court judge.

2 See ss. 535, 536(4), and 536.1(3). Offences within the absolute jurisdiction of the provincial court are listed in s. 553. If the accused elects trial in a provincial court before a preliminary inquiry has been held, he waives the right to a preliminary inquiry.

3 Conversely, if an accused has elected trial in provincial court, the presiding judge has discretion under s. 555(1) to convert the trial into a preliminary inquiry. If a trial has begun on an indictable property offence within the absolute jurisdiction of the provincial court (s. 553), and evidence discloses that the value involved exceeds $5000.00, the judge must put the accused to his election according to s. 536(2). If the accused then elects trial by judge alone or trial by judge and jury, the proceedings shall continue as a preliminary inquiry unless waived by the accused.

titlement to a preliminary inquiry in summary-conviction matters, nor has a justice any jurisdiction to inquire into such offences.

The nature, scope, and purpose of the preliminary are now in flux, and they are becoming both less interesting and less important as a subject of discussion.[4] In principle, one of their central functions is to serve as a screening mechanism for unmeritorious prosecutions. As a matter of fact, though, most preliminary inquiries result in an accused being committed for trial and, in any event, the Crown has the ability to send the accused to trial despite a discharge, as noted above. Preliminary inquiries also long performed a type of disclosure function, but that need is more directly dealt with by *Charter* decisions requiring the Crown to disclose all relevant evidence to the accused. Further, as noted in Chapter 3, *Charter* remedies are not available at a preliminary inquiry. For a long time preliminary inquiries were frequently waived, and recent legislative changes make them available only on request, and potentially only on some issues, further marginalizing the procedure.

Until 2004 the preliminary inquiry was understood chiefly as a test of the sufficiency of the prosecution's case for trial. The central question was whether the prosecution could produce sufficient evidence on the whole of the case to warrant committal for trial.[5] As of right, the accused was entitled to a preliminary inquiry on the whole of the case and, in principle, it served important functions in screening out unsupportable charges and in providing the accused with a fuller understanding of the case to meet. Unless the accused waived the preliminary inquiry, the prosecution was required as a matter of course to produce sufficient evidence. A secondary function of the inquiry was to afford an opportunity to test the quality of evidence taken from witnesses under oath.[6] Among other advantages, this allowed the parties, especially the defence, to have a record of sworn evidence that could later be used at trial to challenge the credibility of a witness.

Since 2004 amendments to the *Code* have altered the nature of the preliminary inquiry and it can no longer be said that its primary func-

---

4   See David Paciocco, "A Voyage of Discovery: Examining the Precarious Condition of the Preliminary Inquiry" (2003) 48 Crim. L.Q. 151.

5   See, for example, *R. v. Hynes*, [2001] 3 S.C.R. 623 [*Hynes*]. Evidence "on the whole of the case" means evidence on each element of an offence. It does not mean that the prosecution must tender all of the evidence that it can produce at trial: *Caccamo v. The Queen*, [1976] 1 S.C.R. 786. Committal for trial can be ordered only if the evidence at the preliminary inquiry is sufficient in the sense that a jury, properly instructed, can find the accused guilty beyond reasonable doubt: *United States of America. v. Shephard*, [1977] 2 S.C.R. 1067 [*Shephard*] (discussed in Section D, below in this chapter).

6   *R. v. Skogman*, [1984] 2 S.C.R. 93 at 105 [*Skogman*].

tion is to test the sufficiency of the prosecution case as a whole.[7] The central feature of those amendments is that a preliminary inquiry will be held only upon the request of a party. That party will almost always be the accused, but a request can be made by the prosecutor. In the absence of a request the accused will simply be committed to stand trial on a date fixed by the court.[8] Nothing in Part XVIII specifically allows a justice to refuse a request for a preliminary inquiry,[9] but this does not imply that a full preliminary inquiry will be held if one is requested. Further, where a request is made, the inquiry will be conducted only with regard to issues and witnesses that are specified in advance.[10] It is contemplated that these points can and should be agreed upon between the parties, and the justice can order a hearing to encourage the parties to reach such agreement.[11] If there is an agreement of this nature, the *Code* provides that the justice may commit the accused without recording evidence on any other issues in the case.[12] The inquiry is thus no longer a test of the prosecution case as a whole because the sufficiency of the prosecution case is assumed, subject to any exception covered by a request. As now conceived, the preliminary inquiry is a limited examination of the sufficiency of the prosecution case with regard to specific issues and the evidence of specific witnesses.

It is important to underscore the importance of the amendments that came into force in 2004. The changes are partly justified by extensive disclosure of the prosecution case to the accused before plea.[13] Another justification is that, in practice, it has always been open to the defence to make admissions and to waive the right to a full preliminary inquiry in favour of a limited inquiry. A third justification was the growing length, in practice, of cross-examination. A fourth is that the right to a full preliminary inquiry was occasionally abused by counsel who, through lack of experience or judgment, could have waived

---

7   S.C. 2002, c. 13.

8   Section 549.

9   Indeed, a perplexing feature of the procedure for making a request is that the provisions do not require or empower the judge to make a decision on the request or on any attempts to narrow the scope of an inquiry. Thus, it would seem to be an open question as to whether a judge who denies any part of a request would lose jurisdiction. It is arguable that he would. This position is consistent with cases that affirm the right of the accused to call evidence at a preliminary inquiry. See, for example, *R. v. Lena* (2001), 158 C.C.C. (3d) 415 (B.C.C.A.).

10   Section 536.3.

11   Section 536.4. This is now commonly called a "focusing hearing."

12   Sections 536.4, 536.5, and 549.

13   This is the effect of jurisprudence after *R. v. Stinchcombe*, [1991] 3 S.C.R. 326.

the inquiry in whole or in part without prejudice to the accused. The amendments address these considerations.

Nevertheless, the reformulation of the preliminary inquiry as a limited examination of specific issues and witnesses significantly changes the nature of the order for committal. This limitation of the scope of inquiry effectively eliminates any test of the sufficiency of the prosecution case from the decision at the end of the inquiry. If the judge does not receive evidence on the case as a whole, it cannot sensibly be said that the decision to commit for trial is a decision based upon evidence that the whole of the case is sufficient. Where a limited inquiry is held on a specific issue, the decision to commit signifies only that the evidence presented on that issue meets the standard for committal. The plain design of the reformed preliminary inquiry is that a limited inquiry will be the norm. The only exception to this conclusion would be the rare case wherein a judge proceeds, upon request, to conduct a preliminary inquiry on the whole of the case. It would be rare because the party that made such a request would seemingly have to assert that the case disclosed by the prosecution included no evidence on all essential elements of the offence charged.

Thus, it is now accurate to say that the function of the preliminary inquiry is to afford the parties an opportunity upon request to test the evidence of specific witnesses on specific issues in preparation for trial. For all practical purposes the preliminary inquiry as it was known before 2004 has been reformed by Parliament as a limited and focused examination to obtain discovery of evidence under oath. For this reason a strong case can be made that Parliament should undertake a more thorough reform of Part XVIII of the *Criminal Code* to redefine this procedure for what it now is. The purpose of such a reform would be to remove traces of the preliminary inquiry as a genuine test of the sufficiency of the prosecution case as a whole.

B. JURISDICTION

The authority of a justice to conduct a preliminary inquiry is strictly statutory under Part XVIII of the *Code*.[14] This means that there is no inherent jurisdiction and the only powers that may be exercised by the judge are those that are explicitly granted in the *Code* or that are necessarily implicit in those provisions. The only additional authority they

---

14   *R. v. Doyle*, [1977] 1 S.C.R. 597 [*Doyle*]; *R. v. Forsythe*, [1980] 2 S.C.R. 268 [*Forsythe*].

have to expand upon the express powers granted to them is found in section 537(1)(i). It provides that the judge at the preliminary inquiry may regulate the course of the inquiry in any way that appears to be desirable and not inconsistent with any other provision of the *Code*. There is an obvious tension between the traditional view of the judge's jurisdiction at a preliminary inquiry and the scope of this discretion. Clearly, this discretion does not expand the scope of a preliminary inquiry, but it does confer broad authority with regards to the manner in which an inquiry is conducted.

The courts have said repeatedly that the preliminary inquiry justice has only the powers given by Parliament in Part XVIII of the *Code*. Thus, a judge who fails to comply with Part XVIII or who exceeds the authority given by the *Code* acts without jurisdiction and may be subject to review in the superior court.[15] This position was fuelled in some measure by the fact that preliminary inquiries were typically held, many years ago, before magistrates without formal legal training. It was also fuelled more generally by the idea that the provincial court is a statutory tribunal that has only those powers in criminal matters that are specifically accorded to it by Parliament. This approach to the jurisdiction of the provincial court is somewhat antiquated, in part because preliminary inquiries are now routinely held before professional judges in the provincial court, and in part because those same judges are competent to exercise all functions for a proper trial. It is not surprising, therefore, that the powers of the justice at the preliminary inquiry have been expanded. Not only is the justice empowered to regulate the inquiry as appropriate, but she is also now entitled to cajole the parties to limit the scope of the inquiry or to do so herself.

Nonetheless, a judge at a preliminary inquiry has no power to grant any remedy other than those contemplated by the *Code*.[16] The Supreme Court has specifically held that the judge cannot grant a remedy under the *Charter*, including remedies for delay, non-disclosure, or the production of evidence obtained in violation of a constitutional right.[17]

1) Commencement

Section 536 states that an accused who is charged with an indictable offence within the absolute jurisdiction of a provincial court judge shall

---

15   *Skogman*, above note 6; *Forsythe*, *ibid*. See *R. v. Deschamplain*, 2004 SCC 76 [*Deschamplain*] and *R. v. Sazant*, [2004] 3 S.C.R. 635 [*Sazant*] for recent considerations of the scope of jurisdictional error at the preliminary inquiry.

16   *Hynes*, above note 5 at para. 33. See also *R. v. Patterson*, [1970] S.C.R. 409.

17   See the further discussion of this issue below at Section B(5).

be remanded to appear before such a judge for trial within the territorial jurisdiction in which the offence was allegedly committed. For all other indictable offences, the justice has jurisdiction to proceed with a preliminary inquiry or to adjourn the preliminary inquiry to a later date. Almost invariably the matter is adjourned at the first appearance and, indeed, there may be frequent adjournments before the preliminary inquiry actually begins with the presentation of evidence.[18] The central point is that the possibility of having a preliminary inquiry in respect of an indictable offence will depend, first, on the classification of the offence and, second, on the election of the accused as to mode of trial.

There can be variations on the prototypical case in which an inquiry proceeds on a single count, in a single information, against a single accused. It is important to bear in mind that the jurisdiction of the judge at the preliminary inquiry is to examine indictable offences charged by the prosecution or disclosed by the evidence. Thus, even if the judge otherwise has jurisdiction over the offences, he cannot conduct a trial and preliminary inquiry for the same accused simultaneously;[19] nor can he try one accused and at the same time conduct a preliminary inquiry in respect of a co-accused.[20] He can, however, conduct a preliminary inquiry in respect of charges in separate informations simultaneously.[21]

At the first appearance of the accused there is an arraignment, in the sense that the charge or charges will be read to the accused. It is not necessary for a formal plea to be recorded because the justice has the power to adjourn the matter. A formalistic reading of the *Code* suggests that the first appearance is the commencement of the preliminary inquiry.[22] In practice, it marks only a *pro forma* commencement of the inquiry at which the accused submits to the jurisdiction of the court, makes a provisional election as to mode of trial,[23] and sets a subsequent date for the actual commencement of the preliminary inquiry. For practical purposes, little turns on whether the preliminary inquiry formally commences at the first appearance or at a later date, such as the date on which the election is recorded. It is important, however, to note that on any account the judge presiding at the inquiry is seized of the matter as

18 *Re R. and Geszthelyi* (1977), 33 C.C.C. (2d) 543 (B.C.C.A.).
19 *R. v. G.(A.M.)* (2000), 142 C.C.C. (3d) 29 (N.S.C.A.).
20 *R. v. Niedzwieki* (1980), 57 C.C.C. (2d) 184 (B.C.S.C.).
21 *R. v. Rutherford*, [1968] 3 C.C.C. 1 (B.C.S.C.).
22 *Doyle*, above note 14; compare *Re Danchella and the Queen* (1984), 19 C.C.C. (3d) 490 (B.C.C.A.) [*Danchella*].
23 In some jurisdictions, there is not even a provisional recording of an election.

soon as evidence is adduced.[24] Until that time, the accused may appear before several justices or judges on various matters. Once evidence is adduced, though, the preliminary inquiry will continue to its conclusion before the same judge.[25]

2) Scope

The scope of the inquiry is defined by section 535 of the *Code*, which directs the justice or judge to inquire into the charge of any indictable offence or any other indictable offence in respect of the same transaction disclosed by the evidence taken in accordance with Part XVIII. Until 1985, the jurisdiction to inquire was limited to the charge recited in the information or any included charge that might be disclosed by the evidence. Accordingly, the jeopardy of the accused in committal proceedings could be no greater than the charge or charges in the information. On a charge of second-degree murder, for example, the presiding judge had no jurisdiction to commit the accused for trial on a charge of first-degree murder.[26] The *Code* was amended in 1985 to allow the judge to commit the accused for trial on any indictable offence disclosed by the evidence at the preliminary inquiry.[27] This extension of jurisdiction implies that the presiding judge and the accused must be alert throughout the preliminary inquiry to the possibility that offences other than those stated in the information may be disclosed by the evidence. Although, in principle, this may seem like a perilous enterprise, it rarely causes difficulty. Moreover, with the shift to limited inquiries focused on specific issues, it is even less likely to pose problems.

The scope of the preliminary inquiry is thus not strictly limited to the offences as charged in the information. The inquiry can extend to any indictable offence disclosed by the evidence, provided that it arises from the same transaction. "Transaction" in this sense is not coextensive with an offence. It refers to a narrative of conduct that may comprise several acts and may disclose several offences. If the information charges only one indictable offence, for example, but evidence of the transaction at the preliminary inquiry supports more, the judge may commit the accused to trial on all of them. The reference to the same

---

24   *Danchella*, above note 22.

25   Section 547.1 provides that when a justice is unable to continue to receive evidence, another justice may do so, if the record is otherwise complete and available, or hear the case afresh.

26   *R. v. Chabot*, [1980] 2 S.C.R. 985.

27   With regard to the scope of the inquiry, see Patrick Healy, "Chabotage: Expanding the Crown's Power to Prefer Additional Counts" (1984) 38 C.R. (3d) 344.

transaction, however, is meant to limit the jeopardy of the accused at the inquiry to a narrative of conduct that is coherent in time or in some other manner.[28]

There is another sense in which the preliminary inquiry can extend beyond an examination of the sufficiency of the prosecution case on the charges in the information. The *Code* expressly allows the accused to call evidence and this can include exculpatory evidence on a matter of defence.[29] For purposes of committal, however, this evidence will not be assessed by the presiding judge or weighed in favour of the accused, not least because the judge has no jurisdiction to examine the validity of defences.[30] The primary purpose of such defence evidence is to allow the accused the opportunity to test it and to record in preparation for trial. Nothing in the recent amendments alters this.

The preliminary inquiry has also been used as an opportunity to lay an evidentiary foundation for an issue that can only be decided at trial. For example, although a justice has no power to order the production of third-party records at the preliminary inquiry, she may allow the accused to cross-examine the complainant on a range of facts that may later support an application at trial.[31] Similarly, although no remedy can be granted under the *Charter* at the preliminary inquiry, the judge may permit cross-examination of a prosecution witness to lay a basis for a motion under the *Charter* at trial. The judge also has discretion to allow the accused to call defence witnesses on trial matters.[32] All of this is consistent with the right of the accused to make full answer and defence, and with the discovery function of the preliminary inquiry, but, it is also strictly beyond an inquiry into the sufficiency of the prosecution case for committal. There has been no serious challenge to the practice of allowing evidence on trial matters to be presented in examination or cross-examination. It may be asked whether this practice will be affected by the recent amendments. It could be argued that a preliminary inquiry that is limited to specific witnesses and specific issues should also exclude issues that can only be decided at trial.

The preliminary inquiry is rarely an occasion for formal challenges to the validity of charges in the information, and even then the only basis would be that the information fails to charge an indictable offence

---

28   See, for example, *R. v. Goldstein; R. v. Caicedo* (1988), 42 C.C.C. (3d) 548 (Ont. C.A.).
29   Section 541.
30   *Hynes*, above note 5.
31   *R. v. B.(E.)* (2002), 162 C.C.C. (3d) 451 (Ont. C.A.).
32   *R. v. Dawson* (1998), 123 C.C.C. (3d) 385 (Ont. C.A.) [*Dawson*].

known to law.[33] The justice has no authority to question whether the information was properly sworn by inquiring into the grounds of belief asserted by the informant.[34] Further, the judge has no jurisdiction to inquire into any special plea based upon principles of double jeopardy.[35] Thus, the scope of inquiry is circumscribed by the content of the charges in the information and the evidence that is produced. This is only underscored by the application of section 601 to the preliminary inquiry. This provision, which is found among those relating to charges at trial, allows for an application to be made to quash a count that fails to charge a known offence or that is otherwise defective on its face.[36]

Of greater importance, however, is that section 601 also gives the judge broad powers to amend the charges in the information at the preliminary inquiry. Thus, quite apart from the judge's jurisdiction to order committal on any indictable offence disclosed by the evidence at the preliminary inquiry, the judge may also amend the information to ensure that the charges conform with the evidence. Although the judge at the preliminary inquiry has no power to order the prosecution to furnish particulars in support of an information,[37] the power of amendment can compensate for this deficiency in all but the most egregious of cases. It is therefore plain that challenges to quash the information at the preliminary inquiry will succeed only in cases where there is a radical jurisdictional defect that lies beyond the power of amendment granted by section 601.[38]

3) Multiple Accused and Multiple Counts

In view of the limited statutory jurisdiction of the judge at the preliminary inquiry, it seems clear that he has no power to order the severance of accused or counts.[39]

If multiple accused are charged in a single information, each is entitled to make a request for a preliminary inquiry, as is the prosecution. If a request is made, the ensuing inquiry must be held in respect of all

---

33   Section 546. See also R. v. Gralewicz, [1980] 2 S.C.R. 493; R. v. Bolduc (1980), 20 C.R. (3d) 372 (Que. C.A.), aff'd [1982] 1 S.C.R. 573.

34   Re Hislop et al. and The Queen (1983), 36 C.R. (3d) 29 (Ont. C.A.).

35   R. v. Prince, [1986] 2 S.C.R. 480.

36   Dallas & Cassidy v. The Queen (1985), 21 C.C.C. (3d) 100 (Ont. H.C.J.); Re Volpi & Lanzino and the Queen (1987), 34 C.C.C. (3d) 1 (Ont. C.A.).

37   R. v. Chew, [1968] 2 C.C.C. 127 (Ont. C.A.).

38   R. v. Webster, [1993] 1 S.C.R. 3. The issue of sufficiency of an information will be discussed at greater length in Chapter 11.

39   Re R. and Legg (1993), 80 C.C.C. (3d) 315 (N.S.S.C.T.D.); Re Peters and the Queen (1982), 2 C.C.C. (3d) 278 (Sask. Q.B.).

accused and each of them will be entitled to participate.[40] In many instances, multiple accused will be concerned about the same issues, but
there are also cases in which various accused persons wish to address
different issues and hear evidence from different witnesses. In such
cases the preliminary inquiry will proceed on the issues and witnesses
identified by the parties, in the same manner as if there were only a
single accused.[41] However, as the law favours prosecution of multiple
accused together, the *Code* specifically empowers a judge not to record
the election of an accused if it would necessarily lead to severance of
the accused.[42] If only one accused elects a mode of trial that entitles
him to a preliminary inquiry, that election will suffice to ensure that
an inquiry will occur.

Multiple counts may be joined in an information for purposes of
a preliminary inquiry, provided that each of them could properly be
the subject of a committal order. Thus, the judge at the preliminary inquiry cannot inquire into summary-conviction offences and indictable
offences within the absolute jurisdiction of the provincial court.[43] Occasionally, however, an information is filed that contains such counts.
Although the judge has no jurisdiction to inquire into them, they can
remain on the information pending the election of the accused. If the
accused elects trial in provincial court, she waives the preliminary inquiry and thus no issue arises because the provincial court judge has
jurisdiction over all of the offences charged. If she elects trial by judge
alone or judge and jury, the preliminary inquiry will proceed on the
electable offences and the others would have to be separately charged
in another information.[44]

---

40   Section 536(4.2).
41   Of particular significance where there are multiple accused will be the cases in
     which one co-accused makes a request to hear the evidence of another.
42   Section 567. Specifically, the judge can fail to record any election other than
     trial by judge with a jury, and so that will be the mode of trial for all the ac-
     cused.
43   Such offences can be joined for purposes of trial if the accused elects trial in
     provincial court and waives the preliminary inquiry.
44   To be clear, the judge's power of committal is only as extensive as his power
     of inquiry, and thus there can be no order of committal on a summary-convic-
     tion offence. In Quebec and Nunavut, the situation would appear to be slightly
     different because the judge with jurisdiction at the preliminary inquiry also
     has jurisdiction when the accused elects trial by judge alone. It would seem to
     follow that multiple counts could remain on the same information pending the
     outcome of the preliminary inquiry. In Quebec, it has been decided that there is
     no objection in principle where the preliminary inquiry and the trial take place
     before the same judge of the Cour du Québec.

4) Presence of the Accused

The accused is entitled to be present at the preliminary inquiry. For many years the courts took the view that the accused must be present.[45] Section 535 refers to an accused who is "before a justice," and this was interpreted to mean that the justice's jurisdiction required the presence of the accused. This position has been changed by amendment of section 537(1)(j.1), which now allows the judge a discretion to excuse the accused from all or part of the inquiry. Even without this amendment, however, the same result might be justified through the exercise of the judge's general power to regulate the conduct of the inquiry. It should also be noted that sections 537(1)(j) and (k) allow the accused to appear by an electronic connection. Therefore, the accused has the right to attend the preliminary inquiry, and will be required to attend unless excused by the justice. As a practical matter, this will follow either upon a request by the accused or the agreement of the parties.

If the accused absconds during the preliminary inquiry, section 544 provides that the accused is deemed to have waived the right to be present.[46] It also provides that the justice may continue the inquiry to its conclusion or, if an arrest warrant has been issued, adjourn it. Even if it is adjourned, the justice may subsequently resume the inquiry. The accused cannot demand that the inquiry be reopened, although the justice is given discretion to make this order if exceptional circumstances justify it. Counsel for the accused is entitled to act for the absconding accused during her absence if the inquiry is continued and this includes calling witnesses. Most important, however, is that if the accused has absconded the justice is entitled to draw an adverse inference.

5) Constitutional Issues

In *Mills*,[47] and again in *Hynes*,[48] the Supreme Court of Canada decided that a court conducting a preliminary inquiry is not a "court of competent jurisdiction" under the *Charter*. Thus, if the accused seeks to apply for a constitutional remedy under section 24 or 52, the only forum for such a motion is the court of trial.

---

45   *Re McLachlan and the Queen* (1986), 24 C.C.C. (3d) 255 (Ont. C.A.).

46   In *Re Plummer and the Queen* (1983), 5 C.C.C. (3d) 17 (B.C.C.A.), it was held that judicial acts undertaken after election by the accused as to mode of trial are acts "during the preliminary inquiry."

47   *R. v. Mills*, [1986] 1 S.C.R. 863.

48   *Hynes*, above note 5.

One reason for reaching this decision was that the jurisdiction granted by the *Code* at the preliminary inquiry does not extend to constitutional issues. This may be true, but it raises the odd spectre that the allocation of jurisdiction under an ordinary statute can relieve the judge of the obligation to observe the supreme law of the country. The exclusion of *Charter* issues from the preliminary inquiry may be defensible as a matter of policy.[49] It is consistent with the idea that the function of the preliminary inquiry is modest: to ascertain whether the prosecution has enough evidence for the matter to be sent to trial. It is also consistent with some notion of economy and efficiency in criminal prosecutions because it would eliminate the time and effort necessary to resolve constitutional questions at a preliminary stage. Further, this position means that the judge at the preliminary inquiry cannot terminate a prosecution by granting a stay under the *Charter.* Particularly given the current limited scope of preliminary inquiries, there are arguments in favour of reserving decisions about *Charter* issues to the trial court.

Nonetheless, this position is anomalous in some regards. As is discussed below, a justice can exclude evidence from the preliminary inquiry on the basis that it does not comply with ordinary requirements for admissibility such as voluntariness. Why, then, should she be prevented from acting in the same way when the statement was obtained through a *Charter* violation? Further, the entitlement to seek a constitutional remedy at the preliminary inquiry would be consistent with a rich and robust concept of full answer and defence.[50] It prevents the accused from seeking an order for disclosure. It prevents any claim of unreasonable delay. In short, it deprives the accused of the opportunity to advance any constitutional claim that may have a material bearing on the outcome of the case. In some cases, efficiency may be better served by having such determinations made at as early a stage as possible.

C. EVIDENCE

1) Admissibility

Evidence at the preliminary inquiry is taken under oath and recorded.[51] As at trial, prosecution witnesses are heard first and may be cross-examined by the accused or counsel. Subsections 540(2) and (3) refer

---

49   These arguments are rehearsed at some length by the majority in *Hynes, ibid.*
50   *Ibid.* at paras. 59*ff.*, Major J., dissenting.
51   Section 540. A court conducting a preliminary inquiry is a court of record.

to the taking of depositions before the presiding justice or judge, but this form of receiving evidence is almost never used. Depositions are statements made and sworn before the justice and they were commonly used long ago when there were few court stenographers and no electronic means for recording the presentation of oral evidence. The modern practice is that evidence taken at the preliminary inquiry is recorded by a stenographer or by electronic means in the same manner as occurs at trial.

As a general proposition, evidence tendered at the preliminary inquiry must comply with principles and rules of admissibility that apply at trial. This means, for example, that any statement made by the accused to a person in authority must prove to be voluntary beyond reasonable doubt.[52] It also means, more generally, that the procedure for receiving evidence at a *voir dire* applies at the preliminary inquiry. There are, however, important qualifications that must be noted concerning the production and admissibility of evidence at the preliminary inquiry. One is that the presiding judge has no authority to call witnesses or to force the parties (notably the prosecution) to produce particular witnesses.[53] Also, as previously noted, the presiding justice or judge has no jurisdiction to hear matters relating to the *Charter*, and so has no jurisdiction to exclude evidence or to grant any other remedy under section 24 of the *Charter*.

However, there is an important qualification concerning the admissibility of evidence in the power granted in section 540(7):

> A justice acting under this Part may receive as evidence any information that would not otherwise be admissible but that the justice considers credible or trustworthy in the circumstances of the case, including a statement that is made by a witness in writing or otherwise recorded.

The section requires prior notice by a party of the intention to tender such evidence, but the judge may dispense with this requirement and order the attendance for examination and cross-examination of any person who will give otherwise inadmissible evidence.[54] This provision would appear to allow a party to tender will-say statements at the preliminary inquiry. For the prosecution, this would be highly efficient because it would eliminate the need to produce witnesses to give *viva voce* evidence. The defence should be expected to object to this practice

---

52   *R. v. Pickett* (1975), 28 C.C.C. (2d) 297 (Ont. C.A.).
53   *Re Phillips and the Queen* (1991), 66 C.C.C. (3d) 140 (Ont. Ct. Gen. Div.); *Re R. and Brass* (1981), 64 C.C.C. (2d) 206 (Sask. Q.B.).
54   Section 540(9).

unless it is content to waive the opportunity of cross-examination and the duty of the prosecution to present oral evidence under oath.

It is hard to say whether any consistent practice has developed yet, but there are some indications of preliminary inquiry judges applying these sections with restraint. Some cases have suggested that there should still be an expectation that witnesses will testify personally, with exceptions permitted. If, for example, the investigating officer who personally took a statement was the one who presented the evidence at the preliminary inquiry, and was in a position to say that the witness had recently confirmed the statement and was willing and available to come to trial, then section 540(7) might apply. However, it should not apply to allow the chief investigating officer to introduce a "will-say" statement with no personal knowledge.[55] Other cases have held that there are matters about which it is reasonable for the accused to want to cross-examine the complainant at the preliminary inquiry in order to assess the case to meet at trial, and that section 540(7) was not meant to give the Crown a virtually unrestricted right to avoid offering *viva voce* testimony.[56]

But section 540(7) is problematic on other grounds. Although the evidence admitted must be considered credible and trustworthy in the circumstances of the case, the provision, in effect, creates an exemption or exception to the ordinary rules of admissibility. The most glaring question is: how far does this exception extend?[57] For example, does it permit the justice to admit an involuntary statement by the accused to a person in authority if it is otherwise credible or trustworthy? Does it extend to any type of evidence that is specifically inadmissible by virtue of an exclusionary rule? Whatever its limits, this provision is peculiar, especially in view of the reform in favour of a limited preliminary inquiry. It allows the decision to commit at the preliminary inquiry to be based, at least in part, upon evidence that cannot be tendered at trial. Indeed, in the ordinary course of events, nothing of evidence admitted at the preliminary inquiry should be heard at trial under the exception in section 540(7). But it is easy to imagine circumstances where precisely this might occur. For example, if an otherwise inadmissible statement is admitted under that section, and the declarant subsequently testifies at trial, can the credibility of the witness be impeached on the basis of the statement admitted at the preliminary hearing? If that statement was unsworn and admitted for the prosecu-

---

55   See R. v. *Sonier* (2005), 201 C.C.C. (3d) 572 (Ont. Ct. J.).
56   See R. v. *Inglis* (2006), 208 C.C.C. (3d) 85 (Ont. Ct. J.).
57   See R. v. *I.(S.P.)* (2005), 27 C.R. (6th) 112 (Nun. Ct. J.).

tion, the result may well cause prejudice to the defence. In short, it would appear that, as it is now drafted, section 540(7) is too broad.

Section 540(7) would be unobjectionable if it were contingent upon the consent of the opposing party, but nothing in the section suggests that this provision would operate only where there is consent. Indeed, if there were consent, it is less likely that there would be a need to present the evidence in question at a preliminary inquiry. The text of section 540(7) would appear to make plain that, even if the opposing party objects to the admission of the evidence, the proponent is entitled to tender it and it may be admitted if the judge considers it credible or trustworthy. In short, this provision provides a party with an opportunity to lower the bar of admissibility, in the form of a case-specific discretion, subject only to considerations of credibility.

There is another troubling difficulty with this provision. The Supreme Court has said repeatedly that it is no part of the justice's function or jurisdiction to assess the credibility of evidence at a preliminary inquiry.[58] It is, to say the least, surprising that section 540(7), by directing the preliminary inquiry judge to consider whether the evidence is "credible or trustworthy," appears in express terms either to contradict this principle or to overlook it.

2) Cross-examination of Prosecution Witnesses

The defence (accused personally or through counsel)[59] is entitled to cross-examine prosecution witnesses at the preliminary inquiry. This is a full right of cross-examination that is constrained not only by a criterion of relevance to the scope of the inquiry as a whole, but also to the sufficiency of the prosecution evidence.[60] Thus, the accused is permitted to cross-examine a prosecution witness on any matter that could lead to the conclusion that the prosecution evidence is insufficient, and is also permitted to cross-examine in a manner that might be useful in a subsequent trial. In this respect, the accused may cross-examine a prosecution witness on a matter that might have central significance at the trial but that is wholly outside the scope of the preliminary inquiry itself.[61] This

---

58   *R. v. Monteleone*, [1987] 2 S.C.R. 154 [*Monteleone*]; *R. v. Yebes*, [1987] 2 S.C.R. 168 [*Yebes*]; *R. v. Charemski*, [1998] 1 S.C.R. 679 [*Charemski*]; *Hynes*, above note 5; *Sazant*, above note 15; *Deschamplain*, above note 15.

59   *Re Zaor and the Queen* (1984), 12 C.C.C. (3d) 265 (Que. C.A.).

60   *R. v. Bayne* (1970), 14 C.R.N.S. 130 (Alta. S.C.A.D.).

61   *R. v. B.(E.)* (2002), 162 C.C.C. (3d) 451 (Ont. C.A.); *Dawson*, above note 32. See also *Re Ward and the Queen* (1976), 31 C.C.C. (2d) 466 (Ont. C.A.); *R. v. George* (1991), 69 C.C.C. (3d) 148 (Ont. C.A.).

occurs most frequently when an accused cross-examines for the purpose of a subsequent challenge at trial to the credibility of a witness, or for the purpose of laying the factual foundation for an issue under the *Charter* to be raised at trial.

With respect to examination and cross-examination, but especially the latter, the justice now has the express power to immediately stop any part of it that is, "in the opinion of the justice, abusive, too repetitive or otherwise inappropriate."[62] This is a broad discretion. While protection against abuse or undue repetition is necessary, it is not clear what is intended by the sweeping phrase "otherwise inappropriate." Given that the *Code* encourages limitations on the scope of preliminary inquiries, this phrase should not be interpreted to restrict the ability of the parties to discover the nature and quality of the opponent's evidence.

In the amendments that came into force in 2004, there is a conspicuous gap that Parliament should have filled that affects the right of cross-examination. If the defence makes a request to hear a prosecution witness on a specific issue, it presumably wishes to cross-examine that witness. Yet there is nothing presently in the *Code* that makes it clear that a witness who will be called at trial by the prosecution is also a prosecution witness for the purposes of cross-examination at the preliminary inquiry, even if the prosecution makes no request to hear that witness before trial. A judge has no jurisdiction at the preliminary inquiry to order the prosecution to call a witness and cannot himself call a witness. Presumably, all that the judge can do is ask the prosecutor to consent to call a witness for the purpose of cross-examination by the accused. It is also arguable that a request from the defence can be considered to have the effect of challenging the prosecution case with regards to a specific witness and specific issue and this, in turn, can be taken to require the prosecution to call its witness on that specific issue. Even if the prosecutor declines to examine the witness, the witness is nevertheless available for cross-examination. Ideally, however, further amendment of the *Code* will be made to clarify that the defence is entitled to cross-examine prosecution witnesses at the preliminary inquiry where there is a request to do so.

3) Address to Accused

At the close of the prosecution evidence the *Code* requires the justice to address an accused who is not represented by counsel as follows, or in like terms:

---

62   Section 537(1.1).

Do you wish to say anything in answer to these charges or to any other charges which might have arisen from the evidence led by the prosecution? You are not obliged to say anything but whatever you do say may be given in evidence against you at your trial. You should not make any confession or admission of guilt because of any promise or threat made to you but if you do make any statement it may be given in evidence against you at your trial in spite of the promise or threat.[63]

This caution is a vestige of ancient law in which magistrates were required to conduct investigations of alleged criminal activity, typically after arrest and before considering bail. As the preliminary inquiry later became a judicial examination of the sufficiency of the prosecution case, the investigative role of the magistrate disappeared. The caution is also a vestige of an era in which an accused person was not competent to testify. For both of these reasons the caution is largely an anachronism.

Section 541(2) only requires this caution to be given to an unrepresented accused, presumably on the assumption that an accused with representation will be competently advised of her position, thus dispensing with the need for the address. Nonetheless, there seems to be no harm in the judge reciting the required address in all cases, unless the defence makes clear that the accused has been apprised of the content of the address. In any case, as a practical matter it is rare for the accused to make a statement after caution, not least because anything she may say by way of defence will not be considered in the decision to commit for trial or discharge.[64]

4) Defence Evidence

The defence is also entitled to adduce evidence on behalf of the accused, including testimony by the accused, but it is not obliged to call witnesses.[65] As the preliminary inquiry is not a trial, and therefore cannot lead to a judgment of acquittal, it is comparatively rare that the accused is discharged at the preliminary inquiry solely on the basis of evidence called by the defence. Indeed, the tactical position of the defence at the preliminary inquiry can be delicate. There is no obligation on the accused to make disclosure of its case, and the production

---

63   Section 541(2).
64   Moreover, the accused who makes a statement after caution cannot be cross-examined, unlike the accused who testifies.
65   Section 541.

of witnesses for the defence can have not only the effect of making disclosure but also of exposing the accused at trial to any weaknesses that may emerge in the evidence of such witnesses.

However, there is often some advantage in the preparation of the defence case if the accused calls evidence of potential prosecution witnesses. Such witnesses may not be essential for the prosecution to succeed at the preliminary inquiry, but they may still be useful for the defence. The advantage lies in hearing and seeing those witnesses, and thus assessing what they can give in evidence and the credibility with which they give it. Even if the effect of calling such evidence is, in some cases, to disclose the strategy of the defence, there may be no disadvantage in doing so if the net effect is to gain a stronger basis for preparing a defence at trial. Once again, these considerations illustrate that the preliminary inquiry provides an opportunity for the defence to acquire further discovery of the case as a whole.

This can be especially important where there is a real risk that the evidence in issue may not be, for any reason, available at trial, and the accused wishes to preserve it. On the other hand, in some cases an accused may be quite content that certain evidence will not be available later. In either event, it is important to take note of the fact that evidence led at the preliminary inquiry (whether by the defence or the Crown) can potentially be admitted at trial.

Section 715 of the *Code* provides that if evidence was taken on oath at the preliminary inquiry in the presence of the accused, and the witness either refuses to testify or is dead, insane, too ill to travel, or absent from Canada, then that evidence can be introduced at trial. This statutory rule depends on the requirement that the accused had a full opportunity to cross-examine the witness. Normally, of course, an accused will have had such an opportunity, but in some cases information about the witness may only become available after the preliminary inquiry, with the result that the opportunity to cross-examine was not a full one.[66]

Section 715, however, does not set out a "comprehensive code" on when preliminary inquiry testimony is admissible. As a result, in some cases it is also possible to admit preliminary inquiry testimony through the principled exception to the hearsay rule. In *R. v. Hawkins*, for example, a witness testified at the preliminary inquiry, but then married the accused and so was incompetent to testify at trial. The Court held

---

66 See, for example, *R. v. Assoun*, 2006 NSCA 47, in which the accused was unaware at the time of the preliminary inquiry that a witness claimed to have obtained some of her information through "psychic visions."

that this did not mean she was "refusing" to testify, and so section 715 did not apply to allow her evidence to be led at trial. Nonetheless, her preliminary inquiry testimony was admissible because it met the criteria of necessity and reliability that make up the principled exception.[67]

5) Publication Bans

As in all other aspects of criminal procedure, proceedings are open unless there is some specific basis for an exception. Thus, the presentation of evidence is conducted in open court and may be the subject of public comment, unless the judge orders otherwise. The *Code* gives the judge discretion to exclude the public from court.[68] This power is occasionally used but it is comparatively rare at preliminary inquiries. As distinct from the general public, witnesses are routinely excluded, at least until they have given their evidence.[69]

Typically, the presentation of evidence at the preliminary inquiry is the subject of a ban upon publication in a newspaper or broadcast. The legislative rationale for these orders is that the accused, who is presumed innocent and is not in jeopardy of conviction at the preliminary inquiry, should be shielded from adverse publicity before trial. The same may be said of other witnesses, especially the complainant. Indeed, there is a general argument that the fairness of any subsequent trial can be ensured only if there is a publication ban at the preliminary inquiry.

A publication ban is imposed by order of the justice before any evidence is taken: it is discretionary if sought by the prosecution, and mandatory if sought by the accused.[70] It has been held that if the order is sought after the presentation of evidence has begun, the presiding judge has discretion in the matter, but there is little apparent justification for this position.[71] If the rationale for allowing any publication ban

---

67   R. v. Hawkins, [1996] 3 S.C.R. 1043. This precise result may now be questionable, given the Court's subsequent ruling on spousal incompetency and the principled exception in R. v. Couture, 2007 SCC 28 [Couture]. However, nothing in Couture casts doubt on the general approach that s. 715 is not a complete code, and that preliminary inquiry evidence is potentially admissible under the principled exception.

68   Sections 537(1)(h) and 486.

69   Re Collette and the Queen; Re Richard and the Queen (1983), 6 C.C.C. (3d) 300 (Ont. H.C.J.); R. c. M.(A.G.) (1993), 26 C.R. (4th) 379 (Que. C.A.); compare Re Armstrong and State of Wisconsin (1972), 7 C.C.C. (2d) 331 (Ont. H.C.J.).

70   Section 539.

71   R. v. Harrison (1984), 14 C.C.C. (3d) 549 (Que. S.P.).

has force in the first place, there is no reason why that rationale should not be given effect after the presentation of evidence has begun.

If the accused is not represented by counsel, the *Code* obliges the judge to inform him of the right to seek a publication ban.[72] When ordered, the ban remains in effect until the accused is discharged or, if the accused is committed for trial, the trial is ended. Although such bans infringe in a material way upon the freedom of expression and the right to know what transpires in the public proceedings of courts, the courts have ruled that they are reasonable limitations upon those rights.[73]

D. COMMITTAL

Section 548 of the *Code* directs the justice or judge at the preliminary inquiry to commit the accused for trial on any indictable offence if the evidence in support of that charge is sufficient. It also requires that the accused be discharged in respect of any charge on which the evidence is not sufficient. Everything turns, therefore, on what is meant by "sufficient" evidence. The courts have provided a test that has been consistently applied for many years but, as will be seen, remains uncertain in some important aspects.

In *Shephard*, the Supreme Court stated that the test of sufficiency at the preliminary inquiry, as for a directed verdict and for committal in extradition matters, is whether a reasonable jury, properly instructed, could find the charge proved beyond reasonable doubt.[74] The core of uncertainty in this test lies in the degree to which an assessment of the evidence permits or requires the presiding judge to consider the probative force of the evidence. It is arguable that a reference to whether the jury could return a finding of guilt is at least some indication that the presiding judge should assess the force of the evidence.

A convenient fashion in which to examine the test of sufficiency is to look at the criteria of completeness and weight. The first of these means only that the prosecution leads evidence corresponding to each of the elements of the offence as defined in the substantive criminal law, including identification.[75] In a case of assault, for example, this would mean that there was evidence led that the accused intentionally applied

---

72   Section 539(2).

73   See, for example, *Dagenais v. Canadian Broadcasting Corporation*, [1994] 3 S.C.R. 835; *Canadian Broadcasting Corporation v. New Brunswick (Attorney General)*, [1996] 3 S.C.R. 480; *R. v. Mentuck*, [2001] 3 S.C.R. 442.

74   *Shephard*, above note 5.

75   *Skogman*, above note 6; *Deschamplain*, above note 15 at para. 23.

force to another person without that person's consent. In the general run of cases, the criterion of completeness poses few difficulties.

It is the criterion of weight that is problematic. The Supreme Court and other courts have said repeatedly that it is not the function of the judge to assess the weight of evidence at the preliminary inquiry.[76] Accordingly, a judge must not assess the credibility of witnesses who testify.[77] This has led some to assert that if there is any evidence on all essential elements in the charge there should be an order of committal.[78] The reason most commonly invoked for this assertion is that the justice or judge at the preliminary inquiry must not usurp the functions of the jury or judge at trial in determining the strength of the case.[79]

On the other hand, if the prosecution evidence is such that no reasonable jury, properly instructed, could find the charge to be proven beyond a reasonable doubt, this seems like a relevant consideration. Whether she is entitled to assess the credibility of witnesses or not, one might argue that the judge should discharge the accused if no reasonable trier of fact could find the accused guilty on the evidence adduced by the prosecution. To reach such a conclusion would not be to usurp the role of the ultimate trier of fact.

The resolution of this problem depends upon the perceived purpose of having preliminary inquiries at all. If the test of sufficiency is restricted to the criterion of completeness, as discussed above, it follows that the justice should not weigh the evidence adduced at the preliminary inquiry at all. It would also follow from this that the test of sufficiency stated in *Shephard* should be reformulated to require that the prosecution evidence need only support an air of reality as regards each of the elements of the charge. But if the primary purpose of the preliminary inquiry is to test the sufficiency of the prosecution case, and thus to protect the accused from being placed on trial pointlessly, it follows that the judge must discharge in any case where no reasonable trier of fact could find the prosecution case proved beyond reasonable doubt.

On the one hand, the Court has regularly ruled that the test of sufficiency at the preliminary inquiry is concerned with the completeness of the prosecution evidence on the elements of the offence. Indeed, the Court has said that if there is direct evidence on all elements, the accused must be committed even where defence evidence has been called.

---

76   *Monteleone*, above note 58; *Yebes*, above note 58.

77   See, for example, *R. v. Arcuri*, [2001] 2 S.C.R. 828 [*Arcuri*]; *Deschamplain*, above note 15; *Sazant*, above note 15.

78   An extreme illustration is *Charemski*, above note 58.

79   *Monteleone*, above note 58.

In this approach, weight would seem to have no part in the test of sufficiency where there is direct prosecution evidence on an element.

On the other hand, where the prosecution case on an element is circumstantial, the Court has said in *Arcuri* that the justice should undertake a limited weighing of the evidence, including any defence evidence, to determine whether a reasonable trier of fact could return a finding of guilt.[80] In doing this, the justice is not entitled to assess reliability or credibility in the evidence and must not draw any inferences from the evidence. A "limited weighing" of circumstantial evidence therefore requires the judge to consider whether, if believed, the evidence could support inferences in favour of the prosecution and whether it could be considered reliable or credible. If so, the accused should be committed.

Further, and once again in the context of an extradition case, the Court has recently commented in *United States of America v. Ferras*:

> 40 . . . I take as axiomatic that a person could not be committed for trial for an offence in Canada if the evidence is so manifestly unreliable that it would be unsafe to rest a verdict upon it. It follows that if a judge on an extradition hearing concludes that the evidence is manifestly unreliable, the judge should not order extradition under s. 29(1). Yet, under the current state of the law in *Shephard*, it appears that the judge is denied this possibility.[81]

In *Ferras* the Court went on to modify the *Shephard* test in the extradition context, but in doing so it indicated that there was no longer symmetry between the extradition and preliminary inquiry tests.

One might hope that the standard of sufficiency will be further reviewed by the Supreme Court, specifically in the context of preliminary inquiries. A purposive interpretation of this test would be that a justice should discharge the accused if no reasonable trier of fact could find the essential elements of the offence proved beyond reasonable doubt. Whether this conclusion is reached by reason of incompleteness or weight should not matter. This approach would not only be consistent with the purpose of the preliminary inquiry, it would also acknowledge the proper role of the trier of fact at a trial. It allows that a case that could come to proof beyond reasonable doubt should go to trial and that a case that could not should simply be dismissed. Given the more limited role that has been provided for preliminary inquiries

---

80   *Arcuri*, above note 77.
81   *United States of America v. Ferras*, 2006 SCC 33.

with the recent legislative changes, however, it is unlikely that major change of this sort is forthcoming.

Assuming that the prosecution case at the preliminary inquiry meets the test of sufficiency, the judge will order committal on any indictable offence charged or supported by the evidence. This is done by endorsing the information in a manner that identifies the appropriate offences.[82] It will be recalled that the judge is not limited to committal on the offences charged in the information, or to lesser or included charges, but is limited to committal upon charges in respect of the same transaction.[83] In general, this means that the committal order must refer to offences that are related to the event or sequence of events that form the factual basis of the charges in the information at the preliminary inquiry. There is some margin in this for flexibility and thus it has been held that if the evidence identifies another victim than that identified in the original charge, there may be an order of committal for an offence in relation to that victim, provided of course that the offence occurred in respect of the same events.[84]

If the accused is discharged at the preliminary inquiry, there is no acquittal and thus he cannot claim protection against double jeopardy if the prosecution should subsequently proceed against him on the same charge or a related charge, either by means of a fresh information or a direct indictment. As the accused was never in jeopardy of conviction at the preliminary inquiry, the discharge cannot constitute a final judgment.[85]

If the accused is committed for trial, the justice who presided at the preliminary inquiry is required to transmit the record of the inquiry to the court of trial.[86] The record comprises the information as endorsed, the evidence (including exhibits), any statement made by the accused after the justice's address, and any paper process relating to compelling the appearance of the accused.

---

82   It is not adequate for the judge simply to say that the accused is committed for trial. Specific offences must be enumerated in the endorsement.

83   The judge has no jurisdiction to commit the accused for trial on any summary-conviction offence that is disclosed by the evidence, but he may commit for any indictable offence, including one that lies within the absolute jurisdiction of the provincial court.

84   *R. v. Stewart* (1988), 44 C.C.C. (3d) 109 (Ont. C.A.).

85   *R. v. Ewanchuk* (1974), 16 C.C.C. (2d) 517 (Alta. S.C.A.D.); *R. v. Fields* (1979), 12 C.R. (3d) 273 (B.C.C.A.).

86   Section 551.

E. REVIEW OF PRELIMINARY INQUIRY DECISIONS

The *Code* sets out no procedure for appealing the decision to commit or discharge at a preliminary inquiry, and so no appeal is possible. This means that review of such a decision can only be made on the basis of an action for *certiorari*. Part XXVI of the *Code* regulates the use of extraordinary remedies in the criminal justice system and attaches some limits on the occasions when *certiorari* is available,[87] but it does remain available in the case of decisions at a preliminary inquiry. In principle, it is open to the Crown to seek *certiorari* in the case of a discharge, and this does sometimes occur.[88] As a practical matter, the Crown also has the usually simpler option, under section 577, of preferring a direct indictment despite the discharge, so more frequently *certiorari* applications involve an accused seeking review of a decision to commit.

Because the preliminary inquiry decision is reviewed by way of *certiorari* rather than appeal, it is not sufficient to show an error of law on the part of the preliminary inquiry judge. Rather, *certiorari* will only be granted if the judge has fallen into jurisdictional error. Many errors of law will simply be errors within a judge's jurisdiction. Erroneously excluding evidence at the preliminary hearing is unlikely to be a jurisdictional error (for example, an error with respect to the application of the rules of evidence will not be a jurisdictional error unless it rises to the level of a denial of natural justice).[89]

Apart from denying natural justice, it is also a jurisdictional error if a trial judge fails to comply with a mandatory provision of the *Code*. In particular, section 548 of the *Code* requires a judge to commit the accused for trial if "there is sufficient evidence." This means that there must be at least some basis in the evidence at the preliminary inquiry that supports the decision to commit.[90] It also means, since a preliminary inquiry judge does not weigh evidence, that where the Crown has adduced direct evidence on all the elements of the offence, the preliminary inquiry judge must commit the accused even if the defence has offered exculpatory evidence.[91] If there is no evidence on some essen-

---

87   See s. 776.
88   See, for example, *Dubois v. R.*, [1986] 1 S.C.R. 366 [*Dubois*]; *Sazant*, above note 15.
89   *Dubois*, *ibid.* at 377; *Forsythe*, above note 14 at 272.
90   *Dubois*, *ibid.*
91   *Arcuri*, above note 77 at para. 29.

tial element of the charge, however, it will be a jurisdictional error for the preliminary inquiry judge to commit the accused to trial.[92]

The existence of evidence at the preliminary inquiry must be understood broadly. Even if the Crown has indicated that evidence led through a preliminary inquiry witness will not be led at trial, that evidence must nonetheless be considered in the decision to commit, and it would be a jurisdictional error to fail to consider it.[93]

Section 548 also requires a preliminary inquiry judge to discharge the accused if "on the whole of the evidence no sufficient case is made out." This means that if a preliminary inquiry judge grants a discharge without considering "the whole of the evidence," that will also be a jurisdictional error.[94] This would constitute a failure to comply with a mandatory statutory provision, and would therefore allow a reviewing court to intervene.

Some guidance on the type of mistakes that can lead to jurisdictional errors was provided relatively recently by the Court with its decision in *Sazant*. The accused had been discharged at the preliminary inquiry on a charge of sexual assault. The preliminary inquiry judge had said there was "absolutely no evidence of non-consent." In fact, the complainant had testified that he did not want to take part in the sexual activity, and so there was no dispute that the preliminary inquiry judge had made an error. The issue was whether it was a jurisdictional error.

The Court held that there were three possible explanations for the preliminary inquiry judge's mistake. He might have misunderstood the elements of the offence and given effect to a non-existent defence. In that event, he would not have tested the Crown's evidence against the actual elements of the offence charged, which would be a jurisdictional error. Secondly, the preliminary inquiry judge might have found the complainant's statement to be ambiguous, capable of interpretation either as an expression of "after-the-fact" regret or as a statement of "during-the-fact" non-consent. If that were the case, though, it was not open to the preliminary inquiry judge to decide which interpretation he preferred — that would be an issue for the trial judge. In that event, the preliminary inquiry judge would again have fallen into jurisdictional error by deciding an issue reserved for another forum.[95] Finally, the preliminary inquiry judge might have simply overlooked the evidence

---

92   *Skogman*, above note 6 at 104.

93   R. v. *Papadopoulos* (2005), 201 C.C.C. (3d) 363 (Ont. C.A.), leave to appeal to S.C.C. refused, [2005] S.C.C.A. No. 314.

94   *Deschamplain*, above note 15 at para. 18.

95   This had also been the rationale in *Dubois*, above note 88, where the preliminary inquiry judge was taken to have decided whether the evidence was capable

of non-consent in the complainant's testimony. In that event he would have failed to consider "the whole of the evidence" as required by section 548, and so again would have committed a jurisdictional error.

FURTHER READINGS

HEALY, PATRICK, "Chabotage: Expanding the Crown's Power to Prefer Additional Counts" (1984) 38 C.R. (3d) 344

PACIOCCO, DAVID, "A Voyage of Discovery: Examining the Precarious Condition of the Preliminary Inquiry" (2003) 48 Crim. L.Q. 151

QUIGLEY, TIM, *Procedure in Canadian Criminal Law*, 2d ed., looseleaf (Toronto: Thomson Carswell, 2005) cc. 14 & 15

of proving the Crown's case beyond a reasonable doubt, a decision reserved for the trial judge.

PRELIMINARY MATTERS AND REMEDIES

A number of matters can or must be dealt with prior to the start of prosecution. First, in some cases an offence is not dealt with by way of prosecution at all, but rather through some alternative. Next, assuming that a prosecution is to occur, some administrative and other matters can be dealt with before the trial begins, either through a pre-trial motion or a pre-trial conference. Finally, in cases that will be tried by a jury, that jury must be selected. All of these issues will be dealt with in this chapter.

A. ALTERNATIVES TO PROSECUTION

In an informal sense, there has long existed an alternative to prosecution in Canada through the exercise of discretion by police in not laying charges in the first place, or by Crown prosecutors in not continuing them.[1] Only relatively recently has that discretion been more formalized in a system of alternative measures authorized by statute.

---

1   Though the general view of the legitimacy of exercising such discretion has varied over time: see the discussion in Bruce Archibald, "Prosecutors, Democracy and the Public Interest: Prosecutorial Discretion and its Limits in Canada" (paper presented at the XVIth Congress of the International Academy of Comparative Law, Brisbane, Australia, 14–22 July 2002) at 17–22 [Archibald].

Statutory alternative measures to prosecution began in 1985 with the *Young Offenders Act*,[2] though under that Act they were available only to young persons. Subsequently in 1995, the provisions of section 4 of the *YOA* were adopted into the *Criminal Code*, thereby creating the potential use of alternative measures for adults as well. The essential theory behind these schemes is that, in certain cases, the interests of society might be adequately protected through measures that are less intrusive to the person alleged to have committed an offence than prosecution. If the person fails to comply with the requirements of the alternative measures program, however, criminal charges can still be laid.

Section 717 of the *Criminal Code* does not require that an alternative measures program exist, but it authorizes the Attorney General of a province to create such a program. The use of these measures is subject to various conditions, in particular the general directive that the use of such measures cannot be inconsistent with the protection of society, and that the person considering their use is satisfied that they are appropriate given "the interests of society and of the victim."[3] Other provisions are aimed at protecting the interests of the person who would otherwise be the "accused." In large part, these provisions are aimed at ensuring that alternative measures are only used in cases that would otherwise have proceeded to prosecution, rather than being used in cases that simply would not have occupied the justice system at all. That is, alternative measures are intended to be a way of diverting some cases out of the criminal justice system, not a way of expanding its scope.

Consistent with this approach, alternative measures cannot be used unless the prosecutor believes that there would be sufficient evidence to proceed with a prosecution, and that the prosecution is not barred at law in any way.[4] The person involved must have been advised of the right to counsel, must accept responsibility for the act or omission constituting the offence, and must fully and freely consent to participate.[5] Alternative measures cannot be used where the person denies involvement in the offence or wants a charge dealt with in court.[6] Further protection for the individual is provided by the rule that no admission, confession, or statement made by a person as a condition of being dealt with by alternative measures is admissible against that person in any later proceedings.[7]

---

2   R.S.C. 1985, c. Y-1, enacted as S.C. 1980–81–82–83, c. 110 [*YOA*].
3   Section 717(1)(b).
4   Sections 717(1)(f) & (g).
5   Sections 717(1)(c), (d), & (e).
6   Section 717(2).
7   Section 717(1)(3).

If a person completes the alternative measures, the court must dismiss any charges laid against that person later in respect of the offence. If charges are later laid against a person who has only partly completed the alternative measures, a court can still stay the charges if it is of the view that "the prosecution of the charge would be unfair, having regard to the circumstances and that person's performance with respect to the alternative measures."[8]

In practice, provinces have tended to consider the use of alternative measures according to various categories of offences. Typically, alternative measures simply will not be used for serious violent offences, serious sexual offences, spousal violence, drug trafficking, organized crime, and so on. Many minor offences presumptively will automatically be referred to alternative measures, while a group of offences in the middle continue to depend on prosecutorial discretion. Normally, this discretion is to be exercised in accordance with criteria established within the province's prosecution service.[9]

Alternative measures programs usually ask the person to undertake community service, personal service for the victim, specialized education programs, counselling, or to write a letter of apology.[10] More ambitious alternatives are also available. In Nova Scotia, for example, relying on the authority of section 717 of the *Criminal Code* and section 4 of the *YOA*, the province has created a restorative justice program. This program creates the possibility for conferences between the offender, the victim, supporters of each of those people, and, potentially, other members of the community or police officers. Supporters of restorative justice argue that the outcomes of such conferences can ultimately be far more beneficial to the offender, the victim, and society as a whole.[11]

More recently the *YOA* has been replaced by the *Youth Criminal Justice Act*.[12] That Act now refers not to "alternative measures" but to "extrajudicial measures." For the most part, the features noted above are unchanged,[13] though they are now classed as "extrajudicial sanctions." However, various additional features, other than sanctions, have

---

8   Section 717(4)(b).
9   See the discussion in Archibald, above note 1 at 29–30.
10   *Ibid*. at 29.
11   *Ibid*. at 34.
12   S.C. 2002, c. 1 [*YCJA*].
13   Two differences should be noted. Section 10(2)(d) requires not only that the young person be informed of the right to consult with counsel, but also that there be a reasonable opportunity to do so. Further, in s.10(2)(b), although the person considering whether to refer must still consider the interests of society, any explicit reference to the interest of the victim has been removed.

been added to the scheme. Most notable is the declaration of principles, in addition to those governing the *YCJA* generally, and specific to extra-judicial measures and clearly aimed at encouraging greater use of the measures. They affirm that extrajudicial measures are often the most appropriate and effective way to address youth crime, and that they allow for effective and timely intervention. In particular, they affirm that extrajudicial measures are presumed to be adequate for non-violent offences where the young person has not previously been found guilty of an offence, and that they can be used even if the young person has previously been dealt with by extrajudicial measures or has been found guilty of an offence.[14]

Consistent with a restorative approach, the *YCJA* also encourages the use of extrajudicial measures that aim to involve the families of the young person and the victim, and the community in their design and implementation.[15]

Finally, the *YCJA* creates a system of "pre-alternative measures," as it were, by allowing the Attorney General of a province to create a system whereby police or prosecutors can administer a caution to a young person rather than starting judicial proceedings. Under the Act, before starting judicial proceedings or taking any other measures, police are to consider the principles set out above and decide whether it would be sufficient to issue a caution. Police can also, with consent, refer a young person to a community agency "that may assist the young person not to commit offences."[16] Provincial programs authorizing Crown prosecutors to administer cautions rather than continue proceedings are also envisioned.[17] The relatively informal, low seriousness of this response to a young person's actions is stressed by the requirement that evidence of a caution or referral given to a young person is not admissible to prove prior offending behaviour in any later proceedings.[18]

B. PRE-TRIAL MOTIONS AND CONFERENCES

1) Timing and Means

Authority over pre-trial motions and conferences is not set out as clearly in Canadian law as one might wish. Potential ambiguity arises even

---

14   *YCJA*, above note 12, s. 4.
15   *Ibid.*, s. 5.
16   *Ibid.*, s. 6(1).
17   *Ibid.*, s. 8.
18   *Ibid.*, s. 9.

with the concept of what counts as "pre-trial." The Court has held on a number of occasions that the phrases "charged with an offence" and "commencement of trial" do not have fixed meanings, and will be adjusted to suit particular contexts.

In *R. v. Chabot*, for example, the Court found the key transition point to be when an indictment was "lodged with the trial court at the opening of the accused's trial, with a court ready to proceed with the trial."[19] In *R. v. Kalanj*, in contrast, the Court notes that the word "charged" has no precise meaning in law, and could reasonably range from being told that one will be charged with an offence to being called upon to plead in court.[20] In the context of the section 11(b) right to trial within a reasonable time the Court rejected the *Chabot* position, holding instead that a person is "charged" for section 11 purposes when an information is sworn or a direct indictment is laid.[21] Similarly, in *Basarabas and Spek v. The Queen* the Court noted that the time of commencement of a jury trial will vary depending on which *Code* section is being considered and what interests are at stake.[22] For example, in dealing with an accused's right to be present for trial, the Court has considered jury selection to be part of the trial,[23] but in dealing with the power to replace a juror, the Court has held that the trial does not commence until the accused is placed in the charge of the jury.[24]

In the context of pre-trial motions, the Court has held that only the trial judge should hear applications to sever counts. In reference to the *Chabot* case in *R. v. Litchfield*,[25] the Court held that only the trial judge has jurisdiction to issue severance orders. However, the Court noted that as long as a trial judge has been assigned, there is no need to wait until the actual trial date to bring the application. Section 645(5) of the *Code* specifically authorizes a trial judge in a jury trial, before the jury has been selected, to deal with any matter that would be dealt with in the absence of the jury. The Court notes that a similar power "was

---

19   [1980] 2 S.C.R. 985 at 999 [*Chabot*].

20   [1989] 1 S.C.R. 1594 at para. 11 [*Kalanj*].

21   The Court rejected the argument that the time should run from the accused's arrest, eight months prior to the laying of charges. Compare *R. v. Connors* (1998), 14 C.R. (5th) 200 (B.C.C.A.), which held that for purposes of the *Identification of Criminals Act*, R.S.C. 1985, c. I-1, an accused had been charged with an offence when he had failed a breathalyzer test and was asked to give fingerprints at the time or return later to do so.

22   [1982] 2 S.C.R. 730 [*Basarabas*].

23   *R. v. Barrow*, [1987] 2 S.C.R. 694 [*Barrow*].

24   *Basarabas*, above note 22.

25   [1993] 4 S.C.R. 333 [*Litchfield*].

always open to a trial judge in a case of trial by judge alone to hear pre-trial motions before preparing to hear evidence."[26] It is likely that the *Litchfield* ruling, regarding the inability of anyone but the trial judge to hear motions concerning severance, applies to pre-trial motions generally. In this context, it is noteworthy that, for *Charter* motions, a preliminary inquiry judge is not a "court of competent jurisdiction" for the purposes of granting the remedy of excluding evidence under section 24(2).[27] However, given the Court's acknowledgment that different considerations apply in different contexts, it is possible that some motions could be permitted at an earlier time or in front of someone other than the trial judge,[28] or, alternatively, that some motions may not be permitted until the trial proper is about to commence.

This is a particlular area of the law that would benefit from rationalization. Some pre-trial motions are specifically permitted in the *Code*, for example: applications for change of venue,[29] for particulars,[30] for exclusion of the public from trial or a publication ban,[31] or to sever counts.[32] Other pre-trial motions are not specifically provided for in the *Code*. For examples, see the general power to hear such motions in non-jury trials referred to above in *Litchfield*, or pre-trial motions for relief under the *Charter*. The latter, among the most significant pre-trial motions made in courts, are subject to rules of court in some jurisdictions, but not to a statutory scheme.[33] Some applications can be made to preliminary inquiry judges,[34] and some cannot.[35] The timing for various applications differs and is sometimes based on wording that does not

---

26 *Ibid.* at para. 27.
27 *R. v. Hynes*, [2001] 3 S.C.R. 623 [*Hynes*]; *Mills v. The Queen*, [1986] 1 S.C.R. 863 [*Mills*].
28 The Court acknowledges in *Hynes*, *ibid.*, that preliminary inquiry judges can exclude evidence that is inadmissable on non-*Charter* grounds.
29 Section 599.
30 Section 587.
31 Section 486.
32 Section 591(3).
33 Compare, for example, *R. v. Blom* (2002), 6 C.R. (6th) 181 (Ont. C.A.) and *R. v. Russell*, [1999] B.C.J. No. 2245 at para. 6 (S.C.).
34 See *R. v. Webster*, [1993] 1 S.C.R. 3, holding that a preliminary inquiry judge has jurisdiction under s. 601 to consider whether an indictment is valid. Indeed, *R. v. Volpi* (1987), 34 C.C.C. (3d) 1 (Ont. C.A.) holds that this application can be made before the accused elects.
35 See *R. v. Chew*, [1968] 2 C.C.C. 127 (Ont. C.A.), dealing with applications for particulars under s. 587.

clearly indicate Parliament's intent (as noted above).[36] Calls for reform of this area have been made.[37]

A further forum in which matters can be discussed pre-trial is through a pre-hearing conference. Section 625.1 of the *Code* permits such hearings:

> to consider matters that to promote a fair and expeditious hearing, would be better decided before the start of the proceedings, and other similar matters, and to make arrangements for decisions on those matters.[38]

Such conferences are mandatory in the case of jury trials.[39]

Pre-hearing conferences provide an opportunity for the parties and the court to see whether an agreement can be reached on issues that will expedite the trial. The conference gives the judge a chance to determine, for example, whether the voluntariness of statements will be

---

36   In addition to the ambiguity noted above concerning phrases like "commencement of trial," note s. 590(2), which allows an accused to apply to divide a count "at any stage of his trial," and the very similar s. 591(3), which allows an accused to request separate trials on separate counts "before or during his trial."

37   See, in particular, Law Reform Commission of Canada, *Trial within a Reasonable Time* (Ottawa: Canada Communication Group, 1994), which recommended a system of pre-trial motions to be heard either by the trial judge or another judge of the same court. In the particular context of pre-trial motions connected with jury selection, see *R. v. Sharma* (1995), 67 B.C.A.C. 241 at para. 23, where the British Columbia Court of Appeal observed that:

> the ancient notion of preferment no longer has any relevance to modern day criminal proceedings . . . . In the interests of public convenience and the efficient operation of the courts, it has been the practice now for many years in this jurisdiction to have juries selected for a number of trials on one day each month. The complexities surrounding the preferment of indictments, when trials begin, when jurors can be replaced and which warrants and judicial interim release powers can be exercised by which judges in such a system, all result from a *Criminal Code* long outdated and over-burdened with half a century of, as I have said before, patchwork revision which does not recognize this practice. A complete overhaul of the procedural provisions of the *Criminal Code*, which would sanctify the sensible innovations developed in this jurisdiction and provide for a simple straightforward way of moving the accused procedurally from committal through to verdict, is long overdue.

38   Section 482(1) of the *Code* creates the authority for superior courts of criminal jurisdiction to create rules of court, and s. 482(2) permits courts of criminal jurisdiction to do so subject to the approval of the Lieutenant Governor in Council. Section 482(3)(c) specifically authorizes rules concerning pre-hearing conferences. Superior courts in every province have, in fact, made such rules.

39   Section 625.1(2).

admitted, whether identity will be an issue, or whether continuity of exhibits will be challenged.[40]

However, in contrast to pre-trial motions, pre-hearing conferences are not intended to determine matters: "s. 625.1 does not bind either the Crown or defence to a particular position."[41] Thus, for example, a Crown prosecutor might indicate at a pre-hearing conference a lack of intention to use a statement given by the accused, but then at trial seek to introduce the statement. Provided that on the particular facts there is no threat to the accused's fair trial right (for example, that the accused has not chosen a jury trial relying on the fact that the statement would not be tendered), the prosecutor is entitled to change strategy despite representations made at the pre-hearing conference.[42] Similarly, a Crown prosecutor can decide after a pre-hearing conference on a joint indictment to file separate indictments against each accused.[43]

The defence is also not bound by representations made at a pre-hearing conference, and can, for example, indicate at a conference that the issue in a sexual assault trial will be consent, but then argue at trial that no sexual relations occurred.[44] Similarly, because the pre-hearing conference is held on a without prejudice basis, indicating an intent to request a transfer hearing to youth court during the conference does not constitute an application.[45]

2) Particular Pre-trial Motions

Pre-trial motions can cover a wide variety of topics, and so the details of each will not be dealt with here. The substantive issues relevant to an application challenging the form of an indictment, or seeking a publication ban, can be found in Chapter 11. Similarly, pre-trial applications dealing with *Charter* issues, such as search and seizure issues or motions regarding disclosure, are dealt with in the chapters that correspond to those topics. However, some pre-trial motions will be discussed at greater length here, in particular applications for change

---

40   *R. v. Christensen* (1995), 100 Man. R. (2d) 25 (C.A.) [*Christensen*].
41   *R. v. Begrand-Fast* (1999), 180 Sask. R. 271 (C.A.), leave to appeal to S.C.C. refused, [1999] S.C.C.A. No. 583 [*Begrand-Fast*].
42   *R. v. K.(M.A.)* (2002), 166 Man. R. (2d) 205 (C.A.).
43   *Begrand-Fast*, above note 41.
44   *Christensen*, above note 40. The Court questions the wisdom of such a strategy, at least without giving prior notice to the court and the Crown of the changed approach.
45   *R. v. A.W.D.* (1999), 126 O.A.C. 334 (C.A.).

of venue, applications regarding fitness to stand trial, and *Charter* applications regarding the right to a trial within a reasonable time.

a)   Change of Venue

At common law, trials are to be held in the area in which the offence occurred. Trial judges typically have jurisdiction throughout the province in which they are appointed, and the only real territorial limitation is that courts should not hear trials of offences committed entirely in another province.[46] Nonetheless, the practice continues to be that trials are held in the area where they occurred, on the basis that this approach serves the interests of both the accused and the community.[47]

In some circumstances, however, it is possible to apply to change the venue in which the trial will be held, in accordance with section 599 of the *Code*. That section allows either the defence or the Crown to apply for a change of venue on the grounds that "(a) it appears expedient to the ends of justice; or (b) a competent authority has directed that a jury is not to be summoned at the time appointed in a territorial division where the trial would otherwise by law be held."[48] As a practical matter, change of venue applications in fact turn on whether pre-trial publicity has made it too difficult for an accused to obtain a fair trial without one.[49]

The essential issue is whether there is strong evidence of a general prejudicial attitude in the community as a whole.[50] In addition, that prejudice must not be capable of being cured by safeguards in jury selection, by instructions from the trial judge to the jury panel, or by the rules of evidence.[51] Because the remedy is discretionary, the judge hearing the application must consider all relevant factors.

The existence of the challenge for cause process, for example, and the ability in some circumstances to question jurors to determine whether

---

46   Section 478(1), but see the various special jurisdiction rules in ss. 7, 476, 477.1, or 478(2) & (3).

47   *R. v. Suzack* (2000), 30 C.R. (5th) 346 at para. 30 (Ont. C.A.) [*Suzack*].

48   Note that s. 2 of the *Code* defines "territorial division" as "any province, county, union of counties, township, city, town, parish or other judicial division or place to which the context applies." Note, as well, that s. 599 is incorporated by reference to apply to summary conviction offences: s. 795.

49   The one distinct circumstance worth noting is when a change of venue is sought under s. 531 of the *Code* to allow a trial to take place more easily in the official language of Canada that is the language of the accused.

50   *R. v. Munson*, 2003 SKCA 28 [*Munson*]; *R. v. English* (1993), 84 C.C.C. (3d) 511 (Nfld. C.A.) [*English*]; *R. v. Alward and Mooney* (1976), 39 C.R.N.S. 281 (N.B.S.C.A.D.).

51   *Suzack*, above note 47 at para.35.

pre-trial publicity has affected their ability to be impartial, has been relied on to dismiss change of venue applications.[52] Indeed, in cases where pre-trial publicity has been province-wide, it has been held that leaving the trial in a larger centre and using the challenge for cause process is more likely to protect the accused's rights than changing the venue to a smaller centre.[53] The date of the media coverage will also be relevant (prejudicial publicity from a year prior might not justify a change in venue).[54] In *R. v. Eng* the British Columbia Court of Appeal upheld a decision not to change venues on a retrial, even though a change of venue had been allowed on the original trial, on the basis that the passage of time had mended any prejudice caused by the media coverage.[55] Further, a change of venue will not be granted if the source of prejudice is the information to come out at trial, rather than the fact of pre-trial publicity: "where the real potential for prejudice lies in the evidence which the jury eventually selected to try the case will hear, a change of venue does not assist in protecting an accused's right to a fair trial."[56]

Where an accused applies for the change in venue,[57] the accused must show that the change is needed. Although this might be considered to place an onus on the accused, the provision has been held not to violate the *Charter*.[58]

b) Fitness to Stand Trial

Another motion potentially made on a pre-trial basis concerns the fitness of the accused to stand trial. This issue looks at whether the accused suffers from a mental disorder, and so is related to the ultimate issue of whether an accused will be found not criminally responsible under section 16 of the *Code*. The fitness to stand trial provisions are found in Part XX.1 of the *Code*. The majority of that Part sets out the procedures to deal with accused who have been found not criminally responsible based on a state of mind at the time of the offence, while the fitness provisions focus on the accused's mental state at the time of trial, and whether it is fair to proceed.[59]

---

52 See, for example, *Suzack, ibid.,* and *Munson,* above note 50. For further discussion of pre-trial publicity and challenges for cause, see below at Section C(3)(c).

53 *Munson, ibid.*

54 *Suzack,* above note 47.

55 *R. v. Eng* (1999), 138 C.C.C. (3d) 188 at para. 6 (B.C.C.A.).

56 *Suzack,* above note 47 at para. 38.

57 This is the typical case, though it is open on the terms of s. 599 for the Crown to apply: see *R. v. Ponton* (1899), 2 C.C.C. 417 (Ont. H.C.J.).

58 *Suzack,* above note 47 at para. 43.

59 Section 141 of the *YCJA,* above note 12, incorporates Part XX.1 of the *Criminal Code* except where those provisions conflict with rules in the former Act.

Everyone is presumed to be fit to stand trial.[60] The definition of "unfit to stand trial" in section 2 of the *Code* requires first that the accused suffers from a mental disorder (the same requirement as in section 16 for an accused to be not criminally responsible). The second requirement is that the accused is unable on that account:

> to conduct a defence at any stage of the proceedings before a verdict is rendered or to instruct counsel, and, in particular, unable on account of mental disorder to (a) understand the nature of the proceedings (b) understand the possible consequences of the proceedings, or (c) communicate with counsel.

This provision is a codification of common law rules concerning fitness.[61] Of these issues, whether the accused is able to communicate with counsel has attracted the most judicial attention.

A consciously low standard has been set for whether an accused can communicate with counsel. All that is necessary is for the accused to be able to communicate the facts relating to the offence: "provided the accused possesses this limited capacity, it is not a prerequisite that he or she be capable of exercising analytical reasoning in making a choice to accept the advice of counsel or in coming to a decision that best serves her interests."[62]

The Court, having jurisdiction over the accused, can order a fitness hearing on its own motion, or on application by the prosecutor or the accused. A party arguing that the accused is unfit has the burden of proof, on a balance of probabilities.[63] The fitness hearing itself is a two-stage process. First, the judge must consider whether there are reasonable grounds to decide whether the accused is unfit to stand trial. If this threshold is met, then the actual question of fitness is decided.[64]

A court can order an assessment to help determine whether an accused is fit to stand trial.[65] This assessment can be ordered on the court's own motion or on application by the prosecutor or the accused. Where the prosecutor applies for an assessment order in a summary conviction case, the court cannot grant the application unless the pros-

---

60 Section 672.22.
61 *R. v. Whittle*, [1994] 2 S.C.R. 914 [*Whittle*]; *R. v. Taylor* (1992), 11 O.R. (3d) 323 (C.A.) [*Taylor*]; *R. v. Brigham* (1992), 18 C.R. (4th) 309 (Que. C.A.).
62 *Taylor*, *ibid.*, approved in *Whittle*, *ibid.*
63 Sections 672.23(2) and 672.22.
64 *R. v. Lovie* (1995), 24 O.R. (3d) 836 (C.A.); *R. v. Bain* (1994), 130 N.S.R. (2d) 332 (C.A.) [*Bain*].
65 Section 672.11(a).

ecutor shows reasonable grounds to believe the accused is unfit or the accused raises the issue.[66]

In non-jury trials or at a preliminary inquiry the judge determines whether the accused is fit.[67] In jury cases where the accused has already been given in charge to the jury, the jury decides fitness.[68] In jury cases where the accused has not been given in charge to the jury, a jury must be sworn to decide the fitness issue, though with consent of the accused that jury can also hear the trial, if one occurs.[69]

Fitness applications need not be made pre-trial, and can be brought any time prior to verdict. There are some restrictions on timing, however. If the offence in question is a hybrid one, the judge must postpone the fitness hearing until after the Crown has elected whether to proceed summarily or by indictment.[70] If the application is brought during a preliminary inquiry, the judge may postpone the application until the time the accused is called upon to answer the charge.[71] Similarly, if the application is brought at trial, the judge has discretion to postpone the application until the opening of the accused's case.[72] The rationale for these delays is found in section 672.3, which notes that, if the accused is discharged at the preliminary inquiry or acquitted at the close of the Crown's case, the fitness issue will not be tried at all. Consistent with this approach is the obligation on the judge, in exercising the section 672.25(2)(b) discretion, to consider first whether the Crown can prove that the accused committed the act alleged in the indictment. If there is dispute over this question the judge:

> may proceed with the trial proper and postpone the fitness inquiry, or he or she may require the Crown to demonstrate at the outset of the fitness hearing that it is in a position to establish that the accused committed the act or acts alleged in the indictment. In either case, a finding that an accused is not fit to stand trial should not be made in the absence of any basis to put that accused on trial.[73]

If the accused is unrepresented, counsel shall be appointed.[74] If the accused is found fit to stand trial, matters continue as if no application

---

66   Section 672.12(2).
67   Section 672.27.
68   Section 672.26(b).
69   Section 672.26(a).
70   Section 672.25(1).
71   Section 672.25(2)(a).
72   Section 672.25(2)(b).
73   *Taylor*, above note 61.
74   Section 672.24.

had ever been made.[75] If the accused is found unfit, however, then a disposition hearing concerning the accused must be held. This hearing is conducted in accordance with essentially the same rules as disposition hearings for an accused found not criminally responsible, under section 16, at the conclusion of trial. The accused cannot be discharged absolutely, but can be confined in a hospital or discharged subject to conditions.[76] Treatment other than electroconvulsive therapy can be ordered for up to sixty days, provided there is specific evidence from a medical practitioner that the treatment will help make the accused fit for trial.[77]

If an accused is found fit to stand trial, it is nonetheless possible to bring a later application concerning the same issue if there is a change in circumstances.[78] If an accused is found unfit to stand trial, there must be regular reviews in which the Crown must show that it could still prove its case against the accused if called upon to do so. These reviews must occur at least every two years, or earlier if the accused shows reason to doubt that the Crown is still able to prove its case.[79] Evidence at these hearings can be by way of affidavits or transcripts, and the exact procedure is not specified in the *Code*. If, at any review, a *prima facie* case against the accused cannot be made out, the accused is entitled to an acquittal.

The defence and the Crown are each entitled to appeal the decision of a fitness hearing.[80]

c)   *Charter* Motions

Many different *Charter* motions can be brought, not necessarily on a pre-trial basis. Applications dealing with a violation of an accused's right to be free from unreasonable search and seizure, for example, might well occur either at the start of a trial or during its course. This chapter will not attempt to deal with all the various substantive issues that could arise on *Charter* motions. Only two motions will be considered here: applications concerning the right to a trial within a reasonable time and applications dealing with abuse of process.

---

75   Section 672.28.
76   Section 672.54.
77   Sections 672.58 and 672.61.
78   See, for example, *R. v. L.S.C.*, 2003 ABCA 105.
79   Section 672.33. This is one of the few places in which the rules for young persons are different. Section 141(10) of the *YCJA*, above note 12, requires that such reviews happen at least every year.
80   Sections 675(3) and 676(3).

i) Trial Within a Reasonable Time

Section 11(b) of the *Charter* guarantees any person charged with an offence the right "to be tried within a reasonable time." It is a motion particularly suited to the pre-trial stage because the minimum remedy for a violation of section 11(d) is a stay of the proceedings.[81] Although there is not complete agreement on the reasoning behind that result, the simplest way to understand the position of the Court is that it is not possible to find that a reasonable time in which to have a trial has already passed, but subsequently to put the accused on trial nonetheless.[82]

The right to trial within a reasonable time is of relatively little significance compared to the impact it might have had. In large measure, this results from the Court's treatment of the section in the context of institutional delay.

Though the section is not drafted in a way to require this reading, it is useful to distinguish between exceptional delay and institutional delay. Exceptional delay refers to delay that is out of the ordinary. In *Rahey*,[83] a decision that normally would have been made in a few days was adjourned by the trial judge nineteen times for a total duration of eleven months. In *R. v. Stensrud*[84] and *R. v. Smith*,[85] delays relating to preliminary inquiries (the preparation of a transcript and the actual scheduling of the inquiry, respectively) both were unusual compared to the norm in those jurisdictions. Institutional delay, on the other hand, refers to delay that is within the ordinary times of the particular jurisdiction, but that is unacceptable compared to some external standard.

R. v. Askov was the first occasion on which the Supreme Court dealt with institutional delay.[86] In that case the Court suggested a guideline of six to eight months delay from the time of committal to the start of a trial. This decision led to very large numbers of cases being dismissed: in a period of less than a year, 47,000 charges were dealt with in this way in Ontario alone. Although the majority of these charges were mi-

---

81 *R. v. Rahey*, [1987] 1 S.C.R. 588 [*Rahey*]. An application can, nonetheless, be brought at a later stage than on a pre-trial motion. In *Rahey* itself, the application was brought in relation to a delay occurring after the close of the Crown's case.

82 Six judges in *Rahey*, *ibid.*, reached the conclusion that a stay is the minimum remedy for a breach of s. 11(b), but for three different sets of reasons. Four of them suggest that a s. 11(b) violation removes the jurisdiction of a court to put the accused on trial. In *R. v. Morin*, [1992] 1 S.C.R. 771 [*Morin*], the Court was asked to reconsider this conclusion, but found it unnecessary to do so since they found no breach of s. 11(b).

83 *Rahey*, *ibid.*

84 [1989] 2 S.C.R. 1115.

85 [1989] 2 S.C.R. 1120 [*Smith*].

86 [1990] 2 S.C.R. 1199 [*Askov*].

nor ones that were withdrawn by Crown prosecutors rather than stayed by judges in accordance with the *Askov* guidelines, the Court appeared to feel some public pressure over this result. In the next case to deal with institutional delay, *Morin*, they adopted a stricter test than had previously existed. In particular, as will be discussed below, the Court gave much greater prominence to the need for an accused to show some particular prejudice in order to succeed in a section 11(b) claim. The net result was that even in the context of exceptional delay, the right was more severely circumscribed than it had been.

The actual scope of the right is fairly limited to begin with. The Court has held that the right does not include pre-charge delay (for example, where an accused has been arrested and fingerprinted but no charges are laid for eight months, that delay is not calculated into the section 11(b) equation).[87] Similarly, since the right is to be "tried" within a reasonable time, it does not protect against delay at the appellate level.[88]

The test for deciding section 11(b) claims was developed in *Smith* and *Askov* and set out in its current form in *Morin*. The Court has noted that "some delay is inevitable. The question is, at what point does the delay become unreasonable?"[89] To determine that question, four general considerations must be weighed:

1)   the length of the delay;
2)   waiver of time periods;
3)   the reasons for the delay, including

   a)   inherent time requirements of the case,
   b)   actions of the accused,
   c)   actions of the Crown,

---

87   *Kalanj*, above note 20. The Court has suggested in *Morin*, above note 82 at 789, that "pre-charge delay may in certain circumstances have an influence on the overall determination as to whether post-charge delay is unreasonable" while reaffirming that "of itself it is not counted in determining the length of the delay." Although this possible use of pre-charge delay has been held open, it does not appear to have actually featured in any Supreme Court of Canada decision. In *R. v. L. (W.K.)*, [1991] 1 S.C.R. 1091, the Court rejected an application based on pre-charge delay and an alleged violation of s. 7 in terms that suggest such motions, while not absolutely barred, are unlikely to succeed, and would require something more than just delay.

88   *R. v. Potvin*, [1993] 2 S.C.R. 880: Whether the accused was acquitted, the charge was stayed, or the accused is appealing a conviction, s. 11(b) affords no protection. The Court did acknowledge that in appropriate circumstances a remedy under s. 7 for abuse of process might be available for appellate delay.

89   *Smith*, above note 85 at 1131.

    d)   limits on institutional resources, and

    e)   other reasons for delay; and

4)   prejudice to the accused.[90]

In effect, the first factor asks whether there is delay that needs explaining, while the remaining three ask whether that delay can be explained. Each factor is worth considering separately.

    "Delay" is an ambiguous term, and could mean either the total time taken from the laying of the charge until the completion of the trial, or the portion of that time that is longer than one would expect. Though the second meaning probably accords more closely with ordinary usage, the Court has been clear that the first is what is intended.[91] The burden of proof to show a *Charter* violation rests on the accused. As a result, if the delay is not unusual, then the section 11(b) analysis might go no further. When delay becomes unusual, however, a secondary burden shifts to the Crown to explain it. The length of time that will require explanation could vary, depending on the circumstances. For example, an accused who is in custody might reasonably seek an earlier trial.[92]

    Waiver is relevant since an accused cannot agree to a certain delay and then later complain of it. Consistent with other contexts, the Court has held that waiver of *Charter* rights can be explicit or implicit, but that it must be clear and unambiguous. The Court has said that consent to a trial date will often constitute a waiver, but this result does not necessarily follow.[93] In particular, if there is no reason to think that an earlier trial date would be available, an accused is not required to make an entirely *pro forma* objection.[94] Further, in some cases acquiescence to a request from the trial judge will be treated differently than

---

90   *Morin*, above note 82 at 787–89.

91   See *Morin, ibid.* at 789, which holds that delay means "the period from the charge to the end of the trial." In *R. v. Collins*, [1995] 2 S.C.R. 1104 [*Collins*] the Court treated the term "delay" as though it meant the unjustified portion of that period, but that appears to be the only exception, and there was no acknowledgment of the change in usage. Unfortunately, recent caselaw from Ontario has wrongly adopted the "unjustified portion" meaning of delay, with the result that the application of the guidelines from *Askov*, above note 86, and *Morin* results in justification of far longer periods than those cases envisioned: see, for example, *R. v. Qureshi* (2004), 27 C.R. (6th) 142 (Ont. C.A.); *R. v. G.(C.R.)* (2005), 206 C.C.C. (3d) 262 (Ont. C.A.).

92   *Morin, ibid.*

93   *Smith*, above note 85.

94   See, for example, *Mills*, above note 27; *Rahey*, above note 81; or *Askov*, above note 86.

requests from counsel, since an accused is likely to defer to the wishes of the trier of fact.[95]

Prior to *Morin*, the reasons for the delay were the most important factors to be considered, and they remain significant. The inherent time requirements of the case, understandably, will vary depending on the circumstances. Complex cases take more time than simple ones,[96] and at the simplest level a case with a preliminary inquiry will take longer than one without. Every case will have certain ordinary requirements, such as the need for the accused to obtain counsel, the time involved in making disclosure, and so on. The Court in *Morin* resisted the call to lay down general guidelines regarding how long these ordinary requirements should take. Instead, it held that courts would need to develop these guidelines locally.[97] On the one hand, it is reasonable to suggest that local courts will be more familiar with local practices and have a better sense of how long it normally takes for disclosure to be made. On the other hand, not setting any such guideline removes most of the incentive for any given region to become more efficient. That is, provided a case does not fall outside the ordinary range for that area, however slow it might be in comparison to similar courts elsewhere in the country, local standards will say there is no problem.

The actions of the accused can be relevant because they can themselves contribute to the delay. An accused may apply for change of venue, change solicitors, request re-election to trial by judge alone,[98] or re-elect to turn a scheduled provincial court trial into a preliminary inquiry.[99] As the Court notes in *Morin*, even though such steps are taken in good faith, they contribute to the total time duration and so must be taken into account in assessing whether that delay was unreasonable.[100]

Much the same is true of actions taken by the Crown. Though the Crown might, perfectly reasonably, request an adjournment to have a particular witness available, the fact that the request was reasonable is

---

95 *Rahey*, ibid.

96 In *Collins*, above note 91, the dissenting judges argued that the seriousness of the offence, a factor similar to, but distinct from, its complexity, ought also to be relevant. They held that since the s. 11(b) right also weighs society's interests in the balance, in principle it should be possible to find unreasonable delay and a serious breach of an accused's right, but nonetheless find that there was no breach of s. 11(b) because the societal interest outweighed the prejudice. The majority in *Collins*, while not specifically addressing this argument, seems clearly to reject it, since they upheld the lower court decision granting a stay.

97 *Morin*, above note 82 at 799–800.

98 The accused in *R. v. Conway*, [1989] 1 S.C.R. 1659 [*Conway*] took all these steps.

99 As in *R. v. Bennett*, [1992] 2 S.C.R. 168.

100 *Morin*, above note 82 at 794.

not a justification to explain away delay that is otherwise unreasonable.[101]

Limits on institutional resources are the factor most relevant in the contrasting decisions of *Askov* and *Morin*, though, on the face of it, there is very little difference in the way in which this factor is described in each. In *Morin* the Court notes that

> The Court cannot simply accede to the government's allocation of resources and tailor the period of permissible delay accordingly. The weight to be given to resource limitations must be assessed in light of the fact that the government has a constitutional obligation to commit sufficient resources to prevent unreasonable delay which distinguishes this obligation from many others that compete for funds with the administration of justice. There is a point in time at which the Court will no longer tolerate delay based on the plea of inadequate resources.[102]

Askov had laid down a guideline of six to eight months from committal to trial. *Morin* affirmed that guideline, and added the further suggestion that the delay in provincial courts should be between eight and ten months. *Morin* also stressed, to avoid the problems that had arisen post-*Askov*, that these times were simply guidelines, not absolute limitation periods. This was not actually a change from what *Askov* had said, but seemingly the Court felt the need to make the point especially clear. Indeed, in *Morin* itself they both laid down the guideline and denied a remedy although that guideline was not met.

The significant way in which *Morin* differed from *Askov* on this issue was in the use that was to be made of comparisons to other jurisdictions. In *Askov*, the Court had relied on statistics showing that the Brampton court in question was dramatically slower than any other court in North America, and, in particular, slower than courts in Montreal. In *Morin* they suggest that this was a misleading comparison, because the manner in which criminal charges are dealt with in Montreal and Brampton is sufficiently dissimilar so as to make statistics drawn from the two jurisdictions of limited comparative value. Comparison with other jurisdictions is therefore to be applied with caution and only as a rough guide.[103]

This was an unfortunate retreat. Montreal had, at the relevant time, a fifteen-year history of using case management in order to deal as ef-

---

101 *Morin, ibid.,* speaking of the facts in *Smith,* above note 85.
102 *Morin, ibid.* at 795–96.
103 *Ibid.* at 799.

ficiently as possible with criminal cases, Brampton did not. Although cases were dealt with differently in the two jurisdictions, one possibility was that that was precisely the source of the problem and not a justification for denying the existence of a problem.[104]

Other factors deal with matters such as those above that cannot be attributed to either the defence or the Crown. When the trial judge in *Rahey* adjourned the decision on a directed verdict nineteen times, for example, that was a factor to be considered under this heading.

It is the change in the way prejudice enters the equation that was of the most significance in *Morin*, and has contributed to the current limited scope of the right. Section 11(b) protects against various forms of prejudice such as threats to security of the person, to liberty, and to the right to a fair trial. The Court stated in *Morin*:

> The right to security of the person is protected in s. 11(b) by seeking to minimize the anxiety, concern and stigma of exposure to criminal proceedings. The right to liberty is protected by seeking to minimize exposure to the restrictions on liberty which result from pre-trial incarceration and restrictive bail conditions. The right to a fair trial is protected by attempting to ensure that proceedings take place while evidence is available and fresh.[105]

In early section 11(b) cases, Chief Justice Lamer argued that prejudice to an accused's security interest — the stigmatization, loss of privacy, stress, and anxiety flowing from being charged with an offence — was inherent in a denial and part of the rationale for the right. Accordingly, prejudice should be presumed and need not be proven. Indeed, he argued that an accused not only did not need to prove prejudice to liberty interests or to fair trial rights, but that such evidence would be "irrelevant"[106] (being held unreasonably long in custody would go to a section 7 violation, not section 11(b), and having lost the ability to call a witness would go to the fair trial guarantee in section 11(d), not to section 11(b)).

However, although the point remained unsettled through many cases,[107] the general view of the Court seemed to be to prefer to allow such additional evidence in. No judge disputed that prejudice to an

---

104   On the other hand, see Carl Baar, "Criminal Court Delay and the *Charter*: The Use and Misuse of Social Facts in Judicial Policy Making" (1993) 72 Can. Bar Rev. 305, where he suggests that for various jurisdictional and statistical reasons, the Court might have been wrong to make the comparison in the first place.

105   *Morin*, above note 82 at 786.

106   *Mills*, above note 27 at 926.

107   *Rahey*, above note 81; *Kalanj*, above note 20; *Conway*, above note 98; *Smith*, above note 85; *Askov*, above note 86.

accused's security interest showed a section 11(b) violation. For example, the unanimous Court in *Smith* held that "'a criminal charge will be hanging over [the accused] for a substantial period of time.' This is the very essence of prejudice to the security interests of a person charged with an offence."[108] Nonetheless, most judges seemed to prefer the view that an accused could also strengthen a section 11(b) claim by showing infringements of a liberty or fair trial interest as well.

The danger in such an approach is that once one argues that evidence of the latter sort makes a claim stronger, it becomes implicit that the absence of such evidence makes a claim weaker. But if prejudice is part of the rationale for the right and is to be presumed, then an infringement of security interests alone should lead to a remedy, whether liberty or fair trial interests have been affected or not.

In fact, the result of *Morin* was to reverse the stand the Court had previously taken on this point. The Court begins by repeating that prejudice should be presumed in the case of section 11(b) violations. However, the Court also gave much greater prominence to a suggestion that had existed in other cases: that many accused do not actually want a trial within a reasonable time, that most accused are content to have delay, and, indeed, would prefer to have unreasonable delay leading to a *Charter* remedy rather than a trial on the merits. Having postulated that this general view existed, the Court then held that the Crown could, therefore, disprove prejudice by showing "that the accused is in the majority group who do not want an early trial and that the delay benefitted rather than prejudiced the accused."[109] On the particular facts of the case, the Court concluded from the accused's failure to try to expedite her trial that she "was content with the pace with which things were proceeding and that therefore there was little or no prejudice occasioned by the delay."[110] Because there was no such prejudice, the Court found that her section 11(b) right was not violated, despite the fact that the delay was outside the reasonable period allowed by the guideline.

To reason in this way, even if some or most accused genuinely do not object to delay,[111] is, in effect, to eliminate the presumption of prejudice. In that case, it is really only the accused who can show some

---

108 *Smith*, *ibid.* at 1138–39.
109 *Morin*, above note 82 at 803.
110 *Ibid.* at 808.
111 It should be noted that the innocent as well as the guilty could hold this attitude. Further, that an accused does not object to delay does not mean that the delay favours the accused: people often put off unpleasant things even if their completion would be of benefit.

tangible form of prejudice, such as prolonged incarceration or loss of witnesses who will benefit from section 11(b). But this amounts to saying that only an accused who can show threats to liberty or fair trial interests (an accused who therefore is already protected by section 7 or section 11(d)) will have a section 11(b) right.

Consequently, the section 11(b) right has attracted relatively little judicial attention, especially in the Supreme Court, since *Morin*. Since that case laid down a guideline but approved departures of it where the accused could not prove prejudice, the task for an accused has become much more difficult. Absent proof of serious prejudice, section 11(b) claims have become less likely to be granted.[112]

ii)   Abuse of Process and Fair Trial Rights

Although the doctrine was in doubt in Canada for many years, the Supreme Court has unequivocally concluded that:

> there is a residual discretion in a trial court judge to stay proceedings where compelling an accused to stand trial would violate those fundamental principles of justice which underlie the community's sense of fair play and decency and to prevent the abuse of a court's process through oppressive or vexatious proceedings.[113]

Motions for a stay based on abuse of process need not be brought on a pre-trial basis, and indeed most typically would not be (many claims, such as entrapment, will depend on the evidence that emerges at trial).[114] However, they are potentially available at a pre-trial stage because the issue in deciding whether to grant a stay for abuse of process is not whether the prosecution can prove its case, but whether the case is "tainted to such a degree that to allow it to proceed would tarnish the integrity of the court."[115] Thus, for example, it is possible to

---

112   There does seem to have been a recent resurgence of claims in Ontario, but as observed above in note 91, the Ontario Court of Appeal has adopted a restrictive interpretation of the meaning of the word "delay" that is at odds with Supreme Court of Canada caselaw and minimizes the likelihood of a successful institutional delay claim even further: See Gerry Ferguson & Steve Coughlan, *Annual Review of Criminal Law 2006* (Toronto: Carswell, 2007) at 146–50 and Gerry Ferguson & Steve Coughlan, *Annual Review of Criminal Law 2005* (Toronto: Carswell, 2006) at 149–51.

113   *R. v. Jewitt*, [1985] 2 S.C.R. 128 at 135 [*Jewitt*].

114   Indeed, the Court held in *R. v. Mack*, [1988] 2 S.C.R. 903 [*Mack*] that an abuse of process claim could not be considered until after the judge had decided whether the Crown had proven the accused guilty beyond a reasonable doubt.

115   *Conway*, above note 98 at 1667.

obtain a stay even at the stage of an extradition hearing to face charges in another country.[116]

Although, as a practical matter the two issues typically arise together of (i) whether there is an abuse of process and, (ii) if there is, whether a stay is the appropriate remedy, they are separate questions.

a.   Abuse of Process

As noted above, the doctrine of abuse of process requires that the proceedings are oppressive or vexatious and that they violate the fundamental principles of justice underlying the community's sense of fair play and decency.[117] At common law, the issue was society's interest in a fair process, and whether proceedings had become so unfair that they were contrary to the interests of justice.[118] In very large measure, the Court has now consciously merged the common law abuse of process doctrine with section 7 of the *Charter*, and for the most part, abuse of process claims can be decided based on whether they violate the accused's right to a fair trial.[119] However, the Court still acknowledged a "residual category" of abuse of process claims that may lead to a stay:

> This residual category does not relate to conduct affecting the fairness of the trial or impairing other procedural rights enumerated in the *Charter*, but instead addresses the panoply of diverse and sometimes unforeseeable circumstances in which a prosecution is conducted in such a manner as to connote unfairness or vexatiousness of such a degree that it contravenes fundamental notions of justice and thus undermines the integrity of the judicial process.[120]

This residual category would be important where the *Charter* does not apply, or where the abuse does not threaten a *Charter* right for some reason.[121]

A pre-trial motion seeking a stay has sometimes been sought on the basis that it will be impossible to empanel an impartial jury, most probably due to pre-trial publicity, though not necessarily only on those

---

116 *United States of America v. Cobb*, [2001] 1 S.C.R. 587.

117 In *R. v. Keyowski*, [1988] 1 S.C.R. 657, the Court appeared to make these criteria alternatives, but in *R. v. Regan*, [2002] 1 S.C.R. 297 at 326 [*Regan*], the Court quoted with approval from the judgment of Justice McLachlin (as she then was) in *Scott*, where she specifically noted that "I would read these criteria cumulatively": *R. v. Scott*, [1990] 3 S.C.R. 979 at para. 70.

118 *R. v. Power*, [1994] 1 S.C.R. 601 at 616.

119 *R. v. O'Connor*, [1995] 4 S.C.R. 411 [*O'Connor*].

120 *Ibid.* at para. 73. See also *Regan*, above note 117.

121 *O'Connor, ibid.* at para. 70.

grounds.[122] The Court has not completely precluded such a motion, though they did hold that such an application brought before jury selection had begun was premature:

> It is only at the stage when the jury is to be selected that it will be possible to determine whether the respondent can be tried by an impartial jury . . . . In an extreme case (and the present certainly qualifies), such publicity should lead to challenge for cause at trial, but I am far from thinking that it must necessarily be assumed that a person subjected to such publicity will necessarily be biased.[123]

On this issue, see the further discussion below, at Section C(3)(c) of challenge for cause in the jury selection process.

In *Jewitt*, the issue was whether the accused had been entrapped, and the Court has subsequently elaborated entrapment as one of the circumstances that might lead to a stay of proceedings based on abuse of process.[124] The list of potential abuses is open-ended, and accused have made applications in a wide variety of situations, including conflict of interest for the accused's lawyers,[125] pre-charge collaboration between police and Crown prosecutors that was alleged to have led to a loss of objectivity on the part of the Crown,[126] reliance by police on advice as to whether their investigation would be illegal,[127] and non-disclosure of evidence.[128] In most cases, these claims are not ultimately successful. Sometimes, this is because the alleged abuse is not found to be made out,[129] but it is also in part because the Court has held that the power to stay proceedings can only be exercised in the "clearest of cases."[130] This leads to the question: when should a remedy be granted?

b.   Stay of Proceedings

Even if an abuse of process has caused prejudice to the accused or threatened the integrity of the justice system, at least two criteria must be met before a stay will be the appropriate remedy:

---

122 See *English*, above note 50; *R. v. Vermette*, [1988] 1 S.C.R. 985 [*Vermette*].

123 *Vermette*, *ibid.* at 992–93.

124 *Mack*, above note 114; *R. v. Barnes*, [1991] 1 S.C.R. 449.

125 *R. v. Neil*, 2002 SCC 70.

126 *Regan*, above note 117.

127 *R. v. Campbell*, [1999] 1 S.C.R. 565.

128 *O'Connor*, above note 119, though the *O'Connor* analysis deals with the issue as implicating the accused's s. 7 rights.

129 See, for example, *Regan*, above note 117, upholding the Nova Scotia Court of Appeal's decision that the Crown prosecutor had remained objective despite pre-trial consultations with the police.

130 *Jewitt*, above note 113 at 137.

(1) the prejudice caused by the abuse in question will be manifested, perpetuated or aggravated through the conduct of the trial, or by its outcome; and

(2) no other remedy is reasonably capable of removing that prejudice.[131]

These criteria have been adopted because the central purpose of a stay is not to remedy prior misbehaviour towards an accused: "the mere fact that the state has treated an individual shabbily in the past is not enough to warrant a stay of proceedings."[132] Rather, a stay is intended to prevent the perpetuation of a wrong that will otherwise continue to affect the parties and the community.[133]

Because abuse of process and the section 7 right to a fair trial are closely aligned, most cases of abuse of process mean that, without a remedy, the trial would not be fair. However, in most of those situations some other remedy such as an order for further disclosure and an adjournment is an adequate solution. Therefore, a stay should only be granted where it is the only remedy that will serve.

Even in the small, residual category of abuses that do not affect an accused's fair trial right, the Court has held that normally a stay should only be granted if the prejudice would be ongoing. It has allowed for the possibility of "cases in which the past misconduct is so egregious that the mere fact of going forward in the light of it will be offensive,"[134] but have stressed that such cases should be "exceptional" and "relatively very rare."[135] If any doubt still exists about whether a stay should be granted in such a case, the Court has directed consideration of a third criterion: a balancing between the interests of the accused served by granting a stay, and the interest of society in having a final decision on the merits. The Court has noted that "in these cases, 'an egregious act of misconduct could [never] be overtaken by some passing public concern [although] . . . a compelling societal interest in having a full hearing could tip the scales in favour of proceeding.'"[136]

---

131 *O'Connor*, above note 119 at para. 75, quoted in *Regan*, above note 117.

132 *Canada (Minister of Citizenship and Immigration) v. Tobiass*, [1997] 3 S.C.R. 391 at para. 91 [*Tobiass*].

133 *Regan*, above note 117 at para. 53.

134 *Tobiass*, above note 132 at para. 91.

135 *Ibid.*; *Regan*, above note 117.

136 *Regan*, *ibid.* at para. 57, quoting from *Tobiass*, *ibid.* at para. 92.

C. JURY SELECTION

1) Introduction

The *Criminal Code* provides for several methods of trial, in particular trial by provincial court judge, trial by superior court judge alone, and trial by superior court judge with a jury (see the discussion in Chapter 3 at section A). Section 471 of the *Code* provides that every indictable offence shall be tried by a judge and jury "except where otherwise expressly provided by law." As a matter of fact, though, various *Code* sections readily provide other choices for every offence except those listed in section 469. The net effect is that a few offences, such as murder and treason, are required to be tried by jury, while a few indictable offences, such as theft not exceeding $5000, cannot have a jury. But, for all other indictable offences an accused can choose between any of the three modes of trial.[137]

Jury selection procedures involve a mixture of federal and provincial legislation. Section 92(14) of the *Constitution Act, 1867*[138] gives provinces jurisdiction over the administration of justice in the province. A jury of twelve members who will hear an individual trial come from a jury array, the larger number of prospective jurors summoned to the courtroom in order for the selection to take place.[139] In each province and territory, a jury act sets out the rules by which the jury array is summoned to the courtroom. These rules include such matters as qualifications and disqualifications for being a juror, sources from which prospective jurors are to be selected, and compensation for jurors. Once the prospective jurors are actually in the courtroom in a criminal matter, the provisions of the *Criminal Code* then govern the actual selection of the jury. These rules deal with challenges for cause, peremptory challenges, excusing jurors, and so on.[140]

---

137 Note as well that s. 11(f) of the *Charter* guarantees an accused the right to "the benefit of trial by jury" for any offence with a punishment of five years imprisonment or more. In *R. v. Turpin*, [1989] 1 S.C.R. 1296, the Court held that although an accused could waive that right, waiver of the right to trial by jury did not amount to a right to trial by non-jury. Accordingly, the *Code* provisions preventing an accused from electing trial by judge alone in a murder case did not violates s. 11(f).

138 (U.K.), 30 & 31 Vict., c. 3.

139 The *Criminal Code* uses both the term "array" and "panel" to refer to this group: see, for example, s. 629, which speaks about challenging a jury panel, but appears under the heading "Challenging the Array."

140 In *Barrow*, above note 23, the Court notes that the provinces have jurisdiction over the "administrative" aspects of jury selection, specifically the authority to

2) Provincial Legislation Jury Selection Procedures — Creating the Jury Array

Although the province has jurisdiction over the administration of justice in the province, it is worth noting that section 626 of the *Criminal Code* specifies that jurors must be qualified in accordance with the laws of the province.[141] That section also states that, notwithstanding any law of a province, no person can be disqualified from jury service based on sex. It is generally accepted today that in any case the jury array should be assembled from as broad and inclusive a source as possible within the province. This desire is manifested in different ways within various statutes. In Nova Scotia, for example, the legislation explicitly sets out that goal, stating that the list should be drawn from a "data base that to the extent possible shall include the entire population."[142] Prince Edward Island, on the other hand, specifies that the *Health Services Payment Act*[143] list should be used.[144] Manitoba contents itself with a direction to the Sheriff to use "appropriate lists."[145] Other provinces do not specify what source is to be used in assembling the array.

---

assemble the array. However, the precise constitutional dividing line between federal and provincial jurisdiction is not entirely clear: see David Pomerant, *Multiculturalism, Representation and the Jury Selection Process in Canadian Criminal Cases* (Ottawa: Department of Justice Canada, Research and Statistics Directorate, 1994) [Pomerant].

141 The Court describes this provision in *R. v. Sherratt*, [1991] 1 S.C.R. 509 [*Sherratt*] as avoiding jurisdictional conflict, but it could equally be seen as contributing to the ambiguity of the situation. It is true that the provision leaves no doubt as to which statutes actually govern the out-of-court portion of jury selection. However, the existence of s. 626 creates doubt as to *why* the provincial jury acts govern the situation. If the provinces have jurisdiction to create those statutes by virtue of s. 92(14) of the *Constitution Act, 1867*, above note 138, then s. 626 is unnecessary: its existence could imply that the *Criminal Code* is the ultimate foundation of authority for the rules in the provincial jury acts. In this regard, the situation could be similar to the definition of "Attorney General" in s. 2 of the *Code*, which in *Canada v. Canadian National Transportation*, [1983] 2 S.C.R. 206 was held to be the provincial Attorney General, not because the province had original jurisdiction over prosecutions, but because valid federal legislation designated the provincial Attorney General. See, generally, Pomerant, *ibid.*, for more on this issue.

142 *Juries Act*, S.N.S. 1998, c. 16, s. 7(1).

143 R.S.P.E.I. 1988, c. H-2.

144 *Jury Act*, R.S.P.E.I. 1988, c. J-5.1, s. 8(1). Note that the Regulations to the Nova Scotia Act, above note 142, similarly specify that the Health Insurance list is an appropriate database.

145 *Jury Act*, C.C.S.M. c. J30, s. 6(1).

There is a reasonable degree of correspondence across the country concerning which people are qualified for jury service. Normally, a juror is required to be of the age of majority in the province, a resident of that province, and a Canadian citizen.[146] Disqualifications frequently appear to be based on two general justifications: (i) that the potential juror would face a conflict in serving on a jury, or (ii) that what the juror does in everyday life is more important than, or for some other reason justifies a general exemption from, serving on a jury. For example, people involved in law enforcement are typically disqualified from jury service, though the exact list of which personnel do and do not qualify varies from province to province. Similarly, judges and lawyers are routinely excluded from juries, as sometimes are articled clerks or those who simply have a law degree. Disqualifications based on some type of criminal record are also routine, though, again, with variation as to how serious an offence it was and how recently it was committed. On a different note, jury acts regularly disqualify the governor general, the lieutenant governor, members of Parliament, members of the provincial government, senators, and so on. In some provinces, doctors, veterinarians, or other health professionals are also disqualified. In addition, most jurisdictions provide scope for an individual assessment of whether it will create a hardship for a particular person to serve on a jury, allow for exemptions based on reasons of religion or conscience, and exclude those with a physical or mental disability that would prevent the person from fulfilling the role of a juror.

3) *Criminal Code* Jury Selection Procedures — Choosing the Jury from the Jury Array

a) Mechanics of Selecting Jurors

Once the jury array has been assembled in court, the *Criminal Code* provisions govern the remaining selection procedures. It is possible for either the accused or the prosecutor to challenge the array itself, though this may only be based on "partiality, fraud or wilful misconduct on the part of the part of the sheriff or other officer by whom the panel was returned."[147] If the array has been accepted, then the selection procedure itself begins, by which the names of those present are pulled randomly from a box in accordance with the procedures set out

---

146 Although, note that Manitoba, for example, has repealed the citizenship requirement: *Charter Compliance Statute Amendment Act*, R.S.M. 1987 Supp., c. 4, s. 14.

147 Section 629: see the discussion of *R. v. Butler* (1984), 3 C.R. (4th) 174 (B.C.C.A.) [*Butler*] and of *R. v. Kent, Sinclair and Gode* (1986), 27 C.C.C. (3d) 405 (Man. C.A.) [*Kent*] at Section C(3)(d), below in this chapter, for more on this issue.

in section 631 of the *Code*.[148] This procedure continues until, after the methods of excluding jurors (discussed below at section C(3)(b)) have been considered, enough jurors have been selected. If the entire jury array is run through without a sufficient number of jurors having been selected, section 644 of the *Code* allows the judge to order the sheriff to "forthwith" summon other jurors to the courtroom. As a practical matter, this can take the form of the sheriff simply going to the street and requiring passersby to attend for potential jury selection. These jurors, known as "talesmen," are then selected from in the same manner as the original array.

Criminal trials must commence with twelve jurors,[149] and in the ordinary course only that number of jurors will be selected. However, particularly given the possibility of pre-trial motions and *voir dires* that can take weeks or even months and occur without the jury, the actual commencement of trial might occur some time after the jury has been selected. As a result, there is a risk that not all twelve jurors will be present when the trial begins.[150] Similarly, circumstances for some juror could have changed in the period between selection and commencement of trial. Section 644(1) of the *Code* allows a judge to discharge a juror based on illness or other reasonable charge, and a juror previously selected might seek to be excused under this section. At that stage the original jury array from which the jury was to be selected will no longer be present. Courts have dealt with this problem in a variety of ways in the past, and two recent *Code* amendments are aimed at the situation. First, under section 644(1.1), provided the jury has not begun to hear evidence, a judge can choose a replacement juror either by using the procedure for selecting talesmen or by selecting a juror from some other

---

148 Section 631 sets out quite precise guidelines concerning how many names are to be randomly drawn at a time, the order in which potential jurors are to be sworn, and so on. However, s. 643(3) provides that failure to comply with s. 631, s. 635 (order of challenges), or s. 641 (calling jurors who have been stood by) does not affect the validity of the proceedings. In essence, this saving provision is only meant to protect against harmless errors: not if the error has deprived the accused of a statutory right or deprives an accused of the right to a trial by a jury lawfully constituted: *R. v. Rowbotham* (1988), 63 C.R. (3d) 113 (Ont. C.A.).

149 The Court has noted that the "commencement of trial" is not a single fixed point, and will vary depending on the *Code* section and interests in question. The accused's right to be present for the entire trial, for example, should be construed to allow the accused to be present for the selection of the jury. In the context of replacing jurors, though, the Court has designated the commencement of trial as the point at which evidence is first heard. See *Basarabas*, above note 22.

150 *R. v. Singh* (1996), 108 C.C.C. (3d) 244 (B.C.C.A.).

jury array that happens to be available.[151] Second, section 631(2.1) of the *Code* allows the judge to direct the selection of one or two alternate jurors at the time of the original selection of twelve jurors.[152] These alternate jurors then attend at the commencement of trial (if a full jury is not present the alternate jurors can be substituted, but if they are not required then the alternate jurors are excused). Alternate jurors cannot be substituted once evidence has been heard. However, although the trial must commence with twelve jurors, section 644(2) directs that the jury remains properly constituted, unless the judge orders otherwise, provided the number of jurors is not reduced below ten.

There are three mechanisms by which a member of the jury array might be excluded from the jury: exemption, challenge for cause, and peremptory challenge. The three occur in that order. First, the trial judge is to decide whether any juror's request to be exempted should be granted. This step is taken first so that the parties are not required to use peremptory challenges to exclude jurors who might not have served in any case.[153] Following that, the parties are called upon to make any challenges, with challenges for cause preceding peremptory challenges.[154]

b) Exemptions

Section 632 of the *Code* allows a trial judge to excuse jurors[155] based on any of three grounds: personal interest in the matter to be tried; relationship with the judge, prosecutor, accused, counsel for the accused, or a prospective witness; and personal hardship or other reasonable cause. Typically, this procedure is carried out before individual juror's names are called, by the judge asking whether any jurors wish to be excused. Although this task is in a sense administrative, it is a part of the trial and the accused is entitled to be present for it.[156]

---

151 In *R. v. Paterson* (2001), 41 C.R. (5th) 278 (B.C.C.A.), the trial occurred before s. 644(1.1) had been placed in the *Code*, though in fact the trial judge did select a replacement juror from a different jury array. The British Columbia Court of Appeal held that s. 644(1.1) merely codified what had already been the law, and refused to allow an appeal.

152 In this event, the Crown and defence receive an additional peremptory challenge for each alternate juror: s. 634(2.1).

153 *R. v. Douglas* (2002), 12 C.R. (6th) 374 (Ont. C.A.) [*Douglas*].

154 *R. v. Bernardo* (2000), 31 C.R. (5th) 368 (Ont. C.A.) [*Bernardo*].

155 Throughout this section, references to a "juror" should be understood where appropriate to mean a "prospective juror": that is, a person on the array whose name is called out for possible selection to a jury.

156 *Barrow*, above note 23.

Strictly the first two grounds upon which jurors can be excused relate to potential partiality, which in general must be dealt with by way of the challenge for cause procedures in the *Code*. However, these grounds are limited to such "obvious situations of non-indifference" that the consent of counsel to the exclusion of the juror can be presumed.[157] In any other circumstances, the challenge for cause procedures must be used. Further, nothing prevents a party from challenging for cause a juror whose request to be excused was not granted by the trial judge.[158]

The trial judge has a further related power under section 633 of the *Code*. Rather than excusing the juror completely, the trial judge can stand jurors aside. In that event, jury selection continues with the remaining members of the array. Jurors that the judge has allowed to stand aside are only re-called for possible selection if the array is exhausted without a complete jury. On its face, the section is limited to standing jurors aside based on personal hardship or other reasonable cause, which is the third of the three grounds upon which jurors can be excused under section 632. However the Ontario Court of Appeal has held that "other reasonable grounds" can include potential partiality on the part of the juror.[159] The section states that it can only be used when a juror is individually called under section 631, rather than in the global manner used for excusing jurors. However, in *Krugel* the Ontario Court of Appeal found that an accused had suffered no prejudice when a trial judge departed from that approach,[160] and in *Douglas* it appeared to approve the practice of a trial judge who, with no objection from counsel, adopted the administrative convenience of informally standing aside, as a group, all jurors who indicated that they would seek an exemption if they were asked.[161]

c) Challenges for Cause

Section 638 of the *Code* sets out the grounds upon which a juror may be challenged for cause. Both the Crown and the accused are entitled to an unlimited number of challenges for cause, but the grounds upon which those challenges can be made are exhaustively defined in subsections (a) through (f) of section 638. Some of the grounds are simply factual questions, such as that the juror's name does not appear on the panel, the juror is an alien, or the juror has been convicted of an offence for which the sentence was death or imprisonment exceeding twelve

---

157 *Sherratt*, above note 141 at 534.
158 *Ibid.*
159 *R. v. Krugel* (2000), 31 C.R. (5th) 314 [*Krugel*].
160 *Ibid.* at para. 36.
161 *Douglas*, above note 153.

months. A juror can also be challenged on the basis either of physical incapacity to perform the duties of a juror, or of an inability to speak the language in which the trial will occur.[162] The only ground that has attracted real controversy is section 638(1)(f), a challenge on the basis that "a juror is not indifferent between the Queen and the accused."

The Supreme Court of Canada has consciously set a limited role for this ground, with one recent exception in cases where race is an issue. In general, though, the Court has observed that there are two approaches to deciding whether a juror is not indifferent:

> The first approach is that prevailing in the United States. On this approach, every jury panel is suspect. Every candidate for jury duty may be challenged and questioned as to preconceptions and prejudices on any sort of trial . . . . Canada has taken a different approach. In this country, candidates for jury duty are presumed to be indifferent or impartial. Before the Crown can challenge and question them, they must raise concerns which displace that presumption.[163]

In other words, challenge for cause is automatic in the United States, and there is a right to question each potential juror to see whether that person is appropriate from the start. Effectively the opposite is true in Canada, where counsel will not be allowed to ask any questions regarding a challenge for cause without first satisfying the judge that there is some reason to doubt the juror's indifference.

"Not indifferent" in this context has been defined to mean "not impartial" or prejudiced.[164] The Court has suggested that there are four relevant types of potential juror prejudice.[165] Interest prejudice arises when the juror has a direct interest in the trial, that is where "the juror

---

162   This requirement is generally (though not uniformly) a provincial criterion for inclusion on a jury array initially, as one might expect. The particular motivation for s. 638(1)(f) is s. 530 of the *Code*, under which a trial can be directed to be in the official language of the accused. That provision is designed for situations where an accused speaks an official language of Canada that is not necessarily the language used daily in the courts of that province and therefore the trial might not ordinarily be in the accused's language. Section 638(1)(f) guarantees that when a trial is ordered to be in one of Canada's official languages, all the jurors will speak that official language. It has only been proclaimed in Manitoba, New Brunswick, Ontario, the Yukon Territory, and the Northwest Territories.

163   *R. v. Williams*, [1998] 1 S.C.R. 1128 at paras. 12–13 [*Williams*].

164   *R. v. Hubbert*, [1977] 2 S.C.R. 267, aff'g [1975] O.J. No. 2595 (C.A.) [*Hubbert*].

165   *Williams*, above note 163 at para. 10, relying on Neil Vidmar, "Pretrial Prejudice in Canada: a Comparative Perspective on the Criminal Jury" (1996) 79 Judicature 249.

is the uncle of the accused, or the wife of a witness," for example.[166] Excluding a juror for this type of prejudice is not controversial, and, as noted above in Section C(3)(b), a trial judge can simply ask about any such relationships and excuse jurors before jury selection commences in such instances with the presumed consent of counsel.[167] Potentially more controversial are the other types: a) specific prejudice, which consists of attitudes or beliefs about the particular case, gained through media coverage or some other source, that might prevent the juror being impartial; b) generic prejudice, consisting of stereotypical attitudes about the accused, victims, witnesses, or the nature of the crime; and c) conformity prejudice, when a juror might feel influenced by strong community feelings about an expected outcome.[168] It is in those contexts that the presumption of impartiality has its most notable impact.

Challenge for cause is not intended to be a means for counsel to find out what type of person the juror is, or to decide whether to use a peremptory challenge.[169] Although the Court has resisted, saying that challenge for cause is limited to extreme cases,[170] the presumption of partiality means that counsel is not permitted to routinely challenge jurors. Rather, a two-step process is involved. First, counsel must satisfy the trial judge that the challenge for cause should be permitted—counsel must tell the trial judge the basis for the challenge.[171] If the trial judge is not satisfied that counsel has provided sufficient reason to doubt the juror's impartiality, the challenge will not occur. This would be true whether counsel wishes to challenge an individual juror or the jury array as a whole. At this stage of the process, the test is whether there is a realistic possibility for partiality.[172] The second stage is the challenge itself, where counsel is permitted to ask questions of the jurors to determine whether the juror will in fact be able to act impartially. Even at this stage, counsel might not have an unrestrained right to question jurors (in some cases only one or two predetermined questions will be allowed).[173]

---

166 *Sherratt*, above note 141 at 534, quoting from the Ontario Court of Appeal level decision in *Hubbert*, above note 164.

167 See s. 632 of the *Code* and *Sherratt, ibid.; Barrow*, above note 23.

168 *Williams*, above note 163 at para. 10.

169 *Hubbert*, above note 164.

170 *Sherratt*, above note 141.

171 *Hubbert*, above note 164 at para. 35 (C.A.): "The *Code* does not require that a challenge, oral or written, be particularized . . . But counsel must have a reason, even a generalized one."

172 *Williams*, above note 163 at para. 32.

173 See, for example, *Hubbert*, above note 164, or the jury selection in the initial trial in *Williams, ibid.* At the Supreme Court in *Williams*, the Court spoke about

Because counsel must state the basis for challenging the juror beforehand, but will likely in fact know very little about the juror, there are practical obstacles that sometimes prevent challenges for cause from even occurring, let alone succeeding. Therefore, cases have often concerned challenges that are relevant to the array as a whole, rather than having particular regard to some individual juror. For example, in *Hubbert* the accused wanted to question every juror to determine whether that juror would be prejudiced by learning that the accused had been detained in mental health institution. Pre-trial publicity has also been a basis upon which counsel have sought to ask questions with a view to making challenges. *Sherratt*, for example, concerned a murder that was particularly notorious in the community, and the accused sought, unsuccessfully, to question jurors to determine whether the pre-trial publicity would prevent jurors being impartial. The Court refused to allow the challenge in that case, holding that there was a distinction between mere publication of the facts of a case on the one hand, and misrepresentation of evidence by the media, wide publicization of discreditable facts from an accused's past, or speculation about the accused's guilt or innocence, on the other hand.[174] It is fair to say that counsel generally have had difficulty persuading judges that it is reasonable to question every member of a jury array with regard to possible prejudice.[175] Precisely because the Canadian approach presumes the impartiality of every juror, showing a realistic potential of partiality is difficult.

Recently, however, the Court has created one exception to this generalization, dealing with situations where partiality might arise due to attitudes about the race of the accused. In *Williams*, the accused was aboriginal and his counsel wanted to challenge jurors for cause based on racial attitudes. The accused did not offer evidence that the particular people on the jury array had racist attitudes. Rather, he led evidence showing that there was widespread bias against Aboriginal

---

"confin[ing] the challenge to two questions, subject to a few tightly controlled subsidiary questions" as "a practice to be emulated" (para. 55). See also the discussion of this approach in *R. v. Gayle* (2001), 154 C.C.C. (3d) 221 (Ont. C.A.) [*Gayle*].

174 For other cases dealing with pre-trial publicity as a ground for challenge, see *R. v. Merz* (1999), 140 C.C.C. (3d) 259 (Ont. C.A.); *Gayle, ibid.*; *R. v. Proulx* (1992), 76 C.C.C. (3d) 316 (Que. C.A.); *R. v. Keegstra* (1991), 3 C.R. (4th) 153 (Alta. C.A.).

175 See V. Gordon Rose & James R. P. Ogloff, "Challenge for Cause in Canadian Criminal Jury Trials: Legal and Psychological Perspectives" (2002) 46 Crim. L.Q. 210 for an overview of types of evidence that has, and has not, been successful in permitting counsel to challenge for cause, as well as a discussion of the potential role of psychologists in such challenges.

peoples in the community. The trial judge accepted that evidence, but held that evidence of general bias in the community did not establish a realistic potential of partiality on the part of jurors at trial, in part because jurors could be expected to set aside their biases. The British Columbia Court of Appeal upheld the decision on the basis that general bias was not the equivalent of a racist attitude of particular concern to a criminal trial.

The Supreme Court of Canada overturned this result for a number of reasons. It held that the lower courts had set too high a standard for showing a realistic possibility of prejudice in these circumstances. Looking for attitudes particularly relevant to the justice system was an unrealistic test, it held, as was the expectation that juror attitudes would be "cleansed" by instructions about how they should discharge their duties. Racist attitudes, the Court pointed out, are insidious and sometimes unconsciously held — a juror might not be able to set them aside, even when trying to do so. Further, the potential effect of the attitude is unpredictable, and therefore hard to guard against:

> It may incline a juror to believe that the accused is likely to have committed the crime alleged. It may incline a juror to reject or put less weight on the evidence of the accused, or it may, in a general way, predispose the juror to the Crown, perceived as representative of the "white" majority against the minority-member accused, inclining the juror, for example, to resolve doubts about aspects of the Crown's case more readily.[176]

Essentially, with *Williams* the Court signaled that trial judges should be more open to being persuaded that there is a realistic potential for partiality (that is, that the first phase of the challenge for cause process is fulfilled) when the challenge is based on possible attitudes about race.[177] Indeed, the Court went so far as to note that widespread racial prejudice, as a characteristic of a community, could be the subject of judicial notice. Once widespread prejudice has been proved in one case, judges in later cases can take judicial notice of it, or indeed simply find that widespread prejudice in a particular community is proven by events of indisputable accuracy, without any need for an accused to provide evidence.[178]

---

176 *Williams*, above note 163 at para 11.
177 On *Williams*, *ibid.*, generally, see David M. Tanovich, "The Future of Challenge for Cause in the Wake of *Williams*" (1998) 15 C.R. (5th) 250 and Stephen G. Coughlan. "Developments in Criminal Procedure: The 1997–98 Term" (1999) 10 Sup. Ct. L. Rev. 273.
178 *Williams*, *ibid.* at para. 54.

Lower courts have carried this finding to its logical conclusion, in a way likely to be approved by the Supreme Court, should the issue indeed reach there. For example in *R. v. Parks* the Ontario Court of Appeal had reached a conclusion similar to that in *Williams*, though on the facts of that case, which dealt with a black accused.[179] In *R. v. Wilson*, that Court subsequently decided that challenges for cause based on the realistic potential for racist attitudes should be allowed to any black accused in Ontario without further empirical evidence of racism.[180] Most recently in *R. v. Koh*, that Court has expanded the finding to allow challenge for cause by any accused belonging to any visible minority. Its intention was not to do away with the need for a finding of a realistic potential for prejudice, but "to find that in the light of the numerous trial and appellate decisions in this jurisdiction concerning various categories of visible minorities, this test has been met wherever the accused is a member of a visible racial minority."[181]

The Court has no intention of making challenge for cause more easily available outside the context of racial prejudice, however. This is clear from the post-*Williams* decision in *R. v. Find*.[182] In that case, the accused wished to be allowed to question jurors in order to decide whether to challenge them for cause, on the basis that the case concerned sexual assaults against children. The accused argued that there was a realistic potential that some jurors would be unable to act impartially because of the nature of the charges. In *Williams*, the Court described racial prejudice as "generic prejudice," which, in turn, it described as "stereotypical attitudes about the defendant, victims, witnesses or the nature of the crime itself."[183] Therefore, *Find* was an attempt to apply the approach in *Williams* to a relatively similar situation (another type of generic prejudice).

The Court rejected the appeal. The accused had argued that there was a realistic potential for partiality on a number of grounds: the wide-

---

179   *R. v. Parks* (1993), 24 C.R. (4th) 81 (Ont. C.A.) [*Parks*]. The Supreme Court refused leave to appeal in *Parks*, but subsequently relied heavily on its reasoning in deciding *Williams*, above note 163. The Court was also able to note in *Williams* that post-*Parks* experience in Ontario had shown no significant delay in jury selection procedures despite the relaxing of the first stage in this context. Given that the efficiency of the system and the spectre of "US style" challenges for cause are a regular concern of the Court, it appears possible that leave to appeal might have been refused in *Parks* precisely to discover what the practical impact of the change would actually be.

180   (1996), 47 C.R. (4th) 61 (Ont. C.A.).

181   *R. v. Koh* (1998), 21 C.R. (5th) 188 at para. 31 (Ont. C.A.).

182   [2001] 1 S.C.R. 863 [*Find*].

183   *Williams*, above note 163 at para. 10.

spread incident of sexual abuse, which meant that previous victims or those close to them were likely to be on the panel; the politicized and gender-based nature of views about sexual assault; myths and stereotypes about sexual assault; the emotional nature of sexual assault trials; the history of challenge for cause in Ontario, which showed that when challenge for cause on this basis was allowed, roughly one third of jurors challenged were disqualified; and social science evidence suggesting widespread bias. Nonetheless the Court was not persuaded on any of these grounds to permit the questioning toward challenge for cause to occur. It found that the evidence presented did not show a realistic possibility of prejudice, and held as well that such a possibility could not be the subject of judicial notice. Further, they concluded that, unlike racial prejudice, any prejudice of this sort could be cured by judicial direction to jurors or other trial safeguards. Although the decision acknowledges the possibility of better evidence being presented in some future case, the case clearly indicates that outside the context of potential racial prejudice, challenge for cause is intended to be no more freely available than it was pre-*Williams*.[184]

Further, in *R. v. Spence*, another post-*Williams* case, the Court refused to allow a *Parks*-like question based on the theory that witnesses might fail to be impartial because they would feel a race-based sympathy for a victim, rather than a race-based antipathy to the accused as in *Williams* and *Parks*.[185] The accused in *Spence* was black and the victim of the robbery was East Indian. The trial judge allowed the accused to challenge potential jurors on the issue of possible bias against him because of his race, but he was not allowed to ask whether jurors would be affected by the fact that he was accused of robbing an East Indian. The accused argued that potential East Indian jurors might feel a natural sympathy for the victim, and that asking this question was simply a natural progression of the *Williams/Parks* approach.

The Court held that the trial judge had acted correctly in refusing to allow the question. It held that the previous cases had only dealt with the issue of potential prejudice *against* a member of a visible minority, and that none of the social science evidence presented in those cases established any kind of bias *in favour of* members of a particular group. The Court also held that such a "natural sympathy" was not a

---

184 Further on this issue, see Steve Coughlan, "*R. v. Find*: Preserving the Presumption of Innocence" (2001) 42 C.R. (5th) 31 and Michael Plaxton, "The Biased Juror and Appellate Review: A Reply to Professor Coughlan" (2001) 44 C.R. (5th) 294.

185 *R. v. Spence*, [2005] 3 S.C.R. 458.

matter of which a court could take judicial notice. Accordingly they rejected the accused's argument.

When challenge for cause is allowed, the process to be followed is set out in the *Code*. For the first juror, the accused decides whether to challenge for cause before the Crown. Then, the Crown and the accused take turns.[186] If the judge permits a challenge for cause to be heard, it is tried by the two jurors most recently sworn or by two people appointed by the judge if no jurors have yet been sworn.[187] The Ontario Court of Appeal has recently observed that these triers often are not adequately instructed in the nature of their task.[188] The trial judge should instruct the triers that they are to decide whether the juror is impartial on a balance of probabilities, they must agree on a decision, they can retire to the jury room or decide where they are, and they are to say so if they cannot agree in a reasonable time.[189] The judge has discretion to exclude the other members of the panel from the jury room while the challenge is heard, and also has discretion to permit submissions by counsel following the questioning.[190]

It will generally be an error that leads to a new trial if the *Code* provisions for challenge for cause are not followed. In *Barrow*, for example, the trial judge permitted jurors to request exemption on the basis that they would be unable to decide impartially, not simply on obvious grounds such as relation to the accused, but based on pre-trial publicity. These exemption requests took place without the accused and were held to usurp a portion of the challenge for cause process.[191] Similarly, in *Guérin* the trial judge largely took over the roles of questioning jurors and deciding their impartiality.[192] In each case a new trial was ordered. There is some dispute, however, as to whether a judge is obliged, when the two triers cannot agree concerning the partiality of a juror, to

---

186 This rule applies to both challenges for cause and peremptory challenges: see s. 635(1). When there is more than one accused, the accused alternate with the Crown as a group, though each accused is separately entitled to challenge: s. 635(2). The accused are required to decide whether to challenge in the order that their names appear on the indictment. Although this requirement might place the first accused at a tactical disadvantage compared to fellow accused, it does not violate the *Charter*: *Suzack*, above note 47.

187 Section 640(2). Where the basis for the challenge is that the juror's name does not appear on the jury panel, the judge personally decides the challenge.

188 *Douglas*, above note 153.

189 *Hubbert*, above note 164.

190 *Hubbert*, *ibid.*; *R. v. Moore-McFarlane* (2001), 47 C.R. (5th) 203 (Ont. C.A.).

191 *Barrow*, above note 23.

192 *R. v. Guérin* (1984), 13 C.C.C. (3d) 231 (Que. C.A.).

appoint two new triers under section 640(4), or whether the judge has discretion to discharge that juror under section 632.[193]

As noted above, both parties make any challenge for cause before either is called on to make a peremptory challenge,[194] though either type of challenge should occur after the judge has decided whether to grant a juror's request for exemption.[195] Although the challenge for cause process is not to be used in order to gain evidence to decide whether to challenge peremptorily, that can indirectly be one of the effects. An unsuccessful challenge for cause does not prevent a peremptory challenge from being used.[196]

d) Peremptory Challenges

Peremptory challenges, which allow the accused or the Crown to dismiss a potential juror without explanation, are governed by section 634 of the *Criminal Code*. Unlike challenges for cause, peremptory challenges are limited in number.[197] Each party has twenty peremptory challenges in cases of high treason or first degree murder, twelve challenges in cases of other offences that carry sentences of five years or more, and four challenges in all other cases. In a trial on more than one charge, the number of peremptory challenges for the most serious offence is provided. If there is more than one accused, each accused receives the prescribed number of peremptory challenges, and the Crown receives the same number as all the accused combined.[198]

There has been no real debate that the accused's use of peremptory challenges is unconstrained. Blackstone offered two rationales for their existence, which have frequently been cited:

> 1. As every one must be sensible what sudden impressions and unaccountable prejudices we are apt to conceive upon the bare looks and

---

193 See *R. v. Brigham* (1988), 44 C.C.C. (3d) 379 (Que. C.A.), holding that s. 640 must be complied with and *Gayle*, above note 173, holding that where the decision to discharge the juror did not result in any prejudice to the accused, and indeed likely saved him a peremptory challenge, a rigidly technical approach should not be followed.

194 *Bernardo*, above note 154.

195 *Douglas*, above note 153.

196 *R. v. Cloutier*, [1979] 2 S.C.R. 709 [*Cloutier*]; *Hubbert*, above note 164.

197 Prior to *Bain*, above note 64, the Crown also had the power to "stand aside" jurors. This allowed the Crown to have a juror put to the bottom of the list, without actually using a challenge, and only to deal with that juror again after the rest of the array had been called. Since normally the entire array was not called, as a practical matter the Crown essentially had a far greater number of peremptory challenges than the accused.

198 Section 634.

gestures of another, and how necessary it is that a prisoner (when put to defend his life), should have a good opinion of his jury, the want of which might totally disconcert him, the law wills not that he should be tried by any one man against whom he has conceived a prejudice, even without being able to assign a reason for such his dislike. 2. Because, upon challenges for cause shown, if the reasons assigned prove insufficient to set aside the juror, perhaps the bare question-ing his indifference may sometimes provoke a resentment, to prevent all ill consequences from which the prisoner is still at liberty, if he pleases, peremptorily to set him aside.[199]

More controversial, and still unsettled, has been the question of whether the Crown is similarly unconstrained in its use of peremptory challenges. The Ontario Court of Appeal has held that the Crown's qua-si-judicial role precludes some uses of peremptory challenges, and that it must exercise that discretion in conformity with *Charter* principles and values: "public confidence in the administration of justice would be seriously undermined if Crown counsel were permitted to exercise the power of peremptory challenge on racial or ethnic grounds."[200] Sim-ilarly, in *R. v. Pizzacalla* the Ontario Court of Appeal ordered a retrial in a case where the Crown used its stand-aside power to produce an all-female jury in a sexual assault case.[201] The Supreme Court of Canada seemed to approve of *Pizzacalla* in *Bain*.[202]

R. v. Biddle presented another case in which the Crown used the stand-aside power to create an all-female jury for a sexual assault case.[203] The majority of the Court declined to comment on the issue, on the basis that the decision in *Bain* to strike down the stand-aside power had rendered the issue of only academic interest. In a concurring judg-ment, however, Justice Gonthier criticized the Crown's behaviour as an attempt to fashion a jury that may seem favourable to it, even if it was in fact impartial. In contrast, Justice McLachlin (as she then was) argued that an all-female jury not only could be, but would be seen by a reasonable observer as impartial.

The principle that the Crown cannot use peremptory challenges to produce a jury that does not appear impartial is not in dispute. What

---

199 See *Cloutier*, above note 196 at 720.
200 *Gayle*, above note 173 at para. 66.
201 (1991), 7 C.R. (4th) 294 (Ont. C.A.) [*Pizzacalla*].
202 All three judgments make reference to *Pizzacalla*, *ibid.*, as an example that Crown prosecutors might sometimes use their powers in an objectionable fashion, seeming, therefore, to agree with the decision by the Ontario Court of Appeal to order a retrial.
203 *R. v. Biddle*, [1995] 1 S.C.R. 761.

will continue to be a source of dispute is whether reasonable people will see the conscious exclusion of one race or one sex from a jury as violating that principle. On this point, Chief Justice McLachlin argues that an all-woman jury would be as capable of being impartial as "all-male juries have been presumed to be for centuries." While that may be literally true, it is not necessarily of any consolation. First, the perception that all-male juries were or are impartial is no longer as accepted as it had been for centuries.[204] Changes in provincial legislation to produce jury arrays from sources that include more women— moving away from municipal assessment rolls, for example—were largely motivated by the desire not to have juries effectively limited to men. Further, the Court has become concerned, particularly in sexual assault cases, with not allowing reasoning to be affected by "myths and stereotypes" that have historically influenced decision-making. Many of those myths and stereotypes arose, one might suppose, precisely because the decision-makers were predominantly or exclusively men.[205] So past practice that the justice system is consciously trying to move away from might not be the best authority.

Further, the Chief Justice suggests that an all-woman jury would be seen as impartial, though some people "might for irrational reasons object." This would be a more persuasive argument in cases where an all-woman jury had resulted simply through some statistical anomaly, rather than in cases like *Pizzacalla* and *Biddle* where the Crown consciously set out to achieve that result. It is undoubtedly true that a jury of women, all of whom have been judged individually to be impartial, could decide a case fairly. But the Crown prosecutors in both *Pizzacalla* and *Biddle* acted on the irrational belief that a juror's decision could be predicted based on sex: in *Pizzacalla*, the Crown prosecutor specifically acknowledged his rationale that male jurors were more likely to believe sexual harassment in the workplace was acceptable than were female jurors. If the belief that a juror's sex is likely to affect that juror's reasoning is unreasonable and objectionable, then of course such a belief cannot support any reasonable apprehension that the jury was not impartial. But in that event, it is surely wrong for the Crown prosecutor to adopt a jury selection strategy hinging on exactly that unreasonable and objectionable belief.

---

204 Note, for example, the inclusion of s. 626(2) in the *Criminal Code* in 1985, preventing anyone from being disqualified, exempted, or excused from a jury panel based on sex.

205 See Bertha Wilson, "Will Women Judges Really Make a Difference?" (1990) 28 Osgoode Hall L.J. 507.

In this context, one might note the Supreme Court's decision in *R. v. Latimer*,[206] where the RCMP, having prepared a questionnaire in cooperation with the Crown prosecutor, administered it to thirty prospective jurors. The questionnaire asked the views of the prospective jurors on a number of issues, including religion, abortion, and euthanasia. The Crown did not disclose the questionnaire or the direct contact with jurors to the defence or the trial judge. In very brief reasons, the Court described this as a "flagrant abuse of process and interference with the administration of justice," which warranted a new trial.[207] The issue, it held, was not whether the RCMP's behaviour actually influenced the jury's deliberations, but that it violated the principle that justice had to not only be done, but be seen to be done.

None of this affects the conclusion that there is no absolute requirement for juries to be representative. As Chief Justice McLachlin observes in *Biddle*, representativeness is generally a good means to try to achieve impartiality and competence, but it is not an end in itself. An accused cannot insist that the jury or jury array contain members of the accused's race.[208] Further, an accused cannot object solely on the basis that the Crown had peremptorily challenged the only jurors of the same race as the accused, without more evidence allowing a court to review the Crown's actions.[209] Although, if there has been a conscious attempt to keep members of one race from the jury array then that will constitute a basis to challenge the array.[210]

A practical difficulty arises for the accused in this context, namely that of proving the motive of the Crown or other actor in the judicial system. In *Butler*, the accused only succeeded in challenging the array because after he had made an initial unsuccessful application, a sheriff spoke to his defence counsel, saying "totally off the record, the reason that Indians do not appear on the jury panels is because we have found them to be unreliable— they may show up one day for trial and then not come the next because they've gone out and gotten drunk the night before."[211] The evidence suggested that the sheriff's office had been acting on this belief for seventeen or eighteen years, and the sheriff only disclosed it at that time in the expectation that the statement would remain confidential. Similarly, in *Pizzacalla* the accused had the benefit of the Crown prosecutor's candid statement that he created an all-wom-

---

206 *R. v. Latimer*, [1997] 1 S.C.R. 217 [*Latimer*].
207 *Ibid.* at para. 43.
208 *Kent*, above note 147.
209 *Gayle*, above note 173.
210 *Butler*, above note 147.
211 *Ibid.* at 177.

an jury because men might be more likely to think sexual harassment was acceptable, and indeed the Crown's concession that this action created the impression of a favourable jury. In *Biddle*, only a few years later, there was no dispute that the Crown prosecutor had consciously produced an all-woman jury, but no reason for doing so was offered and no concession regarding the propriety of the approach was made. The Ontario Court of Appeal speculated that the prosecutor's motive might have been to guarantee the impartiality of the jury, rather than its partiality, and dismissed the appeal partly on that basis.[212]

In *Gayle* as well, the Crown's actions were to peremptorily challenge the only two blacks called as potential jurors. However, there was no evidence of the make-up of the jury array and no evidence of the Crown's reason for challenging those two jurors. Therefore, while stating that, in principle, review of the Crown's use of peremptory challenges should be possible, the Ontario Court of Appeal did not allow a review in that case because there was no factual foundation upon which to conduct it.

In both *Biddle* and *Gayle*, appeal courts have seen it as important that the accused did not object to the Crown's actions at the time. One must be sympathetic to the need for a factual basis for an appeal, but it should be noted that there is not any very clear mechanism at present that an accused could use at trial to object to the Crown's use of peremptory challenges. Presuming that an accused made an application in mid-jury selection, based on an alleged violation of section 11(f) of the *Charter*, a further difficulty arises. The defining feature of a peremptory challenge is that it allows a party to challenge "without showing any cause at all."[213] To ask the Crown to explain the basis upon which it has exercised its peremptory challenges, therefore, is to undermine the nature of the challenge. Further, even if the question were asked, "I just felt like it," would seem to be an acceptable answer.

The difficulty is that although the Crown does not have to have a "good" reason for using a peremptory challenge, some of the "not-good" reasons it might rely on could violate *Charter* values. There will be a significant challenge in finding a method that tests for whether the Crown has acted upon the wrong motives without actually calling on the Crown to explain its motives.

One possibility is judicial creation of a presumption that where the Crown's use of peremptory challenges and the ultimate make-up

---

212 *R. v. Biddle* (1993), 14 O.R. (3d) 756 (C.A.).

213 Sir William Blackstone, *Commentaries on the Laws of England*, vol. 4 (Chicago: University of Chicago Press, 1979) at 1738, cited in *Cloutier*, above note 196.

of the jury suggest that the Crown might have acted on principles that violate *Charter* values, the jury selection should be seen as tainted unless the Crown offers an alternative explanation. This approach would give the accused an effective way to inquire into the issue, without requiring the Crown to explain its use of peremptory challenges routinely. It would also give flexibility to appeal courts in applying the remedy because there would be considerable room for factual dispute as to whether the presumption should be seen to arise. Finally, it would leave unsettled, and therefore open to further development, the issue of what use of peremptory challenges would in fact violate *Charter* values (for example, whether consciously creating an all-man or all-woman jury would do so).

FURTHER READINGS

ARCHIBALD, BRUCE, "Prosecutors, Democracy and the Public Interest: Prosecutorial Discretion and its Limits in Canada" (paper presented at the XVIth Congress of the International Academy of Comparative Law, Brisbane, Australia, 14–20 July 2002)

BAAR, CARL, "Criminal Court Delay and the *Charter*: The Use and Misuse of Social Facts in Judicial Policy Making" (1993) 72 Can. Bar Rev. 305

COUGHLAN, STEVE, "*R. v. Find*: Preserving the Presumption of Innocence" (2001) 42 C.R. (5th) 31

LAW REFORM COMMISSION OF CANADA, *Trial Within a Reasonable Time* (Ottawa: Canada Communication Group, 1994)

PLAXTON, MICHAEL, "The Biased Juror and Appellate Review: A Reply to Professor Coughlan" (2001) 44 C.R. (5th) 294

POMERANT, DAVID, *Multiculturalism, Representation and the Jury Selection Process in Canadian Criminal Cases* (Ottawa: Department of Justice Canada, Research and Statistics Directorate, 1994)

QUIGLEY, TIM, *Procedure in Canadian Criminal Law*, 2d ed., looseleaf (Toronto: Thomson Carswell, 2005) cc. 16, 19, and 20

ROSE, V. GORDON & JAMES R.P. OGLOFF, "Challenge for Cause in Canadian Criminal Jury Trials: Legal and Psychological Perspectives" (2002) 45 Crim. L.Q. 210

STUART, DON, *Charter Justice in Canadian Criminal Law*, 4th ed. (Toronto: Thomson Carswell, 2005) cc. 2 and 6

TANOVICH, DAVID M., "The Future of Challenge for Cause in the Wake of *Williams*" (1998) 15 C.R. (5th) 250

VIDMAR, NEIL, "Pretrial Prejudice in Canada: A Comparative Perspective on the Criminal Jury" (1996) 79 Judicature 249

WILSON, BERTHA, "Will Women Judges Really Make a Difference?" (1990) 28 Osgoode Hall L.J. 507

CHAPTER 11

THE TRIAL PROCESS

A. INTRODUCTION

This chapter focuses on the actual process of a trial. That discussion must begin at the pre-trial stage, with reference to the charging documents that bring a person to court and set out the case to be met at trial. From there we move to a discussion of the pleas an accused can enter, and the various stages of a trial, including opening statements, examination of witnesses, closing arguments, charging the jury, and so on. We will then consider the rules surrounding jury deliberations, and finally conclude with a discussion of the various powers a judge can exercise during the trial.

B. THE CHARGE DOCUMENT

1) Informations, Indictments, and Direct Indictments

When a person is put on trial for an offence, there must be some particular document specifying the charge against that person. Initially, charges are laid by means of an information,[1] which was discussed in Chapter 6. When an accused is tried by a provincial court judge that information is the relevant document, whereas when the accused is

---

1   Section 505.

not tried by a provincial court judge a different document — an indictment — is prepared.[2] Most commonly, the indictment is prepared following the preliminary inquiry and can include any charge on which the person was ordered to stand trial, or any charge founded on the facts disclosed at the preliminary inquiry.[3]

The rule that an indictment can be preferred on a charge where the facts making it out are disclosed at the preliminary inquiry does not allow a prosecutor to prefer an indictment on the very charge for which the accused is discharged. Rather, that power is intended to allow the preferment of charges for other offences that are disclosed at the preliminary inquiry.[4] It does not follow, however, that a prosecutor can never lay an indictment concerning offences for which an accused is discharged. In fact, section 577 permits exactly that.

Section 577 allows for "direct indictments," which permit the prosecutor to prefer an indictment when the accused has not been given the opportunity to request a preliminary inquiry, the preliminary inquiry has been commenced but not concluded,[5] or the accused was discharged following the preliminary inquiry. This power also applies where a committal for trial has been quashed,[6] or where a trial judge has specifically declined to order an accused to stand trial on a charge not laid but disclosed in the evidence at the preliminary.[7] As it is a special power, in effect overriding procedures the accused would otherwise be entitled to benefit from, a Crown prosecutor can only prefer a direct indictment with the personal consent in writing of the Attorney General or Deputy Attorney General.[8]

The Attorney General's power to authorize a direct indictment cannot be reviewed by a court.[9] Also, the power does not violate the *Char-*

---

2   Section 566(1). Note that the power in s. 577 to proceed by direct indictment means that there could be occasions when an indictment is the first charge document prepared.
3   Section 574.
4   *R. v. Tapaquon*, [1993] 4 S.C.R. 535.
5   Courts had already held that the power was available in this situation, but the *Code* has since been amended to explicitly state it. See *R. v. Stewart (No. 2)* (1977), 35 C.C.C. (2d) 281 (Ont. C.A.).
6   *R. v. Charlie* (1998), 126 C.C.C. (3d) 513 (B.C.C.A.).
7   *R. v. McKibbon*, [1984] 1 S.C.R. 131.
8   Section 577(b) also permits direct indictments in private prosecutions where a judge of the court permits the direct indictment to be preferred.
9   *R. v. Balderstone* (1983), 8 C.C.C. (3d) 532 (Man. C.A.), leave to appeal to S.C.C. refused, [1983] 2 S.C.R. v; *R. v. Stolar* (1983), 32 C.R. (3d) 342 (Man. C.A.), leave to appeal to S.C.C. refused, [1983] 1 S.C.R. xiv [*Stolar*].

ter, provided that the accused receives full disclosure and nothing else in the circumstances makes the action an abuse of process.[10]

Once it is preferred, the indictment provides a fresh starting point upon which the future proceedings are based, and an accused is no longer entitled to look behind it, for example to attempt to quash by *certiorari* the committal for trial. The indictment is preferred, and therefore acts as a type of barrier, once it is lodged with the trial court at the start of the accused's trial, in front of a court ready to proceed.[11]

Whether the trial proceeds by information or indictment, it is the starting point for the trial and sets out the case the accused has to meet. The rules set out in Parts XVI and XX of the *Criminal Code* that govern compelling appearance and jury trials also apply to summary conviction offences by virtue of section 795, with only minor variations, so the requirements for informations and indictments can be discussed together. The Court has stressed the importance of this document, holding that "it is fundamental to a fair trial that an accused know the charge or charges he or she must meet."[12] As we will see, though, the general tenor of recent cases has been to considerably downplay the significance of the technical requirements for these documents or any failures to comply with those requirements.

2) Joinder and Severance of Charges

Although many rules surrounding indictments were originally developed to a great extent at common law, they are now primarily set out in the *Code*. There are many rules in the *Code* and there has been a good deal of litigation over these issues, but a good general guideline is that relatively few firm limitations are imposed on the structure of indictments. An indictment (Form 4 from the *Code*) can contain any number of "counts."[13] Each count is to cover a single transaction, though this rule is specifically said to apply "in general" and the concept of a "single transaction" is given a broad interpretation.[14] Further, although for

---

10 *R. v. Ertel* (1987), 58 C.R. (3d) 252 (Ont. C.A.), leave to appeal to S.C.C. refused (1987), 61 C.R. (3d) xxix; *R. v. Arviv* (1985), 45 C.R. (3d) 354 (Ont. C.A.), leave to appeal to S.C.C. refused, [1985] 1 S.C.R. v; *Stolar, ibid.*

11 *R. v. Chabot*, [1980] 2 S.C.R. 985.

12 *R. v. G.R.*, [2005] 2 S.C.R. 371, 2005 SCC 45 at para. 2.

13 "Count" is defined in s. 2 of the *Code* as a "charge in an information or indictment."

14 Section 581(1). See the discussion of *R. v. Lilly*, [1983] 1 S.C.R. 794 [*Lilly*] at Section B(5)(c), below in this chapter, in which twenty-one separate withdrawals from a trust account were the foundation for a single count of fraud, and, in general, the discussion of division of counts.

many years a trial could not concern more than one indictment, more recently the Court has relaxed that requirement. It is now possible to hold a trial on one or more indictments simultaneously, provided that the accused consents, or the trial judge feels that it is in the interests of justice and the charges could have been jointly charged in a single indictment.[15] This latter requirement imposes few restrictions.[16] Section 589 prevents any charge from being joined with murder, though even this rule is subject to exceptions if the other offence arises out of the same transaction or the accused consents to the joinder.[17] Summary conviction and indictable offences can be tried together, provided the accused consents and the accused's election and the other procedures make it possible to do so.[18] Otherwise, the limits on joinder of counts are case-by-case, according to the criteria in section 591(3) of the *Code*. That provision allows a judge to order an indictment to be severed in order to send some counts or some co-accused to a separate trial.

The *Code* gives little in the way of guidance regarding severance decisions, stating only that the court may do so where "the interests of justice so require."[19] A preliminary inquiry judge does not have jurisdiction to sever, it must be done by the trial judge.[20] The judge's decision is subject to review on appeal, but it is not to be interfered with unless the judge has acted unjudicially.[21] Normally, an application to sever is made on a pre-trial basis because the decision will dictate the course of the trial.[22] However, section 591(4) permits the order to be made before or during the trial, with the jury being discharged with regard to any counts or accused that are severed during trial.

Courts have developed considerations to take into account when deciding whether to sever counts. Society has an interest in avoiding a multiplicity of proceedings, and so the onus is on the accused, on a balance of probabilities, to show that separate trials should be held.[23] Particularly with regard to severing counts, other factors to be considered include the factual and legal nexus between the counts, the

---

15   *R. v. Clunas*, [1992] 1 S.C.R. 595 [*Clunas*].
16   See, for example, s. 574 or s. 789(1)(b) of the *Code*.
17   See also s. 473(1.1) that permits an offence in s. 469, which otherwise must be tried by a judge and jury, to be joined with any other offence and tried without a jury, provided the Crown and accused both consent.
18   *Clunas*, above note 15.
19   Section 591(3).
20   *R. v. Hynes*, [2001] 3 S.C.R. 623 [*Hynes*].
21   *R. v. Litchfield*, [1993] 4 S.C.R. 333 [*Litchfield*]. See the further discussion of this issue below, in the context of division of counts.
22   *Ibid.*
23   *R. v. Cross* (1996), 112 C.C.C. (3d) 410 (Que. C.A.) [*Cross*].

complexity of the evidence, whether the accused wishes to testify on some counts but not on others, and whether similar act evidence will be introduced.[24] A decision to hold a single trial on several counts does not automatically make all evidence admissible on each count, admissible on every count. Trial judges must take great care in distinguishing the two issues of severability and similar fact evidence, particularly as the onus is on the accused for the first, but on the Crown for the second.[25]

Where an application to sever is made later in the trial, it ought to be based on some prejudice that was not apparent at the start.[26] For example, an accused could decide at the close of the Crown's case that the Crown's witnesses were not credible on some counts. The accused might therefore feel that it was not necessary to take the stand with regard to those counts, but that it was necessary to testify with regard to other counts. In such circumstances the accused's fair trial right and right to silence may be brought into conflict if the counts were not severed. At such a late stage, however, the burden on the accused is very heavy and an assertion that the accused wished to testify on some counts but not on others would not be sufficient. The accused would be required to outline the basic nature of the proposed defence to justify severance and the consequent re-trial on the severed charges.[27]

3) Joinder and Severance of Accused

Similar considerations arise in deciding whether to sever multiple accused from the same indictment and hold separate trials, though there are additional issues. Even more strongly in these circumstances, the practical goal of avoiding multiple proceedings favours not holding separate trials over the same facts unless it is necessary. The general rule is that accused who are alleged to have committed a crime together should be tried together.[28] This principle is adhered to quite firmly. When co-accused blame one another, they might be able to cross-examine one another in ways not available to the Crown, with regard

---

24   See *R. v. D.A.C.* (1996), 72 B.C.A.C. 227 (C.A.), aff'd [1997] 1 S.C.R. 8 [*D.A.C.*] and *Cross, ibid.*

25   *R. v. Arp*, [1998] 3 S.C.R. 339.

26   *D.A.C.*, above note 24.

27   See *D.A.C., ibid.* and *Cross*, above note 23.

28   *R. v. Chow*, [2005] 1 S.C.R. 384, 2005 SCC 24. See also *R. v. Torbiak and Gillis* (1978), 40 C.C.C. (2d) 193 (Ont. C.A.) [*Torbiak*]; *R. v. Miller and Cockriel* (1975), 33 C.R.N.S. 129 (B.C.C.A.), aff'd on other issues (1976), 70 D.L.R. (3d) 324 (S.C.C.); *R. v. Agawa and Mallett* (1975), 31 C.R.N.S. 293 (Ont. C.A.) [*Agawa*].

to propensity or similar issues, for example.[29] This could result in the fair trial right of one accused conflicting with the pre-trial right to silence of a co-accused, if one accused wants to point to the failure of the other to cooperate with the police. Even then, the Court has held that the solution in such situations is not to sever the trials, but to balance the competing rights of the two accused along with the interest of the state in a joint trial. The Court has held that in such circumstances of a "cut-throat defence," the policy reasons favouring a joint trial apply with equal or greater force than normally. [30]

Nonetheless a trial judge does have discretion to sever the trials in accordance with section 591(3) where it is required in the interests of justice. In deciding the issue, courts should consider not only whether the co-accused will have antagonistic defences, but also other issues, such as the possibility of inconsistent verdicts (which militates against severance) or whether evidence admissible against one accused is inadmissible against another.[31]

The fact that one of the accused would be a compellable witness for the other accused in a separate trial but not in a joint trial is relevant, but not determinative. In *Agawa*, for example, the Ontario Court of Appeal upheld the trial judge's decision not to grant separate trials in such circumstances because there was not sufficient evidence that the co-accused would actually have given evidence useful to the applicant even if he were made compellable.[32] The question is whether the co-accused's evidence could reasonably affect the verdict by creating a reasonable doubt.[33] As with many issues, cases have divided on the proper way to proceed. Some decisions have held that counsel's assertion that a co-accused has made out-of-court statements that would be helpful must be taken at face value and justify severance. Others have held that granting severance simply on the allegation that one co-accused may give evidence in defence of the other is to reverse the presumption in favour of joint trials. Some authority suggests that if an accused shows that a co-accused's evidence is likely to raise a reasonable doubt, there

---

29   R. v. *Kendall* (1987), 57 C.R. (3d) 249 (Ont. C.A.).

30   R. v. *Crawford*; R. v. *Creighton*, [1995] 1 S.C.R. 858 [*Crawford*].

31   *D.A.C.*, above note 24; *Cross*, above note 23.

32   *Agawa*, above note 28.

33   *Torbiak*, above note 28. In that case the trial judge did not apply this test, and refused to sever because the co-accused's testimony would only be corroborative. The Court of Appeal found this to be an error but declined to grant the appeal nonetheless, on the basis that the error did not amount to a miscarriage of justice.

is no longer any discretion to not grant the severance application. Much will depend on the facts of the individual case.[34]

The fact that some evidence will be admissible against one accused but not others is also relevant, but again it is not sufficient to require severance. Where several accused have all made statements, for example, the contents of each statement might become admissible for its truth against the accused making it, but not against each of the co-accused. Particularly in jury trials, the trial judge then has the "added and heavy burden of complete and proper instruction to the jury on the precise limits of the evidence admissible against each of the accused, and hence the limited use to which these statements may be put."[35] The Court has suggested that in conspiracy trials where the evidence is much stronger against one accused, and particularly where a damaging statement will be admissible against one but not the other, the safer course is to order separate trials.[36]

4) Content of Charges

Any given count, whether it is in a multi-count information or dealt with individually, "shall contain in substance a statement that the accused or defendant committed an indictable offence therein specified."[37] Section 581 continues by setting out some rules for that statement, which may be "in popular language without technical averments," in the words of the *Code* provision, or in other words that give the accused notice of the offence that he is charged with. Whatever is done, however, the key rule from section 581(3) is that

> a count shall contain sufficient detail of the circumstances of the alleged offence to give to the accused reasonable information with respect to the act or omission to be proved against him and to identify the transaction referred to but otherwise the absence or insufficiency of details does not vitiate the count.

The *Code* then offers further detail to help determine whether this standard is met. The count may refer to the particular section under which

---

34 See, generally, *R. v. Boulet* (1987), 40 C.C.C. (3d) 38 (Que. C.A.), leave to appeal to S.C.C. refused, [1989] 1 S.C.R. vi; *R. v. Szczerba* (2002), 314 A.R. 114 (Q.B.) and the cases discussed in those cases.

35 *R. v. McFall*, [1980] 1 S.C.R. 321 at 338. The quote is from Justice Estey, who dissented in the result because the majority held that any errors were harmless ones covered by the curative provisions in the *Code*.

36 *R. v. Guimond*, [1979] 1 S.C.R. 960.

37 Section 581(1).

the accused is charged, as a way of helping to give sufficient notice.[38] Further, the *Code* specifies that the absence of details does not automatically render a count insufficient, and lists particular omissions that are not fatal, such as that "it does not name the person injured or intended or attempted to be injured," "it does not specify the means by which the alleged offence was committed," or "it does not name or describe with precision any person, place or thing."[39] The issue of sufficiency of counts is discussed in greater detail below at Section B(5)(b).

The Court has noted that there are two interrelated rules dealing with indictments: section 581(3), dealing with insufficient detail and the "surplusage rule," dealing with additional, unnecessary detail.[40] The general rule is that the purpose of each count in an indictment is to put the accused on notice of the case to be met. Accordingly, a count must have sufficient detail and an accused is normally entitled to expect that the Crown will be required to prove all the details of any allegation made. However, it is open to a court to find that detail actually provided in a count is "surplusage," and therefore that a fact need not be proven, despite being alleged. It is not always clear in practice whether a detail is mere surplusage.

In *R. v. N.C.*, for example, the accused was charged with trafficking in cocaine, though the evidence at trial showed that the substance she had claimed to be cocaine was actually a mixture of baby powder and aspirin. This would have been an offence nonetheless, since the *Narcotic Control Act*[41] provision also made it an offence to traffic in any substance held out to be a narcotic. However, the Court held that, having charged the accused with trafficking in cocaine, the Crown was obliged to prove that the substance actually was cocaine: their failure to do so would mean she must be acquitted.[42] Similarly in *R. v. Saunders*, the Crown charged a number of accused with conspiracy to import heroin. The charge would have been perfectly acceptable had it not specified which narcotic was to be imported. However, having specified heroin, the Crown was obliged to prove that the conspiracy related to that narcotic in particular.[43]

---

38 Section 581(5).

39 Section 583. The *Code* also creates special rules for some particular situations, such as that no one can be convicted of high treason (rather than treason) or first degree murder (rather than second degree murder) without having been specifically charged with that offence: s. 582. See also the special rules in ss. 581(4), 584, and 585.

40 *R. v. Vézina and Côté*, [1986] 1 S.C.R. 2 at para. 54 [*Vézina*].

41 R.S.C. 1985, c. N-1 [since repealed].

42 *R. v. N.C.* (1991), 64 C.C.C. (3d) 45 (Que. C.A.).

43 *R. v. Saunders*, [1990] 1 S.C.R. 1020.

On the other hand, in *R. v. Hanna*[44] the accused was charged with theft of gravel from the Nova Scotia Power Commission and obtained a directed verdict because the only evidence of ownership showed that the gravel was owned by the Power Corporation. This decision was overturned at trial on the basis that there was no possibility that the accused could fail to identify the event that gave rise to the charge against him.

Similarly, in *Vézina* the accused was charged with fraud in an information that specified the Bank of Montreal as the victim. In fact, the Crown was unable to prove that the Bank of Montreal would have suffered any loss from the accused's fraud. The Court held that the information would initially have been valid, even if it had not specified a victim. Accordingly, it did not matter that the Crown was unable to prove the particular allegation, which was mere surplusage.[45]

Whether a detail will be considered surplusage, or whether the Crown will be held to proof of the fact, depends on whether the accused's defence will be prejudiced. In *Saunders*, for example, one accused had taken the stand to testify that he had been involved in one of several conspiracies to import narcotics, but not in the particular conspiracy that was to import heroin. In that case, not holding the Crown to proof of the particular narcotic alleged would have been prejudicial. In *Vézina*, on the other hand, the Court concluded that the accused would not have conducted their defence in any different manner had the allegation that the Bank of Montreal was the victim not been made, and therefore the accused suffered no prejudice. Given the absence of prejudice to the accused, the Crown was not to be held to proof of that fact.

5) Remedies for a Defective Charge

The issue of what to do in the face of a defective charge is intimately bound up with the the nature of the defect. We shall first discuss the potential remedies and then turn to the issue of the types of defect leading to a remedy.

a) Potential Remedies

The real issue is what to do when a charge is alleged not to be sufficient because it does not comply with the necessary requirements. Historically this was a tortuous area, for reasons no longer relevant. Most of these rules developed in Great Britain under a system in which crimes were

---

44 (1991), 109 N.S.R. (2d) 338 (S.C.A.D.).

45 *Vézina*, above note 40.

defined by the common law, a system that created particular difficulties in ensuring that the accused was genuinely given notice of the charge.[46] More importantly, at one point the exploitation of technicalities was the only real mechanism open to courts to guard against unfairness.[47] Accordingly, much of early caselaw dealt with quashing charges against an accused based on defects in form. In Canada, however, there has been "a gradual shift from requiring judges to quash to requiring them to amend in the stead: in fact, there remains little discretion to quash."[48] What we really see in Canada today is a reflection of the fact that the interests of the accused no longer include protection against the death penalty or exile to Australia. Rather, the accused's interests are clarity and sufficient notice in a trial on the merits. Consequently, although breach of these technical requirements can result in an accused avoiding trial occasionally, this is not a normal occurence.

There are three possibilities arising out of an error in an indictment. If it is so flawed that it is an absolute nullity then a trial judge has no jurisdiction to hear the matter, and the charge must be quashed. But in that event the accused was never in jeopardy, and so the Crown can simply lay a new information without violating the double jeopardy rules (here, the accused's only remedy is the greater clarity of the new charge). Alternatively, the charge might be flawed, but not so flawed that it is a nullity; in that event the trial judge is to amend the charge. If the accused has been prejudiced by the error, the trial judge is to grant an adjournment in order to remedy that prejudice. A charge can be quashed only if the prejudice caused by the amending cannot be remedied by an adjournment.[49]

This last possibility is a small subset of the occasions when a charge contains an error, but it is made smaller still by the provisions of section 601 that govern amendments to a defective count. First, that section requires that an objection to an indictment for a defect apparent on its face should be made before an accused has pleaded. At that stage, the likelihood that the accused has already suffered irreparable prejudice is, of course, quite small. Objection can be made after this point, but

---

46   Tim Quigley, *Procedure in Canadian Criminal Law*, 2d ed., looseleaf (Toronto: Thomson Carswell, 2005) at 17-2 [*Quigley*].

47   Quigley, *ibid*. See also *R. v. Sault Ste. Marie*, [1978] 2 S.C.R. 1299 [*Sault Ste. Marie*] and *Vézina*, above note 40 at para. 53: "With the abrogation of the great majority of the capital statutes in the 19th century, however, much of the rationale for the formality and strict adherence to the wording of the indictment disappeared."

48   *R. v. Moore*, [1988] 1 S.C.R. 1097 at 1128 [*Moore*].

49   See *Moore*, *ibid*. and s. 601.

only with leave of the court. Further, the grounds upon which a judge "shall" make an amendment are quite broad and require: a) that the charge is laid under the wrong Act; b) that it fails to state or states defectively an element of the offence, does not negative an exception that should be negatived, or is in any way defective in substance, provided the amendment to be made was disclosed by the evidence; or c) "that the indictment or a count thereof is in any way defective in form."[50] In addition, the *Code* specifies that errors in the time or place at which the offence occurred are not material, provided limitation periods and territorial jurisdiction are complied with.[51] Finally, a trial judge is specifically authorized to amend an indictment to make it conform to the evidence presented at trial.[52]

These provisions do not completely remove the possibility of a charge being quashed. *Moore*, though it stressed the preference for amendment over quashing, presents one of those unusual circumstances in which a technical error led to acquittal. Moore was charged on an information that was incorrectly quashed. The Crown laid a new charge and proceeded to trial on the new information, obtaining a conviction. The Supreme Court of Canada concluded that the original quashing was an error and that the charge should have been amended (had the Crown appealed the first trial judge's decision, this would have been the result). However, the Crown did not appeal that decision, and so the first judge's decision had to stand because the Crown was not entitled to avoid an appeal simply by laying a new information. Therefore, the accused was able to plead *autrefois acquit* at the subsequent trial.

However, it is most likely that the Crown will not be allowed an amendment, if the accused obtains a remedy at all, producing a result that might or might not benefit the accused. In *R. v. Tremblay*, for example, the accused were charged with keeping a bawdy house for the purpose of practicing of acts of indecency.[53] The accused called an expert witness and arranged their entire defence around the argument that the acts performed were not indecent. After all the defence evidence had been presented, the Crown made two applications to amend the charge, first to delete the words "the practice of indecency," and, when that was refused, to change it to "the practice of prostitution." The Supreme Court held that the trial judge had been correct to refuse the amendment. It might have been allowable much earlier in the trial, but it would have caused irreparable prejudice at the stage it was

---

50   Section 601(3).
51   Section 601(4.1).
52   Section 601(2).
53   [1993] 2 S.C.R. 932.

brought. In that particular case, the Court also held that the acts in question were not indecent, and so the acquittal at trial was upheld.

A further remedy potentially available when a count is flawed is to order the Crown to provide particulars under section 587 of the *Code*. Particulars are intended to clarify the charge against the accused, in order to provide clear information as to the offence charged, and also to make the pleas of *autrefois acquit* and *autrefois convict* available in the event that further charges are laid.[54] There is no limit on what can be ordered, but they include requirements like "further describing the means by which an offence is alleged to have been committed" or "further describing a person, place or thing referred to in an indictment."[55] They must be ordered by a judge of the trial court, not by a judge conducting a preliminary inquiry.[56] They need not be ordered at the start of the trial, however, and in considering whether the particulars are needed for a fair trial, the court is to consider the evidence that has been led.[57] Where particulars are ordered, they are entered into the record, and the trial proceeds as though the indictment had been amended in accordance with the particular.[58] There is no actual need to lay an amended information.[59] Of course, although the indictment is taken to be amended, the Crown is still not obliged to prove those things that are surplusage, even if they were provided among the particulars.[60]

Once again, the interest being protected for the accused is clarity at trial. An accused cannot use particulars as a way of limiting the options available to the Crown. In *R. v. Thatcher*, for example, the Crown's theory was that the accused either killed his wife personally or hired another person to do so, but was guilty of murder in either case. The

---

54 *R. v. J.A.H.* (1998), 105 B.C.A.C. 259 (C.A.) [*J.A.H.*]. Dickson J. (as he then was) held in *R. v. Sault Ste. Marie*, above note 47, that there was no problem raising a special plea after a trial on a duplicitous charge, because the rule against multiple convictions would prevent another acquittal arising out of the same facts, and acquittal means acquittal on all the offences charged. In either case, even if a charge was duplicitous, an accused could later point to it to justify pleading *autrefois acquit* or *autrefois convict*. The same argument might be made to say that the special plea justification does not arise in the context of particulars either, though it is a weaker argument here. Providing particulars might make clearer factually what actions are alleged to constitute the offence, thus making clear what "cause or matter" was the substance of a previous conviction.

55 Section 587(1)(f),(g).

56 *Hynes*, above note 20.

57 Section 587(2).

58 Section 587(3)(c).

59 *R. v. J.A.H.*, above note 54.

60 *Vézina*, above note 40.

Crown's position in this regard was made clear from the start, and the accused's application for particulars was rejected on the grounds that:

> the purpose of the application for particulars was not to require the prosecution to provide the accused with additional details with respect to matters referred to in the indictment in order that the accused might be more fully informed of the act or omission charged against them but was to restrict the prosecution to reliance on a part only of the definition of murder contained in the *Criminal Code*.[61]

Still, the most likely result from some defect in a charge is an amendment. The question thus arises: what is considered to be a defect in a charge? In a broad sense, a charge is defective when it departs from the "golden rule," laid down in *R. v. Côté*, that the accused is entitled "to be reasonably informed of the transaction alleged against him, thus giving him the possibility of a full defence and a fair trial."[62]

Consistent with the notion that charges will rarely be quashed for error is the approach to finding error in the first place: generally speaking the rules allow quite a wide range of forms of charge, with the result that no remedy is available because there is not seen to be any problem.

b) Insufficient Charges

The most commonly alleged problem with indictments relates to the requirement in section 581 that a count must contain sufficient detail to give the accused reasonable information and to identify the transaction. In deciding the sufficiency of a count, courts frequently make reference to the test in *R. v. Brodie* that the indictment must lift the charge "from the general to the particular."[63] Though this standard is frequently cited, caselaw makes it clear that it is not attained infrequently. In part, this is because certain omissions (as noted above, omissions such as that the count "does not name the person injured or intended or attempted to be injured . . . does not specify the means by which the alleged offence was committed [or] does not name or describe with precision any person, place or thing"[64]) are specifically noted by the *Code* as not creating insufficiency. Beyond that, courts have generally favoured the view that alleged procedural defects should only rarely prevent a trial.

---

61   *R. v. Thatcher* (1986), 24 C.C.C. (3d) 449 (Sask.C.A.) [*Thatcher*], quoting from *R. v. Govedarov, Popovic and Askov* (1974), 16 C.C.C. (2d) 238 (Ont. C.A.).

62   *R. v. Côté*, [1978] 1 S.C.R. 8 [*Côté*].

63   [1936] S.C.R. 188.

64   Section 583. See also the special rules in ss. 584 & 585.

It is worth being clear that the important meaning of "insufficiency" is insufficiency as spoken of in *Moore*—an error egregious enough that the charge must be quashed. It is not uncommon for courts to speak more loosely of degrees of insufficiency,[65] by which it merely means that a charge could have been clearer or that an amendment might be appropriate. However, for insufficiency to have any greater impact, a count must violate the standard in *Moore* or *Côté* and be so badly drawn up that it does not give the accused notice of the charge. This standard is rarely met.

It has been held that "an information will not be held to be a nullity if the information specifies the time, the place, the victim and the offence."[66] Even that statement suggests a higher standard than is actually insisted upon in practice. It is not surprising that a count suggesting that an offence was committed "on or about" a particular date or "at or near" a particular location should be upheld.[67] Counts charging an offence as having occurred somewhere within a ten-month period eight years earlier[68] or during a sixty-three-month period[69] have also been upheld. The Court has held that "time is not required to be stated with exact precision unless it is an essential part of the offence charged and the accused is not misled or prejudiced by any variation in time that arises."[70]

Indeed, an indictment can be perfectly valid even if the count is not merely broad in its reference to time, but is actually incorrect about the time at which the offence is alleged to have occurred. Unless time is of the essence in a charge, the time that the offence occurred is not an essential element. Therefore, the time of an offence normally does not need to be proven, even if it is stated in the count. Accordingly, it does not matter that the wrong time was stated, and it is not even necessary to amend the indictment. This approach is consistent with the surplusage rule discussed above.

---

65 See, for example, *R. v. Webster*, [1993] 1 S.C.R. 3 at para. 12: "In my opinion, the learned Provincial Court Judge was correct in his conclusion that while 'some measure of insufficiency exists in each of the charges . . . it is not of such a degree as would vitiate the charges.'"

66 *Re MacLean and The Queen* (1988), 68 C.R. (3d) 114 (B.C.C.A.) [*MacLean*], citing in support *Re Regina and R.I.C.* (1986), 32 C.C.C. (3d) 399 (Ont. C.A.); *R. v. Dugdale* (1979), 7 C.R. (3d) 216 (B.C.C.A.); *R. v. Fox* (1986), 50 C.R. (3d) 370 (B.C.C.A.), leave to appeal to S.C.C. refused, [1986] 1 S.C.R. ix [*Fox*]; *R. v. Nadin* (1971), 14 C.R.N.S. 201 (B.C.C.A.), and *R. v. Race*, [1988] B.C.J. No. 1819 (C.A.).

67 *Fox, ibid.*; *R. v. Ryan* (1985), 12 O.A.C. 172 (C.A.), leave to appeal to S.C.C. refused, [1986] 1 S.C.R. ix.

68 *MacLean*, above note 66.

69 *R. v. Colgan* (1986), 43 Man. R. (2d) 101 (C.A.), aff'd [1987] 2 S.C.R. 686.

70 *R. v. Douglas*, [1991] 1 S.C.R. 301 [*Douglas*].

Time could be of the essence where an accused was entitled to take items or perform actions (such as fly a plane) during some periods but not others.[71] In those circumstances, an error in the count with regard to time would be significant because the accused's guilt or innocence would depend upon exactly when the actions in question occurred. But, in most cases, time will not be of the essence, as the Court observes in *R. v. B.(G.) (No. 2)*:

> the date of the offence is not generally an essential element of the offence of sexual assault. It is a crime no matter when it is committed.[72]

Alibi evidence led by the accused can sometimes make the exact time more relevant,[73] and whether the Crown has closed its case before seeking the amendment can also be significant.[74]

It can occur occasionally that a count is struck down on the basis that it does not disclose an offence known to law, though this phrase is not really a term of art.[75] In *Regina v. Fremeau* the Alberta Court of Appeal found that a count in an information did not disclose an offence known to law when it charged that an accused sold "a drug listed or described in Schedule F of the Food and Drug Regulations." The regulation in question did not proscribe selling such drugs, rather, it proscribed selling "*a substance containing* a drug" listed in that Schedule.[76] This somewhat technical approach is uncommon, however, and normally courts will simply look at whether the accused has been reasonably informed of the charge, as required by *Côté*.

Indeed, in *Côté* the charge laid alleged that the accused had refused to provide a breath sample, without explicitly stating that he had done so "without reasonable excuse." Strictly, one could claim that the charge laid, failing to provide a breath sample, was not on its own an offence, but the Court held that the inclusion in the charge of the specific section under which the charge was laid made it impossible for the accused to have been misled.[77] This is consistent with section

---

71 See *R. v. Hamilton-Middleton* (1986), 53 Sask. R. 80 (C.A.) and *R. v. McCrae and Ramsay* (1981), 25 Man. R. (2d) 32 (Co. Ct.).

72 [1990] 2 S.C.R. 30 at para. 11 [*B.(G.)*].

73 See *B.(G.)* itself, *ibid.*; *R. v. Dossi* (1918), 13 Cr. App. R. 158; *R. v. Parkin (No. 1) and (No. 2)* (1922), 37 C.C.C. 35 (Man. C.A.); *Wright v. Nicholson*, [1970] 1 All E.R. 12 (Q.B.), all discussed therein.

74 *R. v. M.B.P.*, [1994] 1 S.C.R. 555 [*M.B.P.*].

75 See Quigley, note 46 at 17-2.

76 *R. v. Fremeau* (1984), 34 Alta. L.R. (2d) 1 (C.A.).

77 *Côté*, above note 62. Note that, in fact, the accused had appealed his conviction at trial on the basis that he did have a reasonable excuse, among other grounds: the error in the charge was raised by the Saskatchewan Court of Appeal.

601(3)(b)(ii) of the *Code*, permitting amendment where a count "does not negative an exception that should be negatived," but goes further. The Court did not find that there would be no prejudice from remedying the defect, but that there was no defect in the first place. Similarly, in *R. v. Henyu* an information was quashed at trial for failing to disclose an offence known to law on the basis that it failed to explicitly allege that the accused had caused bodily harm, one of the elements of the offence. Nonetheless, the Court of Appeal held that in stating that the accused had stabbed the victim, bodily harm was sufficiently implied.[78]

The Court has created some room for arguments about the sufficiency of charges with its decision in *R. v. Wis Development Corp.*[79] It is common for charges to be laid by simply repeating the language of the *Code* section that creates the offence, and this approach is specifically permitted by section 581(2). In *Wis Development*, however, the Court accepted that a charge laid in that form was insufficient when it simply said that the accused "operate[d] a commercial air service," without anything more. That phrase covered a "multitude of activities," ranging from hauling passengers to allowing an aircraft to be photographed for liquor advertisement, and therefore the information was void for not meeting the sufficiency standard of section 510(3).[80] This has caused debate at times over whether the wording in particular *Code* sections also cover a multitude of activities and, therefore, would not be sufficient if used when a charge is laid. The simple fact that an offence can be committed in a number of ways does not make it fall within the *Wis Development* rule, and so charges that an accused had care and control of a vehicle or was keeping a common bawdy house have been found to be unaffected.[81] However, a charge simply asserting that an accused kept a common gaming house was held to violate the rule.[82] Scope for argument regarding when this standard is met remains. However, any problem caused by such a flaw could now be amended (which was not the case for summary offences at the time of *Wis Development*) and so the question has become less important.

---

78 *R. v. Henyu*, [1980] 1 W.W.R. 752 (B.C.C.A.).

79 [1984] 1 S.C.R. 485 [*Wis Development*].

80 This issue merely laid the groundwork for the central issue in the case, which was the ability to amend the information. Since the case was decided under legislation specific to summary conviction offences, and that legislation has since been repealed to allow the general rule to have effect, the case is no longer significant with regard to its main holding. However, that does not affect the initial reasoning concerning whether the information was valid or not.

81 *Fox*, above note 66, and *R. v. Milberg et al.* (1987), 35 C.C.C. (3d) 45 (Ont. C.A.).

82 *R. v. Bingo Enterprises Ltd. (c.o.b. Buffalo Bingo Palace)* (1984), 41 C.R. (3d) 291 (Man. C.A.).

c)   Duplicitous Charges

A potential flaw in counts that is conceptually distinct from insufficiency is duplicity. Where insufficiency asks whether an accused has been given too little information, duplicity in effect suggests that the accused has been given too much information. A duplicitous count is one that charges the accused with committing two different offences, and it is objectionable because the ambiguity prevents the accused from knowing the case to meet. If any ambiguity does not rise to that level, the charge is not duplicitous.[83] This is a distinct requirement from the "single transaction" rule in section 581(1). That rule limits a count to a single factual situation, while the duplicity rule limits it to a single legal issue.

As with the single transaction rule, courts have not found the duplicity rule to be easily violated. In *Sault Ste. Marie*, the Court found a count non-duplicitous that charged the accused did "discharge or cause to be discharged or permitted to be discharged or deposited" pollutants into a river. This charge tracked the wording of the offence section. The Court held that section had not created several different offences but only one offence, polluting, which could be committed in a number of ways. The accused would have no doubt about the case to meet, and so no objection should be taken to the charge.[84] Similarly, a charge that did not differentiate between the general theft section and theft by a person required to account, and suggested the accused was guilty of each, was not duplicitous (again, although two *Code* sections were involved, they were simply two ways of committing theft).[85] This approach is consistent with the idea that a jury must be unanimous to find an accused guilty of an offence, but need not be unanimous with regard to how the accused committed the offence.[86]

Further, an information that contains two counts separated by the word "alternatively" is not duplicitous, since it would not be a single count charging more than one offence.[87] Particular difficulties can arise in conspiracy cases, and a single count charging an accused with more than one conspiracy would be duplicitous. However, even if more than one conspiracy is proven at trial, the charge is not automatically dupli-

---

83   *Sault Ste. Marie*, note 47. See also s. 590(1)(a) of the *Code*, providing that a count is not objectionable if it "charges in the alternative several different matters, acts or omissions that are stated in the alternative in an enactment that describes as an indictable offence the matters, acts or omissions charged in the count."

84   *Ibid.*

85   *R. v. Fischer* (1987), 53 Sask. R. 263 (C.A.) [*Fischer*], dealing with ss. 322 and 330. The potential ambiguity was created by the provision of particulars.

86   *Fischer*, *ibid.*, and *Thatcher*, above note 61.

87   *R. v. Brewer* (1988), 8 M.V.R. (2d) 137 (N.B.C.A.).

citous; if it was not, the only issue will be which conspiracy was the accused charged with, and whether any or all of the conspiracies proven to have been committed are covered by the indictment.[88]

In any event, even if a charge is duplicitous it is not fatally flawed. Section 590(2)(b) allows an accused to apply to have a count that is "double or multifarious" either amended or divided into two or more counts, an application that is to be granted where the ends of justice require it. To divide a count is to make it two or more separate counts (sometimes this is referred to as "severance," though, more strictly, severance is the process under section 591(3)(a) of sending separate counts to separate trials).

Only the trial judge has jurisdiction to divide a count, though the application can be brought on a pre-trial basis.[89] The *Code* allows the count to be divided when it "embarrasses [the accused] in his defence," a criterion broad enough to leave the decision largely in the trial judge's discretion. An appeal court is not to interfere with that discretion unless the judge acted unjudicially or the decision resulted in an injustice. *Litchfield*, for example, dealt with a doctor charged with various sexual assaults arising out of examinations performed on a number of patients. Before trial, a judge divided the counts based on which parts of the complainant's bodies the doctor had been examining, and then severed those counts to be dealt with in different trials. The result, in some cases, was that different parts of a single examination of one patient would be dealt with in separate trials, depending upon which part of the complainant's body was examined. The Court held that this result misapprehended the nature of sexual assault and the order ought not to have been made.[90]

On the other hand, in *Lilly* the Court dealt with a real estate broker who was charged with theft based on a series of withdrawals from a trust account into which a number of deposits relating to real property transactions had been made. In the course of the trial it became apparent that the accused was claiming a colour of right defence with regard to some of the withdrawals, while claiming to be unaware of some of the deposits. The Court held that although it had been acceptable to lay a single count charging the accused with theft, it would have been preferable to divide the count once it became apparent that the accused had two separate defences. Particularly given that it was a jury trial, this approach would have made clearer what was implied in finding

---

88 See *Douglas*, above note 70 and *R. v. Papalia*, [1979] 2 S.C.R. 256.
89 *Litchfield*, above note 21.
90 *Ibid.*

the accused guilty.[91] The matter remains in a trial judge's discretion, though, and so, for example, the fact that an accused's employment has been terminated does not mean that a count of theft must be divided to deal with continuing actions before and after he was fired.[92]

C. PLEAS

The pleas available to an accused charged with an offence are set out in section 606 of the *Code*. An accused can plead guilty, not guilty, or one of the special pleas provided for in the *Code*. The special pleas consist of *autrefois acquit*, *autrefois convict*, and pardon,[93]

The special pleas really amount to the claim that the matter that the accused is called upon to plead is a matter that has already been dealt with—the accused has previously been acquitted, convicted, or pardoned for the offence in question. There can be confused issues around whether the matter the accused is charged with at this time is the same matter that was dealt with by previous charges. They are, in effect, all manifestations of the rule against multiple convictions. The discussion here will focus only on the pleas of guilty and not guilty.

A plea of guilty amounts to an admission by the accused of performing the physical actions that make up the offence, accompanied by the necessary mental state. It is, in effect, a waiver of the right to a trial.[94] A court should inquire into a plea of guilty if there is any reason to doubt that the accused understands its effect, but there is no general obligation to do so.[95]

A plea of not guilty is not a claim of innocence, but is simply a demand that the Crown proves all the elements of the offence and disproves the existence of any defences. Unless a special plea is required, pleading not guilty puts any defence available in issue, including, for example, whether the accused is not criminally responsible by reason of mental disorder.[96]

---

91   *Lilly*, above note 14.
92   *Fischer*, above note 85.
93   Section 607. Section 611 also allows the plea of justification to a charge of defamatory libel.
94   *R. v. Adgey*, [1975] 2 S.C.R. 426 [*Adgey*].
95   See *ibid.*; *R. v. Brousseau*, [1969] S.C.R. 181. Note, however, that s. 36 of the *Youth Criminal Justice Act*, S.C. 2002, c. 1 [*YCJA*] requires a judge to be satisfied that the facts will support a charge before accepting a guilty plea from a young person.
96   Section 613. Although all defences are potentially put in issue by a plea of not guilty, the onus of proof can, in some instances, be on the accused. A plea of not

Where an accused refuses to plead, the judge is to enter a plea of not guilty.[97] An accused can, with the consent of the Crown, enter a plea of guilty to some other offence arising out of the same transaction, whether it is an included offence or not. If the court accepts the plea, the accused will be found not guilty of the offence originally charged.[98]

An accused can later withdraw a guilty plea if "there are valid grounds for his being permitted to do so,"[99] a category the Court has consciously not defined exhaustively. An accused cannot withdraw a plea because the judge rejects a joint sentencing submission, for example, because a co-accused has subsequently been acquitted of the offence, or because the Crown makes a subsequent application to have the accused declared a dangerous offender.[100] Rather, some special circumstance must be in place that suggests the guilty plea should not be accepted at face value as a legitimate concession of guilt. So, for example, if the accused has been pressured by counsel into entering a guilty plea, the accused might successfully withdraw the plea.[101] Similarly, a plea might be withdrawn if it is shown that the accused who wished to plead not guilty actually pled guilty in order to obtain an immediate fine rather than spend a week in custody awaiting trial, or to avoid a more serious charge being laid (first, rather than second degree murder, for example).[102] Circumstances other than improper pressure on the accused could lead to the plea being set aside, however. In *R. v. Fegan*, for example, an accused lost a pre-trial ruling on the admissibility of certain evidence and then entered a guilty plea. The Ontario Court of Appeal held that the guilty plea was not valid because the accused had entered it under the mistaken impression that he would then be able to appeal his conviction and the pre-trial ruling.[103] Alterna-

---

guilty allows an accused to argue entrapment, for example, but the accused will bear the ultimate burden of proof to make out that defence.

97 Section 606(2).

98 Section 606(4).

99 *Adgey*, above note 94, quoted in *R. v. Taillefer; R. v. Duguay*, [2003] 3 S.C.R. 307 at para. 85 [*Taillefer*].

100 *R. v. Rubenstein* (1987), 41 C.C.C. (3d) 91 (Ont. C.A.), leave to appeal to S.C.C. refused (1988), 87 N.R. 77n; *R. v. Hick*, [1991] 3 S.C.R. 383; *R. v. Lyons*, [1987] 2 S.C.R. 309.

101 *R. v. Laperrière*, [1996] 2 S.C.R. 284; *R. v. Lamoureux* (1984), 40 C.R. (3d) 369 (Que. C.A.).

102 *R. v. Cesari* (1986), 50 C.R. (3d) 93 (Que. C.A.); *R. v. Hansen* (1977), 37 C.C.C. (2d) 371 (Man. C.A.).

103 *R. v. Fegan* (1993), 21 C.R. (4th) 65 (Ont. C.A.). Ultimately, the Court of Appeal found it unnecessary to decide whether to set aside the guilty plea, since they held that the pre-trial ruling was correct. See also *R. v. Newman* (1993), 20 C.R. (4th) 370 (Ont. C.A.), where the accused argued, though unsuccessfully, that he

tively, in *Taillefer* an accused received disclosure of significant Crown evidence four years after entering a guilty plea. The Court held that even if a guilty plea was valid—that is, it was voluntary, unequivocal, and based on sufficient information concerning the nature of the charges and the consequences of the plea—it might still be withdrawn if the accused's constitutional rights were violated. The test asks how a reasonable person would have behaved with knowledge of the undisclosed evidence if "there was a realistic possibility that the accused would have run the risk of a trial, if he or she had been in possession of that information or those new avenues of investigation, leave must be given to withdraw the plea."[104]

Guilty and not guilty are, apart from the special pleas, the only pleas available to a person charged with an offence. Experience in the criminal justice system rapidly acquaints counsel with clients who wish to plead "guilty with an explanation," or who want to plead guilty rather than go to trial, but wish to maintain their innocence. In the former case, the accused is required to plead not guilty, and a judge receiving a plea of guilty with an explanation should refuse to accept it. The court should inquire into the accused's intention, and only accept the guilty plea if it is clear that the accused unequivocally wishes to plead guilty.[105]

In general, a judge has no obligation to hear evidence after an accused has pleaded guilty, but can do so. If in doing so it becomes apparent that the accused did not intend to admit some element of the offence, misapprehended the effect of a guilty plea, or did not intend to plead guilty, the trial judge may allow the accused to withdraw the plea or enter a plea of not guilty.

A judge should not permit an accused to plead guilty simply to "get it over with." The judge should only accept a guilty plea when the accused intends to admit all the elements of the offence, and defence counsel has an ethical obligation in this regard.[106] Equally, an accused

---

should be permitted to withdraw his guilty plea for not having been adequately informed of the consequences of pleading guilty due to ineffective representation by counsel.

104 *Taillefer*, above note 99 at para 90.

105 *R. v. McNabb* (1971), 4 C.C.C. (2d) 316 (Sask. C.A.).

106 See, for example, Chapter IX, "The Lawyer as Advocate" in Canadian Bar Association, *Code of Professional Conduct* (Ottawa: Canadian Bar Association, 2006), and the discussion in Michel Proulx & David Layton, *Ethics and Canadian Criminal Law* (Toronto: Irwin Law, 2001), particularly Chapter 8, Section M. See also the discussion there of the plea "*nolo contendere*," which is not permissible in Canada and is in fact a way for an accused to decline to contest a charge without conceding its truth.

cannot enter a "conditional plea." For example, an accused cannot plead guilty to a homicide charge, conditional upon the Crown proving the cause of death.[107] Of course, in a case of theft, it is open to an accused to make factual concessions despite a plea of not guilty, and, for example, admit to having taken items, but advance a claim of colour of right or deny having had the necessary *mens rea*.[108]

Section 650 of the *Code* requires an accused (other than a corporation) to be present in court during the whole trial, and therefore an accused must be present for the plea. Section 800 of the *Code* explicitly permits an accused charged with a summary conviction offence to appear by counsel. Courts have held that a plea entered by counsel to an indictable offence is also, in the normal course of events, binding on an accused who was present at the time.[109]

Recent additions to the *Code* allow an accused to enter a plea via electronic appearance, provided it permits simultaneous visual and oral communication and the accused can still consult privately with counsel.

D. ORDER OF TRIAL

1) Trial Procedures

The procedures governing trial are set out in Parts XIX, XX, and XXVII of the *Criminal Code* and cover indictable offences tried by judge alone or judge and jury and summary conviction trials respectively.[110] Many of the procedures dealing with the actual conduct of trials are common to all three modes.[111]

---

107 *R. v. Lucas* (1983), 9 C.C.C. (3d) 71 (Ont. C.A.), leave to appeal to S.C.C. refused (1984), 9 C.C.C. (3d) 71n.

108 See s. 655 of the *Code*.

109 *R. v. Dietrich* (1970), 11 C.R.N.S. 22 (Ont. C.A.), leave to appeal to S.C.C. refused, [1970] S.C.R. xi; *R. v. Sommerfeldt* (1984), 14 C.C.C. (3d) 445 (B.C.C.A.).

110 Part XIX.1 of the *Code* also sets out the procedures to be used at trials in front of the Nunavut Court of Justice, which is something of a hybrid. Section 573(1) of the *Code* provides that the powers, duties, and function of a provincial court judge may be exercised by the Nunavut Court of Justice, while s. 573(2) clarifies that in doing so the judges of that court are acting as judges of a superior court.

111 Section 572 makes the provisions of Part XX, Jury Trials, applicable to Part XIX, Trial without Jury. Section 795 makes those provisions applicable to summary conviction trials. In each case, the provisions apply to the extent that they are not inconsistent with specific provisions in those Parts and with such modifications as the circumstances require.

A trial is to proceed continuously, though the judge can grant adjournments.[112] The accused is to be present for the trial, but a judge is allowed to excuse the accused from attending.[113] In addition, provisions in the *Code* now permit the attendance of the accused at trial by video link, though this is only permitted for portions of the trial during which no evidence is taken.[114] If an accused absconds during trial, the court can either issue a warrant for the accused's arrest and adjourn the trial, or continue the trial without the accused. In the latter case, defence counsel can continue acting for the accused, and the accused's right to full answer and defence will not have been violated.[115]

The trial judge has discretion as to where the accused will sit during trial. Normally this will be in the prisoner's dock, and the trial judge is not required to permit the accused to sit elsewhere unless the refusal will violate the accused's right to full answer and defence.[116]

The judge can ask questions during the trial, although doing so can raise issues as to whether there is a reasonable apprehension of bias (see the discussion below at section F). Juries are also entitled to ask questions, though within limits. It must be made clear to the jury that the parties are entitled to present the evidence as they want, and so questioning by jurors should not become another interrogation. Jurors' questions are best left to the end, to be submitted in writing to the trial judge who can discuss with counsel whether they should be asked.[117]

2) Opening Statements

The Crown presents its case first, and, as a matter of practice, can begin with an opening statement to the jury explaining its theory of the case and the evidence to be called. The Crown is not actually obliged to call every witness it indicates will be called. The prosecutor, like any

---

112 Sections 571 and 645.
113 Section 645. The presumption of attendance works the other way in the case of summary conviction offences, with s. 800(2) allowing an accused to appear personally or by counsel, but permitting the judge to require the accused's personal attendance.
114 Sections 650(1.1), 650(1.2), and 800(2.1).
115 See s. 475 and *R. v. Zarubin* (2001), 157 C.C.C. (3d) 115 (Sask. C.A.).
116 *R. v. Levogiannis*, [1993] 4 S.C.R. 475 [*Levogiannis*], citing *R. v. Faid*, [1981] 5 W.W.R. 349 (Alta. C.A.), rev'd on other grounds, [1983] 1 S.C.R. 265 [*Faid*].
117 See *R. v. Nordyne* (1998), 17 C.R. (5th) 393 (Que. C.A.) and *R. v. Gagnon* (1992), 47 Q.A.C. 232 (C.A.). See also *R. v. Lam*, [1998] N.W.T.J. No. 79 (C.A.), where defence counsel's decision to ask some questions of his client, after the jury sent a note with those questions to the judge, was found not to form the basis for an appeal.

other counsel at trial, is entitled to modify the trial strategy as the case develops. Short of oppressive prosecutorial conduct amounting to an abuse of process, the accused cannot object to a change of plans on the part of the Crown. In choosing not to call a witness who has been announced, of course, the Crown risks the jury drawing some type of adverse inference, and the accused would normally be entitled to point out the change to the jury when making closing submissions. [118]

Normally the defence is not entitled to make an opening address to the jury immediately following the Crown's opening remarks. However, a trial judge has discretion to let the accused do so, rather than have to wait until the close of the Crown's case. Some authority suggests that making such an opening statement obliges the accused to actually call evidence, essentially because the purpose of the statement is to outline the evidence that will be called. However, the prevailing view appears to be that, in the special circumstances where the accused is allowed an opening statement immediately following the Crown's, there is no obligation to later call witnesses for direct examination, and indeed that "counsel acting responsibly cannot be expected to give an undertaking at that stage to call evidence. That decision must be assessed against the concluded Crown case."[119] Nonetheless, the defence might adduce evidence through cross-examination of Crown witnesses, for example, and in appropriate cases should be allowed an opening statement. Cases returned for a new trial that have a measure of predictability might be ones where such an order is appropriate.[120]

3) Presentation of the Crown Case

Following the opening statement, Crown counsel is required to present evidence proving the charges against the accused. The procedures for taking evidence at trial are the same as at a preliminary inquiry. That is, the evidence is to be taken under oath in the presence of the accused, the accused is entitled to cross-examine the Crown witnesses, and the evidence is recorded.[121]

---

118 R. v. Jolivet, [2000] 1 S.C.R. 751 [Jolivet]; R. v. Cook, [1997] 1 S.C.R. 1113 [Cook]. See R. v. Biniaris, [2000] 1 S.C.R. 381 as an example of the Crown changing its theory of the case during the course of trial.

119 R. v. Sood (1997), 58 O.T.C. 115 (Gen. Div.) [Sood]. See also R. v. Barrow (1989), 91 N.S.R. (2d) 176 (S.C.T.D.) [Barrow], but, in contrast, see R. v. Vitale (1987), 40 C.C.C. (3d) 267 (Ont. Dist. Ct.).

120 Sood, ibid.; Barrow, ibid.

121 Sections 540, 557, and 646. Note that recent amendments to the preliminary inquiry procedures in ss. 540(7), (8), and(9) do not carry over to trials.

Although in principle it is up to the Crown to prove every essential element of the offence, it is open to the accused to concede various parts of the Crown's case.[122] Often this is done through an agreed statement of facts, but not necessarily. An accused can concede the voluntariness of a statement and waive a *voir dire*, for example, without any particular form of words being necessary (as long as it is clear that counsel understood the issue and made an informed decision regarding waiver, that is sufficient). Silence or lack of objection to a statement being admitted is not waiver, however.[123] Even in cases of silence, however, the trial will not necessarily be fatally flawed by the admission of a statement, a trial judge will only have erred if there was clear evidence objectively showing the need to conduct a *voir dire* despite the failure of defence counsel to request one.[124]

The Crown has considerable discretion in deciding how to present its case, consistent with the adversarial nature of the process. The Crown is not required, for example, to call every witness with relevant information, and has no obligation to call a witness it does not consider necessary to the prosecution's case.[125] This rule applies equally even if the witness not called is the complainant. Failing to do so might put the Crown's ability to prove its case at risk, and in some circumstances a trial judge might comment to a jury on the failure to call the complainant, but the decision is still within the Crown's discretion. The defence is not entitled to cross-examine all witnesses, but it can call any witness not called by the Crown as part of the defence case. In some circumstances, the defence can apply under the *Canada Evidence Act*[126] to cross-examine the witness.[127] Further, in some cases the trial judge could choose to call the person as the court's witness, therefore allowing the defence to cross-examine. This might be the right course of action particularly where forcing the defence to call the witness might require the accused to give up the right to speak to the jury last (see the discussion of this issue at section D(8)).

Although evidence typically takes the form of testimony or documents from witnesses on the stand, other forms of evidence are permitted. Provisions in the *Code* create special rules around proof of

---

122 Section 655.

123 *R. v. Park*, [1981] 2 S.C.R. 64.

124 *R. v. Hodgson*, [1998] 2 S.C.R. 449.

125 See *Lemay v. The King*, [1952] 1 S.C.R. 232; *R. v. Yebes*, [1987] 2 S.C.R. 168; *Cook*, above note 118; *Jolivet*, above note 118.

126 R.S.C. 1985, c. C-5.

127 *Cook*, above note 118.

ownership and value of property,[128] expert's reports,[129] dates of birth,[130] and previous convictions.[131] Further, other provisions allow for the use of commission evidence for witnesses who are out of the country or who, through illness or other "good and sufficient cause," cannot attend the trial.[132] In addition, evidence that was taken at a preliminary inquiry can be used at a trial in some circumstances.[133] Videotaped testimony by a person under eighteen or with a physical or mental disability can sometimes be used at a trial for various sexual offences.[134] Further, the use of technology to present evidence is available if it will increase efficiency in any case, not merely in ones with thousands of documents.[135]

Section 652 allows a jury to "have a view," in order to see any place person or thing.[136] This ability is open to the jury any time prior to rendering their verdict, including after they have started their deliberations,[137] and can also be used by a judge conducting a trial without a jury.[138]

A Crown prosecutor will normally have indicated what evidence will be called in the opening address. Failing to actually call that evidence will not necessarily prove fatal to the prosecution. Thus, for example, if hearsay evidence is admitted in anticipation of direct evidence that is expected to be but ultimately is not, called, adequate instructions by the trial judge to the jury can cure any problem.[139]

Section 545 of the *Code* allows a trial judge to imprison a witness who refuses to testify for periods of up to eight days at a time.

4) Presentation of the Defence Case

a) Application for a Directed Verdict
At the close of the Crown's case it becomes the defence's turn to present evidence, if it chooses to do so. Prior to that, however, it is open to an accused to apply for a directed verdict. Although a jury, when there is one, reaches a decision in a trial, in limited circumstances the

128 Section 657.1.
129 Section 657.3.
130 Section 658(3).
131 Section 667.
132 Section 709.
133 Section 715, and see also ss. 657 and 541.
134 Sections 715.1 & 715.2.
135 *R. v. Mackay*, 2002 SKQB 316.
136 Section 652.
137 *R. v. Welsh* (1997), 120 C.C.C. (3d) 68 (B.C.C.A.).
138 *R. v. Prentice* (1965), 47 C.R. 231 (B.C.C.A.), and see s. 572.
139 *R. v. Myers*, [2001] O.J. No. 4258 (C.A.).

trial judge has the authority to direct that an accused will be acquitted. This power is not created by statute, but arises at common law.[140] The directed verdict (sometimes referred to as a "non-suit," or as there being no case to meet) takes its name from the fact that, historically, the trial judge literally directed the jury to retire and return a verdict of not guilty. Recently, the Supreme Court has modified the procedure so that trial judges are instead to withdraw the case from the jury and enter the acquittal personally,[141] but the name has remained.

The test for granting a directed verdict is quite restricted, and is consistent with the differing functions of judge and jury. The jury is the trier of fact, and therefore is called upon to assess the credibility of witnesses, decide whether the Crown's evidence has proven the accused's guilt beyond a reasonable doubt, and so on. A trial judge cannot intrude on that function. However, where the Crown has failed to provide evidence on some essential element of the offence, the trial judge can direct the acquittal of the accused. The accused can make such a motion at the close of the Crown's case, and the judge is to rule on it at that time. The accused is entitled to know the result of that motion before deciding whether to call evidence in defence.[142]

The Court has made clear that this is a limited power, and is not to intrude on the jury's role. A trial judge cannot direct an acquittal on the basis that the Crown's evidence of identification is manifestly unreliable, for example, because the trial judge is not permitted to weigh the strength of the evidence at all.[143] The test for a directed verdict is the same as that for a preliminary inquiry judge in deciding whether to send a matter for trial:

> whether or not there is any evidence upon which a reasonable jury properly instructed could return a verdict of guilty. The "justice" [is] required to commit an accused person for trial in any case in which there is admissible evidence which could, if it were believed, result in a conviction.[144]

Thus, a directed verdict is not available where the Crown's evidence is weak. It is only possible where there is a complete absence of evidence on some point that must be proven. Put affirmatively, the Crown must "adduce some evidence of culpability for every essential definitional

---

140 Judges' common law powers in jury trials are preserved by s. 672 of the *Code*: *R. v. Rowbotham*, [1994] 2 S.C.R. 463 [*Rowbotham* 1994].

141 *Rowbotham* 1994, ibid.

142 *R. v. Boissoneault* (1986), 16 O.A.C. 365 (C.A.).

143 *R. v. Mezzo*, [1986 1 S.C.R. 802 [*Mezzo*].

144 *United States of America v. Shephard*, [1977] 2 S.C.R.1067 at 1080.

element of the crime for which the Crown has the evidential burden," and a motion for a directed verdict will only be granted if it has not done so.[145] That absence turns the question of the accused's guilt into an issue that can be settled by an exclusively legal, not factual, determination.

The rule also applies when the Crown's case rests on purely circumstantial evidence. In such cases the jury can only convict when there is no rational explanation for the circumstantial evidence other than that the accused committed the crime, and must be charged on that basis. Nonetheless, the Court has held that whether that test is met is a question for the jury to decide, not the judge, and so a directed verdict should not be issued.[146] Some ambiguity remains in this context, however. The Court has also held, in assessing the same test in the context of preliminary inquiries, that the judge must engage in a limited weighing of the evidence. Although a judge cannot draw inferences or assess credibility, the judge is to decide whether "if the Crown's evidence is believed it would be reasonable for a properly instructed jury to infer guilt" from that evidence.[147] This formulation of the test seems to create slightly greater scope for a trial judge to decide to grant a directed verdict.[148]

A directed verdict can be granted on the charge laid but the trial must be allowed to proceed in order to decide whether the accused is guilty of any included offences. In *R. v. Titus*, for example, the Court agreed that it would be possible to direct an acquittal on a first degree murder charge, but allow the trial to continue to see whether the accused was found guilty of second degree murder.[149]

b) Defence Presentation of Evidence

An accused who does not make, or does not succeed in, an application for a directed verdict is then entitled to call evidence, or otherwise make full answer and defence.[150] Similar to the Crown, the defence is entitled to exercise discretion as to how to present the case. For example, a trial judge is not permitted to direct the order in which witnesses are to be

---

145 *R. v. Charemski*, [1998] 1 S.C.R. 679 at para. 3 [*Charemski*].

146 *R. v. Monteleone*, [1987] 2 S.C.R. 154; *Mezzo*, above note 143; *Charemski*, ibid.

147 *R. v. Arcuri*, [2001] 2 S.C.R. 828 at para. 30. This issue is discussed in Chapter 9.

148 On this point, generally, see David M. Tanovich, "Upping the Ante in Directed Verdict Cases Where the Evidence is Circumstantial" (1998) 15 C.R. (5th) 21.

149 [1983] 1 S.C.R. 259 [*Titus*]. In *Titus*, the judge erred by failing to grant the motion for a directed verdict, but instructed the jury at the end of the trial that they could not find the accused guilty of first degree murder.

150 Sections 541 and 650(3).

called, insisting that the accused testify first.[151] The defence can call witnesses, including witnesses the Crown has decided not to call.[152] The accused is a competent witness at the trial, but is not compellable, and the failure to testify cannot be made the subject of comment by the judge or the prosecutor.[153] This statutory provision is consistent with the accused's right to silence and the presumption of innocence, both now guaranteed by the *Charter*.[154] Normally, the defence cannot cross-examine its own witnesses, though in certain situations this is permitted.[155]

5) Reopening the Crown's Case

The trial will move to closing arguments once the defence has completed calling all of the evidence it wishes. The Crown is expected to present all of its evidence before the defence is called upon. "Splitting the case" — that is, leading some of the Crown's evidence after the accused's case has been presented — has been prohibited "from the earliest days of our criminal law" for a number of reasons, including that the accused is entitled to know the full case to meet before deciding whether to remain silent or take the stand.[156]

However, in an exceptional case the Crown can apply to reopen its case and call further evidence, at the discretion of the trial judge. The "keystone principle" in deciding whether to allow the Crown to reopen its case is whether the accused will be prejudiced in making a defence.[157] A trial judge's discretion must be exercised judicially in this regard and in the interests of justice, and the Court has laid down guidelines to assist in this task:

> The ambit of a trial judge's discretion to allow the Crown to reopen its case becomes narrower as the trial proceeds because of the increasing likelihood of prejudice to the accused's defence as the trial progresses. During the first stage, when the Crown has not yet closed its case, the trial judge's discretion is quite broad. At the second stage,

---

151   *R. v. Angelantoni* (1975), 31 C.R.N.S. 342 (Ont. C.A.).

152   *Cook*, above note 118.

153   *Canada Evidence Act*, above note 126, s. 4(6).

154   See *R. v. Chambers*, [1990] 2 S.C.R. 1293 and *R. v. Noble*, [1997] 1 S.C.R. 874. Note that, as discussed at Section B(3), above in this chapter, the situation is somewhat different when a co-accused wishes to make reference to an accused's silence: *Crawford*, above note 30.

155   *Canada Evidence Act*, above note 126, s. 9.

156   *John v. The Queen*, [1985] 2 S.C.R. 476 at 480–81; *R. v. Krause*, [1986] 2 S.C.R. 466 [*Krause*].

157   *M.B.P.*, above note 74.

which arises when the Crown has just closed its case but the defence has not yet elected whether or not to call evidence, the discretion is more limited. Finally, in the third phase – where the defence has already begun to answer the Crown's case – the discretion is extremely narrow, and is "far less likely to be exercised in favour of the Crown". The emphasis during the third phase must be on the protection of the accused's interests.[158]

The discretion is most limited in the third stage, of course, because at that point the accused is most likely to be prejudiced by the admission of new evidence on the part of the Crown.

The evidence ought to be new evidence, in the sense that it could not have been foreseen by the Crown and was in the interests of justice. However, that the evidence is new is not sufficient. The Court has held that the type of limited circumstances in which such evidence will be permitted are where the defence directly or indirectly contributed to the Crown's failure to lead the evidence, or where the Crown has made a mistake or omission on a non-controversial issue that was purely formal or technical and that had nothing to do with the substance of the case.[159] Only in those circumstances, or ones closely analogous to them, should the Crown be permitted to reopen its case after the defence has begun to present evidence.[160] It is not relevant that the Crown was not at fault in failing to discover the evidence: the focus is on the prejudice to the accused, which is the same whether the Crown had acted diligently or not.[161] The accused was entitled to know the case to meet before beginning the defence, but that case is at great risk of changing if the Crown is permitted to reopen.[162]

---

158 *R. v. G. (S.G.)*, [1997] 2 S.C.R. 716 at para. 30 [*G.(S.G.)*].

159 *M.B.P.*, above note 74.

160 *G.(S.G.)*, above note 158.

161 *Ibid.* at para. 30.

162 Note the potential interaction, and slight inconsistency, between this rule and the rule on amending indictments, discussed above. An indictment can be amended to conform to the evidence presented, in some cases even after the accused has presented evidence, even alibi evidence. In practical terms, an accused might perceive little difference between the Crown leading new evidence to show that an offence occurred at a different time than the accused's alibi covers, and amending a charge so that the offence is alleged to have occurred at a different time than the accused's alibi covers. In theory, they are different issues: in *M.B.P.*, above note 74, for example, the Court noted that without leading the new evidence, the Crown would not be in a position to apply to amend the information. In that case they held that it was an error to allow the Crown to reopen its case to present new evidence. However, it would not have been an error to amend the charge had the evidence originally presented suggested the

Nonetheless, in appropriate circumstances the Crown can reopen its case. In *R. v. Sylvester*, for example, a police officer received several telephone calls from a person he identified as a witness on a weekend following closing arguments in the case. She told him that she had lied on the stand, and then retracted that claim. The Crown was permitted to reopen its case to present this new evidence, and the defence was allowed to cross-examine, to call the witness herself to the stand once again, and to make further submissions. The Ontario Court of Appeal held that no problem arose with this procedure, since the trial judge had adequately instructed the jury on the limited use they could make of the new evidence.[163]

6) Rebuttal Evidence

A close cousin to the issue of the Crown reopening its case is the possibility of the Crown leading rebuttal evidence. Rebuttal evidence is permitted:

> where the defence has raised some new matter or defence which the Crown has had no opportunity to deal with and which the Crown or the plaintiff could not reasonably have anticipated. But rebuttal will not be permitted regarding matters which merely confirm or reinforce earlier evidence adduced in the Crown's case which could have been brought before the defence was made.[164]

Essentially, rebuttal evidence must concern matters that the Crown is reasonably surprised to find in issue.

This test creates slightly broader scope for admitting rebuttal evidence than for reopening the Crown case. This difference is justified on the basis that, if the test for admitting rebuttal evidence is met, then it cannot be said that the accused did not know the case to meet. If rebuttal evidence only deals with unanticipated matters arising in the defence case, then the evidence led was not part of the original case to meet.[165]

However, to preserve that rationale it is important that rebuttal evidence only be admitted when it truly does concern matters the Crown could not have anticipated. In *R. v. Biddle*, for example, the accused

---

offence occurred at a different date than alleged in the indictment. From the accused's perspective, it might appear that the prejudice to an alibi has greater significance in one context than in the other.

163   *R. v. Sylvester* (1997), 97 O.A.C. 380.
164   *Krause*, above note 156 at 474.
165   *G.(S.G.)*, above note 158 at para. 40.

was charged with an assault that occurred somewhere between 10:00 and 10:30 in the evening. The accused took the stand in his own defence, and his testimony included the claim that he had been at a show between 7:30 and 9:15 p.m., then at several bars later on. The Crown then led rebuttal evidence of a witness who testified that the accused had followed her in his car at 8:30 that evening. The Court held that this evidence should not have been allowed in rebuttal and should have been presented as part of the Crown's original case. The Crown knew that he had given a statement to the police about his whereabouts, and ought to have anticipated that the defence would challenge the identification evidence. The Crown was able to present the witness as part of its case, and its failure to do so prevented the accused from knowing the entire case to meet before testifying.[166]

The accused's right in section 650(3) to make full answer and defence after the close of the Crown's case applies where the Crown has led rebuttal evidence, permitting the accused to lead surrebuttal evidence.[167] However, this opportunity does not eliminate any prejudice caused by improperly led rebuttal evidence. Indeed, the mere fact of entering the witness box a second time can create the impression that the accused was caught in a lie, and so could leave an adverse impression on the jury.[168]

7) Reopening the Defence Case

It is worth noting that it is also open to the defence to apply to reopen its case, though obviously the time in which this could occur is necessarily more restricted because the accused does not present evidence until the Crown's case is done. Whether a trial judge should permit the defence to reopen its case after final argument is a discretionary decision. In *R. v. Scott*, for example, one co-accused sought a bench warrant for a witness who had not responded to a subpoena. Being unsuccessful in the application, the defence entered no evidence and, along with the Crown, made final submissions. The witness then appeared and the accused applied to reopen his case. The Court held that the trial judge had not exercised her discretion improperly in refusing to allow the accused to reopen his case and call the witness. The trial judge had an obligation to conduct the trial in an expeditious and orderly manner, had been given no explanation of the way in which the witness' testi-

---

166 *R. v. Biddle*, [1995] 1 S.C.R. 761 [*Biddle*].
167 *R. v. Ewert* (1989), 52 C.C.C. (3d) 280 (B.C.C.A.).
168 *Biddle*, above note 166 at 776.

mony would be relevant, and had to consider the possible prejudice to the co-accused who objected to an adjournment.[169]

Some authority suggests that it is possible to apply to admit new evidence not only after argument, but indeed sometimes after a verdict has been reached. The Ontario Court of Appeal has held that a case cannot be reopened if the verdict was reached by a jury or if a judge has acquitted an accused, but that it can be reopened following a judge's guilty verdict in "special circumstances."[170] The Saskatchewan Court of Appeal has suggested that if new evidence is to be admitted after a finding of guilt, the test should not vary depending on which court is admitting the evidence. Therefore the test for a trial judge to reopen the defence case after a guilty verdict should be the same as that for admitting fresh evidence on appeal.[171]

8) Addresses to the Jury

a) Closing Arguments by Counsel

Still, in the ordinary course of events all evidence is presented and final submissions are then made. Section 651 of the *Code* sets out the order in which the Crown and the accused are to address the jury. If the defence has not called evidence, then the Crown argues first, but if the defence has called evidence, then it argues first.[172] Although it has been argued that the right to full answer and defence should entitle the accused to address the jury last in all cases, the Court determined, in a closely divided decision, that section 651 of the *Code* does not violate section 7 or section 11(d) of the *Charter*.

Five of the nine members of the Court held that although there was no question that counsel's address to the jury could be of great persuasive significance, there was not sufficient evidence to show that there was an advantage to speaking last. An accused will be reasonably clear, through the Crown's opening arguments and questions to witnesses, as to what argument the Crown will make. In general, therefore, the rule requiring an accused to speak first sometimes did not cause *Charter* problems. In individual cases where irregularities in Crown counsel's address to the jury or other issues threatened an accused's fair trial right, two options are available. The trial judge, who in any event addresses the jury last in charging them, could give curative instructions,

---

169   *R. v. Scott*, [1990] 3 S.C.R. 979.
170   *R. v. Lessard* (1976), 33 C.R.N.S. 16 (Ont. C.A.).
171   *R. v. Mysko* (1980), 2 Sask. R. 342 (C.A.).
172   Where there is more than one accused, all accused are equally affected by the decision of any one of them to call evidence, and the Crown will argue last.

instructing the jury to ignore improper aspects of an argument. Further, a court's inherent jurisdiction would allow it to grant to the defence a limited right of reply following the Crown's address, where not doing so would prejudice the accused's right to a fair trial and to make full answer and defence. This situation might arise where, for example, the accused has been misled by the Crown as to the argument to be advanced, or where the Crown's argument has changed so dramatically that the defence could not reasonably have anticipated and answered it.[173] The right of reply would be confined to addressing the issues improperly dealt with by Crown counsel.

Note that although a majority of the Court found that section 651 was not so unfair that it violated the *Charter*, all nine members of the Court expressed the view that better alternatives could be found. Various proposals have been put forward, such as always allowing the accused to speak last or giving the accused a choice as to when to speak.[174]

b) Charging the Jury

Once counsel have argued, if there is a jury the judge then gives them instructions, usually referred to as the "charge to the jury." Section 650.1 of the *Code* permits a judge to confer with the Crown and the defence with regard to what matters should be explained to the jury. The purpose of the charge to the jury is to "decant and simplify" the case, and leave the jury with a sufficient understanding of the facts as they relate to the relevant legal issues.[175] In general, the trial judge has considerable discretion regarding the content and form of the charge to the jury, though with some limits. An accused has a right to a properly instructed jury, but not to a perfectly instructed jury.[176]

The organization of a jury charge is a matter of common law, and so trial judges do have some latitude in structuring them. Trial judges are permitted to experiment with new approaches to instructing a jury,

---

173 *R. v. Rose*, [1998] 3 S.C.R. 262 [*Rose*]. Note that Justice L'Heureux-Dubé, one of the five judges making up the majority in the result, disagreed with the other four judges as to whether a trial judge had inherent jurisdiction to grant a limited right of reply, holding that this jurisdiction had been ousted by s. 651. However, the reasons of the four judges who held that s. 651 violated the *Charter* (particularly their arguments concerning s. 11(d)) suggest that they would agree with the four members of the majority regarding inherent jurisdiction.

174 See, for example, Tim Quigley, "Principled Reform of Criminal Procedure" in Don Stuart, R.J. Delisle, & Allan Manson, eds., *Towards a Clear and Just Criminal Law* (Toronto: Carswell, 1999); Law Reform Commission of Canada, *The Jury* (Ottawa: Law Reform Commission, 1982).

175 *R. v. Jacquard*, [1997] 1 S.C.R. 314 [*Jacquard*].

176 *Ibid.*, reaffirmed in *R. v. Daley*, 2007 SCC 53 at para. 31 [*Daley*].

provided that at the end the jury understands the nature of their task and have been given the necessary help from the instructions. In R. v. Ménard, for example, the trial judge gave his instructions in four parts, instructing the jury on substantive law at the start of the trial, giving instructions on two other specific matters during the course of the trial, and reviewing the evidence without reviewing the other instructions (though distributing transcripts of them) at the end of the trial. The Court decided that in the particular circumstances of the case no miscarriage of justice occurred, but did make several comments on the approach taken. They suggested that long and detailed instructions at the start of a trial might be more confusing than helpful, and that they increase the risk of a jury being confused by instructions concerning matters that ultimately do not arise in the case. Similarly, where an erroneous statement of law is made at the outset of the trial, the error might have a much greater effect on the trial and be much more difficult to correct, if it can be corrected at all. The Court also held that the principles of reasonable doubt, the presumption of innocence, and the burden of proof were too important to be dealt with at the end, by simply referring the jury to the transcript of the earlier instructions.[177]

The judge's charge should be fair, dispassionate, and should be the last thing said to the jury before they commence their deliberations. Judges generally ask counsel, following the charge, whether they felt any portion was unclear or needed clarification, but it is an error to actually allow counsel to address the jury directly again.[178] Similarly, a judge should not divide the charge in two, instructing the jury on some matters, then allowing counsel to speak, then finally completing the charge.[179] However, beyond these types of issues, a trial judge's discretion as to how to structure the charge will rarely be interfered with.

A judge cannot leave the jury to their own devices in deciding what evidence must be considered:

> The rule which has been laid down, and consistently followed is that in a jury trial the presiding judge must, except in rare cases where it would be needless to do so, review the substantial parts of the evidence, and give the jury the theory of the defence, so that they may appreciate the value and effect of that evidence, and how the law is to be applied to the facts as they find them.[180]

---

177 R. v. Ménard, [1998] 2 S.C.R. 109 [Ménard].

178 R. v. C. (J.D.) (2003), 186 O.A.C. 234 (Ont. C.A.).

179 R. v. Levene (1983), 36 C.R. (3d) 386 (Ont. C.A.).

180 Azoulay v. The Queen, [1952] 2 S.C.R. 495 at 497–98, recently reaffirmed in Daley, above note 176 at para. 54.

This does not mean, however, that an exhaustive review of every piece of evidence is required in every case. Rather, the judge must see to it that the jury is able to fully appreciate the issues and the defence presented, which may be best served by omitting reference to some peripheral evidence.[181]

Thus, a judge still has a considerable amount of discretion as to exactly how to review the facts. A judge can decide to review particular facts only once in the charge, for example, even though they might be relevant to more than one issue. Indeed, restating the facts each time they are relevant could make the charge worse, not better.[182] On the other hand, charges that are very long will not necessarily be an error either. In *R. v. Fell*, for example, the trial judge gave a four-day charge to the jury. Although the Ontario Court of Appeal suggested that such a length for a charge might be more exhausting and confusing than helpful, they held that there was nothing inaccurate in the charge, and that this exercise of the trial judge's discretion did not make the trial unfair.[183]

Much caselaw concerns jury instructions. This is in part because appeals generally focus on legal issues, and so whether a judge has accurately described the law to the jury is a potentially fruitful source of argument. A charge should review the facts, the prosecution's theory of the case, the accused's theory of the case, and the defences which arise for the jury. The trial judge should charge on all defences that arise on the facts, whether the accused has raised them or not.[184] It will also be necessary to charge the jury on whatever particular issues are relevant to the trial, such as the use that can be made of an accused's criminal record, or issues surrounding circumstantial evidence, identification evidence, and alibi evidence. Recently, a considerable number of cases have focused on whether trial judges adequately explain the concept of "proof beyond a reasonable doubt" to juries.[185] In reviewing a trial judge's instructions to the jury, the charge must be viewed as a whole,

---

181 *Daley, ibid.* at paras. 56–57.

182 *Jacquard*, above note 175.

183 *R. v. Fell* (1990), 40 O.A.C. 139. See also *R. v. Rideout* (1999), 182 Nfld. & P.E.I.R. 227 (Nfld. C.A.), aff'd on other issues, [2001] 1 S.C.R. 755, reaching a similar conclusion concerning a thirteen-hour jury charge.

184 *Faid*, above note 116.

185 A non-exhaustive list includes *R. v. Lifchus*, [1997] 3 S.C.R. 320; *R. v. Starr*, [2000] 2 S.C.R. 144; *R. v. Beauchamp*, [2000] 2 S.C.R. 720; *R. v. Russell*, [2000] 2 S.C.R. 731; *R. v. Avetysan*, [2000] 2 S.C.R. 745, rev'g (1999), 174 Nfld. & P.E.I.R. 34 (Nfld. C.A.) [*Avetysan*]; *R. v. Rhee*, [2001] 3 S.C.R. 364; and *R. v. Feeley*, 2003 SCC 7.

and inadequacies in one portion might be compensated for sufficiently in other parts so that the entire charge is acceptable.[186]

The Court has recently summarized the principles relating to whether a charge to the jury was adequate:

> 30 . . . The cardinal rule is that it is the general sense which the words used must have conveyed, in all probability, to the mind of the jury that matters, and not whether a particular formula was recited by the judge. The particular words used, or the sequence followed, is a matter within the discretion of the trial judge and will depend on the particular circumstances of the case.

> 31 In determining the general sense which the words used have likely conveyed to the jury, the appellate tribunal will consider the charge as a whole. The standard that a trial judge's instructions are to be held to is not perfection. The accused is entitled to a properly instructed jury, not a perfectly instructed jury . . . . It is the overall effect of the charge that matters.[187]

Instructions should also cover the procedural aspects of the jury's deliberation. Confusion in juror's minds over how long they are expected to deliberate before a "hung jury" could be declared, for example, might improperly affect their deliberations.[188]

Even though the jury is the trier of fact, a trial judge is entitled to offer opinions on matters of fact in the course of the instructions to the jury. However, the trial judge must not remove the decision from the jury by instructing them to convict. Such an instruction violates an accused's section 11(f) right to trial by jury.[189] That is, there is no "directed verdict of conviction" that is analogous to a directed verdict of acquittal.

Following the charge to the jury, judges tell juries not to begin their deliberations immediately. First, the judge consults with counsel to see whether they have any objections or feel that any matters need clarification. It remains within the judge's discretion whether to act on

---

186 This principle is stated in virtually every case dealing with jury instructions, but see, for example, *Jacquard*, above note 175; *R. v. W.(D.)*, [1991] 1 S.C.R. 742; *R. v. S.(W.D.)*, [1994] 3 S.C.R. 521 [*S.(W.D.)*].

187 *Daley*, above note 176.

188 *R. v. Pan*, [2001] 2 S.C.R. 344 at para. 98 [*Pan*].

189 *Boulet v. The Queen*, [1978] 1 S.C.R. 332; *R. v. Sims*, [1992] 2 S.C.R. 858 [*Sims*]; *R. v. Krieger*, 2006 SCC 47 [*Krieger*]. In *Krieger*, the trial judge deliberately directed the jury to retire and return with a verdict of guilty. See also *R. v. Gunning*, [2005] 1 S.C.R. 627, where the trial judge directed the jury that one of the elements of the offence in question had been proven by the Crown; this too was an error.

the comments of counsel. Failure by counsel to raise an objection at the time does not automatically prevent that matter from later being a basis for appeal, nor does it mean that the error was a harmless one to which the curative provision in section 686(1)(b)(iii) can be applied. However, failure by counsel to object at the time will enter into an appellate court's decision about the overall accuracy of the instructions and the seriousness of the alleged misdirection.[190]

c)   Re-charging the Jury

Where a judge re-charges following submissions from counsel, essentially the same criteria apply to as to the original charge. In most instances, that re-charge will simply be considered as part of the charge, and the question will be whether, taken as a whole, the jury has been properly instructed. A re-charge might rectify an error in the original charge, meaning that, as a whole, the charge is satisfactory.[191] Similarly, in W.(D.) an error in a re-charge did not form the basis for an appeal, largely because the re-charge was quite short and followed only a few minutes after the original charge, the original charge had instructed the jury correctly, and the trial judge said in the re-charge that the jury should not give special emphasis to the re-charge and should be mindful of the duties he had outlined in the charge.

On the other hand, sometimes it is necessary to re-charge a jury after they have begun their deliberations because the jury has sent a question to the judge. In these circumstances the re-charge takes on much greater significance. If the jury has asked a question, it will generally relate to an important point in their reasoning. Even if they were correctly instructed on the point earlier, if they have asked a question, they have forgotten or did not understand the instruction. Therefore, when a question is received from a jury it must be considered to be significant. Counsel must be heard as to what response should be made to the question, and the answer must be correct and comprehensive. Since the jury has asked about the issue, instructions must be repeated even if they were given in the original charge, and the need for the re-charge to be correct and comprehensive increases with the greater the delay. Finally, an error in a re-charge following a question from the jury generally cannot be saved by a correct original charge because the fact that a question was asked shows that the jury did not adequately understand the original instructions.[192]

---

190 *Jacquard*, above note 175; *Thériault v. The Queen*, [1981] 1 S.C.R. 336.
191 See, for example, *R. v. G.(R.M.)*, [1996] 3 S.C.R. 362 [*G.(R.M.)*].
192 *R. v. S.(W.D.)*, above note 186.

E. JURY DELIBERATIONS

1) Jury Sequestration

Following the jury charge and any re-charge, the *Code* permits a trial judge to allow the jury to separate rather than commence deliberations immediately, and in this event a publication ban is imposed.[193] Once the jury begins its deliberations it is sequestered (isolated in a way to keep from it any potential sources of information). At this stage the jury is essentially to be left alone until it has reached a verdict, or until it is apparent that it will not be able to do so. The verdict, whether for conviction or acquittal, must be unanimous. If the jury is ultimately unable to reach unanimity then, as will be pursued below, section 653 of the *Code* permits the trial judge to discharge the jury and order a new trial.

The jury is not completely isolated, in the sense that it is able to initiate contact with the judge. When a judge receives a non-administrative inquiry from the jury, the judge is to "(a) read the communication in open court in the presence of all parties; (b) give counsel an opportunity to make submissions in open court prior to dealing with the question; (c) answer the question for the jury in open court in the presence of all parties."[194] Such requests can concern a variety of things.

Juries sometimes request copies of the *Criminal Code*, or portions of it, for example. A trial judge is permitted to give short sections of the *Code* to the jury, but must be careful not to prejudice the outcome of the trial by doing so.[195] It is likely to be a mistake to give the *Code* provisions to the jury and leave them to work out the meaning for themselves, but it could be acceptable to provide photocopies of some sections if it is accompanied by an explanation.[196] However, where giving the jury sections of the *Code* will also involve a complete and lengthy re-charge on the issues relating to those sections, it will usually be better to see whether the jury's concerns can be addressed in some other fashion. A trial judge might be better advised to ask the jury to be more specific about the particular concern that motivates the request, and then try to answer that concern. Similarly, re-reading the sections of the *Code*

---

193 Sections 647 & 648.

194 *R. v. Fontaine*, [2003] 1 W.W.R. 634 at para. 59 (Man. C.A.), quoting from *R. v. Dunbar and Logan* (1982), 68 C.C.C. (2d) 13 (Ont. C.A.).

195 *Cathro v. The Queen*, [1956] S.C.R. 101.

196 See, for example, *R. v. Flewwelling* (1984), 63 N.S.R. (2d) 382 (C.A.); *R. v. McCormack* (1984), 28 Man. R. (2d) 29 (C.A.); *R. v. Vawryk*, [1979] 3 W.W.R. 50 (Man. C.A.); and *R. v. Crothers* (1978), 43 C.C.C. (2d) 27 (Sask. C.A.).

and explaining them to the jury might be a sufficient response to the request.[197]

Juries can also take other material into the jury room in some cases, such as transcripts of wiretaps or chronologies prepared by counsel to help organize material. However, the caselaw is not consistent on when this is advisable or permissible and whether juries should be required to re-hear evidence in its entirety.[198]

Similar considerations arise if the jury requests transcripts of the trial judge's instructions or of the argument by counsel. It is not necessarily an error to provide them to the jury, even to provide the argument of only one side if that is all that was requested, though the better choice might be to provide both counsel's argument nonetheless.[199] Distributing transcripts raises the likelihood of error, particularly if the jury receives only part of the judge's instructions. The Court has noted that judges must be sure that the jury receives the entire charge in clear and legible form, and that all members of the jury are capable of reading it. It has held: "it may well be that the dangers associated with such an approach outweigh the potential benefits."[200]

The same types of considerations govern when the jury asks to re-hear evidence or asks for clarification of the legal issues during its deliberations. A trial judge has discretion and is not obliged to answer every request from the jury precisely as asked. So, for example, where a jury requests transcripts of the evidence of all the witnesses shortly after commencing deliberations, a trial judge will not err by refusing this request. However, since questions from the jury must be given particular consideration, it is not sufficient to simply refuse (as noted above at Section D(8)(b)). A trial judge should consult with counsel on how to respond, and propose alternatives or ask the jury to deliberate further to decide more specifically what their concern is, for example.[201] Where

---

197 *R. v. Keegstra*, [1996] 1 S.C.R. 458.

198 See, for example, *R. v. Quashie* (2005), 198 C.C.C. (3d) 337 (Ont. C.A.); *R. v. D.J.* (2004), 190 C.C.C. (3d) 529 (Ont. C.A.); and *R. v. Robert* (2004), 25 C.R. (6th) 55 (Que. C.A.). See also *R. v. Latoski* (2005), 200 C.C.C. (3d) 361 (Ont. C.A.); *R. v. Pleich* (1980), 16 C.R. (3d) 194 (Ont. C.A.); *R. v. Rowbotham* (1988), 63 C.R. (3d) 113 (Ont. C.A.) [*Rowbotham* 1988]; *R. v. Bengert (No. 13)* (1979), 15 C.R. (3d) 62 (B.C.S.C.), aff'd on other grounds (1980), 15 C.R. (3d) 114 (B.C.C.A.), leave to appeal to S.C.C. refused (1980), 53 C.C.C. (2d) 48n (S.C.C.) [*Bengert*].

199 *R. v. Ferguson*, [2001] 1 S.C.R. 281.

200 *Ménard*, above note 177.

201 *R. v. Ostrowski*, [1990] 2 S.C.R. 82; or see, for example, *R. v. Holden* (2001), 159 C.C.C. (3d) 180 (Ont. C.A.), leave to appeal to S.C.C. refused, [2001] S.C.C.A. No. 574; *R. v. K. (B.A.)* (1998), 19 C.R. (5th) 400 (B.C.C.A.); *R. v. Perry* (1995), 54 B.C.A.C. 275 (C.A.).

the jury's question is unclear, the judge should request clarification in order to be able to answer it appropriately.[202]

Other considerations arise when the jury is not seeking a review of the evidence at trial but is actually seeking additional evidence. The basic rule is that this is simply not permitted: no additional information that did not come out at trial can be given to the jury once they have begun deliberating, and it might be necessary to tell the jury that there was no evidence led on the point in question.[203] So, for example, a jury cannot have a demonstration that was conducted at trial repeated for them after the close of both cases.[204] Nor should the jury have material that, although it was used at trial, did not form part of the evidence.[205] However, once again a refusal of the jury's request might well be an error, and the trial judge should try to determine whether the jury's concern can be satisfied in some other way.

Requests from jurors sometimes do not concern the law or the evidence, but the jury's own deliberations or concerns by one juror about the behaviour of another juror. In *R. v. Côté*, for example, two jurors sent notes to the trial judge that questioned the honesty of two other jurors. The judge consulted with counsel on how to proceed, but without their agreement, and in the absence of the accused, met with the two jurors who had complained and decided that the jury's deliberations could continue. The Court held that the judge erred by meeting with the jurors in the absence of the accused. At any point where the accused's vital interests are at issue the accused is entitled to be present. Had the trial judge received communications that might have concerned purely administrative questions, it would have been permissible to meet with the jurors privately. But even in those circumstances, once it became apparent that the integrity of a juror was being questioned, the accused would be entitled to be present and the judge should adjourn the meeting.[206]

In the absence of these types of requests that necessitate some response, the jury is to be left unhindered to perform its function without communication from others. In *R. v. Mercier*, for example, a new trial

---

202 *R. v. H.(L.I.)*, 2003 MBCA 97.

203 *R. v. Templeman* (1994), 40 B.C.A.C. 76 (C.A.).

204 *R. v. Kluke* (1987), 22 O.A.C. 107 (C.A.). But see *R. v. Clair* (1995), 143 N.S.R. (2d) 101 (C.A.), leave to appeal to S.C.C. refused (1996), 151 N.S.R. (2d) 240n, where it was held that allowing a jury to have a measuring tape did not affect the fairness of the trial, because it merely allowed them to estimate distances, something they could have done without the tape, more accurately.

205 *Rowbotham* 1988, above note 198.

206 *Vézina*, above note 40.

was necessary when a Crown prosecutor entered the jury room in the jury's absence and erased some words from the blackboard.[207] Not all communication has that result, however. Where there has been contact between the jury and anyone else, the trial judge must conduct an inquiry to determine whether the jury, or perhaps an individual juror, cannot continue. It might be that no prejudice has actually been caused because the contact was relatively harmless or because it had no actual impact on the deliberations.[208] On the other hand, where the improprieties are so serious that they affect public confidence in the system, no prejudice needs to be shown. Thus where a jury, during its deliberations, was taken to dinner with a group of people including a close relative of the murder victim, the absence of actual prejudice was irrelevant.[209]

2) Exhorting the Jury

It can occur that deliberations continue so long as it appears, or notes are sent from the jury stating, that the jury is deadlocked and will be unable to reach a unanimous verdict. Although the trial judge can discharge the jury under section 653 and order a new trial, normally the first step is to call the jury in and exhort them to reach a verdict. Principles have developed around such exhortations, so that they do not present a threat to the independence of the jury or the interests of the accused. Exhorting a jury properly is a delicate task. A judge should not express an opinion on the facts during an exhortation, even though that is permissible in the original charge.[210] The exhortation also should not suggest that one or another group's opinions on the evidence is preferable. Rather, the exhortation is to focus on the process of deliberation itself, and encourage the jury members to listen to and consider one another's views.[211] No pressure should be placed on the jury, and no factors that are extraneous to the task of reaching a verdict should be introduced. Jurors should not be encouraged to change their minds for

---

207 (1973), 12 C.C.C. (2d) 377 (Que. C.A.) [*Mercier*].

208 In *R. v. Taillefer* (1995), 40 C.R. (4th) 287 (Que. C.A.), for example, a juror contacted a witness on the second day of deliberations, but was questioned by the judge and allowed to stay on the jury. The jury did not reach a decision for another eleven days, suggesting that the communication had been of no effect and that the trial judge had not erred in the exercise of his discretion.

209 *R. v. Cameron* (1991), 2 O.R. (3d) 633 (C.A.), leave to appeal to S.C.C. refused, [1991] 3 S.C.R. x. See also *R. v. Hertrich* (1982), 137 D.L.R. (3d) 400 (Ont. C.A.), leave to appeal to S.C.C. refused (1982), 45 N.R. 629n (S.C.C.).

210 *Sims*, above note 189.

211 *Ibid.*

the sake of conformity, and no deadline should be imposed.[212] It is an error, therefore, to tell the jury to consider the expense of a new trial, or to consider the benefit to the accused of a verdict being reached. It is also an error to direct the minority to reconsider the views of the majority. Rather, it is better to direct all the jurors to reconsider one another's views.[213]

Nonetheless, it is appropriate for a trial judge to remind the jurors of their oath and encourage them to try to reach a verdict. In effect, as long as it is clear that the jurors do retain the right to disagree, and provided improper pressures and irrelevant considerations are not brought to bear, a trial judge can urge them to try to find a way not to.[214] Further, not every improper exhortation will lead to a new trial. Other factors, such as the length of the deliberations, the question asked by the jury, and the length of the subsequent deliberations following the exhortation, will all help determine whether the exhortation coerced the jury or caused some jurors to accept a verdict that they did not agree with.[215]

3) Rendering a Verdict

Once the jury has finished its deliberations and indicated that it is ready to return, the jury announces its verdict in court. The announcement is made by the jury foreman. It is possible to request that the jury be polled — that is, that every juror be asked individually about the verdict. There is no legal requirement for this procedure, however, which is usually allowed where some doubt as to whether unanimity exists.[216]

After the jury has been discharged by the trial judge neither it nor the trial judge has any further authority to act. In the vast majority of circumstances, that causes no difficulty, but it can do so in the rare situation where an error is alleged to have occurred in recording the verdict but is not discovered until after the jury is discharged. In *R. v. Head*, for example, the jury foreman announced a verdict of not guilty,

---

212 *G.(R.M.)*, above note 191.

213 *Ibid.*

214 See, for example, *R. v. Littlejohn* (1978), 41 C.C.C. (2d) 161 (Ont. C.A.).

215 *G.(R.M.)*, above note 191 at para. 50. Also "While a short lapse of time between an exhortation and the verdict might well be an indication that a judge has influenced a jury's decision, the reverse is not necessarily true. A large time gap between the exhortation and the verdict may or may not indicate the independence of the jury": *R. v. Jack* (1996), 113 Man. R. (2d) 84 at para. 91 (C.A.), Justice Helper dissenting. Her decision was adopted by the Supreme Court of Canada when the decision was reversed on appeal: [1997] 2 S.C.R. 334.

216 *R. v. Laforet*, [1980] 1 S.C.R. 869.

and the judge discharged the jury and acquitted the accused. The foreman then indicated that he thought the jury could have found the accused guilty of an included offence. The Court held that the trial judge was *functus officio* and no longer had jurisdiction to inquire into the matter or correct any error, and, therefore, that the acquittal had to stand.[217]

More recently in R. v. Burke, while reaffirming the general rule that a trial judge has no jurisdiction to alter a recorded verdict once a jury is discharged, the Court found a rare residual jurisdiction to be used when there has been an irregularity.[218] In that case, the jury had reached a guilty verdict, but the trial judge and many others in the court misheard the foreman, understanding him to say "not guilty." The error was discovered almost immediately after the jury was discharged, and was brought to the judge's attention within minutes, but most jurors and the accused had already left. The Court held that there were a number of ways to proceed when such errors occur, but that sometimes the trial judge has a limited jurisdiction to correct errors in the recorded judgment. If the circumstances would require the jury to reconsider its verdict, then the ordinary *functus* rule applies and the trial judge has no jurisdiction to correct. But if no reconsideration of the verdict is involved, then the trial judge must decide whether there is, in the circumstances, a reasonable apprehension of bias. If there is no such apprehension, then the judge can correct the error. But if there is a reasonable apprehension of bias the trial judge must either allow the verdict that was recorded to stand or declare a mistrial. The incorrect verdict must stand unless it is necessary to declare a mistrial to prevent a miscarriage of justice. In *Burke*, no question of the jury reconsidering its verdict arose, and so there was jurisdiction to potentially correct the error. However, since many of the jurors had gone home and had been exposed to media coverage of the case after their discharge, even if there was no actual bias there was a reasonable apprehension of it, and so the verdict could not simply be changed to guilty. Since leaving the incorrect acquittal in place would have led to a miscarriage of justice, a mistrial was declared and a new trial ordered.

4) Jury Secrecy

Finally, it is worth observing section 649 of the *Code*, which makes it an offence for anyone present in the jury room to disclose any information

---

217 R. v. Head, [1986] 2 S.C.R. 684.
218 R. v. Burke, [2002] 2 S.C.R. 857 [Burke].

about the jury's deliberations, other than in connection with an investigation of obstructing justice.[219] This law closely reflects the common
law rule on jury secrecy that is to the same effect, though it also prevents anyone who overhears, even accidentally, the jury's deliberations
from disclosing that information. The Court has recently considered
whether these rules violate section 7 of the *Charter*. It concluded that
they do not, and discussed the policy behind jury secrecy in *Pan*.[220]

The facts of *Pan* are complex. He was tried for murder three times,
the first two trials having been declared mistrials. At the appeal of his
conviction at the third trial, Pan objected to the process by which a
mistrial was declared at his second trial. Investigations of a possible obstruction charge revealed that one juror at that trial had, among other
things, been following media coverage and seeking other information
outside of court and reporting the information to the other jurors. The
mistrial resulted when that same juror sent a note to the trial judge asking that the jury be polled once it reported its verdict—her intention, it
appeared, was to feign agreement in the jury room and then disagree in
open court. The trial judge consulted with counsel as to how to respond
and ultimately declared a mistrial. Pan's argument hinged on the claim
that the mistrial should not have been declared and that he should have
been entitled to the acquittal that would have resulted if the second
trial continued. To make this argument, it would have been necessary
for Pan to lead evidence that section 649 prevented being led.

The Court reviewed the reasons why a guarantee of jury secrecy is
a valuable thing: it promotes candour in discussions, and lets the jury
consider all possibilities without fear of later recriminations from the
public. This rationale is particularly valuable to an unpopular accused
or an individual charged with a particularly heinous crime. Related
to that rationale was the need to protect jurors from harassment, cen-
sure, and reprisals, which would permit them to perform their function
more confidently. Finally, jury secrecy promotes finality, though the
Court held that this rationale alone would not be sufficient to justify
the rule.[221]

However, it held that the common law jury secrecy rule does not
prevent every conceivable piece of information relevant to what has

---

219 Section 649. There is an exception allowing such information to be disclosed in
    connection with a prosecution for obstructing justice under s. 139(2).

220 *Pan*, above note 188.

221 The jury secrecy rule has been criticized as overly restrictive: see, for example,
    Sonia R. Chopra & James R.P. Ogloff, "Evaluating Jury Secrecy: Implications for
    Academic Research and Juror Stress" (2000) 44 Crim. L.Q.190; Paul Quinlan,
    "Secrecy of Jury Deliberations—Is the Cost Too High" (1993) 22 C.R. (4th) 127.

gone on in a jury room from being disclosed. The Court drew a distinction between matters extrinsic to the jury's deliberations and those intrinsic to them. An extrinsic matter would be that some third party had contact with the jury or gave particular information to a juror, whereas an intrinsic matter would be the effect that the contact or information had on the jury's deliberations. The common law rule and section 649 only prevent intrinsic matters from being disclosed. In *Mercier*,[222] therefore, it was possible to lead evidence that the Crown prosecutor had erased words from the blackboard in the jury room, since that was an extrinsic matter. However, evidence concerning any effect this action might have had on the jury's reasoning was intrinsic and therefore not admissible. The Court acknowledged that in practical terms it may sometimes be difficult to draw the distinction, but nonetheless held that the jury secrecy rule applies only to intrinsic matters.

Understood in this way the Court held that the common law jury secrecy rule accorded with the goals of jury secrecy and was in accordance with the principles of fundamental justice. Since the statutory rule was consistent with the common law rule, it too passed *Charter* scrutiny.

F. POWERS OF THE COURT

A trial judge has a variety of powers to control the process in the courtroom. Many of these arise at statute, though some come from the common law. In addition, section 482 of the *Code* permits superior courts to make rules of court, which can govern, among other things, matters regarding the pleading, practice, and procedure at trial. Such rules, of course, must not be inconsistent with the *Criminal Code*.

1) Control over the Court Process

A trial judge has fairly significant discretion in how a trial runs, including the ability to curtail cross-examination, prevent irrelevant or harassing questions, and ask questions of witnesses. However, these powers must be exercised with caution and can be taken too far. Ultimately, such interventions can violate an accused's right to a fair trial. The test is not whether the accused was actually prejudiced, but "whether a

---

222 *Mercier*, above note 207.

reasonably minded person who had been present throughout the trial would consider that the accused had not had a fair trial."[223]

The *Code* gives judges the power to grant adjournments during trials or other proceedings.[224] At one time the rules concerning adjournments, and particularly the issue of whether a court lost jurisdiction over the accused or the offence by failing to proceed properly, were quite complex. Further, the *Code* formerly contained a provision preventing any adjournment of more than eight days without the accused's consent. Now, however, section 485 specifically preserves the court's jurisdiction over an accused despite a failure to comply with any of the *Code's* provisions concerning adjournments or remands. Indeed, subsequent to a decision that found the predecessor of section 485 to not preserve a court's jurisdiction where it adjourned a case but failed to proceed on the set date,[225] the provision now more broadly preserves the court's jurisdiction despite a failure "to act in the exercise of that jurisdiction." Where a court does lose jurisdiction over an accused, it can regain it by issuing a summons or warrant for the accused within three months. However, if this is not done, the proceedings are considered dismissed for want of prosecution and the Crown cannot lay new charges without the personal consent in writing of the Attorney General or Deputy Attorney General.[226]

A trial judge also has some discretion around the circumstances in which evidence will be heard. The judge can decide to exclude any or all members of the public from all or part of the trial. This power can be used where it is "in the interest of public morals, the maintenance of order or the proper administration of justice."[227] The *Code* specifically notes that the "proper administration of justice" includes ensuring the interests of witnesses under the age of eighteen in sexual assault trials and of justice system participants.[228] A trial judge who does not grant a request for exclusion in a sexual offence case must give reasons for not having done so.[229]

This power conflicts with the principle that court proceedings should be open, which is one of the hallmarks of a democratic society,

---

223 *R. v. Valley* (1986), 26 C.C.C. (3d) 207 at 232 (Ont. C.A.).
224 Sections 537 and 645. See also the discussion in *R. v. J.C.G.* (2004), 189 C.C.C. (3d) 1 (Que. C.A.) and *R. v. M.V.* (2004), 189 C.C.C. (3d) 230 (Que. C.A.).
225 *R. v. Krannenburg*, [1980] 1 S.C.R. 1053.
226 Sections 485(2), 485(3), and 485.1.
227 Section 486(1). The section also permits exclusion of the public "to prevent injury to international relations or national defence or national security."
228 Section 486(2).
229 Section 486(3).

and can also conflict with freedom of the press since it might prevent journalists from being present for and reporting on some portion of a trial. The Court has held that the provision therefore violates section 2(b) of the *Charter*, but nonetheless is saved as a reasonable limit, provided the discretion to use the section is exercised properly. Accordingly, the Court held:

(a) the judge must consider the available options and consider whether there are any other reasonable and effective alternatives available;

(b) the judge must consider whether the order is limited as much as possible; and

(c) the judge must weigh the importance of the objectives of the particular order and its probable effects against the importance of openness and the particular expression that will be limited in order to ensure that the positive and negative effects of the order are proportionate.[230]

The burden is on the person seeking the exclusion to provide a sufficient factual foundation, and to show that the particular order is necessary, that it is as limited as possible, and that the salutary effects of the order are proportionate to its deleterious effects.

Section 486.1 of the *Code* also gives a judge some powers over the manner in which some witnesses are allowed to testify. A witness under the age of eighteen, or with a mental or physical disability, can be permitted to have a support person of their choice nearby while testifying, though this is only allowed if the judge is of the opinion that it will not interfere with the proper administration of justice. The judge can order that the support person and the witness not communicate during the witness' testimony.[231] Further, a judge can allow a witness under the age of eighteen or with a mental or physical disability that interferes with their ability to communicate evidence to testify from outside the courtroom or from behind a screen or other device that prevents the witness from seeing the accused. However, the order can only be made where the judge believes that the exclusion is necessary to obtain a full and candid account from the witness.[232] The provision is only designed to avoid a face-to-face confrontation between the witness and the accused, and so although the screen allows the witness

---

230 *Canadian Broadcasting Corp. v. New Brunswick (Attorney General)*, [1996] 3 S.C.R. 480 at para. 69.

231 Sections 486.1(1) and (4).

232 Section 486.2(2). Note that ss. 486.2(4) & (5) create a similar ability concerning any witness in the case of terrorism and organized crime offences.

not to see the accused, the accused is still able to see the witness.[233] The trial judge has substantial latitude in ordering this procedure, which has been found not to violate the *Charter*.[234] At the time the section was challenged, however, the use of screens was available only in the case of a sexual offence. The section no longer contains that limitation, and so it is not perfectly clear that the same conclusion would follow in a new challenge.

A judge also has a great deal of general discretion in the course of the trial, from intervening to ask questions personally to expressing opinions on the facts. Further, a judge has a trial management power which includes:

> the power to place reasonable limits on oral submissions, to direct that submissions be made in writing, to require an offer of proof before embarking on a lengthy *voir dire*, to defer rulings, to direct the manner in which a *voir dire* is conducted, especially whether to do so on the basis of testimony or in some other form, and exceptionally to direct the order in which evidence is called.[235]

An overriding rule, however, is that the trial judge's behaviour must not create a reasonable apprehension of bias. Rudeness on the part of a judge to either the Crown or the defence may or may not cross the threshold, and the fact that the rudeness was equally distributed may or may not help prevent a reasonable apprehension of bias.[236] A judge who expresses an opinion on whether the accused has presented any defence while the Crown decides whether to cross-examine, might be seen as making the trial proceed expeditiously.[237] A judge can ask questions of the accused or other witnesses without creating a reasonable

---

233 *Levogiannis*, above note 116. Similarly, where the witness testifies from outside the courtroom, arrangements must be made to permit the accused to watch the testimony by closed circuit television: s. 486.2(7).

234 *Levogiannis*, ibid. In general on this subject, see Nicholas Bala & Hilary McCormack, "Accommodating the Criminal Process to Child Witnesses" (1994) 25 C.R. (4th) 341. In addition, see N. Bala, R.C.L. Lindsay, & E. McNamara, "Testimonial Aids for Children: The Canadian Experience with Closed Circuit Television, Screens and Videotapes" (2001) 44 Crim. L.Q. 461 for a survey of judges, lawyers, and victim-witness workers on their experience in court with these various devices.

235 *R. v. Felderhof* (2003), 17 C.R. (6th) 20 at para. 57 (Ont. C.A.).

236 See, for example, *R. v. Hossu* (2002), 167 C.C.C. (3d) 344 (Ont. C.A.); *R. v. Rose* (2001), 42 C.R. (5th) 183 (Ont. C.A.); *R. v. Callocchia* (2000), 39 C.R. (5th) 374 (Que. C.A.); *Avetysan*, above note 185. See also Wayne K. Gorman, "Judicial Intervention in the Trial Process" (2003) 47 Crim. L.Q. 481.

237 *R. v. Currie* (2002), 3 C.R. (6th) 377 (Ont. C.A.).

apprehension of bias, but, in some cases, a judge can carry this too far and a new trial will be necessary.[238] Whether this will be so very much depends on the facts of the individual case.

2) Publication Bans

A trial judge has the ability, in various circumstances, to order a publication ban. Such bans should be seen as exceptional, since they prevent public knowledge of court proceedings, and therefore are in conflict with the open court principle. The Court has described the open court principle as a "hallmark of a democratic society" and a "cornerstone of the common law,"[239] but, nonetheless, in certain circumstances publication bans are permitted. Most of these bans have a statutory base, although there is also a common law ability to issue publication bans.

Most noteworthy is the ban outlined in section 486.4, which allows a judge to ban the publication of any information that would identify the complainant or a witness in a trial for a variety of listed sexual offences. A trial judge is required to inform any witness under eighteen and the complainant of the right to make such an application, and where one of those persons or the prosecutor applies, the judge is required to order the ban. An earlier version of this provision was upheld under the *Charter* on the basis that, although the provision violated freedom of the press, it was saved under section 1.[240] It is also of note that at the time, only prosecutors and complainants could make applications under the section. The Court's reasoning focused on the need to encourage victims of sexual assault to report the crime both in finding that there was a sufficiently important objective and in determining whether the provision was minimally impairing. Indeed, the Court specifically noted that it was not deciding whether the section would survive a *Charter* challenge if the prosecutor were not applying on the complainant's behalf. Since that time, the section has been expanded to include publication bans on behalf of witnesses under the age of eighteen. It is possible that a *Charter* challenge to the section in this context might succeed.

A similar power to seek a ban on publication of information disclosing the identity of a victim or witness is found in section 486.5. In this case, however, the ban is discretionary, and the trial judge must consider a variety of factors, including the right to a fair and public

---

238 *R. v. Brouillard*, [1985] 1 S.C.R. 39.
239 *Vancouver Sun (Re)*, [2004] 2 S.C.R. 332, 2004 SCC 43 at paras. 23–24.
240 *Canadian Newspapers Co. v. Canada (Attorney General)*, [1988] 2 S.C.R. 122.

hearing, the risk of harm to the witness if her identity were disclosed, the impact of the order on freedom of expression, and a number of other matters. In addition, this type of publication ban can sometimes be issued to protect the identity of justice system participants, such as jurors, prosecutors, or police officers. The power is only available in trials for certain offences, such as those dealing with criminal organizations or terrorism offences.[241]

There are other particular bans within the *Code* as well. For example, section 276.3 prevents reporting of information regarding an application to admit evidence of previous sexual activity, and section 648 prevents the publication of evidence from a trial while jurors are separated before beginning deliberations.

The *YCJA* also bans the publication of some information. Subject to exceptions dealing with public safety, no one is to publish information that could identify a young person as one being dealt with under the Act. Similarly, no one may publish information identifying a young person who was a victim or a witness at proceedings concerning another young person. In the latter case the young person can apply to be permitted to publish such information personally, and is entitled to do so after reaching the age of eighteen.[242]

Finally, the Court discussed a trial judge's common law power to grant a publication ban in *Dagenais v. Canadian Broadcasting Corp.*,[243] and later cases. An application for a ban can be made to the trial judge, to another judge of that court if no trial judge has been appointed, or to a judge of the superior court if the level of court for trial cannot yet be established. The application is to be made in the absence of the jury, and the judge has discretion to decide whether to give notice of the application to the media. The trial judge also has discretion as to whether to grant the media standing in the application, whether to permit them to cross-examine or present evidence, and so on. The judge also, of course, has discretion in deciding whether to grant the publication ban itself or not. In exercising that discretion, however, the trial judge is required to act in accordance with the *Charter*. Thus, the Court held, the traditional common law rule that a ban would be granted if there was a real and substantial risk of interference with the right to a fair trial needed to be modified to recognize the *Charter* guarantee of freedom of expression and freedom of the press.

---

241 Sections 486.5(2) and 486.2(5).
242 *YCJA*, above note 95 at ss. 110 & 111.
243 [1994] 3 S.C.R. 835 [*Dagenais*].

Subsequently, in *R. v. Mentuck* the Court returned to the subject of publication bans, but this time in circumstances where the ban was sought by the Crown and no fair trial right was at issue. *Mentuck* involved an undercover police investigation of the type usually referred to as the "Mr. Big" scenario. In this technique, a suspect is induced, on one of a variety of pretexts, to give the details of an offence he has committed to what he believes to be the members of a criminal organization to which he is being recruited. The Crown sought a publication ban both on the names of the particular police officers who had been involved in Mentuck's undercover operation, as well as on the release of information about the technique itself. The Court upheld the former ban, but not the latter.

In the course of discussing the appropriate test for a publication ban, the Court observed that the *Dagenais* test was not phrased in a way that would always address the underlying issue. In *Dagenais*, the question had been whether a fair trial right was compromised, and the Court had formulated a test that only asked about that interest. In *Mentuck*, it recognized that a broader range of interests might need to be contrasted to the freedom of expression. The Court therefore concluded that the real question was of finding a balance between the many possible interests that made up the proper administration of justice on the one hand, and freedom of expression on the other. Accordingly, the "*Dagenais/Mentuck*" test for publications bans is:

A publication ban should only be ordered when:

(a) such an order is necessary in order to prevent a serious risk to the proper administration of justice because reasonably alternative measures will not prevent the risk; and

(b) the salutary effects of the publication ban outweigh the deleterious effects on the rights and interests of the parties and the public, including the effects on the right to free expression, the right of the accused to a fair and public trial, and the efficacy of the administration of justice.[244]

The person seeking the publication ban has the onus. The first step requires that the ban is as narrowly circumscribed as possible while still achieving the objectives, and that no other effective means would achieve the objectives. The second step involves weighing the importance of the objectives of the particular ban and its probable effects against the importance of the particular expression that will be limited. In *Dagenais*, the publication bans were not justified because there

---

244 *R. v. Mentuck*, 2001 SCC 76 at para. 32.

were various alternatives such as adjourning trials, changing venues, sequestering jurors, allowing challenges for cause and *voir dires* during jury selection, and providing strong judicial direction to the jury. In *Mentuck*, the ban on the names of particular officers was justified since they were using their real names, and therefore their safety and the integrity of other undercover investigations would have been jeopardized. The ban on reporting the technique in general was not justified because the Court was unconvinced that a serious risk to the effectiveness of the technique would arise if its existence were reported in newspapers.[245]

3) Contempt of Court

Judges have the power to find people in contempt of court. This common law power is expressly preserved by section 9 of the *Code*, and appeal procedures from it are set out in section 10. Contempt is divided into contempt committed in the face of the court and contempt not committed in the face of the court, a distinction still reflected in section 10 of the *Code*. Superior courts have jurisdiction over both types of contempt, while inferior courts can only punish the former. The *YCJA* gives youth justice courts very broad jurisdiction, including contempt in the face of and not in the face of either the youth justice court or any other court, when it is committed by a young person.[246] It is only contempt in the face of the court that will concern us here.

Contempt can cover a variety of behaviours, including insolence to the court or refusal to answer questions while under oath, for example.[247] The accused, a witness, or counsel all can be cited in contempt. The power to punish for contempt is intended to maintain the dignity of the court and to ensure a fair trial. A judge can respond to contemptuous behaviour in either of two ways: (i) through the ordinary procedure, which gives the accused the usual procedural guarantees of a criminal trial, or (ii) through a more summary procedure.[248] The summary procedure can only be used where it is urgent and imperative to act immediately and, other than in exceptional circumstances, that procedure must comply with the requirements of natural justice. In general terms, this means that "only '[t]he least possible power ad-

---

245 *R. v. Arradi*, 2003 SCC 23 [*Arradi*].
246 *YCJA*, above note 95, s. 15.
247 See *R. v. K.(B.)*, [1995] 4 S.C.R. 186 [*K.(B.)*] and *Arradi*, above note 245.
248 *Arradi, ibid.* at para. 29. See *R. v. Vermette*, [1987] 1 S.C.R. 577 for an example of contempt being dealt with through the ordinary procedure of a separate trial on the charge.

equate to the end proposed' should be used."[249] In particular, it means that normally a three-step process is to be followed. First, the person is to be put on notice that she will be required to show cause as to why she should not be found in contempt of court. This is referred to as being "cited" in contempt. Second, an adjournment should be given, long enough to allow the person an opportunity to consult with counsel, and possibly be represented by counsel. Finally, a person who is found in contempt should be allowed to make representations as to sentence. Although in some cases not all these steps need be followed, departure from this model is only permitted in exceptional circumstances. Failure to follow this process is an error of law.[250]

The contempt proceedings can also be conducted in the jury's presence where the contempt has occurred in front of it, since the jury helps make up the court.[251] However, it must be made clear to the jury that the accused's guilt in the contempt proceeding cannot be used to assess guilt in the actual trial.

4) Mistrials

One particular judicial power worth discussing separately is the authority to declare a mistrial. A trial judge has the authority to declare a mistrial at virtually any point in the proceedings, from as early as the jury selection stage[252] to as late as the post-conviction but pre-sentence stage.[253] Indeed, a trial judge still has jurisdiction to declare a mistrial after an appeal has been launched, provided a sentence has not yet been handed down.[254]

A wide variety of issues can lead to a mistrial application, among them are inappropriate publicity or other errors during jury selection, improper comments by the Crown prosecutor during an opening statement or closing submission, or inadmissible evidence accidentally being given to the jury.[255] A mistrial is not automatically granted in the case of such errors, and in fact is more a remedy of last resort. Where

---

249 *Arradi, ibid.* at para. 33, quoting *K.(B.),* above note 247 at para. 13, itself quoting *United States v. Wilson,* 421 U.S. 309 at 319 (1975).

250 *Arradi, ibid.*

251 Note, similarly, that another judge of the same court is not permitted to hear the contempt proceeding: *R. v. Doz,* [1987] 2 S.C.R. 463.

252 *R. v. Williams,* [1998] 1 S.C.R. 1128 [*Williams*] and *Bengert,* above note 198.

253 *R. v. McAnespie,* [1993] 4 S.C.R. 501.

254 *R. v. MacDonald* (1991), 107 N.S.R. (2d) 374 (S.C.A.D.) [*MacDonald*].

255 See, for example, *Williams,* above note 252; *R. v. Dore* (2002), 4 C.R. (6th) 81 (Ont. C.A.); *Grabowski v. The Queen,* [1985] 2 S.C.R. 434; *Pisani v. The Queen,* [1971] S.C.R. 738 [*Pisani*]; *R. v. Khan,* [2001] 3 S.C.R. 823.

possible, a trial judge should first try to remedy whatever prejudice has arisen by less drastic means. Other remedies might include an adjournment, reopening the case, or, quite commonly, clearly instructing the jury that they are to ignore the submissions or information they ought not to have heard. It is only where such other remedies are insufficient that a mistrial should be granted.[256] Put another way, "the general principle is that a mistrial is declared if the Crown's jury address is so improper that it deprives the accused of the right to a fair trial."[257]

Although it is typically the accused who applies for a mistrial, it is also open to the Crown to do so.[258] Similarly, although circumstances leading to a mistrial application are more likely to arise in a jury trial, in principle the power exists in trials held by judge alone as well.[259]

For the most part, the authority to order a mistrial comes from the common law. It is a discretionary decision, and, although it is subject to appeal, an appeal court is not to interfere with the trial judge's exercise of discretion unless clearly satisfied that the judge proceeded on some wrong principle or was wrong.[260] As noted above, there is also a discretion in section 653 of the *Code* for a trial judge to declare a mistrial if satisfied that a jury is unable to agree on a verdict. Although section 653(2) says that this discretion is not reviewable, there are suggestions that the subsection might not withstand *Charter* scrutiny.[261]

As a general rule, a new trial can be held following a mistrial, and the fact of a mistrial does not allow an accused to plead *autrefois ac-*

256 See, for example, *R. v. D.(L.E.)*, [1989] 2 S.C.R. 111 at para. 28: "should inadmissible evidence be adduced, the trial Judge should either instruct the jury immediately to disregard it or, if it is of so prejudicial a nature that the jury would not have the capability of disregarding it, he should discharge the jury and order a new trial . . . . If the trial judge was of the view that an immediate caution to the jury to disregard the evidence was insufficient to ensure a fair trial, then his course was to direct a mistrial rather than admit the evidence of similar acts which had previously been excluded," quoting in part from *R. v. Ambrose* (1975), 25 C.C.C. (2d) 90 (N.B.S.C.A.D.), aff'd [1977] 2 S.C.R. 717.
257 L'Heureux-Dubé J., dissenting in *Rose*, above note 173 at para. 66, citing *Pisani*, above note 255.
258 The Crown applied successfully for a mistrial in *Williams*, above note 252, for example.
259 In *MacDonald*, above note 254, for example, the judge contacted the Crown and a Crown witness, without the knowledge of the accused, following conviction but before sentencing, and the trial judge granted a subsequent application for a mistrial brought by the Crown and the defence.
260 *Bengert*, above note 198. See also *R. v. Khan*, [2001] 3 S.C.R. 823.
261 See *Pan*, above note 188 at para. 111. The section was challenged in that case, but the *Charter* issue was not decided since the Crown did not dispute the ability of appeal courts to review the initial decision.

quit or *autrefois convict*. In particular circumstances, the *Charter* might prevent a new trial from being held after an improper declaration of a mistrial, but only where the principles of fundamental justice are in issue. Where a trial judge declares a mistrial to save a floundering Crown case and give it time to obtain further witnesses, for example, the *Charter* might prevent a new trial, but in ordinary circumstances new proceedings can be commenced.[262]

FURTHER READINGS

BALA, NICHOLAS, & HILARY MCCORMACK, "Accommodating the Criminal Process to Child Witnesses" (1994) 25 C.R. (4th) 341

BALA, N., R.C.L. LINDSAY, & E. MCNAMARA, "Testimonial Aids for Children: The Canadian Experience with Closed Circuit Television, Screens and Videotapes" (2001) 44 Crim. L.Q. 461

CHOPRA, SONIA R., AND JAMES R.P. OGLOFF, "Evaluating Jury Secrecy: Implications for Academic Research and Juror Stress" (2000) 44 Crim. L.Q. 190

GORMAN, WAYNE K., "Judicial Intervention in the Trial Process" (2003) 47 Crim. L.Q. 481

LAW REFORM COMMISSION OF CANADA, *Double Jeopardy, Pleas and Verdicts* (Ottawa: Law Reform Commission of Canada, 1991)

LAW REFORM COMMISSION OF CANADA, *The Charge Document in Criminal Cases* (Ottawa: Law Reform Commission of Canada, 1987)

LAW REFORM COMMISSION OF CANADA, *The Jury* (Ottawa: Law Reform Commission, 1982)

PROULX, MICHEL, & DAVID LAYTON, *Ethics and Canadian Criminal Law* (Toronto: Irwin Law Inc., 2001)

QUIGLEY, TIM, *Procedure in Canadian Criminal Law*, 2d ed., looseleaf (Toronto: Thomson Carswell, 2005) cc. 17, 18, 20, & 21

QUIGLEY, TIM, "Principled Reform of Criminal Procedure" in Don Stuart, R.J. Delisle, & Allan Manson, eds., *Towards a Clear and Just Criminal Law* (Toronto: Carswell, 1999)

---

262 *Pan, ibid.* at para. 113.

QUINLAN, PAUL, "Secrecy of Jury Deliberations—Is the Cost Too High" (1993) 22 C.R. (4th) 127

STUART, DON, *Charter Justice in Canadian Criminal Law*, 4th ed. (Toronto: Thomson Carswell, 2005) cc. 2 and 6

TANOVICH, DAVID M., "Upping the Ante in Directed Verdict Cases Where the Evidence is Circumstantial" (1998) 5 C.R. (5th) 21

CHAPTER 12

APPEALS

A. INTRODUCTION

Rights of appeal in the Canadian criminal justice system are entirely a creature of statute. Various appeal provisions are set out in the *Criminal Code*, and in addition the *Code* provides that only appeals authorized in Parts XXI and XXVI can be brought with regard to indictable offences.[1] In fact, however, that has not operated to completely restrict the methods of review of decisions of the lower courts.

First, applications for extraordinary remedies such as *certiorari* can be brought in some cases, though the scope of such applications is more limited than an appeal (see the discussion of this issue in Chapter 9). In addition, in some unusual circumstances an appeal to the Supreme Court might be possible through section 40 of the *Supreme Court Act*.[2] In *Dagenais v. Canadian Broadcasting Corp.* the Court held that a literal interpretation of section 674 of the *Code* would exclude relying on section 40, and that such a literal interpretation could not be adopted.[3] In that case, section 40 was used to allow a third party (the media) to appeal a publication ban, an appeal that would not have been possible under any of the *Code*'s appeal provisions. See also *R. v. Laba*, where section 40 permitted the Crown to appeal a ruling that overturned a

---

1 Section 674.
2 R.S.C. 1985, c. S-26.
3 *Dagenais v. Canadian Broadcasting Corp.*, [1994] 3 S.C.R. 835.

reverse onus provision in the *Code*, even though they had been successful in the result at the Court of Appeal. In effect, the Crown was appealing a case that it had won.[4] The provision is sometimes used in cases
where an appeal of an interlocutory order is in issue, such as when a
third party challenges an order for production of privileged communications, as in *R. v. McClure* or *R. v. Brown*.[5] In the latter case, the Court
noted that such appeals reach it without having been considered by any
court of appeal, which denies the Court the benefit of a fuller record,
and input from that lower court. They suggested that this gap in the
Code's appeal provisions was anomalous and an "unnecessary encum-
brance" that should be fixed by Parliament.[6]

The focus of this chapter, however, will be on the statutory appeal
powers set out in the *Criminal Code* itself. Although some issues, such
as time limits and procedures, are set by rules of court,[7] for the most
part the *Code* determines what can and cannot be done.

The *Code* creates separate sets of rules for appeals of indictable offences and of summary conviction offences. However, as a matter of
convenience it does permit the appeal of a summary conviction matter
to be heard along with that of an indictable offence where the two offences were tried together.[8] In the case of indictable offences, different
appeal rights are given to an accused and the Crown. For summary
conviction offences, on the other hand, the appeal rights are essentially
parallel. The *Code* provisions deal with appeals of the result in the trial,
as well as findings that a person is not criminally responsible or is not
fit to stand trial, as well as appeals of sentence. It is the first of these
that is of primary interest in this chapter.

B. APPEALS OF INDICTABLE OFFENCES

1) Appeals by the Accused

a) Overview of Appeal Provisions
At first glance, it would appear that an accused appealing a conviction
has an enormously broad right of appeal. Section 675(1)(a) says that a
person can appeal a conviction based on a question of law alone, (with
leave of the court of appeal) on a question of fact, on a mixed ques-

---

4   *R. v. Laba*, [1994] 3 S.C.R. 965.
5   *R. v. McClure*, 2001 SCC 14; *R. v. Brown*, 2002 SCC 32 [*Brown*].
6   *Brown, ibid.* at para. 110.
7   Section 678.
8   Sections 675(1.1) and 676(1.1).

tion of law and fact, or on any ground of appeal "that appears to the court of appeal to be a sufficient ground of appeal."[9] In fact, the right is not nearly as expansive as that section alone suggests. These bases for appeal pass through at least three "filters," each limiting the grounds upon which an appeal might succeed.

The first two filters are found in section 686(1)(a). Section 675 set out the bases upon which an appeal can be *made*; the grounds upon which an appeal can be *granted* are considerably narrower. Section 686(1)(a) sets out those grounds:

(i)   the verdict should be set aside on the ground that it is unreasonable or cannot be supported by the evidence,

(ii) the judgment of the trial court should be set aside on the ground of a wrong decision on a question of law, or

(iii) on any ground there was a miscarriage of justice.

It is important to note the differences between the scope of this provision and section 675.

Appeals can be made under section 675 on the basis of an error relating to a question of fact or mixed fact and law. However, appeals will not necessarily be granted under section 686(1) simply because such an error is shown. Rather, only such an error that results in an unreasonable verdict or a miscarriage of justice will be sufficient. That is the first filter.

The second filter relates to the primary remaining ground of appeal in section 675, appeals based on a question of law. At face value, section 686(1)(a)(ii) says that demonstrating a wrong decision on such a question will lead to a successful appeal. However, there is some ambiguity in the meaning of the phrase "question of law." In essence, it has a broader meaning in the context of section 675 than it does in the context of s. 686(1)(a). As a result, the conclusion that an issue is a question of law for the jurisdictional purpose of deciding whether a ground of appeal exists, does not mean, therefore, that it is a question of law for the purpose of deciding whether the appeal should be granted.[10] In that latter context, it may be treated as a question of mixed law and fact. This change in

---

9   Section 675(1)(a). Questions of fact or mixed law and fact can also be appealed "on the certificate of the trial judge that the case is a proper case for appeal."

10 See, for example, *R. v. Biniaris*, 2000 SCC 15 at para. 22 [*Biniaris*]: "The sole purpose of the exercise here, in identifying the reasonableness of a verdict as a question of fact, law or both, is to determine access to appellate review. One can plausibly maintain, on close scrutiny of any decision under review, that the conclusion that a verdict was unreasonable was reached sometimes mostly as a matter of law, in other cases predominantly as a matter of factual assessment.

characterization may cause the first filter to be relevant. In addition, since the latter question will involve greater deference to the trial judge (see the discussion of standard of review, below at Section B(1)(b)(i)), it further acts to limit the possibility of a successful appeal.[11]

The third filter is found in the fact that even if an appeal meets the conditions of section 686(1)(a), it may not be granted, nonetheless. The grounds upon which an appeal might succeed are narrowed even further by section 686(1)(b), which sets out the grounds upon which the court of appeal can dismiss an appeal. Most obviously, a court can dismiss an appeal if none of the above grounds for granting it are made out. However, that is not the only basis for dismissing an appeal. That is, even if the accused does succeed in showing that one of the grounds of appeal in section 686(1)(a) is made out, the appeal might fail nonetheless.

Another, further basis for dismissing an appeal is that, although there was an error, the accused "was properly convicted on another count or part of the indictment."[12] In addition, section 686(b) contains two other bases upon which an appeal might be dismissed despite an error:

(iii) notwithstanding that the court is of the opinion that on any ground mentioned in subparagraph (a)(ii) the appeal might be decided in favour of the appellant, it is of the opinion that no substantial wrong or miscarriage of justice has occurred, or

(iv) notwithstanding any procedural irregularity at trial, the trial court had jurisdiction over the class of offence of which the appellant was convicted and the court of appeal is of the opinion that the appellant suffered no prejudice thereby.

The former of these two is often referred to as the "curative proviso." The effect of it, along with section 686(1)(b)(iv), is that not all errors of law will lead to a successful appeal either. Errors in law that cause no substantial wrong, do not create a miscarriage of justice, or are mere procedural irregularities will not lead to a successful appeal by the accused.

These last two provisions are discussed in greater detail below at Sections B(1)(b)(iv) and (v). For the moment, it is sufficient to note that only an error of law under section 686(1)(a)(ii) could be saved by the curative proviso in 686(1)(b)(ii). If the appeal was based on either an unreasonable verdict or a miscarriage of justice then the harmless error

---

But when that exercise is undertaken as a jurisdictional threshold exercise, little is gained by embarking on such a case-by-case analysis."

11   See *R. v. Grouse*, 2004 NSCA 108 at paras. 33–43, for a detailed explanation of this point.

12   Section 686(1)(b)(i).

exception has no application. It has been suggested that the underlying theory of this section is that appeals are fundamentally concerned with miscarriages of justice. Sections 686(1)(a)(i) and (iii) (unreasonable verdicts and other miscarriages of justice) necessarily fall into that category, and errors of law are presumed to fall into it unless the Crown shows otherwise.[13]

One other point of difference arises depending on the basis upon which an appeal is granted or dismissed. If an appeal is granted under section 686(1)(a), then the court of appeal quashes the conviction and can either acquit the accused or order a new trial. If, on the other hand, the appeal is dismissed on the basis that the accused was properly convicted on some part, then the appeal court can substitute a verdict, affirm the sentence, impose a new sentence, or remit the matter back to the trial court for sentencing.[14] A court of appeal has no more ability to find that an accused is factually innocent than a trial court does, though they are able to express the reasons for acquittal "in clear and strong terms."[15]

Finally, note that appeal courts can deal with issues other than whether the accused was convicted or acquitted. Section 686 also gives the appeal court the ability to hear appeals relating to findings that an accused was unfit to stand trial, that an accused was not criminally responsible by reason of mental disorder, or with regard to special verdicts.[16] In addition, of course, a court of appeal can vary a sentence imposed on an accused.[17]

b) Appeal Provisions in Depth

i) Standard of Review
Since the grounds for an appeal by an accused extend beyond errors of law to include unreasonable verdicts and miscarriages of justice, appeal courts must review a variety of findings from lower courts. Specifically, it can be necessary to review questions of law, questions of fact, inferences of fact, and questions of mixed fact and law. The Supreme Court considered the standard of review for each of these issues in *Housen v. Nikolaisen*.[18]

---

13   See *R. v. Morrissey* (1995), 38 C.R. (4th) 4 (Ont. C.A.) [*Morrissey*].

14   Sections 686(2) & (3).

15   *R. v. Mullins-Johnson*, 2007 ONCA 720 at para. 24.

16   Sections 686(1)(c) & (d).

17   Section 687.

18   [2002] 2 S.C.R. 235 [*Housen*]. *Housen* is a civil case, but the Court has noted the relevance of its discussion of these issues to criminal matters: see *R. v. Buhay*, 2003 SCC 30.

With regard to pure questions of law, the standard of review is correctness, and so an appellate court can substitute its opinion for that of the trial judge. Questions of fact, on the other hand, are only reviewable on a higher standard. A finding of fact should not be overturned in the absence of a "palpable and overriding error," which amounts to "prohibiting an appellate court from reviewing a trial judge's decision if there was some evidence upon which he or she could have relied to reach that conclusion."[19] The Court has offered three basic rationales for this approach. First, given the number, length, and cost of appeals, there should be limits on how readily available they should be—deferring to a trial judge's findings of fact helps to impose a limit and does so on a principled basis. Second, trial judges are presumed to be competent and able to decide cases justly and fairly—allowing regular appeals would undermine that presumption as well as public confidence in the trial process. Finally, trial judges are better situated to make factual findings because they hear the testimony being given, are exposed to all the evidence, and are familiar with the case as a whole. Their primary role is to weigh and assess evidence, and so their expertise should be respected.

For essentially the same reasons, inferences of fact are held to the same standard of review as findings of fact. The issue is not whether there is evidence that reasonably supports the inference, but rather whether some palpable and overriding error can be shown from drawing the inference.

Questions of mixed law and fact are, in some ways, the most complicated. The Court has noted that these issues fall on a spectrum. Some things that may, at first, appear to be a question of mixed fact and law may actually be reduced to a question of law, in which case the correctness standard would apply. However, in other cases the higher standard of review is required, and so the general rule is that where an issue on appeal involves the trial judge's interpretation of the evidence as a whole, it should only be overturned in the case of palpable and overriding error.

ii) Unreasonable Verdicts

The basic standard for assessing whether a verdict is unreasonable is "whether the verdict is one that a properly instructed jury acting judicially, could reasonably have rendered."[20] This test entails both subject-

---

19   *Housen, ibid.* at paras. 1 and 10.
20   *R. v. Yebes*, [1987] 2 S.C.R. 168 at para. 16 [*Yebes*], reaffirmed more recently in *Biniaris*, above note 10, and *R. v. Beaudry*, 2007 SCC 5 [*Beaudry*].

ive and objective elements, and the Supreme Court has been reluctant to label it as one or the other. It does require the court of appeal to engage in some weighing of the evidence, and not simply to consider the question of the sufficiency of the evidence.[21] However, the court of appeal cannot merely substitute its view for that of the trier of fact, rather it must ask whether the trier of fact could reasonably have reached the conclusion it did on the evidence before it.[22]

Although, in principle, this same standard applies whether the verdict was reached by a jury or by a judge sitting alone, there are some differences that make the two situations worth discussing separately.

Juries do not give reasons, and indeed jurors and everyone else are precluded from revealing anything concerning the deliberations in the jury room.[23] Further, if the jury was charged incorrectly, then there would be an error of law and the appeal would be based on section 686(1)(a)(ii) rather than (i). Accordingly, the issue of unreasonable verdicts in jury cases arises when the jury has been charged correctly, but nonetheless returns with a verdict that seems questionable.

The Supreme Court has held that a general sense of unease or lurking doubt about a jury's decision is not a sufficient basis for a court of appeal to intervene. Such a feeling might trigger a closer inquiry, but cannot be the end of the analysis. The appeal court must proceed further and articulate as precisely as possible what features of the case suggest that the jury's verdict was an unreasonable one.

Where a jury has been properly instructed but has returned an unreasonable verdict nonetheless, it means that the jury was not acting judicially. It might, for example, have failed to adequately apply advice that it was given about the frailties of eyewitness identification evidence or the limited use of similar fact evidence. To act judicially in this context requires that the jury act dispassionately, apply the law, and adjudicate on the basis of the record and nothing else. It also requires that the jury arrive "at a conclusion that does not conflict with the bulk of judicial experience."[24] This assessment would allow an appeal court to conclude, for example, that no jury could properly have been satisfied that identification was proved given the nature of the evidence led.

---

21 *Biniaris*, *ibid.* at para. 36. See also *Yebes*, *ibid.* at para. 25: "While the Court of Appeal must not merely substitute its view for that of the jury, in order to apply the test the Court must re-examine and to some extent reweigh and consider the effect of the evidence."

22 *R. v. Burns*, [1994] 1 S.C.R. 656.

23 See s. 649 of the *Code* and the discussion of this issue in Chapter 11, Section E(4).

24 *Biniaris*, above note 10 at para. 40.

The same standard applies to concluding that a judge has rendered an unreasonable verdict, but the task is different because in this case the trial judge should have issued reasons showing the reasoning process by which the verdict was reached. Those reasons have an impact on an appeal court's ability to assess the reasonableness of the verdict.

The Supreme Court considered this issue quite recently with its decision in *Beaudry*.[25] The point is not entirely free from doubt, but the Court appears to have slightly expanded the circumstances in which a verdict by a trial judge can be found to be unreasonable. The Court noted in *Biniaris* that

> [t]he review for unreasonableness on appeal is different, however, and somewhat easier when the judgment under attack is that of a single judge, at least when reasons for judgment of some substance are provided. In those cases, the reviewing appellate court may be able to identify a flaw in the evaluation of the evidence, or in the analysis, that will serve to explain the unreasonable conclusion reached, and justify the reversal.[26]

In *Beaudry*, all nine judges agree with this statement, but they disagree over its exact significance. The disagreement is over the consequence of finding that the trial judge's reasoning process was unreasonable. That is, is that conclusion alone sufficient or is something more needed?

Justice Charron, for four of the judges, concludes that finding an error in the trial judge's reasoning is potentially useful in pointing to whether a verdict is unreasonable, but has no greater significance. A judge could make errors in the reasoning process but that does not necessarily mean that the final result is unreasonable. That is, the question is whether the ultimate verdict is unreasonable, not whether the judge's reasoning process was unreasonable. In that event, an appeal based on section 686(1)(a)(i) should fail if, despite the fact that the trial judge's approach was unreasonable, the verdict was nonetheless reasonably available on the evidence.

On the other hand, Justice Fish for four other judges holds that, as section 686(1)(a)(i) refers to verdicts that are "unreasonable *or* cannot be supported on the evidence," there are really two different bases upon which such an appeal could succeed. Hence, even though a verdict might be supported on the evidence in some fashion, it could still be unreasonable. On this view:

---

25   *Beaudry*, above note 20.
26   *Biniaris*, above note 10 at para. 37.

No one should stand convicted on the strength of manifestly bad reasons — reasons that are illogical on their face, or contrary to the evidence — on the ground that another judge (who never did and never will try the case) could *but might not necessarily* have reached the same conclusion for *other reasons*.[27]

Justice Binnie votes with Justice Charron in the result, making those reasons the majority conclusion on whether the appeal succeeds or fails. However, he appears to accept Justice's Fish approach to section 686(1)(a)(i) in principle, with the result that this broader understanding of the scope of that section now applies. In that event, flaws by a trial judge in the evaluation and analysis of evidence, entirely apart from any legal error, could lead to a successful appeal on the basis of an unreasonable verdict.

One particular circumstance in which a verdict can be found to be unreasonable is when there are multiple accused or multiple counts and there are inconsistent verdicts. The same evidence could not reasonably lead both to a conviction and an acquittal. This basis of proving unreasonableness is a difficult one, however, because jury members are not bound by any particular theory of the case, need not all agree with one another on how to reach the same conclusion, and are allowed a very wide latitude in accepting some, all, or none of each witness's testimony. Therefore, it is unusual to be able to say that the "same evidence" was in play in both cases.

In essence, it will only be a rare case, one where the evidence on two different charges is not logically separable, where an inconsistent verdict appeal will succeed. Since the question is whether the verdicts are supportable on any theory of the evidence that is consistent with the law, it is difficult to show that two verdicts are clearly inconsistent with one another. In the case of multiple accused charged with the same offence, it will typically be difficult to prove that verdicts are inconsistent even if some are convicted and some are acquitted (the jury could well have accepted evidence against one accused but not against the other).[28]

iii) Errors of Law and Miscarriages of Justice

Section 686(1)(a)(ii) permits an appeal to be granted in the case of "a wrong decision on a question of law," while section 686(1)(a)(iii) permits an appeal based on "a miscarriage of justice." It is convenient to consider these two grounds of appeal together because, although distinct, they share many features in common. Indeed, it has been suggest-

---

27   *Beaudry*, above note 20 at para. 97 [emphasis in original].
28   See, for example, *R. v. Pittiman*, 2006 SCC 9.

ed that the same rationale underlies all three bases of appeal in section 686(1)(a) — that of miscarriage of justice. Section 686(1)(a)(i) sets out one basis upon which a verdict would be a miscarriage of justice (that it is unreasonable). Section 686(1)(a)(iii) explicitly includes any other miscarriage of justice as a basis for appeal. It has been suggested that section 686(1)(a)(ii), combined with the curative proviso, is an expression of the idea mentioned above that any error of law is presumed to be a miscarriage of justice unless the contrary is shown by the Crown.[29]

One feature that errors of law and miscarriages of justice have in common with one another, but which is distinct from unreasonable verdicts, is that there is no requirement that the verdict was not supportable on the evidence. That is, even if the court of appeal concludes that a jury could have convicted despite the legal error or miscarriage, that fact is not a basis for rejecting the appeal.[30]

Most errors that are not based on the unreasonableness of a verdict will relate to an error of law. The primary reason for distinguishing between an error of law and a miscarriage of justice, as noted above, is the availability of the curative proviso — it cannot be resorted to in the latter case. However, to a certain extent this distinction is a formal one, rather than one of any real substance. Any mistake at trial that amounts to a miscarriage of justice would, in any case, fail to meet the test for the curative proviso. As a result, the underlying theory of the two subsections is really the same.

An error of law is "any decision . . . that was an erroneous interpretation or application of the law."[31] There is no requirement that the error by itself must have led to any unfairness or prejudice; that is only an issue at the curative proviso stage.[32] So, for example, whether there is an air of reality to a defence is a legal question. It is therefore an error of law to instruct a jury on a defence when there is no air of reality to it, or to fail to instruct when there is.[33] The provision of flawed instructions to a jury is an error of law, as is an improper exhortation.[34] Using the summary procedure for contempt of court proceedings unnecessarily is an error of law.[35] Failing to give a *Vetrovec* warning where one is required is also an error of law.[36]

---

29   *Morrissey*, above note 13.
30   *R. v. Lohrer*, 2004 SCC 80 at para. 1 [*Lohrer*].
31   *R. v. Khan*, 2001 SCC 86 at para. 22 [*Khan*].
32   *Ibid.*
33   *R. v. Cinous*, 2002 SCC 29.
34   *R. v. G. (R.M.)*, [1996] 3 S.C.R. 362.
35   *R. v. Arradi*, 2003 SCC 23.
36   *R. v. Bevan*, [1993] 2 S.C.R. 599 [*Bevan*].

The distinction between an error of law and a miscarriage of justice can be seen to some extent in the facts of *Khan*. There, the jury was provided with a transcript that included an exchange between counsel and the judge that had taken place in the jury's absence. This was discovered a few hours later and the transcript was replaced, and the trial judge rejected a motion for a mistrial application. The Supreme Court held that this appeal was properly brought on the basis of error of law. The issue was whether the trial judge had made a correct legal decision in rejecting the mistrial application. On the other hand, had the error regarding the transcript not been discovered until afterward, so that there was no decision regarding the matter at trial, then the appeal would be framed in terms of whether there was a miscarriage of justice.

A miscarriage of justice can be either substantive or procedural. Any error that deprives an accused of a fair trial is a legal error.[37] Further, if the error at trial is not purely one of law, but one of mixed law and fact, then the issue is also whether a miscarriage of justice thereby arose. So, for example, an allegation of ineffective assistance of counsel that is only raised on appeal would concern a possible miscarriage.[38] A failure to limit cross-examination would raise issues of miscarriage, as would an appeal based on the claim that the trial judge had misapprehended the evidence.[39]

Although the underlying theory of sections 686(1)(a)(ii) and (iii) is the same, they are not quite identical in application. In some cases the same conclusion would be reached no matter which route was followed. For example, if an error of law causing prejudice is a miscarriage then the curative proviso does not apply, but if the error causes prejudice then the curative proviso potentially applies, but would not succeed. That is, one could say either that the error is a miscarriage not subject to the curative proviso, or that the error is an error of law that was not harmless in the first place.

However, there are some differences between the two sections. First, as noted, some miscarriages of justice are matters of mixed law and fact. Beyond that, the curative proviso has been interpreted so that it can actually be satisfied in two different ways, one of which does not amount to suggesting that the error was harmless in itself. It is to that question we now turn.

---

37 *Fanjoy v. The Queen*, [1985] 2 S.C.R. 233 at para 11 [*Fanjoy*].
38 *R. v. G.D.B.*, 2000 SCC 22.
39 See, respectively, *Fanjoy*, above note 37 and *Lohrer*, above note 30.

iv) The "Curative Proviso"

Section 686(1)(b)(iii) allows an appeal court to dismiss an appeal despite an error of law provided that "no substantial wrong or miscarriage of justice has occurred." The test for whether this section is met is well-established, and requires that there is a "reasonable possibility that the verdict would have been different had the error . . . not been made."[40]

Caselaw has established that there are two entirely different ways of satisfying this test, both of which are quite fact dependent. The first is to show that the error is harmless in itself. If that is so, then the error would not have been capable of causing prejudice to the accused. The other possibility is to show that the evidence against the accused is so overwhelming that even if the appeal was granted and a retrial ordered, the result would inevitably be a conviction. In such cases the error itself might not have been incapable of causing prejudice, but any theoretical prejudice has no genuine impact.

Various types of errors can fall into the first, "harmless error" branch of the curative proviso. Some mistakes could actually be of benefit to the accused. For example, if the trial judge articulates a stricter standard for guilt than is actually required, there will have been an error of law, but it will certainly not have prejudiced the accused.[41] In other cases, the error might fail to benefit the accused, but be of no real consequence. For example, a failure to permit cross-examination might be in error, but if it is on a point not really in any doubt, then the error is harmless.[42] Similarly, if hearsay evidence is improperly admitted, but on some point that is of no consequence to the accused's guilt, then the curative proviso can be applied.[43] Generally speaking, the harmless error criterion is more likely to be met when only a single error is at issue, rather than the cumulative effect of a number of errors, but there is no absolute rule.[44]

The other ground for applying the curative proviso is on the basis that the rest of the evidence is so overwhelming that a conviction on a retrial is inevitable. The most important point to bear in mind is that this branch of the curative proviso imposes a very high standard. It has long been noted that this aspect of the provision must be used with great circumspection or the accused will be deprived of the right to trial

---

40　*Khan*, above note 31 at para. 28, quoting *Bevan*, above note 36 at 617. *Khan* contains a very full summary of the correct approach to s. 686(1)(b)(iii).

41　See, for example, *R. v. MacGillivray*, [1995] 1 S.C.R. 890.

42　*United Nurses of Alberta v. Alberta (Attorney General)*, [1992] 1 S.C.R. 901.

43　*Gunn v. The Queen*, [1974] S.C.R. 273.

44　*R. v. Jacquard*, [1997] 1 S.C.R. 314.

by jury.[45] So, for example, where evidence has been improperly admitted it is not open to a court of appeal simply to conclude that the remainder of the evidence could or ought to result in a conviction. If that were the case, then there would be no need for section 686(1)(b)(iii).[46] Rather, the appropriate standard is an "onerous" one, and the Supreme Court has restricted use of the provision on very stringent terms.[47] It has said that the provision should only be applied if conviction would be "inevitable" or "invariable,"[48] or that the result would "necessarily" have been the same.[49] Most recently it has stated that the proviso can be used

> only if it is clear that the evidence pointing to the guilt of the accused is so overwhelming that any other verdict but a conviction would be impossible.[50]

Whether the test is made out in any given case will be very much a factual question. In general, courts of appeal should be more cautious in cases involving questions of credibility and should avoid speculating about the bases upon which a jury may have accepted some evidence or rejected other evidence.[51]

v) Procedural Irregularities
Section 686(1)(b)(iv), it will be recalled, allows an appeal court to dismiss an appeal on the basis that

> notwithstanding any procedural irregularity at trial, the trial court had jurisdiction over the class of offence of which the appellant was convicted and the court of appeal is of the opinion that the appellant suffered no prejudice thereby.

The section is best understood by discussing not what it adds to the analysis of an appeal, but what it takes away from that discussion. The purpose of the subsection is to remove from consideration a wide variety of issues that might technically have been errors though they

---

45 See. R. v. B.(F.F.), [1993] 1 S.C.R. 697 [B.(F.F.)]. See also Colpitts v. The Queen, [1965] S.C.R. 739 at 744, noting the danger that "the judges would in truth be substituted for the jury, the verdict would become theirs and theirs alone, and would be arrived at upon a perusal of the evidence without any opportunity of seeing the demeanour of the witnesses and weighing the evidence with the assistance which this affords."
46 R. v. S.(P.L.), [1991] 1 S.C.R. 909 [S.(P.L.)].
47 R. v. Broyles, [1991] 3 S.C.R. 595.
48 S.(P.L.), above note 46.
49 B.(F.F.), above note 45.
50 Khan, above note 31 at para. 31.
51 B.(F.F.), above note 45.

caused no prejudice to the accused, but that could not have been dealt with under the curative proviso. Accordingly, it simplifies the appeal process by eliminating those questions from the analysis.

Prior to the enactment of section 686(1)(b)(iv) it was possible for errors of law to be cured by the harmless error provision in section 686(1)(b)(iii). Most procedural irregularities would be errors of law. However, caselaw concluded that some particular types of errors went to the jurisdiction of the court, and that some of these instances could not be classified as "errors of law" and, as such, the curative proviso could not be applied. Some of these jurisdictional errors were of no real consequence—the exclusion of the accused from a small portion of the trial might be a jurisdictional error, but, if nothing of significance occurred during that time, the accused suffered no prejudice. Nonetheless, since the curative proviso did not apply, the appeal had to be granted.

Section 686(1)(b)(iv) now allows appeals based on such technicalities to be dismissed, provided there is no harm to the accused's interests in doing so. In part, this is accomplished by the fact that the section does not apply if the trial court did not have jurisdiction over the *class* of offence, as opposed to losing jurisdiction over the particular offence or particular offender through some procedural irregularity. Accordingly, the section would not apply if an indictable offence under section 469 somehow were tried in provincial court, for example.

More importantly, though, the section only applies if the procedural irregularity caused the accused no prejudice. The Court has held that it is appropriate to infer that the irregularity *did* cause prejudice, and therefore that this inference must be rebutted. The analysis of that question is the same as that conducted under the curative proviso in section 686(1)(b)(iii).[52] As a result, section 686(1)(b)(iv) is largely parallel to section 686(1)(b)(iii), but applies only to a narrow range of procedural irregularities creating a jurisdictional error that could not be classified as a pure error of law.

The Court has helpfully summarized the correct approach to applying sections 686(1)(b)(iii) and (iv):

> If the procedural irregularity amounts to or is based on an error of law, it falls under ss. 686(1)(a)(ii) and 686(1)(b)(iii).
>
> If the procedural irregularity was previously (before 1985) classified as an irregularity causing a loss of jurisdiction: s. 686(1)(b)(iv) provides that this is no longer fatal to the conviction, and an analysis of prejudice must be undertaken, in accordance with the principles set out in s. 686(1)(b)(iii).

---

52 *Khan*, above note 31 at para. 16.

If the procedural error did not amount to, or originate in an error of law, which is rare, s. 686(1)(*a*)(iii) applies and the reviewing court must determine whether a miscarriage of justice occurred. If so, there are no remedial provisions in s. 686(1)(*b*) that can cure such a defect, and the appeal must be allowed and either an acquittal entered or a new trial ordered.[53]

2) Appeals by the Crown

Crown appeals can be brought under section 676 of the *Code*. The first thing to note is that the appeal rights in that section are not parallel to the appeal rights given to an accused in the case of a conviction. The Crown's right of appeal is narrower, and, in particular, contains nothing equivalent to the accused's right under section 686(1)(a)(i). That is, the Crown cannot appeal on the basis that an acquittal was unreasonable or could not be supported on the evidence.[54]

The Crown's right of appeal is primarily set out in section 676(1)(a): "any ground of appeal that involves *a question of law alone*" (emphasis added). This right specifically applies in section 676(1)(a) to verdicts of acquittal or of not criminally responsible on account of mental disorder. Other portions of section 676 allow appeals of most decisions that could bring an end to a prosecution, such as an order of a superior court of criminal jurisdiction that quashes an indictment or fails to exercise jurisdiction on an indictment, and an order of a trial court that stays proceedings or quashes an indictment.[55] These latter powers of appeal would capture situations where the accused has received a *Charter* remedy, such as a stay of proceedings based on entrapment or a violation of the right to a trial within a reasonable time. Similarly, where a trial judge has dismissed charges against an accused on the basis that the offence in question was invalid or *ultra vires*, this will amount to an acquittal that is appealable,[56] as will accepting a plea of *autrefois acquit*.[57] In addition, the Crown can appeal an accused's sentence with leave.[58]

---

53   *Ibid.* at para. 18.
54   See *Biniaris*, above note 10 at para. 32 and *Sunbeam Corporation (Canada) Ltd. v. The Queen*, [1969] S.C.R. 221.
55   Sections 676(1)(b) & (c). Note that these provisions do not include a discharge at a preliminary inquiry, which therefore can only be reviewed through *certiorari*, or overridden through preferring a direct indictment: see the discussion in Chapter 9.
56   See *Cheyenne Realty Ltd. v. Thompson*, [1975] 1 S.C.R. 87 and *Re Regina and Kripps Pharmacy Ltd.* (1981), 60 C.C.C. (2d) 332 (B.C.C.A.).
57   *R. v. Sanver* (1973), 12 C.C.C. (2d) 105 (N.B.S.C.A.D.).
58   Section 676(1)(d).

The Court has noted that many countries do not permit acquittals to be appealed at all, but, nonetheless, a right of appeal by the Crown does not violate the *Charter*.[59] However, the Court has stressed on a number of occasions that acquittals should not be lightly overturned. The Crown is required to satisfy the court that the verdict would not necessarily have been the same had the errors not occurred, and the Crown has a heavy onus in doing so.[60] In *R. v. Graveline*, for example, the accused's defence at trial had been based on non-mental disorder automatism and she did not argue self-defence. The trial judge instructed the jury on self-defence nonetheless, and therein erred on a question of law. However, the Supreme Court held on these facts that the Crown did not satisfy its onus to show that the legal error was of any consequence. It noted that an abstract or purely hypothetical possibility that the accused would have been convicted was not sufficient, rather the Crown must show how "in the concrete reality of the case at hand" the error had a material bearing on the acquittal.[61] Something like an error that calls for the wrong standard of proof to be applied, for example, would be needed.[62]

Obviously, a crucial consideration, given the relatively limited nature of the Crown's right of appeal, is exactly what constitutes a question of law.[63] Some straightforward examples include the admissibility of evidence, the interpretation of a statute, and whether evidence is capable of being corroborative.[64] A decision concerning the application of a legal standard, such as investigative necessity, is also a question of law.[65] Whether a correct conclusion has been reached on a *Charter* question, such as whether there has been a section 10(b) violation or whether evidence should be excluded under section 24(2), is also a question of law.[66] In addition, matters can still be classed as questions of law even if they involve the consideration of the evidence in some way.

---

59   See *R. v. Graveline*, 2006 SCC 16 at para. 13 [*Graveline*]; and *R. v. Morgentaler*, [1988] 1 S.C.R. 30.

60   See *R. v. Sutton*, 2000 SCC 50 at para. 2 [*Sutton*] relying on *Vézeau v. The Queen*, [1977] 2 S.C.R. 277; and *R. v. Morin*, [1988] 2 S.C.R. 345.

61   *Graveline*, above note 59 at para. 14.

62   See *Sutton*, above note 60.

63   It is worth recalling here the discussion above concerning the ambiguity over the meaning of "question of law": see above notes 10 and 11. Here we are dealing with the broader meaning of a question of law for jurisdictional purposes.

64   *R. v. B.(G.)*, [1990] 2 S.C.R. 57 [*B.(G.)*].

65   *R. v. Araujo*, 2000 SCC 65 at para. 18. See also *Biniaris*, above note 10.

66   See *R. v. Baig* (1985), 46 C.R. (3d) 222 (Ont. C.A.) and *R. v. Genest* (1986), 54 C.R. (3d) 246 (Que. C.A.).

In particular the Court has identified three ways in which the treatment of evidence can be a question of law.[67] First, a question of law could concern the legal effect of undisputed facts. The facts might be agreed, or the trial judge might have made all necessary findings of fact (in that even a court of appeal could disagree with the trial judge's conclusion without engaging in fact-finding itself). In such a case, the nature of the disagreement would really concern the law rather than the facts. Secondly, in some cases misdirection as to the evidence can be a question of law, but only in limited circumstances. The failure of a trial judge to direct herself to all the evidence is a question of law if it is based on a misapprehension of some legal principle, but only in that instance. Finally, it is an error of law for a trial judge to instruct a jury to consider individual pieces of evidence separately to decide whether they constitute proof beyond a reasonable doubt. The proper approach is to instruct the jury to consider the whole of the evidence and determine on that basis whether the guilt of the accused had been established beyond a reasonable doubt. The same is also true of a judge reasoning in a trial by judge alone.

Where the court of appeal grants an appeal from an acquittal in a trial by judge alone, it has two choices: to order a new trial or to enter a conviction. In the latter case, the court can either impose sentence or remit the matter to the trial court for sentencing. A court of appeal should only choose to enter a conviction where the trial judge has already made all the findings necessary to support a guilty verdict, or where those facts are not in dispute.[68] However, the court of appeal is not permitted to enter a conviction where the trial was by judge and jury; in that case the only option is to order a new trial.[69]

3) Other Appeal Related Issues

a) Statutory Powers on Appeal

Various *Code* provisions create particular powers relating to appeals. Most generally under section 683, a court of appeal can order exhibits or other items produced, hear witnesses or admit an examination of a witness, and refer questions to a special commissioner.[70] That section also permits an appeal court to amend the indictment where the accused has not been misled or prejudiced.

---

67   See *R. v. Morin*, [1992] 3 S.C.R. 286 and *B.(G.)*, above note 64.

68   *R. v. Cassidy*, [1989] 2 S.C.R. 345.

69   Section 686(4). Giving this greater protection in the case of trial by jury does not violate the *Charter*: *R. v. Skalbania*, [1997] 3 S.C.R. 995.

70   See the discussion at Section B(3)(b), below in this chapter.

In addition, a court of appeal can assign counsel for an accused or order an accused released pending an appeal.[71] In the case of an appeal from conviction, to be released the accused must demonstrate that: the appeal is not frivolous; he will surrender himself into custody in accordance with the terms of the order; and his detention is not necessary in the public interest.[72] Note that although the "public interest" criterion was found to be unconstitutionally vague in the pre-trial context (see the discussion in Chapter 6), it has been upheld with regard to bail pending an appeal.[73]

Note as well that an accused has the right to be present at the appeal. However, that right may not apply if the appeal is based on a question of law alone and the accused is both in custody and represented by counsel. In addition, the appeal court can order that an accused in custody can only appear by electronic means.[74] In some circumstances it is also possible for an appeal to be brought even though the accused is deceased. A court of appeal has the jurisdiction to do so, but should only choose to exercise that jurisdiction where it is in the interests of justice.[75]

b)   Fresh Evidence on Appeal

It is possible for evidence to be introduced on appeal that was not before the trial court. However, this cannot be done in an unconstrained way, and, in *R. v. Palmer*, the Court laid down guidelines for the introduction of fresh evidence on appeal:

1) The evidence should generally not be admitted if it could have been adduced at trial by due diligence, (but this principle is not to be applied as strictly in a criminal case as in civil cases);

2) The evidence must be relevant in the sense that it bears upon a decisive or potentially decisive issue in the trial;

3) The evidence must be credible in the sense that it is reasonably capable of belief; and

4) It must be such that if believed it could reasonably, when taken with the other evidence adduced at trial, be expected to have affected the result.[76]

---

71   Sections 684 and 679.

72   See the discussion of these criteria in *R. v. Mapara* (2004), 186 C.C.C. (3d) 273 (B.C.C.A.).

73   *R. v. Farinacci* (1993), 25 C.R. (4th) 350 (Ont. C.A.).

74   Section 688.

75   *R. v. Smith*, 2004 SCC 14.

76   *R. v. Palmer*, [1980] 1 S.C.R. 759 [*Palmer*].

Note that the evidence sought to be introduced must have been capable of admission at the initial trial; hearsay or opinion evidence that would not have been admissible at trial is no more admissible on appeal.[77]

The due diligence requirement is, to some extent, intended to prevent the reassessment in hindsight of a strategic decision made at trial.[78] The requirement that the evidence bears upon a potentially decisive issue does not mean that it must relate directly to guilt or innocence in the sense that it is a new witness that can offer the accused an alibi — the evidence could also give reason to doubt other evidence that had been relied on at trial. In R. v. Trotta, for example, fresh evidence was admitted and a new trial was ordered in light of evidence that the testimony of a pathologist called by the Crown was unreliable.[79] On the other hand, evidence that could only bear on a peripheral issue will not, due to the fourth criterion above, be admitted.[80]

The Court has also commented on the procedure to be used in fresh evidence applications. It has directed that, unless the application is dismissed immediately, judgement should be reserved on whether to admit the evidence until after the appeal is heard. In that way, the appeal court will be better able to decide whether the evidence could reasonably have been expected to affect the result of the case. If it could, the appeal court can also consider how great an impact it might have had in order to decide whether to order a new trial or, relying on the fresh evidence, decide the matter itself.[81]

Note, as well, that the Palmer criteria do not create the only test by which new evidence can be introduced on appeal, though it is the most common one. However, in some cases, evidence showing that the validity of the trial is in issue, rather than evidence relating to guilt or innocence. In such cases, the Palmer criteria do not apply. In Taillefer (discussed more fully in Chapter 8) the fresh evidence was evidence that had, wrongly, not been disclosed to the accused earlier. In those circumstances the Court held that the less strict test from Dixon, relating to disclosure, was more appropriately applied.[82] More generally,

---

77 See, for example, R. v. Assoun (2006), 207 C.C.C. (3d) 372 (N.S.C.A.), leave to appeal to S.C.C. refused, [2006] S.C.C.A. No. 233, or R. v. Archer (2005), 34 C.R. (6th) 271 (Ont. C.A.) [Archer].

78 See, for example, Archer, ibid. or R. v. Perlett (2006), 212 C.C.C. (3d) 11 (Ont. C.A.) [Perlett].

79 2007 SCC 49.

80 See Perlett, above note 78, or R. v. Flis (2006), 205 C.C.C. (3d) 384 (Ont. C.A.).

81 R. v. Stolar, [1988] 1 S.C.R. 480.

82 See R. v. Taillefer; R. v. Duguay, 2003 SCC 70; and R. v. Dixon, [1998] 1 S.C.R. 244.

when the trial process itself is in issue the strict *Palmer* criteria do not apply.[83]

c) Duty to Give Reasons

Although there is no general duty for a trial judge to give reasons in every case, the Court made clear in *Sheppard* that in many circumstances the failure to do so, or to do so adequately, will be an error of law giving rise to a ground of appeal.[84]

A trial judge's reasons do not need to be the equivalent of a jury instruction, and should not be held up against some abstract standard.[85] They are to be assessed as a whole, and a misstatement will not necessarily be fatal. Further, an appeal court is not to intervene "simply because it thinks the trial court did a poor job of expressing itself."[86] Trial judges are not required to explain their entire reasoning process in detail, rather they are only required to give reasons that the parties can understand and that permit appellate review.[87]

It is possible, though, to appeal a trial judge's decision on the basis that the reasons do not comply with that standard. The Court noted in *Sheppard* that

> . . . the requirement of reasons is tied to their purpose and the purpose varies with the context. At the trial level, the reasons justify and explain the result. The losing party knows why he or she has lost . . . . Interested members of the public can satisfy themselves that justice has been done, or not, as the case may be.[88]

In addition, a trial judge is not permitted to prevent meaningful appellate review by failing to explain the reasons behind a verdict. Accordingly, it can be an error of law to provide insufficient reasons.

Determining that there is an error of law based on insufficient reasons is a two-stage analysis. First, the appeal court must ask whether the reasons are inadequate. Second, it must be determined whether that inadequacy prevents appellate review. That is, even if reasons are objectively inadequate, that will not necessarily prevent appellate review.

---

83   See, for example, *R. v. Schneider* (2004), 192 C.C.C. (3d) 1 (N.S.C.A.); *R. v. Wolf* (2005), 197 C.C.C. (3d) 481 (Ont. C.A.); *R. v. MacInnis* (2006), 212 C.C.C. (3d) 103 (N.S.C.A.).

84   *R. v. Sheppard*, 2002 SCC 26 [*Sheppard*].

85   *Ibid.*; *R. v. Rhyason*, 2007 SCC 39; *R. v. Gagnon*, [2006] 1 S.C.R. 621 at para. 19 [*Gagnon*].

86   *Sheppard, ibid.* at para. 26.

87   *Ibid.* and *R. v. Boucher*, 2005 SCC 72.

88   *Sheppard, ibid.* at para. 24.

The basis for the verdict might be obvious on the face of the record. However, if both stages of the test are met then a new trial should be ordered.[89]

In *Sheppard* itself, there were significant inconsistencies and conflicts in the evidence, as well as issues of credibility. The trial judge delivered "boiler plate" reasons that indicated, in a single sentence, that he had considered the testimony and the burden on the Crown. The Court held that these reasons were insufficient for the accused, or an appeal court, to know the basis for the conviction, and therefore it overturned the conviction. The Court also laid down general guidelines surrounding when a trial judge had a duty to give reasons, including that:

1.   The delivery of reasoned decisions is inherent in the judge's role. It is part of his or her accountability for the discharge of the responsibilities of the office. In its most general sense, the obligation to provide reasons for a decision is owed to the public at large.

2.   An accused person should not be left in doubt about why a conviction has been entered. Reasons for judgment may be important to clarify the basis for the conviction but, on the other hand, the basis may be clear from the record. The question is whether, in all the circumstances, the functional need to know has been met.

3.   The lawyers for the parties may require reasons to assist them in considering and advising with respect to a potential appeal. On the other hand, they may know all that is required to be known for that purpose on the basis of the rest of the record.

    . . .

5.   Reasons perform an important function in the appellate process. Where the functional needs are not satisfied, the appellate court may conclude that it is a case of unreasonable verdict, an error of law, or a miscarriage of justice within the scope of s. 686(1)(a) of the *Criminal Code*, depending on the circumstances of the case and the nature and importance of the trial decision being rendered.

6.   Reasons acquire particular importance when a trial judge is called upon to address troublesome principles of unsettled law, or to resolve confused and contradictory evidence on a key issue, unless the basis of the trial judge's conclusion is apparent from the record, even without being articulated.

    . . .

8.   The trial judge's duty is satisfied by reasons which are sufficient to serve the purpose for which the duty is imposed, i.e., a deci-

---

89   *Gagnon*, above note 85.

sion which, having regard to the particular circumstances of the case, is reasonably intelligible to the parties and provides the basis for meaningful appellate review of the correctness of the trial judge's decision.[90]

The duty to give reasons also applies to acquittals, but in a different fashion. There is no "unreasonable acquittal" ground of appeal, and the Crown and the accused have different tasks at trial. A conviction requires proof of every element beyond a reasonable doubt, but an acquittal only requires that there be reasonable doubt. Reasonable doubt need not be based on factual findings supporting it, and can arise simply because an inadequate foundation for guilt has been laid. In that event, it takes less for reasons to be adequate in the case of an acquittal.[91]

Note, in addition, that issues can arise because of the timing with which reasons are released. Although reasons need not always be given contemporaneously with the decision, when there is delay the possibility of problems increases. In some cases it might seem that reasons were no longer drafted with an open mind, but rather to justify the conclusion of guilt that had already been reached. This is a danger particularly where reasons are not issued until after the accused has launched an appeal. In such a case, there could be cause to think that the reasons were designed to justify the verdict, rather than actually reflecting the decision-making process that was used. Delay itself is not a deciding factor, but it increases the possibility that reasons will not be seen to have been impartial.[92]

C. APPEALS OF SUMMARY CONVICTION OFFENCES

Appeals from summary conviction offences share many qualities with appeals from indictable offences, though there are some differences worth noting. The most notable difference is the court to which the appeal is brought. Indictable offences are appealed to the court of appeal for the province. Generally speaking, summary conviction appeals are taken to the province's superior court of criminal jurisdiction that is *not* the court of appeal.[93] There are also differences in the grounds upon

---

90 *Sheppard*, above note 84 at para. 55.
91 *R. v. Walker*, 2008 SCC 34.
92 *R. v. Teskey*, 2007 SCC 25.
93 See the definitions in ss. 2, 673, and 812. See, however, the discussion of appeals under s. 830, below in this section.

which an appeal can be brought, which are broader for both accused (called the "defendant" in the case of summary conviction offences) and the Crown, and are essentially parallel. Under section 813 a defendant can appeal a conviction or order made against her, and the Crown can appeal "an order that stays proceedings on an information or dismisses an information." In addition, that section lets both parties appeal sentences, verdicts of not criminally responsible, and fitness to stand trial decisions. No explicit limits are attached to any of these grounds.

As with indictable offences, though, the bases for granting appeals are narrower than the grounds for launching them. Indeed, they are narrower in precisely the same way. Section 822(1) incorporates most of section 683 to 689 by reference. As a result, all of the rules in section 686(1) that concern appeals from convictions or acquittals are equally applicable to summary conviction offences. Recall as well that when a summary conviction offence is appealed along with an indictable offence, the appeals can, with leave, be combined.[94]

As a result of this incorporation others provisions applicable to indictable offences, such as the powers of the court in section 683, also apply. In addition, bail pending a summary conviction appeal can also be granted, though under the specific provisions in section 816 rather than those governing indictable offences.

There are, however, other notable differences between summary conviction and indictable appeals, which include the possibility of other methods of appeal. First, under section 822(4) it is possible for an appeal of a summary conviction matter to take place by trial *de novo*. Proceeding in this way can be justified if, because of the condition of the record—a grounds of decreasing relevance given the methods of recording proceedings in common use today—or "for any other reason," the interests of justice would be better served in this way. As a practical matter trials *de novo* are a rarity.

In addition sections 829 to 838 create an alternative method of appeal, though again these provisions are little used. They incorporate many of the provisions regarding other summary conviction appeals, but the grounds upon which they can be brought are more limited. Either party can appeal a decision in this way on the basis that it is erroneous in point of law, it is in excess of jurisdiction or it constitutes a refusal or failure to exercise jurisdiction. All of these are grounds upon which an appeal could have been launched under section 813.[95] A de-

---

94   Sections 675(1.1) and 676(1.1).

95   Tim Quigley, *Procedure in Canadian Criminal Law*, 2d ed., looseleaf (Toronto: Thomson Carswell, 2005) [Quigley] notes at 24–39 the possibility that the quashing of an information prior to plea might be appealable only under s. 830,

fendant is only permitted to opt for one of the two methods of appeal.[96] Appeals under Section 830 can be brought either on a transcript or an agreed statement of facts.[97] In such cases, the appeal could, in some provinces, go directly to the provincial court of appeal.[98]

Finally, whichever method of appeal is brought at the first level, the *Code* permits a potential second level of appeal from summary conviction matters to the court of appeal. Such appeals depend on leave of the court and can be brought only on a question of law.[99] The rules in sections 673 to 689, which govern appeals of indictable offences, are incorporated by reference to these appeals.[100]

D. APPEALS TO THE SUPREME COURT OF CANADA

Sections 691 to 695 create a right to appeal decisions of a court of appeal regarding indictable offences to the Supreme Court of Canada.[101] The grounds upon which such appeals can be brought, and the circumstances in which they are permitted, are much narrower than the first level of appeal.

An appeal to the Supreme Court of Canada can only be based upon a question of law, no other ground of appeal is permitted. When an issue constitutes a question of law, as opposed to a question of mixed law and fact, as has already been discussed in the context of appeals to the court of appeal then that analysis is equally applicable here. However, there are some considerations that are unique to the Supreme Court context.

A court of appeal can, under section 686(1)(a)(i), allow an appeal based on a finding that it was unreasonable or cannot be supported by the evidence. This question obviously could involve some considera-

---

though he also observes that a new information could simply be laid in such circumstances.

96 Section 836.

97 Section 830(2).

98 This result follows because s. 829 defines "appeal court" for s. 830 appeals as the superior court of criminal jurisdiction for the province, but the definition of that term in s. 2, for some provinces, includes the court of appeal.

99 Section 839. Once again, it is a question of law for jurisdictional purposes that is in issue.

100 Section 839(2).

101 In an appropriate case, presumably the appeal power under s. 40 of the *Supreme Court Act*, above note 2, could be used to appeal a decision of a court of appeal concerning a summary conviction matter: see Quigley, above note 95 at 24–40.

tion of facts, and the unreasonableness of a particular verdict might raise questions of mixed law and fact. However, as a class, the question of whether a court of appeal has properly applied section 686(1)(a)(i) is a question of law. It is therefore possible to bring an appeal to the Supreme Court based on whether the court of appeal ought to have allowed the appeal.[102]

Similarly, under section 686(1)(b)(iii) a court of appeal can use the curative proviso and dismiss an appeal based on the finding that there was no substantial wrong or miscarriage of justice. Once again, whether the court of appeal has made a correct decision in applying the curative proviso is a question of law and so is appealable to the Supreme Court.[103] Presumably, the same rationale should apply to the "procedural irregularity" saving provision in section 686(1)(b)(iv).

Apart from the fact that the only ground of appeal is on a question of law, there is also the issue of when the accused or the Crown will be permitted to appeal. For the most part, appeals are permitted in only two circumstances: i) where a judge of the court of appeal dissents on a question of law, or ii) when the Supreme Court gives leave to appeal a question of law. These are the only circumstances in which the Crown can appeal or in which an accused, who was convicted at trial and on appeal, can appeal. However, if an accused was acquitted at trial but that acquittal was replaced with a conviction on appeal, then a further basis for appeal is allowed. In that case, the accused can appeal on any question of law, whether there was a dissent in the court of appeal or not.[104]

Note that one option for a court of appeal is to overturn the actual conviction at trial, but substitute a conviction on some other count. In such a case, both the Crown and the accused will have a right of appeal.[105] Note as well that, even if the Supreme Court grants leave to appeal on a question of law, that does not preclude it from ultimately concluding that the issue raised is not one of law after all, and dismissing the appeal on that basis.[106] Like a court of appeal, the Supreme Court has the power to appoint counsel for an accused and has the power to make any order that the court of appeal could have made.[107]

---

102 See *Yebes*, above note 20 and *Biniaris*, above note 10.
103 See *R. v. Mahoney*, [1982] 1 S.C.R. 834; and *R. v. Jolivet*, 2000 SCC 29.
104 Sections 691(1), 691(2), and 693.
105 *Biniaris*, above note 10 at para. 18.
106 *R. v. Demeter*, [1978] 1 S.C.R. 538.
107 Sections 694.1 and 695.

FURTHER READINGS

SOPINKA, JOHN, & MARK GELOWITZ, *The Conduct of an Appeal*, 2d ed. (Toronto: Butterworths, 2000)

QUIGLEY, TIM, *Procedure in Canadian Criminal Law*, 2d ed., looseleaf (Toronto: Thomson Carswell, 2005) c. 24

GLOSSARY

absolute jurisdiction offence: An offence listed in section 553 of the *Code*. These offences can only be tried by a provincial court judge, and so the accused has no election.

ancillary powers doctrine: The process through which new police powers can be created at common law. The test for the creation of ancillary powers is drawn from the British case *R. v. Waterfield*, which is applied in Canada today in a way quite distinct from the approach in its country of origin.

arrest: An arrest consists of words of arrest accompanied either by the touching of the person with a view to detention or by the person submitting to the arrest. The word "arrest" need not actually be used, provided the accused can be reasonably supposed to have understood that she was under arrest. Arrest powers are given in the *Criminal Code* to everyone, including private citizens, and additional arrest powers are given to property owners and peace officers.

Attorney General: A member of cabinet and the chief law officer for a jurisdiction. The Attorney General has jurisdiction over all or most matters of criminal law, including law-making and prosecutions. In most jurisdictions, the Attorney General is also responsible for policing, although this role is sometimes taken on by the Solicitor General or some other minister. The Attorney General is given various discretionary powers in the *Criminal Code*, some of which must be exercised personally and some of which can be exercised on his behalf by a Crown prosecutor.

bail: The name in common usage for the process by which a justice can release a person who has been accused of an offence until the trial is held. Bail can be granted either unconditionally or on various conditions. Properly known as "judicial interim release."

challenge for cause: The process by which the Crown or the accused can challenge a potential juror in order to suggest that the person should not serve on the jury. The most common basis for challenge for cause is that the juror is not indifferent between the Queen and the accused, which amounts to a claim that the juror will not act impartially.

change of venue: Moving the location of a trial from one territorial jurisdiction to another.

charge document: The document setting out the charges based upon which an accused will stand trial: see **information** and **indictment**.

Charter of Rights and Freedoms: Sections 1–34 of the *Constitution Act, 1982*, setting out various guaranteed rights which, subject to the justification clause in section 1 of the *Charter*, take priority over any other legislation. The most important sections for criminal law purposes include the fundamental freedoms guaranteed in section 2 (such as freedom of expression), the legal rights provisions in sections 7–14 (such as freedom from unreasonable search and seizure, the right to counsel, and so on), and the remedies provisions in sections 24 and 52.

common law: Judge-made law, as distinct from laws set out in statutes or regulations.

Constitution Act, 1867: An Act of the British Parliament that is the first of Canada's constitutional documents, and initially created Canada as a separate country from Great Britain. It is the source of the division of powers between the federal and provincial governments.

count: An individual charge within a single information or indictment.

court of appeal: The highest court in a jurisdiction for indictable offences, but designated differently in various provinces and territories. For summary conviction matters, the court of appeal is the jurisdiction's superior court of criminal jurisdiction that is not the highest court in the jurisdiction. See the definitions in sections 2, 673, and 812 of the *Code*.

court of criminal jurisdiction: A trial-level court hearing criminal matters, but designated differently in various provinces and territories. See the definition in section 2 of the *Code*.

Crown prosecutor: A lawyer responsible for the carriage of public prosecutions on behalf of the Crown. Most public prosecutions are conducted by provincially appointed Crown prosecutors, but federal Crown prosecutors also conduct some prosecutions, particularly with regard to narcotic offences.

criminal offence: A violation of any non-regulatory offence, whether summary conviction or indictable, which is found in the *Criminal Code* or in other federal legislation, and which is constitutionally justified under section 91(27) of the *Constitution Act, 1867*.

Crown election: Hybrid offences can be tried either by indictment or on summary conviction. The Crown elects which mode of trial will be used.

curative proviso: A portion of the rules governing appeals that permits an appeal to be dismissed despite the presence of a legal error at trial, if it is found that the error is harmless and does not cause a miscarriage of justice.

curtilage: The area surrounding and associated with a dwelling house.

detention: A restraint of liberty other than arrest in which a person may reasonably require the assistance of counsel, but might be prevented or impeded from retaining and instructing counsel without delay. The restraint of liberty might arise because of physical constraint, or because a police officer or other agent of the state assumes control over the movement of a person by a demand or direction. See also **psychological detention**.

direct indictment: A Crown prosecutor has the ability, under section 577 of the *Code*, to prefer a "direct indictment," which has the effect of requiring an accused to be placed on trial for the indictable offence charged therein, either without a preliminary inquiry having been held or completed, or despite a discharge at the preliminary inquiry. This power can only be used with the personal consent in writing of the Attorney General or Deputy Attorney General. Also referred to as a "preferred indictment."

disclosure: The right of a person charged with an offence to be informed of all relevant evidence, whether incriminatory or exculpatory, in the hands of the Crown.

division of powers: The manner in which legislative jurisdiction is divided between the federal and provincial governments in accordance with sections 91 and 92 of the *Constitution Act, 1867.*

DNA warrant: A warrant issued under section 487.05 authorizing the taking of bodily samples from a person for the purpose of DNA analysis.

election: An accused who is charged with an indictable offence is in most cases offered a choice as to mode of trial: superior court judge with a jury, superior court judge alone, or provincial court judge. In such cases, the accused is said to have an election as to mode of trial. See **absolute jurisdiction offence** and **exclusive jurisdiction offence**.

exclusive jurisdiction offence: An offence listed in section 469 of the *Code*. These offences (barring prosecutorial consent) can only be tried through a jury trial in a superior court of criminal jurisdiction, and so the accused has no election.

general warrant: A warrant issued under section 487.01 of the *Criminal Code* that authorizes the bearer to use any device, investigative technique, procedure, or any thing described in the warrant that would constitute an unreasonable search and seizure if it were not authorized by warrant.

hybrid offence: An offence that may be prosecuted either on indictment or as a summary conviction offence. See **Crown election**.

implementational duties: The obligation imposed on the police to act toward a person who has been arrested or detained and has asserted the right to counsel in particular ways, including facilitating that person's contact with counsel, and holding off from attempting to elicit incriminating information until the person has had a reasonable opportunity to do so.

indictable offence: The more serious category of offences, which have no minimum penalty but can carry sentences as severe as life imprisonment without possibility of parole for twenty-five years. Indictable offences are tried on an indictment and might have a preliminary inquiry. In most cases, an accused has an election as to mode of trial, though this is not the case for absolute jurisdiction offences or exclusive jurisdiction offences.

indictment: A document prepared once an accused has been committed for trial after a preliminary inquiry, though it can also be laid without a preliminary inquiry having been conducted (see **direct indictment** or preferred indictment). This document specifies the particular offence or offences with which the accused is charged, and is the document based upon which the trial for an indictable offence will occur.

information: A document sworn in front of a justice of the peace, alleging that a person has committed an offence. An information is required for the issuance of some process, such as an arrest warrant, and is the document based upon which the trial for a summary conviction offence will occur.

informational duties: The obligation imposed on police to inform a person who is arrested or detained of particular pieces of information, such as the right to counsel, the existence of legal aid, and the telephone numbers for duty counsel.

investigative detention: The common law police power to briefly detain an individual, where on an objective view of the totality of the circumstances there is a clear nexus between the individual to be detained and a recent or on-going criminal offence, and the decision to detain is reasonable based on all the circumstances, including the extent to which the interference with individual liberty is necessary to perform the officer's duty, the liberty interfered with, and the nature and extent of that interference.

joinder: Joining more than one count, or more than one accused, on a single information.

judicial interim release: See **bail**.

jurisdiction: The legal authority to act in certain manners. Parliament must have jurisdiction to legislate over particular criminal matters, and courts and judges must have jurisdiction in various ways (for example, territorially) to conduct a trial.

jury: The triers of fact in some criminal trials. Juries normally consist of twelve individuals drawn from the community where the trial takes place, selected after a process involving challenge for cause and peremptory challenges.

jury array: A large number of potential jurors summoned to court from whom the actual jurors for a particular trial will be chosen.

justice: As used in the *Criminal Code*, a justice of the peace or a provincial court judge.

peace officer: A person exercising authority under the *Criminal Code* to investigate criminal offences and exercise powers such as arrest. In most instances a peace officer will be a police officer, but the definition also encompasses others, including, for example, some customs officers, correctional officers, pilots while an aircraft is in flight, and others. See the definition in section 2 of the *Code*.

peremptory challenge: The right of the accused or the Crown to object to a member of the jury array being chosen to serve on the jury, without being required to offer any explanation for the objection. The Crown and the accused each have a limited number of peremptory challenges, which varies with the offence charged: see section 634 of the *Criminal Code*.

preferred indictment: Another term for a direct indictment.

preliminary inquiry: A hearing conducted in accordance with Part XVIII of the *Code*, before an accused is placed on trial for an indictable offence. An accused either can be committed for trial or discharged at the end of the preliminary inquiry. Originally a preliminary inquiry was presumptively required in the case of all indictable offences, although it could be waived, but in its current form the preliminary inquiry is held on request and might be restricted to particular issues.

private prosecution: A criminal charge laid and pursued by a private individual.

production: The right of a person accused of a criminal offence to be provided, in some cases, with information that is in the hands of third parties but not in the hands of the Crown.

promise to appear: A written promise in accordance with Form 10 of the *Criminal Code* to attend court at a particular place and time. A potential basis upon which bail can be granted.

prosecutor: The person who carries forward criminal proceedings. In public prosecutions, the prosecutor will be the Attorney General, and in private prosecutions the prosecutor will be the person laying the charge. In either case, the term includes counsel acting on behalf of the prosecutor, and, in the case of a private prosecution for a summary conviction offence, will also include an agent acting for the person who laid the charge.

psychological detention: The term used to describe a situation when a person is not in fact required by law to comply with the demands of a peace officer, but is unaware of that fact and reasonably believes that she has no choice but to comply.

public prosecution: A criminal charge laid and pursued on behalf of the state by a Crown prosecutor.

quash: To set aside a decision (such as discharging an accused at a preliminary inquiry or issuing a search warrant) so that it no longer has effect.

reasonable expectation of privacy: The amount of privacy which a person is entitled to expect in a free and democratic society. Privacy consists of at least personal, territorial, and informational privacy.

recognizance: A written acknowledgement in accordance with Form 11 of the *Criminal Code* of responsibility for a debt not to exceed $500, to be forfeited upon failure to appear in court. A potential basis upon which bail can be granted.

reverse onus: A statutory provision requiring that the accused be responsible for providing evidence on some relevant point, either to raise a doubt about whether the point is true or to show on balance of probabilities that it is not true.

search: Any investigative technique that infringes on a person's reasonable expectation of privacy. A search conducted without a warrant is *prima facie* a violation of the right in section 8 of the *Charter* to be free from unreasonable search and seizure.

search warrant: A warrant issued under section 487 of the *Criminal Code* authorizing the bearer to search a building receptacle or place and seize evidence or other specified items.

severance: A judicial decision not to try more than one accused, or more than one count, on the same information.

stay of proceedings: An order preventing, either temporarily or permanently, any further action on a prosecution. Crown prosecutors have a power under the *Criminal Code* to temporarily stay proceedings for a period not exceeding one year, and judges can permanently stay proceedings as a remedy for a *Charter* breach.

summary conviction offence: A generally less serious category of offences that carry less severe penalties (in most cases a maximum of six months imprisonment) and that cannot be prosecuted more than six months after the date of the offence. Summary conviction offences are tried on an information and the trial necessarily takes place in front of a provincial court judge.

summons: A written notice issued by a judge or justice in accordance with Form 6 of the *Criminal Code*, requiring the person to whom it is given to appear in court at the stated place and time.

superior court of criminal jurisdiction: A trial level court hearing criminal matters, sometimes with a jury, and designated differently in various provinces and territories. See the definition in section 2 of the *Code*.

surety: A third party who agrees to forfeit a sum of money if the person for whom she stands surety fails to appear in court in accordance with the terms of a recognizance.

telewarrant: A procedure authorized under section 487.1 of the *Criminal Code* allowing certain types of warrants to be obtained by means of telecommunication where it is impracticable for the peace officer to appear personally to make application.

undertaking: A written promise given by an accused person to a peace officer (Form 11.1) or a judge or justice (Form 12) to appear in court at a stated place and time and to comply with other conditions.

warrant: A judicial authorization given to peace officers empowering them to perform particular actions, such as to search a location or arrest a person.

TABLE OF CASES

INDEX

ABOUT THE AUTHOR

Stephen Coughlan is a professor of law at Dalhousie University in Halifax. He received an LL.B. from Dalhousie Law School and a Ph.D. in philosophy from the University of Toronto, both in 1985. He has practised law with the Metro Community Law Clinic and with the Dalhousie Legal Aid Service, and has also worked with the criminal procedure project of the Law Reform Commission of Canada. Having worked at Dalhousie Law School in a variety of capacities, he was appointed to a tenure-track position in 2000, was promoted to Associate Professor in 2001, and became a full Professor in 2004. His areas of teaching have included criminal law and procedure, constitutional law, health law, and appellate advocacy. His students have won many prizes at competitive moots, including first place overall in the Commonwealth Law Moot. Prof. Coughlan has received the Dalhousie Law School Teaching Excellence Award, the Hannah and Harold Barnett Award for Excellence in Teaching First Year Law, the Dalhousie University Alumni Association Award of Excellence for Teaching, and the Association of Atlantic Universities Distinguished Teacher Award.

Professor Coughlan is an editor of the *Criminal Reports* and an author of the National Judicial Institute Criminal Law e-Letter. He is one of the authors of the *Carswell Annual Review of Criminal Law* and of *Learning Canadian Criminal Law* (10th ed.). In addition, he is a member of the Law and Technology Institute at Dalhousie Law School and is one of the authors of the Canadian IT Law Association's newsletter on law and technology issues. The majority of his more than 100 articles, annotations, chapters, reports, and books have been in the criminal law field, but he has also published in other fields, including health law (particularly with regard to issues of elder abuse) and the future of the legal profession.